AF797615

CANON LAW SOCIETY OF AMERICA

PROCEEDINGS OF THE SEVENTY-SECOND ANNUAL CONVENTION

Buffalo, New York
October 11-14, 2010

Canon Law Society of America
Office of the Executive Coordinator
The Hecker Center, Suite 111
3025 Fourth Street, NE
Washington, DC 20017-1102

© Copyright 2011 by Canon Law Society of America

ISBN: 978-1-932208-28-3
OLD ISBN: 1-932208-28-3
ISSN: 0277-9889
SAN: 237-6296

The Canon Law Society of America's programs and publications are designed solely to help canonists maintain their professional competence. In dealing with specific canonical matters, the canonist using Canon Law Society of America (CLSA) publications or orally conveyed information should also research original sources of authority.

The views and opinions expressed in this publication are those of the individual authors and do not represent the views of the CLSA, its Board of Governors, staff or members. The CLSA does not endorse the views or opinions expressed by the individual authors. The publisher and authors specifically disclaim any liability, loss or risk, personal or otherwise, which is incurred as a consequence, directly or indirectly, of the use, reliance, or application of any of the contents of this publication.

Unless otherwise noted, all canons quoted are from the *Code of Canon Law, Latin-English Edition* (Washington, DC: Canon Law Society of America, 1999)

Printed in the United States of America

Canon Law Society of America
Office of the Executive Coordinator
The Hecker Center, Suite 111
3025 Fourth Street, NE
Washington, DC 20017-1102

TABLE OF CONTENTS

FOREWARD

The Canon Law Society of America (CLSA) is pleased to present the *Proceedings* of the seventy-second annual convention held in Buffalo, New York, October 11-14, 2010. The CLSA annually publishes for its members and others in the canonical community the major addresses, seminars and reports presented at the annual meting. The 2010 convention was a simultaneous convention with the Canadian Canon Law Society. The keynote address was delivered in French and appears here in English and in French.

We are grateful to the presenters who provided their final texts in a timely fashion. Texts have been edited for consistency in conformity with the CLSA Style Sheet and Publications Guidelines including capitalization, use of footnotes, gender-inclusive language, and citation of canons. Included in this edition of *CLSA Proceedings* is a listing of the participants who attended the Buffalo convention.

The CLSA, established on November 12, 1939 as a professional association dedicated to the promotion of both the study and the application of canons law in the Catholic Church today, numbers over 1,300 members who reside in the United States and thirty-five other countries. *CLSA Proceedings 72* (2010) should take its place among previous volumes as a professional resource. Additional copies of this volume may be purchased from the CLSA website, www.clsa.org.

For CLSA membership information, please visit the CLSA website or contact the Office of the Executive Coordinator.

Sr. Sharon A. Euart, RSM
Executive Coordinator
Canon Law Society of America
3025 4th Street, NE
Suite 111
Washington, DC 20017-1102

KEYNOTE ADDRESS

THE STABILITY AND DYNAMISM OF THE CANONICAL JURIDICAL SYSTEM*

Most Reverend Juan Ignacio Arrieta

To speak of the characteristics of canon law, I have at times used a paragraph from the book "*Lo spirito del diritto canonico*" (The Spirit of Canon Law), with which Pio Fedele begins corresponding to the certainty of the law. In that work published in 1962 Fedele expresses in a flexible way a sort of paradox which, in my opinion, identifies with considerable precision some of the external manifestations of the law of the Church which I should like to draw your attention.

> "To him who considers - says Fedele - the immutable and eternal principles on which the canonical structure is founded and the endless veins in which it sinks its profound roots it will seem to be, among all of the juridical structures, the most static, unmovable and inflexible, the most refractory to any political, economic or social changes which weave the tapestry of human history, the least sensitive to the unavoidable dissimilarity of the cases and the peculiarity of the situations which make up its perpetual flow. On the other hand, to him who considers the impressive diversity of peoples which it embraces and the rich variety of the historical eras which its secular existence has run, it will seem to be the most dynamic, mutable and elastic, that which best adheres to the unrepeatability of the cases of individual and social life."[1]

In effect, canon law is a system which, on the one hand, rests on foundations that are not available and are off-limits to any transaction or possibility of pact. On the other, that same Law has the aspiration to be applied coherently in the whole world and to resolve whatever situation of justice which might present itself within the ecclesial society. The history of canon law, furthermore, shows that despite the deficiencies which might have existed in one period or another, that very aspiration of universal applicability has been, as a general rule, reached in the diverse eras of history, having at times to replace the inexistence or vacuum of civil juridical systems, thanks to the peculiar structure of the Church which integrates an incomparable plurality of legislative levels - Popes, Bishops, particular and plenary Councils, and now episcopal conferences - which connect the universal with the most concrete and varied of places.

---

* This presentation was delivered in French and has been translated by the author into English. The French text follows this text.

[1] Cfr. Pio Fedele, *Lo spirito del diritto canonico* (Padua, 1962) 197.

Furthermore, if that law has been able to respond in a generalized way to the questions of justice of the ecclesial society, it has been first of all thanks to the intrinsic characteristics of the juridical system and to the way in which canon law should be applied in the Church.

In this paper I will attempt to recall the substantial dynamism which characterizes the canonical order and the demand which it entails to harmoniously integrate diverse juridical levels and elements not consistent with canonical relevance in each new circumstance which presents itself to resolve the concrete situations of justice. I will attempt to underline the complete opposition of the legal system of the Catholic Church to any form of juridical positivism, and I will attempt to show the vital force which, in turn, the juridical organization and elaboration of the canonist receives from being consistent with the theological principles and with the divine law which are at the base of every canonical norm and which should always guide the solution of conflicts.

1. The substantial juridical level: foundation and guide of the juridical order

Fedele rightly affirms that canon law is based on immutable factors which are not subject to the free arrangement by those who practice it. Such elements constitute, so to speak, the essential nucleus and the source from which the peculiar juridical nature of canon law flows, its obligatory nature. They are at once the "title" from which the authority and the faithful respectively exercise their functions and the guide to later develop the positive norms of the canonical juridical order in each of the diverse areas which pertain to the ecclesial society.

Herein is rooted the first level or substantial level of the juridical nature which we need to consider.[2]

In effect, the main singularity which, in this sense, the canonical order has, regarding any other juridical system, is rooted in the very source from which its legitimacy proceeds, and from which it derives also all of its capacity to establish juridical bonds among the faithful.[3] The juridical structure of the Church is, in effect, that of a social group which springs from a revealed religion and which, also as a group, has its origin in the divine will expressed in that revelation, which is transmitted, as taught by Catholic theology, through sacred scripture, through tradition and through the magisterium of the Church. The will of Christ is, ultimately, the source of legitimacy of the institutions of the Church

---

[2] Cfr. J. Hervada, *Introducción al estudio del derecho canónico* (Eunsa: Pamplona, 2007) 69ff.; F. Coccopalmerio, "Riflessioni sull'identita del diritto ecclesiale," in *Codice de Diritto Canonico Commentato* (Ancora: Milan, 2009) 38ff; G. Lo Castro, "La dimensione umana del diritto divino," in *Diritto divino e legislazione umana*, ed. A. R. Coppola et al. (G. Giappichelli: Turin, Italy, 1998) 50ff.

[3] Cfr. P. Lombardía, "Sobre las características peculiares del ordenamiento canónico," in *Escritos de Derecho Canónico y de Derecho Eclesiástico del Estado*, vol. 1 (University of Navarra: Pamplona, 1973) 173-222; K. Morsdorf, "Sulla fondazione del diritto canonico," in *Fondamenti del Diritto canonico*, ed. K. Mörsdorf (Marcianum Press: Venice, 2008) 141ff.

and of the entire canonical system, and it is what, ultimately, allows them to have juridical relevance in each and every element that constitute the canonical order.[4]

As opposed to what happens in the civil legislations, the bond which exists in the Church between the leader and the subject is not derived from any type of "social pact", but rather proceeds "exactly"—we can say now with the theology of Vatican II—from the sacramental and hierarchical structure which Christ has willed to establish in his Church. For that reason, he institutes the sacred orders and constitutes shepherds to lead the communities, identifying and teaching with authority the contents of the communion which animate all. It is from there, as we all know well, that the position of authority of the institutions and the persons which occupy them proceed; and it is also there that their respective mandates find their foundation, which, otherwise, would lose legitimacy.

From the sacramental structure of the Church, from the tapestry which the sacraments form in her—especially baptism and holy orders—and from the funding will of Christ which persists alive in the Church, where, in summary, the central nucleus of the canonical juridical nature comes from; a nucleus made up of principles, rarely of normative formulas, more or less related among themselves, which are obligatory and which frequently are not possible to derogate.

But it is not only the law and the authority who receive in the Church legitimizing force from the divine will and the sacraments. But also the other components of the canonical order, the positions which the faithful occupy in the Church and the juridical efficacy of the manifestations of their free will, acquire from that same source the potential which the canonical juridical system recognizes for them.

Just as the sacred order constitutes positions of authority and hierarchy, the sacrament of baptism establishes the base position of the Christian faithful, the root of their rights and fundamental duties, and the basis of their capacity to efficaciously generate canon law with the manifestations of their own will, for example, when one decides to found an association in the Church or to personally adhere to one, or when one freely binds oneself by a free vow, or when, expressing one's own consent, constitutes a marital union.[5]

All of these factors which are present in the different areas of canon law—in the law of association or in the hierarchical structure; in the area of the *munus docendi* in marriage or penal law—represent what we should recognize as a first level of effect of the canonical juridical nature, made up of principles and binding rules which have a proper system of knowledge and a proper method of elaboration, and which must always be considered whatever the nature of the

[4] Cfr. Hervada, 31ff.

[5] Cfr. P. Lombardía, "Derecho divino y persona física en el ordenamiento canónico," in *Escritos de Derecho Canónico*, vol. 1 (University of Navarra: Pamplona, 1973) 225-253.

juridical operation which is to be undertaken. The one who elaborates general norms as well as the one who shall apply them to each specific case, should proceed consistent with these principles.

The principles to which I refer are found in the very sources of revelation. This is why their knowledge and maturity follows the same historical avatars as the development of dogma. They have been gradually made explicit throughout history, allowing a juridical formulation in every moment consonant with the state of Catholic theology. We have witnessed it recently with the doctrinal development of the Second Vatican Council on the sacramentality of the episcopacy, which has made it possible to formulate more precisely the statute of the episcopal college, of the particular church, etc.; or also with the development of the theology of the people of God which has made it possible to formulate for the first time the fundamental rights of the faithful arising from baptism.

The progress in knowledge of that primary nucleus of *ius divinum*—as we must externally qualify it—which gives a foundation to the functioning of the canonical juridical nature and gives direction to the development of its order, appears thus bound to the magisterium of the Church. For this same reason, the activity of this magisterim appears also as an element of dynamism and expansion of canon law.[6]

It is fitting that what we have just seen regarding the doctrine of the Vatican Council II should, for the same reason, be made evident with the successive expressions of the ordinary magisterium in several areas. For example, when one reflects today on the structure or the competencies of episcopal conferences, would it be appropriate to ignore the *motu proprio Apostolos suos* of 1998 which reconsidered the entire doctrine on the collective dimension of the episcopate?[7] Or, how could the position of the local churches and that of their respective shepherds in the womb of the *communio ecclesiarum* be treated today without taking into consideration the letter *Communionis notio* that the Congregation for the Doctrine of the Faith published in 1992 which extensively developed precisely this question?[8] Both documents are expressions of a magisterium which determines the substantial interpretation of those institutions and of others related to them. And for the same reason, how can the full range of the diverse factors which intervene in the situations of consensual incapacity contained in canon 1095 of the code be interpreted without keeping in mind the constant pontifical magisterium on this matter?

---

[6] P.J. Viladrick, "El ius divinum como criterio de autenticidad en el Derecho de la Iglesia," in *Ius Canonicum* (Rome: 1976) 16:104.

[7] Cfr. John Paul II, motu proprio *Apostolos suos*, May 21, 1998: *AAS* 90 (1998) 641-658; cf. Thomas Green, "The legislative competency of the Episcopal Conferences: present situation and future possibilities in light of Eastern Synodal experience," *The Jurist* 64 (2004) 284-331.

[8] Cfr. Congregation for the Doctrine of the Faith, letter *Communionis notio*, May 28, 1992: *AAS* 85 (1993) 838-850.

On various occasions the Roman Pontiff has recalled the binding character of the magisterium[9], precisely because it makes explicit the divine law on the nature of the person, and thus, of the exercise of the individual's freedom in the context of marriage. However, this teaching has later been taken up by the jurisprudence of the Roman Rota, which adds to the magisterium, which maneuvers on the substantial level, a new juridic element in this case, which belongs to a different level: the obligation to follow the jurisprudence.

The substantial nucleus of the canonical juridical nature proceeds then from the sacramental structure of the Church: from the very product of the sacraments instituted by Christ. It is understood, therefore, that throughout history the most virulent attacks against the legitimacy of canon law have sought to deny all relation between the visible aspects of the Church and her invisible dimension; between the sacraments, the Word, the law and the effective action of the grace of God, seeking to reduce all of those factors to purely symbolic elements without an effective relation with the divine action in history.[10]

To my understanding, this is the substantial or fundamental level of the canonical order, integrated with elements of divine law. In this sense, Pio Fedele was very right when he held that such principles and external rules were refractory to the social changes or to the flowing of time, since, to a large extent, they are part of the deposit of faith.

2. Integration of the canonical norm in its historical evolution

The other part of the paradox of the Roman canonist recognized on the other hand that, despite the fundamental immutability, the canonical order had shown throughout history a singular capacity to adapt to the various situations in different countries and historical periods, thus manifesting a dynamism and an elasticity which have no comparison with the secular juridical systems.

I think this characteristic responds above all to the pluri-centric character of its legislative system, as was said above. Together with norms emanating from the Supreme Authority of the Church—the Pope and the ecumenical councils—the ecclesial structure is integrated, in every historical moment, by a particular law of diocesan dimensions which proceeds from the various types of provincial or plenary councils. This makes it possible for the system of norms to maintain contact with the reality of the diverse places and times.

However, I am not going to make a presentation of a historical nature. Rather, I want to make reference to what is happening in our present times.

In the legislative order, as is well known, the 1983 code "consecrated" juridically the doctrine on the episcopacy of the Second Vatican Council. Consequently, the diocesan bishop, who represents Christ in the particular Church, it is acknowledged—not given—to have a wide legislative capacity

---

[9] John Paul II, *Allocution to the Roman Rota*, January 29, 2005: *AAS* 97 (2005) 166.

[10] Cfr. C.J. Errázuriz, *Corso fondamentale su diritto della Chiesa* (Giuffrè: Milan, 2009) 3-7.

which he should exercise in harmony with the canonical system as a whole,[11] and is limited only by matters which affect the ecclesial unity and communion or which the Roman Pontiff has expressly reserved to himself. Furthermore, the Holy See confers a certain legislative capacity upon the episcopal conferences—they are habitual faculties[12]—so that they may establish in each country a common normative nucleus to ensure cohesion among the dioceses. To make all of this possible, the 1983 code, significantly modifying the criteria followed by its 1917 predecessor, habitually kept itself on a more doctrinal and general level, letting the particular law determine the less substantial details of the institutions.

A very practical consequence of this: the need to request authentic responses of the universal legislator has decreased, for the interpretative problems more directly associated with the "everyday" juridical experience have been left now in the hands of the particular legislator.

Facing this decentralized process, it is proper to ask oneself what have been the results this has had in the legislative area? What use have the bishops and the episcopal conferences made of the competencies which have been acknowledged in them, or which they have received from the Holy See, respectively?

A large portion of episcopal conferences have legislated in matters which the code assigned to their competence; one-forth of them, however, have not after twenty-seven years. Almost always it is a matter of countries of mission territories which have undergone or are still undergoing difficult social periods, if not open persecution of the Church. Nevertheless, as a general rule, it should be pointed out that the determinations of the episcopal conferences, the general decrees, have not developed the specific aspects of their respective tradition very much; by and large they have limited themselves to enact norms similar to those of other conferences of their same geographical, linguistic or cultural area.[13]

Nor can a different appraisal be given of particular diocesan legislation; although on this point the evidence is more fragmented, it would be safe to affirm that, except for a few isolated cases, the expectations which the code put forward in the development of the diocesan legislation have not yet been verified. Apart from the obligatory norms of an institutional nature, like the statutes of diocesan organisms, the production of particular diocesan law has been characterized by its occasional and fragmentary character, responding primarily to the passing demands of each place, without anything that could be

---

[11] Cfr. W.L. Daniel, "The Principle of Legality in Canon Law," *The Jurist* 70 (2010) 29-85.

[12] Cfr. Juan I. Arrieta, *Diritto dell'organizzazione ecclesiastica* (Giuffré: Milan, 1997) 507-508; Juan I Arrieta, *Governance Structures within the Catholic Church* (Wilson & Lafleur: Montreal, 2000) 32, 36, 284-287.

[13] Cfr. J.T. Martion De Agar, et al., *Legislazione delle Conferenze episcopali complementari al CIC*, 2 ed. (Rome, 2009).

called a "encompassing project" which, without a doubt, in many places it was illusory to attempt.

What has been particularly incisive on this point, in my view, has been the lack of institutional use, as a general rule, which has been made of the convocation of the diocesan synods, which almost always have received the focus of a pastoral event, missing the opportunity to use them, as was their erstwhile purpose in the Church, to establish or renew, *in toto*, the body of the particular law of the dioceses.[14]

Whether for lack of necessary juridical sensibility, or for absence of technically prepared personnel or for the almost material impossibility to face such demands, above all in mission countries, it must be noted that the decentralizing effort of the 1983 code has as yet to be realized on the normative level.

The general decrees of the episcopal conferences and diocesan law are thus elements which integrate and give new dynamism to the universal norm in their respective places. But, on the other hand, it must also be noted that throughout time the meaning of the universal legislation changes and receives new applications. For example, today it is not possible to interpret the institutions of the code as we would have just after the promulgation of the text in 1983. In some cases, as we have seen, because there have been doctrinal documents which have changed the entire "paradigm" which corresponds to concrete institutions. But that itself has also happened in the strictly normative area: practically in all of the material sectors of interest to the code, there now exist new technical elements and new normative dispositions which in some way have developed the originating norm and which need to be integrated with it.

It is a matter, as a whole, of normative dispositions of very unequal nature, which possess an unequal juridical relevance which the good sense of the canonist should know how to integrate; the canonist cannot attempt pure mathematics, nor demand total formal rigor: here also the key to integration shall proceed from the relationship between the different planes of the canonical juridical nature.

At times they are *motu proprios* or apostolic constitutions, as the recent one on Ordinariates for the Anglicans,[15] or the one which approved the *Lex propria* of the Apostolic Signatura,[16] which add elements to the way of conceiving

---

[14] Cfr. Thomas Green, "Selected Issues in Developing Structures of Diocesan Communion," *The Jurist* 69 (2009) 418-441; Juan I. Arrieta, "Los sínodos españoles tras la promulgacion del código de derecho canónico de 1983," in *Actes du VII Congres de la Consociatio Internationalis Studio Iuris Canonici Promovendo*, vol. II (L'Annee canonique: Paris, 1992) 561-574.

[15] Cfr. Benedict XVI, apostolic constitution *Anglicanorum coetibus*, November 4, 2009: *AAS* 101 (2009) 985-900; Juan I. Arrieta, "Gli ordinariati personali," *Ius Ecclesiae* 22 (2010) 151-172.

[16] Cfr. Benedict XVI, motu proprio *Antiqua ordinatione*, June 21, 2008, promulgates the *Lex propria Supremi Tribunalis Signaturae Apostolicae*: *AAS* 100 (2008) 513-538; Juan

personal circumscriptions or which modify the deadlines of recourse established in *Pastor bonus*[17] or the norms given for the Roman vacant see.[18] In other cases it is a matter of dispositions of a lesser juridical nature, like the diverse instructions or directories, which on occasion develop unforeseen, or at times forgotten, aspects in the canons of the code. For example, the 2004 Directory *Apostolorum successores* for the pastoral ministry of the bishops explicitly invokes the figure of the "sede plena apostolic administrator"—not present in the code, —or declares what is the position of the auxiliary bishops in the meetings of the ecclesiastical province, to give just some examples.[19] Art. 101 of the 2008 *Lex propia* of the Signatura is another example, which finally makes efficacious the generic provisions of the code on the possibility to demand reparation for damages resulting from illegitimate administrative acts.[20]

In all these years, furthermore, there has been a succession of responses from the Congregation for Divine Worship on certain aspects of discipline about the administration of the sacraments;[21] the Apostolic Signatura has emitted a good number of decrees about procedural discipline, and the same has been done by the other Dicasteries—Doctrine of the Faith,[22] Catholic Education,[23]

I. Arrieta, "La 'Legge propria' della Segnatura apostolica," in *Ius et Iura: Escritos de Derecho Eclesiastico y de Derecho Canoni co en Honor del Profesor Juan Fornes*, ed. María Blanco, et at. (University of Navarra: Granada, 2010) 61-75; *La Lex propria del Supremi Tribunalis della Segnatura Apostolica*, ed. P.A. Bonnet, et al. (Vatican Publishing House: Vatican City, 2010).

[17] Cfr. John Paul II, apostolic constitution *Pastor bonus*, June 28, 1988, art. 123 §1: *AAS* 80 (1988) 845-930, modified by the art. 74 §1 *Lex propria Supremi Tribunalis Signaturae Apostolicae*.

[18] Cfr. John Paul II, apostolic constitution *Universi Dominici gregis*, February 22, 1996, n. 26: *AAS* 88 (1996) 305-343, now made precise in art. 2 §2 *Lex propria Supremi Tribunalis Signaturae Apostolicae*.

[19] Cfr. Congregation for Bishops, Directory *Apostolorum successores*, February 22, 2004, nn. 73 and 23 a; Thomas Green, "Contemporary Challenges to Episcopal Governance: Reflections on the 2004 Directory on the Ministry of Bishops and Other Pertinent Texts," *The Jurist* 68 (2008) 418-459.

[20] Art. 123 §2 *Pastor bonus* had given the Signatura competence to judge on the reparation for damages produced by illegitimate acts of the ecclesial administration (cc. 57 §3, 128 CIC). Now articles 101-103 of the *Lex propria Supremi Tribunalis Signaturae Apostolicae* defines the procedure.

[21] Cfr. Congregation for Divine Worship and Discipline of the Sacraments, *Responsa ad dubia proposita*: Notitiae 44 (2007) 182-183; Notitiae 45 (2009) 170, 171.

[22] Cfr. Congregation for the Doctrine of the Faith, *Risposte a quesiti riguardanti alcuni aspetti circa la dottrina sulla Chiesa*, June 29, 2007: *AAS* 99 (2007) 604-608; *Responsa ad quaestiones circa cibum et potum artificialiterprebenda,* August 1, 2007: *AAS* 99 (2007) 820-821; *Nota doctrinalis de quibusdam rationibus evangelizationis,* December 3, 2007: *AAS* 100 (2008) 489-504; *Responsa ad proposita dubia,* February 1, 2008: *AAS* 100 (2008) 200; instruction *Dignitas personae*, September 8, 2008: *AAS* 100 (2008) 858-887.

[23] Cfr. Congregation for Catholic Education, instruction *Sugli istituti superiori di scienze religiose,* June 28, 2008, ed. Vatican, 2008; "Orientamenti per l'utilizzo delle competenze psicologiche nell'ammissione e nella formazione dei candidati al

Religious,[24] etc.—in their areas of competence, giving general norms or developing praxis of action in very precise directions. Generally, it has not been necessary to alter the text of the canonical norm so that now a more defined interpretation might be given of the content of its norms. All of those interventions developed the norm of the code, indicating also its appropriate meaning, correcting other less adjusted interpretations.

The Pontifical Council for Legislative Texts—in addition to the promulgation of the instruction *Dignitas connubii*[25]—has also intervened on diverse occasions by way of authentic interpretations through the "Notes" or "Declarations."[26] The latter are surely not interpretations of the universal law which attempt to have equal binding as the law itself; but neither are they merely academic pronouncements without juridical relevance. Such notes, well known in the civil arena as ways to orientate the application of the laws, indicate what the position of the pontifical council is on specific points of the law and commit its future action on that point. Consequently, at least, they had to be given the juridical force that canon 19 grants to the *praxis Curiae Romanae* when the specific norm to be applied is lacking.

Practically every new disposition given in an area of the legislative order entails, at least, a small variation in the entire group of norms of the respective sector, at least to corroborate with new force the meaning they previously had. Thus, the faculties granted to nuncios suppose, for example, a modification of the intervention of the dicasteries of the Holy See;[27] each one of the concordats is also canon law and, seen as a whole, sketches inevitable lines of normative action of the Church.[28] The habitual faculties granted to some dicasteries in disciplinary matters, not to mention the norms of the recently revised *motu proprio Sacramentorum sanctitatis tutela* have undoubtedly altered the general framework of the penal system sketched by the code.[29]

---

secerdozio," *Communicationes* 40 (2008) 322-335.

[24] Cfr. Congregation for the Institutes of Consecrated Life and the Societies of Apostolic Life, instruction *Il servizio dell'autorita e l'obbedienza*, May 11, 2008: *L'Osservatore Romano*, May 29, 2008, appendix; *Linee orientative per la stesura della relazione periodica*, June 8, 2008: *AAS* 100 (2008) 580-584.

[25] Cfr. Pontifical Council for Legislative Texts, instruction *Dignitas connubii*, January 26, 2005; cfr. R. Page, "L'instruction *Dignitas connubii*: Questions and choices," *Studia Canonica* 41 (2007) 309-343.

[26] Cfr. J. Otaduy, "Los medios interpretativos de la ley canónica, y su relación con las distintas doctrinas de la interpretación," *Ius Canonicum* 35 (1995) 447-500.

[27] Cfr. *Index Facultatum Legalitis Pontificiis tributarum, Typis Polyglottis Vaticanis*, 1986; *Index Facultatum Legatis Pontificiis in territoriis missionum tributarum, Typis Polyglottis Vaticanis*, 1999.

[28] Cfr. C. Corral, *Derecho internacional concordatario* (Tecnos: Madrid, 2009) 131ff.

[29] Cfr. D. Cito, "Il diritto canonico di fronte ai reati (in particolare di fronte agli abusi sui minori)" *Iustitia* 63 (2010) 253-263; D.G. Astigueta, "Facoltà concesse alla Congregazione per il Clero," *Periodica* 99 (2010) 1-33; A. Bettetini, "Il diritto a un'adeguata tutela diurisdizionale (can 221) e it processo penale canonico per i 'delicta gravior'," in *Il diritto ecclesiastico*, vol. 1-2 (2008) 113-132.

On the other hand, neither can the incidence of the *praxis* of the Roman dicasteries[30] be forgotten, which canon 19 indicates in the case of a *lacuna*, and, is also an interpretive element of the norms and of the meaning of the institutions. With all the more reason, nevertheless, attention should be given to the jurisprudence of the Roman Rota—the only tribunal which establishes jurisprudence in the Church[31]—and it should be expected that the duty to periodically publish its decisions, which art. 11 of the new *Lex propria* of the Tribunal of the Apostolic Signatura now establishes, should make it possible in the future to know and use the jurisprudence in administrative matters.[32]

In summary, we find ourselves thus with a normative system in continual development, in which each new element makes more precise or modifies something of the preceding situation; it is up to the canonist to know how to integrate all these elements, giving to each one its different corresponding juridical weight in the design of the whole.

Returning to Pio Fedele's paradox, if on the one hand the eternal foundations appear immutable, their formal expressions—that is, the norms, the sentences and the other objective elements which develop them—are in constant evolution, to be applied to diverse situations but also as a means to better and more completely adjust the positive norms with those foundations that confer vitality to the whole system and were its first juridical level.

3. The interrelation between the substantial elements and the formal norm

Thus far, we have presented two levels of the juridical nature, and we have also indicated what their elements of knowledge are and how they are developed over time. These two levels come together in the juridical norm, or in the body of juridical norms which constitute the system of a canonical institution, as for example marriage, since the normative development of the institutions and the specific options adopted by the legislator contain the essential principles by which they are inspired.

Now we should ask ourselves how both levels become related; that is, what interrelations are established between the substantial elements and the formal norms with the other elements of the objective law of the Church?

The first point to which it is necessary to acquire awareness in this field is that both levels—the substantial and the normative, as we are calling them—which come together in the juridical norm, represent two levels of the juridical nature which should always be kept parallel, even though they are in close relation between themselves and even though the first level might in fact be the interpretative guide to the second.

---

[30] Cfr. Juan I. Arrieta, "Il valore giuridico della prassi nella Curia romana," *Ius Ecclesiae* 9 (1996) 97-117.
[31] Cfr. *Pastor bonus*, art. 126.
[32] *Lex propia del Supremo Tribunale della Segnatura Apostolica*, art. 11 §4: *AAS* 100 (2008) 517.

Next, it is necessary to warn that each level demands a diverse hermeneutical treatment, since the knowledge of the substantial principles, despite being juridical and obligatory, demands a method of abstraction akin to that which is proper to ecclesiology.

And thirdly, it is necessary to underline that between these two levels there exists an ontological type of hierarchy and dependence, and according to that hierarchy, divine law should always prevail.

Although the norm should be interpreted as a unit, it is necessary to keep a sort of "double reading" of the principles and of the normative formulations, whatever the juridical operation it may be that must be undertaken. I speak of a "double reading" in the sense that in this intellectual process each one of the two levels should maintain its proper autonomy and its influence upon the other.

(a) In the normative moment,[33] when a norm must be elaborated, the substantial elements of law mark which are the priority interests which should be protected and the finalities which the new law should try to reach, which throughout its articulation it should maintain itself in dialogue with close consistency with those principles. The legislator, whoever he may be, is closely bound to the theological "reality" sketched by the principles and criteria of divine, natural or positive law.

The human norm cannot change the substantial theological reality: this would be a positivistic illusion in which the one who has power could fail if there is no distinction between the interdependence of the two levels of the juridical nature. It is rather the substantial reality—which in the Church is theological—which guides the norm and shows how it should be integrated, showing the limits and the errors of the human legislator.[34]

Thus, Pio Fedele was right when he affirmed that "in no order like in the canonical order is the omnipotence of the legislator a myth."[35]

(b) On the doctrinal level, the canonist who dedicates himself or herself to making the canonical science progress, could not be content with a merely technical study of the norms or with the elaboration of those other principles or criteria adopted by the human legislator to give consistency to the system of norms; because upon ignoring the existence of the level which fundamental of

---

[33] Cfr. In this regard R.E. Jenkins, "Nulla Lex Satis Commoda Omnibus Est: The Implementation of the Penal Law of the 1983 Codex Iuris Canonici in Light of Four Principles of Modern Legal Codification," *The Jurist* 69 (2009) 615-645.

[34] "Las normas jurídicas que el legislador humano establece no pueden tener un contenido caprichoso sino que encuentran el fundamento de su juridicidad en su concordancia con el derecho divino, natural y positivo. Es más, la misión del legislador humano consiste precisamente en llevar a cabo un proceso de concreción y adecuación del Derecho divino a unas circunstancias históricas. No es posible, por tanto, escindir las normas de Derecho divino, natural y positivo, de las de Derecho humano, ya que es en función de su adecuación al Derecho divino como el Derecho humano encuentra la razón de su juridicidad" (Lombardía, "Derecho divino," 243).

[35] Fedele, 214.

the very norm it is deprived of the direct function which that level exercises in the interpretation of the norms and in the dogmatic reconstruction of the institutions.

(c) Particularly from the point of view of the application of the law, the canonical system seems like a type of hybrid, half way between the codified European system and the Anglo-Saxon juridical system. Certainly, the law exists and should be applied, but that does not free the canonist from the duty to confront it with the imperatives of substantial justice. The duty to apply the law does not free the canonist from verifying the demands of substantial justice, and in conformity with them, to interpret positive law and to choose the right way to apply it to the specific case.

In that way it is recognized that the rules and the norms of divine law maintain an autonomous juridical vigor, always making themselves present when specific situations have to be resolved, and imposing specific demands. That is what happens, above all, when from the cold application of the norm there comes forth a specific case of injustice and then harm to souls or the occasion of sin might objectively arise. For this reason, canon 1608 demands of the judge "moral certitude" before passing sentence on a matter which he must solve.

In such circumstances, the demands of divine law lead the one who should apply the norm to employ the technical elements of elasticity that canon law has elaborated throughout history precisely for this end: *epicheia*, dispensation, *disimulatio*, *aequitas*. They are, in the moment of application of the law the instruments to be used—or which the canonist should recommend to the ordinary, who would be the one who would have the juridical power to enact it—so that the demands of the substantial juridical nature should prevail which were in reality the *ratio legis* of the norm, but which might have been left behind.

All of this leads to an important characteristic of canon law in the area of the "certainty of the law": a demand that proceeds from these two levels of the juridical nature. In effect, the need to recognize an autonomous juridical nature to non-formalized elements of divine law clashes with the assumptions of the "certainty of the law" which the present juridical culture understands as an absolute dogmatic principle and a quasi-mathematical criterion.

Also, canon law, logically, seeks to reach that type of certitude, but not in an absolute way; that is, not when from a formal application of the norms, an injustice from a substantial point of view might ensue. They would obviously be greatly exceptional circumstances, but they presuppose the breaking of the absolute character of the principle.

This point was the object of a passionate debate among canonists of the middle of the last century.[36] The stakes were high: that the modern culture

---

[36] Cfr. R. Bidagor, "El espíritu del derecho canónico," in *Revista española de Derecho canónico* 13 (1958) 8ff.; P. Ciprotti, "Il fine Della Chiesa e il diritto," in *Archivo de*

should recognize the juridical nature of the canonical discipline. Whence the effort of an ample sector of canonists, most of whom taught in civil faculties of law, to greatly limit the influence of the demands of divine law, demanding the canonization of its principles[37] as a way to redirect its concrete juridical force through the routes of formalized law. [38]

However, there was no lack of who knew how to underline the capital role that divine law plays in the canonical system as well as the radical relevance that it has, which does not require any canonization. In canon law, this requires, however, to search elsewhere, to meet the demands of consistency and certainty which every juridical system claims for itself.[39]

With great intuition, it seems to me, the great jurist Giuseppe Capograssi indicated that it is in keeping in mind the two levels of the juridical nature which we are reviewing, it belongs to canon law to look no longer for "formal certitude", but rather to pursue above all "substantial certitude," which does not proceed only from the relationship between the decision and the external form of canon law, but above all with its conformity with the principles of the law[40] and with the *ratio* from which it proceeds.

In other words, the formal dictation of the norm, deprived of its agreement with the substantial principles and rules, would be inadequate to respond to the demands of justice in the Church.

4. On the priority of the substantial norm

One example of the priority which the substantial level has over the normative in the revisions of the canons of the code occurred recently with the

---

diritto eclesiástico 4 (1942) 36ff; J. De Salazar, *Lo jurídico y lo moral en el ordenamiento canónico* (Publicaciones del Seminario de Vitoria: Vitoria, 1960); P. Fedele, "Diritto canonico," in *Enciclopedia del diritto*, vol. XII (Giuffrè: Milan, 1964) 871-904; J. Hervada, *El ordenamiento canónico. Aspectos centrales de la construcción del concepto* (University of Navarra: Pamplona, 1966); O. Robleda, "Fin del derecho de la Iglesia," in *Revista española de Derecho canónico* 2 (1947) 283ff.; M.E., Casellati Alberti, "Note sulla salus animarum come fine della norma giuridica," in *La norma en el Derecho canónico* (University of Navarr: Pamplona, 1979) 683-690; V. Bertolone, *La "Salus animarum' nell'ordinamento giuridico della Chiesa* (New Coletti: Rome, 1987).

[37] Cfr. V. Del Guidice, "Canonizatio," in *Scritti giuridici in onore de Santi Romano*, vol. IV (Padua, 1939).

[38] Cfr. P.A. D'Avack, *Trattato di diritto canonico* (Giuffrè: Milan, 1978) 113ff.; Fedele, "Diritto canonico," 871-9044; E. Corecco, "Valore dell'atto contro legem," in *La norma en el Derecho canónico* (Pamplona, 1979) 845ff.; O. Giacchi, "Diritto canonico e domatica giuridica moderna," in *Annali della R. Universita di Macerata* 12-13 (1939) 193-194.

[39] Cfr. P. Lombardía, "Aportaciones de Vincenzo Del Giudice al studio sistemático del Derecho canónico," *Ius Canonicum* 2 (1962) 289-325.

[40] G. Capograssi, "La certezza del diritto nell'ordinamento canonico," in *Ephemerides iuris canonici* 5 (1949) 24ff.; S. Berlingo, "Il diritto divino nella dinamica dell'esperienza giuridica della Chiesa," in *Diritto divino e legislazione umana*, ed. A. R. Coppola et al. (G. Giappichelli: Turin, Italy, 1998) 160ff.

motu proprio Omnium in mentem. This was the second time that the text of the Code of Canon Law had been directly modified. In both cases, the attempt was to make adequate the legal norms with the demands of the substantial norms. Other initiatives are underway with precisely the same motive.

As is known, in 1998 the texts of canons 750 and 1371 of the Latin code were modified, and the corresponding canons of the Eastern code as well, through the *motu proprio Ad tuendam fidem* to make adequate its redaction,[41] in the substantive and penal aspects, to the text of the *Professio fidei* which was in effect since 1989.[42] The normative change of the *motu proprio* was only a consequence of the doctrinal clarification of the ordinary magisterium, which had previously modified the text of the *Professio fidei*.

However, it is no secret that it was the doctrinal formulation of the *Professio fidei* and not the *motu proprio* which in a binding way indicated the precise areas of the content of the Catholic faith.

The same reason has led now to the change of five canons of the Latin code with the *motu proprio Omnium in mentem*;[43] in the Eastern code it has not been necessary to intervene because the redaction of these texts did not present problems. On one hand, it was necessary to rectify canons 1008 and 1009 to avoid the extension to the diaconate of the faculty of "*agere in persona Christi Capitis*" reserved solely for presbyters and bishops, as the Congregation of the Doctrine of the Faith had precisely determined upon modifying in the typical edition, the redaction of the n. 875 of the *Catechism of the Catholic Church*.

For a like doctrinal reason, at least in part, it was necessary to modify the canons 1086 §1, 1117 and 1124 of the code, and to suppress the clause "*actus formalis defectionis ab Ecclesia Catolica*." The clause, which does not belong to the canonical tradition, had been originally introduced with the idea of saving the canonical validity of the marital unions of baptized Catholics who contracted marriage outside the Church. After consultation with all of the episcopal conferences in the late nineties, it was clear that the experience of the diocesan tribunals on this point had not been positive and that, in order to avoid juridical uncertainty and abuses of the marital discipline, it was appropriate to modify the text. But, above all, a deeper doctrinal problem emerged from those studies, related to the departure of the Church on the occasion of the so-called religious tax. It was an issue in Germany, Austria and Switzerland, with outstanding repercussions in the ecclesial legislation of each of these countries:[44] a most

---

[41] Cfr. John Paul II, *motu proprio Ad tuendam fidem*, May 8, 1998: *AAS* 90 (1998) 457-461.

[42] Cfr. Congregation for the Doctrine of the Faith, *Professio fidei et Iusiurandum fidelitatis*, January 9, 1989: *AAS* 81 (1989) 104-106.

[43] Cfr. Benedict XVI, *motu proprio Omnium in mentem*, October 26, 2009: *AAS* 102 (2010) 8-10; F. Coccopalmerio "Ragioni di due interventi," in *Communicationes* 41 (2009) 334-338; J. Werckmeister, "Le motu proprio Omnium in mentem et le mariage des ex-catholique," *Revue de Droit Canonique* 57/2 (2010) 241-254.

[44] Cfr. J.P. Durand, "Questions ethiques et pastorals des sorties d'eglise" in *L'Année*

interesting issue that I cannot elaborate on in this presentation.

For several years, the Pontifical Council for Legislative Texts and the Congregation for the Doctrine of the Faith studied the problem from a doctrinal point of view, also in dialogue with the respective episcopates. As a result, in March 2006 the Pontifical Council, with the approval of the Holy Father, sent out a circular letter, prepared in agreement with the Congregation for the Doctrine of the Faith.[45] In essence the document clarified from a doctrinal perspective that in order for the abandonment of the Church to take place a declaration made before a civil authority was not enough, but it was necessary that the manifestation of the will had to be verified in its proper pastoral context, that is, by means of a conversation with the pastor or with another minister who agreed to evaluate with certainty the intention of the subject.

It is known that the circular letter led to various reactions in each of the three mentioned countries. Thank God in the three countries mentioned, more adequate juridical alternatives are being found to express the consequences of this type of declaration. But what is of interest here is that that doctrinal declaration of 2006 and the resulting inquiry undertaken by the episcopal conferences determined the modification of the three canons of the code on formal abandonment of the Church. In what refers to abandonment on the occasion of the religious tax the *motu proprio Omnium in mentem* did not do anything except formalize the consequences of that declaration.

In the countries mentioned it was passively considered, at least since the promulgation of the 1983 code, that the Catholic who declared not to belong to the Catholic Church in the tax office, among other consequences, could not contract canonical marriage; but it was commonly understood that this civil marriage would receive full canonical recognition, since that person was not bound by canonical form in virtue of canon 1117. Furthermore, the diriment impediment for disparity of cult would not apply to that person either (c. 1086 §1) nor did the person need to ask permission to licitly contract a mixed marriage (c. 1124).

The entire situation has now changed, but in regards to the rejection on the occasion of the religious tax, the change did not occur from the *motu proprio* but rather from the 2006 declaration: that is, when it was clarified that the doctrinal point which was the root of the problem.

The point was brought out with all of its juridical force when months after the *motu proprio Omnium in mentem* was published, an episcopal Conference posed to the Pontifical Council the necessity to give "retroactive effect" to the

---

canonique 48 (2006) 11-17; R. Puza, "Les sorties de l'eglise: la situation allemande (kirchenaustritt)," *L'Année canonique* 48 (2006) 19-35; A. Borras, "Questions theologiques a propos des sorties de l'eglise catholique," *L'Année canonique* 48 (2006) 37-52; Ph. Toxe, *Les consequences de la definition de l'actus formalis defecionis sur le droit au marriage*," *L'Année canonique* 48 (2006) 53-59.

[45] Cfr. Pontifical Council for Legislative Texts, circular letter *Quad verba actus formalis defectionis ab Ecclesia catholica, Communicationes* 38 (2006) 170-172.

motu proprio and declare its juridical efficacy beginning at the entering into effect of the code in November 1983. Otherwise, it was argued, the civil unions of the baptized Catholics celebrated since 1983 until the *motu proprio* would be canonically valid in manifest disparity with the treatment of similar unions before 1983 or after the efficacy of *Omnium in mentem* which are invalid on the grounds of defective form.

The response of the Pontifical Council—which that episcopal conference immediately understood, completely resolving the problem[46]—has a close relation with what we are seeing here. There is no need for any intervention of the authority declaring the *motu proprio* retroactive because the canonical validity of those unions does not depend on the *motu proprio* but rather on the 2006 declaration which, in clarifying the doctrinal elements which make up the formal act of abandonment, with juridical effects declared *ex tunc*—from always—that the statement to the civil authority did not produce a formal abandonment and thus it did not exempt the baptized catholic from the substantial form of the celebration of marriage.

Therefore, *Omnium in mentem* has been a consequence which, with *ex nunc* effects, henceforth, reestablishes in this entire matter the juridical situation which existed before the code, when no other abandonment of the faith was recognized except for apostasy: a type of person who is probably not very concerned about whether the canonical legislation recognizes the validity of his eventual civil union.

The lesson is important. It is not the human norm which establishes the *ex nunc* determinate juridical effects, but rather the doctrinal declaration which clarifies the demands of the substance of law and which, with the *ex tunc* effect imposes itself in the canonical structure to the legislator, to the governing body,[47] and above all, to the judge who should apply the content of the doctrinal declaration of 2006 to see if a specific baptized person was subject to the canonical form even though he might have declared his abandonment of the Church before a civil authority.

Furthermore, the subordination of the *motu proprio* to the doctrinal declaration of 2006 has lessened the consequences of a technical problem of no small importance, as it rendered juridically irrelevant—at least in the cases related to the taxes, which were the most frequent—the date of the entering into effect of the *motu proprio* as such. It just so happens that, in effect, the editions of the *Acta Apostolicae Sedis* are at this moment six months behind, and that the *motu proprio Omnium in mentem* which was made known in November 2009 was just published in these weeks with the edition which has the date of January 2010. The *vacatio legis* prescribed by canon 8 §1 being three months from the

---

[46] Cfr. Österreichischen Bischofskonferenz, "Erklärende Ausführungen nach c. 34 CIC," in *Die Osterreichischen Bischofe*, 19 (2010) 15-16; idem., "Feststellung" in *Die Osterreichischen Bischofe*, 19 (2010) 17.

[47] Cfr. H. Pree, "The Divine and the Human of the Ius divinum," in *In diversitate unitas*, ed. Rik Torfs (Peeters Publishers: Leuven, 1997) 26.

date of the number of the *Acta Apostolica Sedis*, technically the *motu proprio* went into effect last April, four months before coming out in the *Acta.*

Although this defect should be avoided in future occasions, in the context of the topic which we are treating it seems an irony which underscores the limit of human technique in the face of reality.

The different efficacy of either document, and the anthological dependence which they maintain among themselves show the need to cultivate our sensibility regarding these two levels of the juridical nature: the substantial level, of divine law and of permanent principles which should always prevail in each situation of justice, and the legal level, which gives form and develops the principles of the substantial law from which it draws all of its juridical force, its capacity to oblige.

5. Positivism, exegesis and the quest for informing principles

This way of doing canon law, which forces us to consistently scrutinize the entire whole of elements which form the juridical nature of the Church also explains the difficulties our discipline has experienced faced with the increasing imperative of positivism in modern culture. For being true to its proper identity,[48] canon law has found itself on the periphery of the trends which have profoundly altered the framework of the secular juridical culture,[49] and it has had to suffer, for a century, the consequences of a cultural ostracizing which considers it a non juridical discipline.[50]

But the canonical science has not remained in a negative position, one of mere resistance. During that same period canon law has been able to achieve the reconstruction of its own law in a more modern key and much more consistent with the essence of the Church and with the sacramental system, as we see here. Despite the risks attached to two codification processes, and of the limitations incumbent on its scientific development—to which I will refer next, to conclude—canonicity has been able to substantially keep its original instruments intact minted by a bi-millennial tradition with the precise objective of insuring to the reason of the jurist of the Church direct contact with reality and with the truth, freeing the canonist from a rigid subjection to the mechanical dictation of the norms which would prohibit from weighing the correspondence of these with the substantial justice.

This characteristic of seeing oneself immune from juridical positivism, and

---

[48] Cfr. Juan I. Arrieta, "Ius divinum e ruolo della canonistica," in *Il Ius divinum nella vita della Chiesa: XIII Congresso Internazionale di Diritto Canonico* (Marcianum Press: Venezia 2010) 1395. Other works which treat the question from different perspectives can be found within this publication.

[49] Cfr. J.P. Schouppe, "Convergences et differences entre le droit divin des canoniste et le droit naturel des jurists," in *Ius Ecclesiae* 12 (2000) 29-67.

[50] Cfr. J. Hervada, "Il diritto naturale nell'ordinamento canonico," in *Ius Ecclesiae* 1 (1989) 493-508; ibid., "La 'lex naturae' e la 'lex gratiae' nella base dell'ordinamento giuridico della Chiesa," in *Ius Ecclesiae* 3 (1991) 49-66.

of having to cultivate direct contact with the substantial justice, with the natural law or the positive divine law, is today a patrimony almost exclusive of the canonist, and this makes the canonist particularly responsible in the face of the general juridical culture. For this reason, it is a duty for all of us to keep it and work for its progress.

How can one not be alarmed, for example, when after thirty years, based on canon 1095, consensual incapacity should be declared of one who has lived that time in peaceful family stability and having begotten offspring from that union? The harmony between the two levels of the juridical nature cannot leave the canonist at ease in such cases. He should ask himself, could it not be that the marriage system has concentrated above all on one of the interests, certainly constitutive of marriage, while, however, ignoring that at the same time other substantially relevant interests have emerged equally worthy of juridical protection?

But I move to my final point.

I have alluded above to the limitations placed on the scientific development of canon law, and should like to finish this presentation by making explicit reference to this point.

When in 1917 the *Codex Iuris Canonici* was promulgated, the then Sacred Congregation for Seminaries and University Studies issued two decrees which have marked the posterior course of teaching of Canon Law and also the way in which many canonists relate to the canonical norm. In one decree the Congregation indicated that in teaching canon law each of the canons should be analyzed, presenting the structure of the Code according to its books, titles and chapters, and diligently explaining the content of the canons regarding their origin and their history.[51] In the second decree the Congregation indicated that canon law exams should focus on the exegesis of the canons isolated from one another as well as from the origin of the institutions and their historical evolution.[52]

These two decisions, which speak eloquently about the fears of the age regarding the reception of the code, have had an influence through the following century, crystallizing in the majority of the curricula in faculties, in the course outlines, and in the text-books of canon law. In light of what has been discussed here, this other perspective offers rather a static vision of the canonical norm, elevating it almost to an inaccessible archetype, without drawing out the structural elements to confront the new situations.

Instead of perceiving the norm in its course, integrating it with those other norms which appeared later, one focuses on the origin, trying to understand the meaning of the expressions which it uses. Undoubtedly this exercise is

---

[51] Cfr. S. Congregation for Seminaries and Educational Institutions, Decree, August 7, 1917: *AAS* 9 (1917) 439.

[52] Cfr. S. Congregation for Seminaries and Educational Institutions, Decree, October 31, 1918: *AAS* 11 (1919) 19.

necessary, but it represents only the starting point because later it must be integrated with the successive elements which the juridical experience offers. If the effort is solely concentrated on the genesis of the norm and only on its exegesis, as often happens, one falls into a worship of the legal text, which would prevent us from facing what is represented by the substantial law, leading us almost without realizing it, to some of the dangers of juridical positivism.

Furthermore, concentrating on the positive norm is a risk because it is then difficult to give consistent answers to new problems, on which no precise juridical regulation may yet exist. Accustomed to reason exclusively from the norm, the absence of a legal decree leads to an incapacity to resolve new situations.

The only alternative is to give primary attention to the principles which guide the system. As opposed to the proposition which we have just seen, the systematic consideration of the juridical order, in addition to dealing with the concrete laws, tries to elaborate the principles around which each group of norms is organized, giving them consistent unity and harmony. Such principles drawn from the canonical order are added to those others of the substantial law which we saw at the beginning, and give the key to face new situations.

The juridical life of the Church, which frequently sees itself increasingly obliged to respond to unforeseen situations in the norm, imposes the need to systematize and resolve the cases in a way consistent with these principles of the canonical order. To them also refers canon 19 of the code when it indicates what is to be done when norms are lacking.

Recently we have witnessed examples of this situation with regard to the emergency in the matter of the sexual abuses by the clergy in some countries and the urgency to establish protocols which would guarantee safe external conduct and pastoral activity with young people. It has frequently occurred that to resolve these questions it has been entrusted to the civil jurists to prepare adequate programs in accord with the administrative system of each country. It is exactly what any multinational corporation would have done. But the fact is that the Church is not a corporation. The Church is an originating society, with a law with two thousand years of history, and with juridical principles which must be applied, which can incorporate without difficulty many elements of the administrative system of each country, but which cannot renounce, for example, to the hierarchical direction of the initiative and the ecclesial authority that has to act; to the way in which the Church envisions the relationship between the presbyter and his bishop; to her own understanding of the paternal power (*patria potestas*) of parents over their children, or the demands and the limits of intimacy between persons.

It is true that other factors have influenced this abdication of canon law, not the least of which has been, in my opinion, the misguided conviction that the structure of the legislative order of the ecclesial society does not have the necessary elements to consistently and efficaciously deal with new situations. I believe this is an erroneous conviction. For this reason, the canonists' task to search and elaborate the inspiring principles of the canonical system becomes particularly important.

KEYNOTE ADDRESS

STABILITE ET DYNAMISME DU SYSTEME JURIDIQUE CANONIQUE

Most Reverend Juan Ignacio Arrieta

Afin du présenter les caractéristiques du Droit canonique j'ai utilisé, à l'occasion, le paragraphe du livre *Lo spirito del diritto canonico*, avec lequel Pío Fedele débute le chapitre sur la certitude du droit. Dans cet ouvrage, publié en 1962, Fedele exprime d'une façon plutôt poétique une espèce de paradoxe identifiant avec précision, selon mon opinion, des manifestations externes du Droit de l'Église sur lesquelles je souhaite attirer votre attention.

> « Celui qui considère – disait Fedele – les principes immuables et éternels sur lesquels l'ordonnancement canonique prends appui, ainsi que les veines interminables à l'intérieur desquelles il plonge ses racines profondes, pourra penser qu'en comparaison avec les autres ordonnancements juridiques, le canonique soit le plus statique, immobile e inflexible, le plus réfractaire à tout type de changement politique, économique ou social que puisse tisser le canevas de l'histoire humaine. Il leur paraîtra le moins sensible à l'incontournable inégalité des cas et à la spécificité des situations qui constituent le perpétuel flux de l'histoire. En revanche, pour celui qui considère l'immense diversité des gens que l'ordonnancement canonique englobe et la riche variété d'époques historiques qu'il a parcouru dans son existence séculaire, ce même ordonnancement canonique apparaîtra, au delà de tout autre ordonnancement juridique, comme le plus dynamique, muable et flexible, celui qui répond le mieux à la spécificité de chaque cas de la vie individuelle et sociale »[1].

En effet, le Droit canonique est un système qui, d'une part, s'appuie sur des fondements qu'on ne peut pas modifier à sa guise et qui sont hors de portée de toute transaction ou de toute possibilité de pacte. D'autre part, ce même Droit prétend à son application de façon cohérente dans le monde entier; il vise aussi à solutionner toute situation juridique qui puisse se présenter dans la société ecclésiale. En outre, l'histoire du Droit canonique montre qu'en dépit des déficiences qui aient pu exister à certaines périodes, en règle générale, la prétention à l'universalité de son application a été atteinte tout au long des différentes époques de l'histoire. Plus encore, le Droit canonique a même joué un rôle de suppléance devant l'inexistence ou les lacunes des systèmes juridiques

---

[1]Cfr. P. FEDELE, *Lo spirito del diritto canonico*, Padova 1962, p. 197. Traduction de l'auteur.

civils. Cela a été rendu possible grâce à la structure spécifique de l'Église qui comprend une incomparable pluralité d'instances législatives (le Pape, les évêques, les conciles particuliers et pléniers, et maintenant les Conférences épiscopales). Ces instances mettent en rapport l'universel avec les aspects les plus concrets et diversifiés en différents endroits.

De plus, si de façon générale ce Droit a su répondre aux interrogations de justice de la société ecclésiale, cela est dû surtout aux caractéristiques intrinsèques du système juridique et à la façon dont il doit être appliqué dans l'Église.

Dans cet exposé je souhaite rappeler le dynamisme substantiel caractéristique de l'ordonnancement canonique : un dynamisme qui, pour résoudre les situations concrètes de justice, doit intégrer, en harmonie avec chaque nouvelle circonstance, la diversité de niveaux juridiques et les multiples éléments d'importance canonique variable. Je viserai donc à mettre en évidence la plus complète opposition entre le système légal de l'Église catholique et toute forme de positivisme juridique. Je souhaite montrer la force vitale que l'ordonnancement et l'élaboration juridique du canoniste reçoivent de la cohérence par rapport aux principes théologiques et au droit divin, qui en tant que fondement de toute norme canonique doivent toujours orienter la résolution des conflits.

1. Le plan de la juridicité substantielle: fondement et guide de l'ordonnancement

Fedele affirme, avec à propos, que le Droit canonique s'appuie sur des facteurs immuables qui ne sont pas laissés à la libre disposition des individus. Ces éléments constituent, pour ainsi dire, le noyau essentiel et la source d'où jaillissent les caractères juridique (juridicité) et obligatoire (obligatoriété) spécifiques du Droit canonique.[2] Ces éléments sont, en même temps, le « titre » en vertu duquel aussi bien l'autorité que les fidèles exercent respectivement leurs fonctions et leur guide pour développer par la suite les normes positives de l'ordonnancement canonique, dans chacune des sphères qui intéressent la société ecclésiale.

Voilà où s'enracine un premier plan ou niveau substantiel de la juridicité, qu'il nous faut considérer[3].

En effet, la spécificité principale dont jouit l'ordonnancement canonique, en comparaison avec tout autre système juridique, est ancrée dans la source même

---

[2]Bien que je ne trouve pas les mots « juridicité » et « obligatorieté » dans le dictionnaire de la langue française, ils manifestent d'une façon plus succincte les notions que j'utiliserai tout le long de cette exposée.

[3] Cfr. J. HERVADA, *Introduction to the Study of Canon Law*, Gratianus Series, Montreal 2007, p. 57 ss. *(Introducción al estudio del derecho canónico*, Pamplona 2007, pp. 69 ss.); F. COCCOPLAMERIO, *Riflessioni sull'identità del diritto ecclesiale*", in *Codice di Diritto Canonico commentato*, Milano 2009, pp. 38 ss.; G. LO CASTRO, *La dimensione umana del diritto divino*, in "Diritto divino e legislazione umana", a cura di A. Filipponio-R. Coppola, Turin 1998, pp. 50 ss.

d'où provient sa légitimité et d'où découle également sa capacité d'établir des liens juridiques parmi ses fidèles[4]. L'ordonnancement juridique de l'Église est, en effet, celui d'un groupe social provenant d'une religion révélée et en tant que groupe, tire son origine de la Volonté divine exprimé dans cette Révélation. Cette Révélation est transmise, comme l'enseigne la théologie catholique, à travers l'Écriture Sainte, la Tradition et le Magistère de l'Église. En dernière instance, la Volonté du Christ est la source de la légitimité des institutions de l'Église ainsi que de tout le système canonique en tant que tel. C'est cette Volonté du Christ qui donne à chacun des éléments qui constituent l'ordonnancement toute leur importance juridique[5].

Le lien existant dans l'Église entre les gouvernants et les sujets, ne découle d'aucun 'pacte social', comme dans les ordonnancements civils. Dans l'Église, ce lien procède 'exactement' (pouvons-nous dire maintenant avec la théologie du Concile Vatican II) de la structure sacramentelle et hiérarchique que le Christ a voulu établir pour son Église. Ainsi, Il a institué le sacrement de l'Ordre et constitué des Pasteurs pour diriger les communautés, identifier et enseigner les contenus de la communion qui doivent animer tous ses membres. C'est là aussi qu'est sa source, comme on le sait, de la position d'autorité des institutions et des personnes qui occupent les fonctions; dans cette même structure nous retrouvons le fondement des mandats qu'elles reçoivent; puisque sans ce fondement elles n'auraient pas leur légitimité.

De la structure sacramentelle de l'Église constitué par les sacrements, principalement du Baptême et de l'Ordre sacré, tout comme de la Volonté fondatrice du Christ qui demeure vivante dans l'Église, provient en résumé le noyau central de la juridicité canonique. Ce noyau est formé de principes (rarement de normes) ayant plus ou moins de relations réciproques, de principes obligatoires et le plus souvent inabrogeables.

Mais, la force de la Volonté divine et des sacrements ne légitime pas seulement la loi ou l'autorité. Les autres composantes de l'ordonnancement canonique, la place des fidèles dans l'Église et l'efficacité juridique de leurs déclarations de volonté, acquièrent, de cette même source, la reconnaissance dans le système juridique canonique.

De la même façon que l'ordre sacré est à la base des positions d'autorité et de hiérarchie, le sacrement du baptême établi la position juridique fondamentale de base du fidèle chrétien, la racine de ses droits et de ses devoirs fondamentaux et l'assise de sa capacité pour générer efficacement du droit canonique avec ses manifestations de volonté : lorsqu'il décide par exemple de fonder une association dans l'Église ou d'adhérer personnellement à une association existante, ou lorsqu'il s'engage librement par un voeu, ou encore lorsqu'il

---

[4] Cfr. P. LOMBARDÍA, *Sobre las caracteristicas peculiares del ordenamiento canónico*, in *Escritos de Derecho Canónico* I, Pamplona 1973, pp. 173-222, spec. 221; K. MÖRSDORF, *Sulla fondazione del diritto canonico*, in "Fondamenti del Dirito canonico", Venecia, 2008, pp. 141 ss.

[5] Cfr. J. HERVADA, *Introduction ...,* cit, note 2, pp. 19 ss (*Introducción,* pp. 31 ss.)

manifeste le consentement pour constituer l'alliance conjugale[6].

Tous ces facteurs, présents dans les différents secteurs du Droit canonique (dans le droit des associations ou dans la structure hiérarchique; dans la sphère du *munus docendi*, dans le droit matrimonial ou dans le droit pénal) représentent ce qu'on peut reconnaître comme un premier niveau de la juridicité canonique. Ce premier niveau est composé de principes et de règles à caractère obligatoire; ces principes et ces règles ont leur propre système de connaissance et leur propre méthode d'élaboration, qui doivent toujours être pris en compte, quelle que soit la nature de l'opération juridique à accomplir. C'est ainsi que ceux qui élaborent des normes générales, comme ceux qui veillent à leur application dans des cas concrets, doivent toujours agir en cohérence avec les principes que nous venons d'exposer.

Ces principes auxquels je me réfère sont aux sources mêmes de la Révélation. Leur connaissance et leur développement ont suivi les mêmes aléas historiques que l'élaboration du dogme. Ils ont été explicités peu à peu au long de l'histoire. Cela a conduit à une formulation juridique en accord avec la théologie catholique au cours des siècles. Le Concile Vatican II donne un bon exemple de ce développement doctrinal. Ainsi, l'approfondissement de la dimension sacramentelle de l'épiscopat a permis de formuler, avec plus de précision notamment, le statut du Collège épiscopal et de l'Église particulière. De même, le développement de la théologie du Peuple de Dieu a permis d'articuler, pour la première fois, les droits fondamentaux des fidèles enracinés dans le baptême.

Le progrès dans la connaissance du noyau primaire du *ius divinum*, qui donne son fondement à la juridicité canonique et oriente le développement de son ordonnancement, apparaît ainsi lié au Magistère de l'Église. Ainsi l'activité du Magistère se présente comme l'élément dynamique et un facteur d'expansion du Droit canonique[7].

Ce que nous venons de voir en rapport avec la doctrine du Concile Vatican II, peut être vérifié avec les expressions successives du Magistère ordinaire dans divers domaines. Par exemple, lorsqu'aujourd'hui on réfléchit sur la structure et les compétences des Conférences épiscopales, il n'est plus possible d'ignorer le *motu proprio Apostolos suos* de 1998, qui a reconsidéré toute la doctrine sur la dimension collective de l'épiscopat[8]. Ou comment traiter aujourd'hui, par exemple, la position des Églises locales au sein de la *communio ecclesiarum*, ainsi que celle de leurs Pasteurs respectifs, sans prendre en compte la Lettre

---

[6] Cfr. P. LOMBARDÍA, Der*echo divino y persona física en el ordenamiento canónico*, in "Escritos de Derecho Canónico", Pamplona 1973, pp. 225-253.

[7] P.J. VILADRICH, Ius divinum *como criterio de autenticidad en el Derecho de la Iglesia*, in "Ius Canonicum" 16, 1976, p. 104.

[8] Cfr. JEAN-PAUL II, m.p. *Apostolos Suos*, du 21.V.1998, AAS 90 (1998) 641-658; cfr. T.J. GREEN, *The legislative competency of the Episcopal Conferences: present situation and future possibilities in light of Eastern Synodal experience*, in "The Jurist" 64, 2004, pp. 284-331.

Communionis Notio, publiée par la Congrégation pour la Doctrine de la Foi en 1992, qui a développé amplement cette question spécifique[9]? Ces deux documents sont des expressions du Magistère déterminant l'interprétation substantielle de ces institutions et d'autres en rapport avec elles. Pour la même raison, comment pourrait-on interpréter aujourd'hui la portée des divers facteurs qui interviennent dans les situations d'incapacité consensuelle envisagées au canon 1095 du Code sans avoir à l'esprit le constant Magistère pontifical sur cette matière?

Le Pontife romain a rappelé à plusieurs reprises la force juridiquement contraignante que possède ce Magistère[10], précisément parce qu'il explicite le droit divin sur la nature de la personne et par conséquence aussi sur l'exercice de sa liberté dans le contexte matrimonial. En outre, un tel enseignement a été accueilli par la jurisprudence de la Rote Romaine, et telle intégration dans la jurisprudence ajoute au Magistère (au niveau substantiel) un nouvel élément de juridicité, appartenant à un autre niveau (le devoir de suivre la jurisprudence).

C'est ainsi que le noyau substantiel de la juridicité canonique provient de la structure sacramentelle de l'Église: c'est le produit des Sacrements institués par le Christ. L'on comprend alors, que tout au long de l'histoire les attaques les plus virulents contre la légitimité du Droit canonique aient cherché à nier toute relation entre les aspects visibles de l'Église et sa dimension invisible; entre les Sacrements, la Parole, la Loi et l'action efficace de la grâce de Dieu, visant à réduire tous ces facteurs à des éléments purement symboliques, sans aucune relation efficace avec l'action divine dans l'histoire[11].

Voilà ce que je considère comme le niveau substantiel ou fondamental de l'ordonnancement canonique, incluant des éléments de droit divin. Pio Fedele avait, donc, grandement raison, dans ce sens, lorsqu'il soulignait que ces principes ou ces règles éternelles étaient réfractaires aux changements sociaux ou historiques, puisque pour une large part ils manifestent le dépôt de la Foi.

2. L'intégration de la norme canonique dans le devenir historique

Un autre axe du paradoxe mis en évidence par Fedele, reconnaissait, en revanche, que malgré ces fondements immuables, l'ordonnancement canonique avait démontré au long de l'histoire une haute capacité d'adaptation aux multiples situations de nombreux pays et de périodes historiques. Il manifestait alors son dynamisme et sa flexibilité qui dépassent, sans comparaison possible, tous les systèmes juridiques séculiers.

Cette caractéristique, me semble-t-il, répond avant tout aux caractères de son système législatif. En effet, à côté des normes émanant de l'Autorité Suprême

---

[9] Cfr. CONGR. POUR LA DOCTRINE DE LA FOI, Lettre *Communionis Notio*, nº 8, 28.V.1992, AAS 86 (1993) 838-850.

[10] Cfr. JEAN-PAUL II, alloc. du 29 janvier 2005 au Tribunal de la Rote Romaine, AAS 97 (2005) 166.

[11] Cfr. C.J. ERRÁZURIZ, *Corso fondamentale sul diritto della Chiesa*, I, Milano 2009, pp. 3-7.

de l'Église (le Pape ou les Conciles Œcuméniques), l'ordonnancement ecclésial comprendra, à chaque moment historique, le droit particulier diocésain ou résultant des divers types de Conciles provinciaux ou pléniers. Tout cela permet au système des normes de se maintenir toujours en contact étroit avec la diversité spatio-temporelle.

Je ne compte toutefois pas faire une réflexion de nature historique. Je souhaite plutôt me centrer sur ce qui se produit dans notre temps.

Comme l'on sait, dans l'ordre législatif, le Code de droit canonique de 1983 a consacré juridiquement la doctrine du Concile Vatican II sur l'épiscopat. En conséquence, l'évêque diocésain représente le Christ dans l'Église particulière et on lui reconnaît (on ne lui octroie pas) une grande capacité législative qu'il doit exercer en harmonie avec l'ensemble du système canonique[12]. Cette capacité n'est limitée que par les matières qui affectent l'unité et la communion ecclésiale, ou encore par celles réservées au Pontife Romain. En outre, le Saint Siège accorde aux Conférences épiscopales une certaine capacité législative (des facultés habituelles[13]) afin qu'elles puissent établir dans le pays un noyau normatif commun assurant la cohésion entre les diocèses. Afin de rendre possible cette façon de procéder, le Code de 1983, a modifié notablement le critère suivi par le Code de 1917. Il s'est ainsi maintenu habituellement sur un plan plus doctrinal et général, laissant au droit particulier le soin de donner solutions aux aspects moins substantiels des institutions.

Une des conséquences pratiques de cette façon de procéder est la diminution du « besoin » de recourir auprès du législateur universel pour obtenir des réponses authentiques, puisque les problèmes d'interprétation reliés directement à l'expérience juridique quotidienne reviennent à la juridiction du législateur particulier.

Devant cette décentralisation, il est légitime de se demander quels ont été les résultats de cette façon de procéder dans le domaine législatif ? Quel a été l'usage que les évêques et les Conférences épiscopales ont fait de cette compétence qui leur était reconnue ou qu'ils recevaient du Saint-Siège?

Nombre de Conférences épiscopales ont légiféré dans les domaines que le Code confiait à leur compétence. En revanche, au moins vingt-cinq pour cent de ces Conférences à travers le monde, n'ont pas exercé ce pouvoir, 27 ans après la promulgation du Code. Il s'agit presque toujours de pays de territoires de mission ou encore de pays qui ont traversé ou traversent toujours de difficiles périodes sociales et, dans certains cas, une persécution ouverte contre l'Église. En règle générale, cependant, on constate que les interventions des Conférences épiscopales, par les décrets généraux, n'ont pas exposé en détail les aspects

---

12 Cfr. W.L. DANIEL, *The Principe of Legality in Canon Law*, in "The Jurist" 70, 2010, pp. 29-85.

13 Cfr. J.I. ARRIETA, *Diritto dell'organizzazione ecclesiastica*, Milano 1997, pp. 507-508; ID, *Governance Structures wthin the Catholic Church,* Gratianus Series, Montreal 2000, pp. 32, 36, 284-287

spécifiques de leur propre tradition nationale. Une bonne partie des Conférences s'est limitée à édicter des normes similaires à celle d'autres Conférences de leur aire géographique, linguistique ou culturelle[14].

Il ne semble pas que l'on puisse donner une évaluation différente par rapport à la législation particulière diocésaine, bien que dans ce domaine l'information soit plus fragmentaire. Il n'est pas risqué d'affirmer que, sauf dans des cas isolés, les attentes que le Code plaçait dans la législation diocésaine ne se sont pas encore concrétisées.

Outre les normes obligatoires de type institutionnel, tels les statuts des organismes diocésains de participation, la production de droit particulier diocésain se caractérise par son caractère conjoncturel et fragmentaire, principalement en réponse aux exigences contingentes de chaque lieu, sans traduire ce qu'on pourrait appeler 'un projet d'ensemble', qu'il était sans aucun doute illusoire d'envisager dans bien des endroits

À mon point de vue, cela a eu pour conséquence notable la soous-utilisation institutionnelle des Synodes diocésains. En règle générale, ceux-ci ont été convoqué davantage comme un événement pastoral, perdant ainsi l'opportunité de les utiliser pour établir ou renouveler en bloc le droit particulier diocésain, fonction qu'ils avaient accomplie jadis dans l'Église[15].

Ainsi, que ce soit par manque de la nécessaire sensibilité juridique, ou par l'absence de personnel techniquement préparé, ou encore par la presqu'impossibilité matérielle de relever de telles exigences, principalement dans des pays de mission, force nous est de constater que l'effort de décentralisation du Code de 1983, n'a pas encore eu le succès escompté au plan de la dynamique normative.

Les décrets généraux des Conférences des évêques et le droit diocésain constituent des éléments qui intègrent et donnent un nouveau dynamisme, dans leurs lieux respectifs, à la norme universelle. Mais il faut tenir compte également des changements de sens et des nouvelles déterminations que la législation universelle reçoit au cours du temps. Aujourd'hui il est impossible d'interpréter les institutions du Code de droit canonique comme nous l'aurions fait au moment de sa promulgation en 1983. Outre l'impact que puisse avoir le CCEO de 1990,

---

[14] Cfr. J.T. MARTÍN DE AGAR-L. NAVARRO, *Legislazione delle Conferenze episcopali complementari al C.I.C.*, 2ª ed., Roma, 2009. On peut consulter celles des Conférences de dix pays francophones dans *Code de droit canonique bilingue et annoté,* 3e éd.(2e tirage révisé), E. Caparros et H. Aubé (éd), Collection Gratianus, Montréal 2009, Appendice III, pp. 1791-1973; et celles des Conférences de treize pays anglophones dans *Code of Canon Law Annotated*, 2nd edition revised and updated, E. Caparros et H. Aubé (ed), Gratianus Series, Montréal, 2004, Appendix III, pp. 1637-1817.

[15] Cfr. T.J. GREEN, *Selected Issues in Developing Structures of Diocesan Communion*, in "The Jurist" 69, 2009, pp. 418-441 (spec. pp. 427-429); J.I. ARRIETA, *Sínodos españoles tras la promulgación del código de derecho canónico de 1983*, in Actes du VII Congrès de la Consociatio Internationalis Studio Iuris Canonici Promovendo, "L'Année canonique", hors serie, vol. II, Paris 1992, pp. 561-574.

thème qui sera traité dans une autre conférence, il convient de signaler que dans quelques cas, comme nous l'avons vu, il y a eu certains documents doctrinaux qui ont complètement modifié le « paradigme » correspondant à des institutions concrètes. Mais cela est arrivé aussi dans le champ strictement normatif: pratiquement dans tous les secteurs matériels qui intègrent le Code il y a maintenant des nouveaux éléments techniques et des nouvelles disposition normatives qui, d'une façon ou d'une autre, ont déployé la norme originaire et doivent être intégrés dans cette norme.

Il s'agit, dans l'ensemble, de dispositions normatives de nature très diverse et qui possèdent un impact juridique très diffèrent. Le bon sens du canoniste doit le conduire à les intégrer.

Parfois ce sont des *motu proprio* ou des constitutions apostoliques, comme la récente constitution sur les Ordinariats pour les Anglicans[16] ou celle qui a approuvé la *Lex propria* de la Signature Apostolique,[17] ajoutant des éléments sur la façon de concevoir les circonscriptions personnelles ou modifiant les délais du recours établi par *Pastor Bonus*[18] ou encore les normes concernant la vacance du Siège de Rome[19]. Dans d'autres cas, il s'agit de dispositions d'une nature juridique secondaire tels les diverses instructions et directoires qui, à l'occasion, développent des aspects imprévus ou encore oubliés dans les canons du Code. Par exemple, le Directoire *Apostolorum successores* sur le ministère pastoral de évêques de 2004 rétablit explicitement la figure de « l'administrateur apostolique *sede plena* », absent du Code, ou déclare quelle est la position des évêques auxiliaires lors des réunions de la Province ecclésiastique, pour ne donner que ces exemples.[20] Un autre exemple: l'article 101 de la *Lex propria* de la Signature, de 2008, rend finalement efficaces les prévisions génériques du Code sur la possibilité d'exiger la réparation pour les dommages causés par des actes illégitimes de l'administration.[21]

---

[16] Cfr. BENOÎT XVI, *const. ap. Anglicanorum coetibus*, 4.XI.2009, AAS 101 (2009) 985-990; J.I. ARRIETA, *Gli ordinariati personali*, in “Ius Ecclesiae” 22, 2010, pp. 151-172.

[17] Cfr. BENOÎT XVI, *motu proprio Antiqua ordinatione,* 21.VI.2008, promulguant la *Lex propria Supremi Tribunalis Signaturae Apostolicae*, AAS 100 (2008) 513-538; J.I. ARRIETA, *La ‘Legge propria' della Segnatura apostolica*, in *In charitate iustitia,* Rivista giuridica del Tribunale ecclesiastico Regionale Calabro, XVII, 2009, pp. 33-54; AA.VV., *La Lex propria del S.T. della Segnatura Apostolica*, a.c. P.A. Bonnet, C. Gullo, Roma 2010.

[18] Cfr. JEAN-PAUL II, *const.* ap. *Pastor Bonus*, art. 123 §1, 28.VI. 1988, AAS 80 (1988) 8451-930, modifié par l'art. 74 §1 *Lex propria Supremi Tribunalis Signaturae Apostolicae.*

[19] Cfr. JEAN-PAUL II, *const. ap. Universi Dominici gregis*, nº 26, 22.II.1966, AAS 88 (1996) 305-343, maintenant précisé dans l'art. 2 §2 *Lex propria Supremi Tribunalis Signaturae Apostolicae*.

[20] Cfr. CONGR. POUR LES ÉVÊQUES, Directoire *Apostolorum Successores*, nºs 73 et 23.a), 22.II. 2004; cfr. T.J. GREEN, *Contemporary Challanges to Episcopal Governance : Reflections on the 2004 Directory on the Ministry of Bishops and Others Pertinent Texts*. In “The Jurist” 68, 2008, pp. 418-459.

[21] L'art. 123 §2 *Pastor Bonus* avait donné à la Signature la compétence pour juger de la

Durant toutes ces année, il y a eu aussi des Réponses de la Congrégation pour le Culte concernant des aspects concrets de la discipline de l'administration des Sacrements,[22] la Signature Apostolique a porté un nombre important de décrets dans le domaine de la procédure et d'autres Dicastère on fait de même (la Doctrine de la Foi,[23] l'Éducation catholique,[24] les Religieux[25]), chacun donnant des normes générales ou développant une praxis pour des actions précises dans son champ de compétence. De façon générale, il n'a pas été nécessaire de modifier le texte des normes du Code, mais il faut désormais donner une interprétation plus nuancée au contenu de ces normes. Toutes ces interventions développaient les normes du Code et en indiquaient aussi le sens adéquat, tout en corrigeant d'autres interprétations moins justes.

Le Conseil pontifical pour les Textes Législatifs – autre a la promulgation de l'Instruction *Dignitas connubii* de 2005[26] – est intervenu également à plusieurs reprises en apportant des interprétations authentiques et au moyen de « Notes » ou de « Déclarations ».[27] Certes, ces dernières ne sont pas des interprétations de la loi universelle qui puissent avoir la même force obligatoire que la loi elle même; toutefois, elles ne sont pas non plus des opinions purement académiques sans portée juridique. Ces Notes (présentées dans certains cas sous d'autres appellations) sont bien connues dans le monde civil. Elles orientent la façon d'appliquer la loi et indiquent la position du Conseil pontifical sur des points spécifiques du droit; elles engagent le Conseil dans ses interventions futures sur ce point. Ainsi, au minimum, on peut donc reconnaître à ces

---

réparation des dommages produits par des actes illégitimes de l'administration ecclésiastique (cc. 57 §3, 128 CIC). Maintenant les art. 101-103 de la *Lex propria Supremi Tribunalis Signaturae Apostolicae* définissent la procédure.

[22] Cfr. CONGR. POUR LE CULTE DIVIN ET LA DISCIPLINE DES SACREMENTS, *Responsa ad dubia proposita, Notitiae* 44 (2007) 182-183; *Notitiae* 45 (2009) 170; *Notitiae* 45 (2009) 171.

[23] Cfr. CONGR. POUR LA DOCTRINE DE LA FOI, *Risposte a quesiti riguardanti alcuni aspetti circa la dottrina sulla Chiesa,* 29.VI.207, AAS 99 (2007) 604-608; *Responsa ad quaestiones circa cibum et potum artificialiter prebenda,* 1.VIII.2007, AAS 99 (2007) 820-821; *Nota doctrinalis de quibusdam rationibus evangelizationis,* 3.XII.2007, AAS 100 (2008) 489-504; *Responsa ad proposita dubia,* 1.II.2008, AAS 100 (2008) 200; Instr. *Dignitas personae,* 8.IX.2008, AAS 100 (2008) 858-887.

[24] Cfr. CONGR. POUR L'ÉDUCATION CATHOLIQUE, Instr. *Sugli istituti superiori di scienze religiose,* 28.VI.2008, Ed. Vaticana 2008; *Orientamenti per l'utilizzo delle competenze psicologiche nell'ammissione e nella formazione dei candidati al sacerdozio,* 29.VI.2008, in *Communicationes* 40, 2008, 322-335.

[25] Cfr. CONGR. POUR LES INSTITUTS DE VIE CONSACRÉE ET LES SOCIÉTÉS DE VIE APOSTOLIQUE, Instr. *Il servizio dell'autorità e l'obbedienza,* 11.V.2008, in "L'Osservatore Romano", *29.V.2008, adnexo; Linee orientative per la stesura della relazione periodica,* 8.VI.2008, AAS 100 (2008) 580-584.

[26] Cfr. CONSEIL PONTIFICAL POUR LES TEXTES LEGISLATIFS, *inst. Dignitas connubii*, 26.I.2005 ; cfr. R. PAGE, *L'instruction Dignitas connubii : questions choisies*, in "Studia Canonica " 41, 2007, pp. 309-343.

[27] Cfr. J. OTADUY, *Los medios interpretativos de la ley canónica, y su relación con las distintas doctrinas de la interpretación*, in "Ius Canonicum" 35, 1995, pp. 447-500.

interventions la même force juridique que le canon 19 donne à la *praxis Curiae Romanae* en l'absence de norme concrète à appliquer.

Se on regarde l'ordonnancement canonique comme un système unitaire et cohérent, toute nouvelle disposition dans un secteur déterminé apporte une variation - plus grand o plus petite - de l'ensemble des normes du ceux secteur, au moins pour corroborer avec une nouvelle force le sens e l'interprétation qu'elles avaient auparavant. Ainsi, les facultés concédées aux Nonces supposent, par exemple, une modification des interventions des Dicastères du Saint-Siège.[28] Les Concordats sont aussi des lois canoniques et, considérés dans leur ensemble, ils présentent, sans aucun doute, des lignes de l'action normative de l'Église.[29] Les facultés habituelles octroyées à certains Dicastères en matière disciplinaire, pour ne pas mentionner les normes de la toute dernière réforme du *motu proprio Sacramentorun sanctitatis tutela,* ont certainement altéré le cadre général du système pénal établi par le Code.[30]

D'un autre côté, on ne peut pas oublier l'incidence de la *praxis* des Dicastères romains,[31] signalée par le canon 19 en cas de lacune de la loi. Cette pratique est aussi un élément servant à l'interprétation des normes et du sens des instructions. À plus forte raison, on doit prendre en compte la jurisprudence de la Rote Romaine, seul tribunal établissant la jurisprudence dans l'Église.[32] On peut toutefois espérer que le devoir imposé par l'article 11 de la nouvelle *Lex propria* au Tribunal de la Signature Apostolique de publier leurs décisions périodiquement, puisse permettre, dans un avenir rapproché, de connaître et d'utiliser la jurisprudence administrative.[33]

Dans l'ensemble, nous sommes devant un système normatif en constant développement, dans lequel chaque nouvel élément précise ou modifie quelque nuance de la situation antérieure. Il revient au canoniste de savoir intégrer tous ces éléments, en accordant à chacun le poids spécifique juridique qui lui correspond dans le plan d'ensemble.

Revenant au paradoxe de Pio Fedele, présenté au début, les fondements éternels demeurent immuables, ses expressions formelles, c'est-à-dire les normes, les sentences et les autres éléments objectifs qui les développent, sont

---

[28] Cfr. *Index Facultatum Legatis Pontificiis tributarum, Typis Polyglottis Vaticanis,* 1986; *Index Facultatum Legatis Pontificiis in territoriis missionum tributarum, Typis Polyglottis Vaticanis*, 1999.

[29] Cfr. C. CORRAL, *Derecho internacional concordatario*, Madrid 2009, pp. 131 ss.

[30] Cfr. D. CITO, *Il diritto canonico di fronte ai reati (in particolare di fronte agli abusi sui minori)*, in "Iustitia" 63, 2010, 253-263; D.G.ASTIGUETA, *Facoltà concesse alla Congregazione per il Clero*, in "Periodica" 99, 2010, pp. 1-33; A. BETTETINI, *Il diritto a un'adeguata tutela giurisdizionale (can 221) e il processo penale canonico per i* delicta graviora, in "Il diritto ecclesiastico" 1-2, 2008, pp. 113-132.

[31] Cfr. J.I. ARRIETA, *Il valore giuridico della prassi nella Curia romana*, in "Ius Ecclesiae" 9, 1996, pp. 97-117.

[32] Cfr. *const. ap. Pastor Bonus*, art. 126.

[33] *Lex propria* du Tribunal Suprême de la Signature Apostolique, art. 11 §4, 21.VI. 2008, AAS 100 (2008) 517.

en évolution constante, afin d'être appliquées à des situations diverses, mais aussi comme un moyen pour mieux ajuster, de façon plus raffinée, les normes positives aux fondements qui vivifient le système dans son ensemble et qui constituent le premier niveau de la juridicité

3. L'interrelation entre les éléments substantiels et la norme formelle

Jusqu'ici, nous avons présenté les deux plans ou niveaux de la juridicité canonique et nous avons indiqué comment on les connaît et comment ils évoluent dans le temps. Ces deus niveaux, ils confluent dans la norme, ou dans l'ensemble de normes qui constituent le système d'une institution canonique (par exemple, le mariage), car le développement normatif des institutions et les options concrètes adoptées par le législateur contiennent les principes plus essentiels ou s'en inspirent.

Maintenant, nous devons nous interroger sur la façon dont ils entrent en relation; c'est-à-dire les interrelations qui se tissent entre les éléments substantiels et les normes, et les autres éléments du droit objectif de l'Église.

Le premier point à retenir dans ce domaine est que les deux plans (le substantiel et le normatif, comme nous les appelons), qui comme je l'ai dit confluent dans la norme, représentent deux plans ou niveaux de juridicité qui doivent toujours se maintenir en parallèle, même si il sont en étroit rapport et même si le premier représente de fait le guide d'interprétation du second.

Par la suite, il faut garder à l'esprit que chacun de ces nivaux exigent un traitement herméneutique différent, étant donné que la connaissance des principes substantiels, bien qu'ils soient juridiques et obligatoires, exige une méthode d'abstraction voisine de l'ecclésiologie.

Et, en troisième lieu, il convient de souligner qu'entre ces deux plans il y a une hiérarchie et une dépendance de type ontologique, qui conduit à toujours reconnaître la priorité au droit divin.

Même si la norme doit être interprétée dans son unité, il est nécessaire de maintenir une sorte de « double lecture » des principes et des formalisations normatives, quelle que soit l'opération juridique à accomplir. Je parle de « double lecture » en ce sens que, dans ce processus intellectuel chacun des deux plans doit maintenir sa propre autonomie et son influence sur l'autre plan.

(a) Au moment d'élaborer une norme,[34] les éléments de droit substantiel manifestent les intérêts prioritaires qui doivent être protégés et les finalités que la loi doit chercher à atteindre; c'est pour cela qu'on devra maintenir tout au long de la rédaction des textes normatifs un dialogue d'étroite cohérence avec les principes substantiels. Le législateur, quel qu'il soit, se trouve alors étroitement lié à la « réalité » ecclesiale tracée par les principes et les critères de

[34] Cfr. a ce propos R.E.JENKINS, *Nulla Lex Satis Commoda Omnibus Est: The Implementation of the Penal Law of the 1983 Codex Iuris Canonici in Light of Four Principles of Modern Legal Codification*, in "The Jurist" 69, 2009, pp. 615-645.

la loi divine, naturelle ou positive.

La norme humaine, en effet, ne peut changer la réalité théologique substantielle: cela serait une « illusion positiviste ». En revanche, la réalité substantielle doit guider la norme et montrer la façon de l'intégrer, tout en signalant également les limites et les erreurs du législateur humain.[35]

C'est pour cela que Pio Fedele affirmait avec raison: « plus que dans aucun autre ordonnancement, c'est dans l'ordonnancement canonique que la toute-puissance du législateur est un mythe ».[36]

(b) Au plan doctrinal, le canoniste qui souhaite faire progresser la science canonique, ne pourra pas non plus se limiter seulement à l'étude technique des normes ou à trouver ces autres « principes » ou « critères » adoptés par le législateur humain que donnent cohérence au système des normes ; puisqu'en ignorant l'existence du niveau qui en constitue leur fondement, il se prive de la fonction « directrice » que ce fondement exerce dans l'interprétation des normes et dans la reconstruction dogmatique des institutions.

(c) Concrètement, du point de vue de l'application du droit, le système canonique apparaît comme une sorte de droit hybride, à mi-chemin entre le système codifié européen et le système prétorien anglo-saxon. Certes, la loi existe et doit être appliquée, mais cela ne dégage pas le canoniste du devoir de la confronter aux impératifs de la justice substantielle. Le devoir d'appliquer la loi ne le libère pas de son obligation de vérifier les exigences de la justice substantielle et, en fonction de cette vérification, d'interpréter la loi positive et de choisir le mode juste de l'appliquer aux cas concrets. Nous reconnaissons ainsi que les principes ou les normes du droit divin entretiennent une force juridique autonome, toujours présente lorsqu'il faut résoudre des situations concrètes, et à même d'imposer des exigences spécifiques. C'est ce qui arrive surtout, lorsque l'application « froide » de la norme à un cas concret risque de

---

[35] Les normes juridiques que le législateur humain édicte ne peuvent pas avoir un contenu capricieux; elles doivent trouver le fondement de leur juridicité dans leur concordance avec le droit divin, naturel et positif. Plus encore, la mission du législateur humain [et en tout premier lieu celui du législateur ecclésiastique] consiste précisément à mener à terme un processus de concrétisation et d'adéquation du Droit divin à des circonstances historiques. Il n'est donc pas possible de scinder les normes de Droit divin, naturel et positif, de celle du Droit humain, puisque c'est en fonction de son adéquation au Droit divin que le Droit humain trouve la raison de sa juridicité. (Notre traduction). Original: "Las normas jurídicas que el legislador humano establece no pueden tener un contenido caprichoso sino que encuentran el fundamento de su juridicidad en su concordancia con el derecho divino, natural y positivo. Es más, la misión del legislador humano consiste precisamente en llevar a cabo un proceso de concreción y adecuación del Derecho divino a unas circunstancias históricas. No es posible, por tanto, escindir las normas de Derecho divino, natural y positivo, de las de Derecho humano, ya que es en función de su adecuación al Derecho divino cómo el Derecho humano encuentra la razón de su juridicidad". (P. LOMBARDÍA, *Derecho divino y persona física en el ordenamiento canónico*, *op. cit.*, p. 243).

[36] P. FEDELE, *Lo spirito del diritto canonico*, *op. cit.* p. 214.

provoquer une injustice, un dommage aux âmes ou une occasion de péché.

Dans ces circonstances, les exigences du droit divin conduisent celui qui doit appliquer la norme à avoir recours aux éléments techniques que la souplesse du Droit canonique a élaborés au long de son histoire dans ce but précis: l'*epicheia*, la dispense, la *disimulatio*, l'*æquitas*. C'est au moment de l'application de la loi que le canoniste devrait les employer ou les recommander à l'Ordinaire. Ce dernier, avec le pouvoir juridique qui est le sien, fera usage de ces moyens afin que puissent prévaloir les exigences de la juridicité substantielle, la vraie *ratio legis* de la norme, mai qui pourrait être mise de côté.

Tout cela conduit à mettre en évidence une caractéristique importante du Droit canonique dans le domaine de la « certitude du droit ». En effet, le besoin de reconnaître une juridicité autonome aux éléments de droit divin qui n'ont pas été formalisés choque avec les postulats de la « certitude du droit » érigée en principe dogmatique absolu et quasi mathématique par la culture juridique contemporaine.

Logiquement, le Droit canonique poursuit également ce type de certitude, mais non de façon « absolue », surtout quand de l'application formelle des normes, il peut résulter une injustice du point de vue substantiel. Il s'agit, de toute évidence, de circonstances tout à fait exceptionnelles, mais elles portent atteinte au caractère absolu du principe.

Cette question a été au cœur d'un débat passionné entre canonistes au milieu du dernier siècle.[37] La marche était haute: la reconnaissance de la dimension juridique (juridicité) de la discipline canonique par la culture moderne. De là l'effort d'un bon nombre de canonistes, principalement de ceux qui enseignaient dans les facultés de droit de l'État, pour limiter au maximum l'influence des exigences du droit divin, en exigeant la canonisation de ses principes[38] comme une façon de contrôler sa force juridique par la voie du droit mis en forme par le législateur.[39]

---

[37] Cfr. R. BIDAGOR, *El espíritu del derecho canónico*, in "Revista española de derecho canónico" 13, 1958, pp. 8 ss.; P. CIPROTTI, *Il fine della Chiesa e il diritto*, in "Archivio di diritto ecclesiastico" 4, 1942, pp. 36 ss.; J. DE SALAZAR, *Lo jurídico y lo moral en el ordenamiento canónico*, Vitoria 1960; P. FEDELE, *Diritto canonico*, in "Enciclopedia del diritto" XII, Milano 1964, pp. 871-904; J. HERVADA, *El ordenamiento canónico. Aspectos centrales de la construcción del concepto*, Pamplona 1966; O. ROBLEDA, *Fin del derecho de la Iglesia*, in "Revista española de derecho canónico" 2, 1947, pp. 283 ss.; M.E., CASELLATI ALBERTI, *Sulla* salus animarum *come fine della norma giuridica*, in "La norma en el derecho canónico", Pamplona 1979, 683-690; V. BERTOLONE, *La 'salus animarum' nell'ordinamento giuridico della Chiesa*, Roma 1987.

[38] Cfr. V. DEL GIUDICE, *Canonizatio*, in "Scritti giuridici in onore di Santi Romano", vol. IV, Padua 1939.

[39] Cfr. P.A. D'AVACK, *Trattato di diritto canonico*, cit., pp. 113 ss.; P. FEDELE, *Diritto canonico*, in *Enciclopedia del diritto* XII, cit.; E. CORECCO, *Valore dell'atto contra legem*, in "La norma en el derecho canónico", Pamplona 1979, pp. 845 ss.; O. GIACCHI, *Diritto canonico e dogmatica giuridica moderna*, in "Annali della R. Università di Macerata" 12-13, 1939, pp. 193-194.

Par ailleurs, il y a eu aussi des canonistes qui, dans ce contexte, ont su souligner le rôle capital que le droit divin remplit dans le droit canonique, ainsi que sa force obligatoire sans qu'aucun type de canonisation ne soit nécessaire. Dans le cas du droit canonique, il faut donc chercher ailleurs les exigences de cohérence et de certitude requises pour tout système juridique.[40]

Avec une profonde intuition, me semble-t-il, le grand juriste Giuseppe Capograssi, avait signalé que, si l'on prend en considération les deux niveaux ou plans de la juridicité que nous avons soulignés, ce qui revient au Droit canonique est de chercher non pas la « certitude formelle », mais plutôt la « certitude substantielle ». Celle-ci ne provient pas seulement de la correspondance de la décision avec la forme « externe » de la loi canonique, mais aussi et surtout de sa conformité avec les principes de la loi[41] et avec la *ratio* de laquelle la loi procède.

En d'autres mots, si elle était privée de sa concordance avec les principes et les règles substantielles, la disposition formelle de la norme serait inadéquate pour répondre aux exigences de la justice.

4. À propos de la priorité de la norme substantielle

Un exemple de la priorité du niveau substantiel sur le normatif se trouve dans les réformes des canons du Code, et récemment à propos du *motu proprio Omnium in mentem*. Cette réforme a été la deuxième à modifier directement le Code de droit canonique. Dans les deux occasions, on a cherché à faire l'adéquation de la norme légale aux exigences des normes substantielles. D'autres initiatives analogues sont en route, précisément pour la même raison.

Comme l'on sait, les textes des canons 750 et 1371 du Code latin on été modifiés en 1998 par le *motu proprio Ad tuendam fidem*[42] afin de rendre conforme sa rédaction, dans la partie substantive et pénale, au texte de la *Professio fidei* qui était en vigueur depuis 1989.[43] Le changement normatif du *motu proprio* n'était qu'une conséquence de la clarification doctrinale du Magistère ordinaire, qui avait auparavant modifié la norme concernant la *Profesio fidei*.

Cependant, de toute évidence, c'était la formulation doctrinale de la *Professio fidei,* et non pas le *motu proprio,* qui indiquait de façon contraignante des contenus de la foi catholique.

---

[40] Cfr. P. LOMBARDÍA, *Aportaciones de Vincenzo Del Giudice al estudio sistemático del Derecho canónico*, in "Ius Canonicum" 2 (1962) 289-325.

[41] G. CAPOGRASSI, *La certezza del diritto nell'ordinamento canonico*, in "Ephemerides iuris canonici" 5, 1949, pp. 24 ss; S. BERLINGÒ, *Il diritto divino nella dinamica dell'esperienza giuridica della Chiesa*, in "*Diritto divino e legislazione umana", op. cit.,* pp. 160 ss.

[42] Cfr. JEAN-PAUL II, m.p. *Ad tuendam fidem*, 8.V.1998, AAS 90 (1998) 457-461.

[43] Cfr. CONGR. POUR LA DOCTRINE DE LA FOI, *Professio fidei et Iusiurandum fidelitatis*, 9.I.1989, AAS 81 (1989) 104-106.

Pour ces mêmes raisons, on a procédé maintenant à la modification de cinq canons du Code latin avec le *motu proprio Omnium in mentem.*[44] Il n'a pas été nécessaire d'intervenir dans le Code oriental, puisque la rédaction des canons correspondants ne soulevait pas les mêmes difficultés. D'un côté, il a fallu rectifier les canons 1008 y 1009 afin de réserver la faculté de « *agere in persona Christi Capitis* » seulement aux prêtres et aux évêques, et non au degré du diaconat. C'est ainsi que la Congrégation pour la Doctrine de la foi l'avait précisé lors de la modification du nº 875 de l'*editio typica* du Catéchisme de l'Église Catholique.

Pour la même raison, il fallait modifier du moins en partie les canons 1086 §1, 1117 et 1124 du Code, et supprimer la phrase « *actus formalis defectionis ab Ecclesia Catholica* ». Cette clause, que n'appartient pas à la tradition canonique, été mis pour assurer la validité canonique des unions matrimoniales des baptisés qui se mariaient après avoir abandonné l'église. À la suite d'une consultation de toutes les Conférences épiscopales à la fin des années quatre-vingt-dix, il est devenu clair que l'expérience des tribunaux diocésains dans ce domaine n'avait pas été positive. Dans le but d'éviter l'insécurité juridique et les abus dans la discipline matrimoniale, il convenait donc de modifier le texte.

Mais, surtout, ces études ont permis de découvrir un problème doctrinal plus profond, en rapport avec l'abandon de l'Église motivé par ce qu'on a appelé l'impôt religieux. La situation était vécue principalement en Allemagne, en Autriche et en Suisse, avec ses répercussions d'importance dans la législation ecclésiastique de chacun de ces[45] pays: un sujet de grand intérêt sur lequel nous ne pouvons pas nous arrêter maintenant.

Pendant plusieurs années, le Conseil pontifical pour les textes législatifs et la Congrégation pour la doctrine de la foi ont étudié ce problème du point de vue doctrinal, en dialogue avec les Conférences épiscopales de ces pays. Le résultat a été une Lettre circulaire de mars 2006 diffusée par le Conseil pontifical, avec l'approbation du Saint-Père, préparée en accord avec la Congrégation pour la doctrine de la foi. En substance, le document clarifiait, dans une perspective doctrinale, que la déclaration faite à un fonctionnaire de l'État ne suffisait pas à provoquer l'abandon de l'Église. Il fallait pour ce faire, que la manifestation de volonté soit vérifiée dans le contexte pastoral adéquat, à savoir lors d'une conversation avec le curé ou avec un autre ministre, dans le but de pouvoir évaluer avec certitude l'intention du sujet.

---

[44] Cfr. BENOÎT XVI, *m.p. Omnium in mentem*, 26.X.2009, AAS 102 (2010) 8-10; F. COCCOPALMERIO, *Ragioni di due interventi*, in *Communicationes* 41, 2009, 334-338; J. WERCKMEISTER, *Le motu proprio Omnium in mentem et le mariane des ex-catholiques*, in "Revue de Droit Canonique" 57/2, pp. 241-254.

[45] Cfr. J.P. DURAND, *Questions éthiques et pastorales des sorties d'église*, in "L'année canonique", 48, 2006, pp. 11-17 ; R. PUZA. *Les sorties de l'église : la situation allemande (kirchenaustritt)*, loc. cit., pp. 19-35 ; A. BORRAS, *Questions théologiques à propos des sorties de l'église catholique*, loc. cit., pp. 37-52 ; Ph. TOXE, L*es conséquences de la définition de l'actus formalis defectionis sur le droit au mariage*, loc. cit., pp. 53-59.

Comme l'on sait, les réactions a cette Lettre circulaire on été différentes dans chacun de ces trois pays. Mais, ce qui est intéressant à mettre en lumière est que la Déclaration doctrinale de 2006 été « définitive », du point de vue juridique, par rapport à question de l'abandon occasionné par l'impôt religieuse, et elle n'avait pas besoin du *motu proprio Omnium in mentem.* Ces la discipline matrimoniale canonique para rapport a la forme du constitution à avoir changée avec ce motu proprio.

Dans certains lieux on considérait pacifiquement, au moins depuis la promulgation du Code de 1983, que le catholique qui déclarait ne plus appartenir à l'Église Catholique devant un fonctionnaire des impôts, parmi d'autres conséquences, ne pouvait pas contracter le mariage canonique. Toutefois, on considérait communément que son mariage civil recevait la pleine reconnaissance canonique, puisque le fidèle n'était pas obligé à la « forme canonique », par l'application du canon 1117 CIC. On n'appliquait pas, non plus à cette personne, l'empêchement dirimant de disparité de culte (canon 1086 §1 CIC) et elle n'avait pas besoin non plus de demander la permission de contracter licitement un mariage mixte (canon 1124 CIC).

Cette situation est maintenant changée. Toutefois, en ce qui concerne la sortie formelle de l'Eglise à l'occasion de l'impôt religieux, le changement n'est pas provenu du motu proprio, mai bien de la Déclaration que le Dicastère avait faite en 2006, à savoir lorsqu'il a clarifié le point doctrinal qui était à l'origine du problème.

La question a surgi avec toute sa force juridique lorsque, quelques mois après la publication du *motu propio Omnium in mentem*, on a proposé au Conseil pontifical le besoin de donner un « effet rétroactif » au *motu propio*, et de déclarer son efficacité juridique rétroactivement à la date de l'entrée en vigueur du Code le 28 novembre 1983. L'on soutenait que, dans le cas contraire, les unions civiles de baptisés catholiques célébrées entre novembre 1983 et la date de l'entrée en vigueur du *motu propio* seraient canoniquement valides. Cela mettrait en évidence une disparité de traitement par rapport aux unions similaires antérieures au 28 novembre 1983 ou à celles célébrées après l'entrée en vigueur de *Omnium in mentem* qui, elles, sont invalides par défaut de forme.

La réponse du Conseil pontifical manifestait une étroite relation avec ce que nous sommes en train de développer. Une intervention de l'autorité, afin de déclarer l'effet rétroactif des ces normes, n'était pas nécessaire. En effet, la validité canonique de ces unions ne dépend pas du *motu proprio*, mais plutôt de la Déclaration de 2006 qui, en clarifiant les éléments doctrinaux qui configuraient l'acte formel d'abandon, avait déclaré, avec effet juridique *ex tunc* (depuis toujours), que la déclaration au fonctionnaire civil ne produisait pas un abandon formel et par conséquence ne libérait pas le baptisé catholique de la forme substantielle de la célébration du mariage.

Omnium in mentem, a été donc une conséquence, avec des effets *ex nunc*, à partir de maintenant, qui rétablit dans cette matière la situation juridique qui existait avant le Code, alors qu'on ne reconnaissait pas d'autre abandon formel de l'Église catholique que l'apostasie.

L'enseignement est important. Ce n'est pas la norme humaine qui établit *ex nunc* des effets juridiques spécifiques, mais la déclaration doctrinale qui, après avoir clarifié les exigences du droit substantiel, s'impose avec effet *ex tunc*, dans l'ordonnancement canonique. Elle s'impose au législateur, au gouvernant[46] et, encore davantage, aux juges, qui doivent appliquer le contenu de la Déclaration doctrinale de 2006, afin de vérifier si un baptisé de façon concrète est assujetti à la forme canonique, en dépit du fait d'avoir déclaré au fonctionnaire civil son abandon de l'Église.

L'efficacité différente de chacun des documents et la dépendance ontologique qu'ils maintiennent entre eux, démontrent le besoin de cultiver notre sensibilité par rapport à ces deux plans ou niveaux de juridicité: le substantiel, soit le droit divin et les principes permanents qui doivent toujours prévaloir dans chaque situation juridique, d'un côté, et de l'autre le plan légal, qui donne la forme et développe les principes du droit substantiels où se trouve enracinée toute sa force de juridicité contraignante.

5.- Positivisme legaliste, exégèse et recherche des principes informateurs

Cette façon de procéder du Droit canonique, obligeant à scruter d'une manière cohérente l'ensemble des éléments qui constituent la juridicité dans l'Église, explique aussi les difficultés éprouvées par notre discipline face à la poussée du positivisme régnant dans la culture moderne. Parce qu'il était fidèle à son identité propre,[47] le Droit canonique a été placé en marge des courants qui ont altéré profondément le cadre de la culture juridique séculière.[48] Il a dû subir depuis un siècle les conséquences d'un ostracisme culturel, qui l'a considéré comme une discipline non juridique.[49]

Mais la science canonique ne s'est pas pour autant repliée dans une position négative, de simple résistance. Dans cette même période, elle a réussi à mener à bien la reconstruction du Droit propre dans une perspective plus moderne et beaucoup plus cohérente avec l'essence de l'Église et avec sa structure sacramentelle, comme nous sommes en train de le voir. Malgré les risque inhérents aux deux processus de codification et aux limitations posées à son développement scientifique, dont je parlerai pour finir, la science canonique a

---

[46] Cfr. sur la praxis et le *privilegium fidei*, H. PREE, *The Divine and the Human of the Ius Divinum*, in "In diversitate unitas", Leuven 1997, p. 26.

[47] Cfr. J.I. ARRIETA, *Ius divinum e ruolo della canonistica*, in "Il Ius divinum nella vita della Chiesa", Atti del XIII Congresso Internazionale di Diritto Canonico organizzato dalla *Consociatio Internationalis Studio Iuris Canonici Promovendo* e la Facolté di Diritto Canonico San Pio X, Venezia, 2010, p. 1395. Dans le même volume on trouve plusieurs ouvrages traitant de la question.

[48] Cfr. J.P. SCHOUPPE, *Convergences et différences entre le droit divin des canoniste set le droit naturel des juristes*, in « Ius Ecclesiae » 12, 2000, pp. 29-67 (spéc. P. 45).

[49] Cfr. J. HERVADA, *Il diritto naturale nell'ordinamento canonico*, in "Ius Ecclesiae" 1, 1989, pp. 493-508; ID., *La lex naturae e la lex gratiae nella base dell'ordinamento giuridico della Chiesa*, in "Ius Ecclesiae" 3, 1991, 49-66.

réussi à conserver substantiellement intactes ses instruments originaux. Ciselés par une tradition bimillénaire, ces instruments ont pour objectif précis d'assurer à la raison du juriste de l'Église le contact direct avec la réalité et avec la vérité, le libérant d'une soumission rigide au mécanisme littéral des normes, qui pourrait l'empêcher d'évaluer la correspondance des textes formels avec la justice substantielle.

Cette caractéristique, restée immunisée contre tout positivisme juridique, doit cultiver le contact direct avec le droit substantiel, avec la loi naturelle ou le droit divin positif, qui est des nos jours patrimoine presqu'exclusif de la science canonique. Cela nous impose une grande responsabilité face à la culture juridique générale. C'est donc pour nous un devoir de maintenir cette caractéristique si importante et de la faire progresser.

Comment ne pas tirer la sonnette d'alarme, par exemple, lorsque, après trente ans de mariage, on puisse déclarer, sur la base du canon 1095 CIC, l'incapacité contractuelle d'une personne ayant vécu pendant tout ce temps dans une stabilité familiale pacifique, l'union ayant aussi engendré des enfants? Le manque de concorde entre les deux plans de la juridicité ne peut pas satisfaire le canoniste dans ces types de cas. Ne devrions-nous pas nous interroger afin de savoir si le système matrimonial ne s'est pas centré sur l'un des intérêts, certainement constitutif du mariage, ignorant, en revanche, d'autres intérêts substantiellement importants et dignes également de tutelle juridique que le temps a fait aussi émerger?

Je passe à mon dernier point.

J'ai mentionné auparavant les limites imposées au développement scientifique du Droit canonique et je souhaite conclure mon intervention en me référant expressément à cette question. Lors de la promulgation du *Codex Iuris Canonici de* 1917, la Sacré Congrégation pour les Séminaires et les Universités d'études avait porté deux décrets qui ont marqué l'évolution ultérieure de l'enseignement du Droit canonique, ainsi que la façon dont beaucoup de canonistes ont abordé les normes canoniques. Dans l'un de ses décrets la Congrégation indiquait que l'enseignement du Droit canonique devait se faire en analysant chacun des canons, tout en présentant le Code de façon ordonnée selon ses livres, titres et chapitres, en exposant diligemment le contenu des canons en accord avec son origine et son histoire. Tandis que dans le second décret, la Congrégation établissait que les examens de Droit canonique devaient porter sur l'exégèse des canons, isolés ou réunis avec d'autres, ainsi que sur l'origine des institutions et leur évolution historique.

Ces deux décisions illustrent bien les craintes de l'époque à propos de la réception du Code. Elles ont eu une incidence marquante tout au long du XXe siècle sur la majorité des plans d'étude des Facultés, ainsi que sur les programmes des matières et des manuels de Droit canonique. À la lumière de ce que nous avançons depuis le début de cet exposé, cette perspective découlant des deux Décrets de la Congrégation offre, en revanche, un vision statique de la norme canonique, qui est ainsi élevée au rang d'archétype intangible, devenant un obstacle pour extraire de l'ordonnancement des éléments qui puissent répondre aux nouvelles situations.

Ainsi, au lieu de percevoir la norme dans son devenir, en l'intégrant dans la mouvance des normes postérieures, cette méthode se centre sur la genèse de la norme, cherchant à capter le sens des expressions qu'elle utilise. Certes, cette opération est nécessaire, mais elle ne représente que le point de départ, car par la suite il faut l'intégrer avec les éléments successifs offerts par l'expérience juridique. Autrement, si l'effort se limite seulement à la genèse de la norme et à son exégèse, comme cela se produit si fréquemment, on risque de tomber dans un culte indu du texte légal, qui empêchera la confrontation avec tous les élément du droit substantiel. Cette manière de procéder expose à plusieurs inconvénients du positivisme juridique.

En outre, se centrer sur la norme positive comporte un risque important: la difficulté à trouver une réponse cohérente aux nouveaux problèmes sur lesquels il n'y a pas encore une règlementation juridique précise. En effet, dés lors que l'on est habitué à raisonner exclusivement à partir de la norme, l'absence d'une disposition légale conduit à l'incapacité de résoudre des situations nouvelles d'une façon cohérente avec l'ensemble dell'ordonnancement.

La seule véritable alternative consiste à accorder une attention prioritaire aux principes qui président au système. Au contraire de ce que nous venons d'exposer, la considération systématique de l'ordonnancement, en plus de prendre grand soin des dispositions concrètes, cherche à élaborer les principes autour desquels chaque groupe de normes est organisé, leur donnant ainsi cohérence, unité et harmonie. Ces principes, extraits de l'ordonnancement, s'ajoutent aux autres du droit substantiel, dont on parlait au début, et qui constituent la clé de voûte pour affronter les nouvelles situations.

La vie juridique de l'Église est obligée, assez fréquemment, de répondre a des situations imprévues dans les normes. Cela demande de se tourner vers le système canonique et de résoudre les cas de façon cohérente, en ayant recours aux principes de l'ordonnancement. Le canon 19 du Code réfère précisément à ces principes lorsqu'il indique comment agir dans les cas d'absence de norme.

Ces dernières années nous avons assisté à des exemples de ces situations (notamment en matière d'abus sexuel). L'urgence s'est fait sentir d'établir des protocoles destinés à garantir des conduites sûres lors d'activités pastorales avec des jeunes. Pour résoudre ces questions, on a souvent mandaté des juristes civils pour préparer les programmes adéquats en accord avec le système administratif de chaque pays. C'est précisément ce qu'aurait fait n'importe quelle multinationale. Mais, l'Église n'en est pas une; elle est une société originaire avec un droit riche de deux mille années d'histoire et comportant des principes juridiques à appliquer. Des principes permettant d'incorporer sans difficulté un bon nombre des éléments provenant des systèmes administratifs de chaque pays, mais qui ne pourraient pas renoncer, par exemple, au gouvernement hiérarchique de l'initiative en question, à sa propre façon de concevoir les relations du prêtre avec son évêque, ou de comprendre la *patria potestas* des parents ou, encore, les limites à l'intimité des personnes.

Certes, dans cette défaillance du Droit canonique, d'autres facteurs ont aussi eu une influence. Je pense, en particulier à l'erreur importante consistant à considérer que l'ordonnancement de la société ecclésiale, ne possède pas les éléments nécessaires pour répondre de façon cohérente et efficace aux nouvelles situations. Je considère que cette conviction est erronée. C'est la raison pour laquelle il est particulièrement important que les canonistes s'efforcent de chercher et d'élaborer les principes inspirateurs du système canonique.

Major Address

The Renewal of Canon Law in the Spirit of a Church of Communion

Most Reverend V. James Weisgerber

The tradition of the seminary which I attended was to treat all the sacraments in the last year of our formation, the deacon year. Traditionally there were three parallel tracks: dogmatic, moral and canonical. This was 1962 and the anticipation of the Second Vatican Council was already shaking things up, so the faculty of theology decided that more integration was needed. Henceforth one professor would handle all aspects of a sacrament, so the professor of canon law, an eminent scholar, taught us the dogmatic, moral and canonical aspects of penance and marriage. His bias showed as he tried to demonstrate to us that the Code of Canon Law was a font of revelation! Baptism and Eucharist were handled by the professor who taught dogmatic theology. He knew very, very little canon law and as he ended his attempts at instructing us in respect to the canonical aspects of the sacraments, he would always give us this sage bit of advice: When in a jam, do what you think is reasonable, and then check the code.

While this would not be a recommended approach, it has a certain merit, because the canonical law of the Church is above all reasonable. It is essential for the well-being of the community. While my own study of the law has been somewhat limited, I am happy to report, that no matter what position of ministry I exercised within the Church, diocesan pastoral officer, pastor of a parish, general secretary of the conference of bishops, or bishop, I have always enjoyed the support of good canonists, men and women who profoundly understood the law and the law's ultimate end, which is the "salvation of souls." For this I am deeply grateful. I must add that as I was preparing for this address I read quite a lot of canonical studies and I discovered a very intriguing and interesting field of endeavor. A challenge for my years of retirement?

So I come before you today not as an expert or trained canonist, but rather as a pastor. The task I have selected is to reflect on the life of the Church, specifically the role of the laity, fifty years after the council and twenty-five years after the Special Synod of Bishops which was called to study the implementation of the council. My remarks will obviously reflect my own experience, my own hopes, and disappointments. I have, over the last twenty years, been intimately involved in the work of the Canadian Conference of Catholic Bishops and in several capacities been privileged to participate in many national and international gatherings of bishops and other church leaders. I believe these experiences have enriched my understanding of where we are and where we are going.

As a pastor I recognize that canon law contains guidelines for actions, not beliefs. The law presents norms for conduct, not the content of faith; it is concerned with the patterns of practice within the community. Obviously these patterns of practice must find their root and foundation in the teaching of the Church. To quote Ladislas Orsy, "Values discovered by faith became the objects of legal norms."[1] Therefore the Code of Canon Law must guarantee that our institutional life follows and supports the teaching of the Church and, for the Church today, this means especially the teachings of the Second Vatican Council. Pope John Paul II tells us: "The Second Vatican Ecumenical Council was truly a prophetic message for the Church's life; it will continue to be so for many years in the third millennium which has just begun. The Church, rich in the eternal truths entrusted to her, will still speak to the world, proclaiming that Jesus Christ is the one Savior of the world: yesterday, today and forever!"[2]

Just a word about the council. Canon 337 reminds us that an ecumenical council is the most solemn form in which the college of bishops exercises leadership within the Church and so it follows that the Second Vatican Council and its teaching are the most important expression of God's word to the Church today. We see today much discussion about the meaning and the interpretation of the council. This is all probably necessary and salutary, but only insofar as these discussions help us fully embrace the council and it's teaching as the pre-eminent work of the Holy Spirit in the Church today. There is not, nor can there be any other vision for the Church today than the vision set before us in the teachings of the Second Vatican Council.

The implementation of the council, however, can elicit very different opinions. Is the glass half full or half empty? Many critics see the council as having unleashed forces that have led the Church astray. We are lost and need to return to the certitudes of the past. The glass is half empty. Others, recognizing many of the same limitations and shortcomings, also see how much good has been accomplished. The glass is half full and we must redouble our efforts to endeavor to become the community envisaged by the council.

The centerpiece of the council is the Dogmatic Constitution on the Church, *Lumen gentium*. The council moves away from a historically narrow consideration of the Church simply as a juridical institution to a much larger, richer view which sees the Church as mystery, a sacrament, a communion. The 1985 Synod of Bishops' final document underscores that the ecclesiology of communion is the central and fundamental idea of the council's documents. The Congregation for the Doctrine of the Faith confirmed this in 1992 stating that: "The concept of communion which appears with a certain prominence in the texts of the Second Vatican Council is very suitable for expressing the core of the mystery of the church and can certainly be a key for the renewal of Catholic

---

[1] Ladislas Orsy, *Theology of Canon Law* (Collegeville: Liturgical Press, 1972) 103.

[2] John Paul II, "Address of the Holy Father to the Conference Studying the Implementation of the Second Vatican Council," (Vatican City: Libreria Editrice Vaticana, February 27, 2000; http://www.vatican.va/holy_father/john_paul_ii/speeches/documents/hf_jp-ii_spe_20000227_vatican-council-ii_en.html) 9.

ecclesiology."[3]

The second chapter of *Lumen gentium*, on the People of God, speaks of the gift and the mission of the Church as the common patrimony of *all* the baptized. A fundamental unity and dignity of all the baptized precedes all distinctions and responsibilities. In the communion of the Church there are no first and second class members, no professionals and amateurs. All are gifted, all are mandated, and all are responsible. This is at the heart of the theology of communion.

While this teaching appeared radically new in the mid-twentieth century, it was really a retrieval of much that characterized the Church at her beginnings. Through historical challenges and developments, the clergy assumed more and more space with a consequent marginalization of the laity. When I was a youth one would hear the expression, "the role of the laity is to pray, pay, and obey." While this was said in jest, it often came uncomfortably close to the truth. The council offers a much richer truth. All the baptized share in the one priesthood of Christ and together with Christ the Head, all are the People of God, the Church. This renewed vision of the dignity and responsibility of the laity pervades all the council's teaching, rooted as it is in a theology of communion.

The Constitution on the Sacred Liturgy imparts this same message, insisting that it is the whole Church which offers the Eucharist. All the baptized, exercising the royal priesthood, join the spiritual sacrifice of a life of conversion to the one offering made on the cross by the Redeemer. All the baptized are summoned to full, conscious, and active participation in the Eucharist, the source and life of the Church. Further, "the council concludes, it is evident to everyone that all the faithful of Christ of whatever rank or status are called to the fullness of the Christian life and to the perfection of charity."[4] The laity share in the work of the gospel, not through delegation by the clergy, but through the anointing of the Spirit which they receive in baptism. Each of the baptized shares in the prophetic role of the Church when, "thanks to a supernatural sense of the faith which characterizes the people as a whole, it manifests this unerring quality when, 'from the bishops down to the last member of the laity' it shows universal agreement in matters of faith and morals."[5] Everyone is called to be involved; everyone is important. Both the pastoral constitution of the Church in the Modern World, *Gaudium et spes*, and the 1988 post-synodal apostolic exhortation, *Christifideles laici*, insist that the vocation of the laity has a secular character in the sense that they are called to sanctify from within the world in which they live out their lives. These declarations, however, do not invite the

[3] Congregation for the Doctrine of the Faith, "Letter to Bishops of the Catholic Church on Some Aspects of the Church Understood as Communion," (Vatican City: Libreria Editrice Vaticana, May 28, 1992; http://www.vatican.va/roman_curia/congregations/cfaith/ documents /rc_con_cfaith_doc_28051992_communionis-notio_en.html) 1.

[4] Vatican II, dogmatic constitution *Lumen gentium* (Vatican City: Libreria Editrice Vaticana, November 21, 1964; http://www.vatican.va/archive/ hist_councils /ii_vatican_council/documents/vat-ii_const_19641121_lumen-gentium_en.html) 40.

[5] Ibid., 12.

laity to be less present and active in all the dimensions of the Church's life.

I think one can glean the vision of the new role of the laity inspiring the fathers of the council and their great desire and hope in their conclusion to the chapter on the role of the laity. "The laity have the right … to receive from their sacred pastors the spiritual goods of the Church, especially the assistance of the word of God and the sacraments. Every layperson should openly reveal to their pastor his needs and desires with that freedom and confidence which befits a child of God and a brother or sister in Christ."[6] A Church of communion is foreseen: "A great many benefits are to be hoped for from this familiar dialogue between laity and their pastors: in the laity, a strengthened sense of personal responsibility, a renewed enthusiasm, a more ready application of their talents to the projects of their pastors. The latter, for their part, aided by the experience of the laity, can more clearly and more suitably come to decisions regarding spiritual and temporal matters. In this way, the whole Church, strengthened by each one of its members, can more effectively fulfill its mission for the life of the world."[7]

In his homily for the Mass of beatification of Cardinal John Henry Newman, Pope Benedict XVI approvingly quotes Newman: "I want a laity, not arrogant, not rash in speech, not disputatious, but men who know their religion, who enter into it, who know just where they stand, who know what they hold and what they do not, who know their creed so well that they can give an account of it, who know so much of history that they can defend it."[8] This vision has strong roots in the tradition and was a precursor to the vision of a church of communion so central to the teaching of the Second Vatican Council.

How have we fared? The Second Vatican Council ended forty-five years ago, a blink of the eye in the history of the Church. The new code has been guiding us for a mere twenty-seven years. While history will enable us to see more clearly where we have been and where we find ourselves now, it is certainly possible to get some idea about the faithfulness of our present Church to the hopes and aspirations of the council. Clearly any conclusions will be tentative and will be based on personal experience, listening to others, and on reading and reflection. Each of us will probably insist on variations, but I believe we can arrive at some common conclusions.

Let us begin, as did the council, with the liturgy. Much has been accomplished. Many church leaders, today, are unnerved by the imminent introduction of a new translation of the Roman Missal. This challenge is a small matter compared to the task facing the Church in 1965 as it was called to implement the Constitution on the Sacred Liturgy. Books had to be prepared,

---

6 Ibid., 37.

7 Ibid.

8 Pope Benedict XVI, "Homily during the Beatification of Cardinal Newman," (Vatican City: Libreria Editrice Vaticana, September 19, 2010; http://www.vatican.va/holy_father/benedict_xvi/homilies/2010/documents/hf_ben-xvi_hom_20100919_beatif-newman_en.html).

presiders had to be retrained, people had to learn to sing, lectors, Communion ministers had to be recruited and trained, sanctuaries had to be rearranged, and we had little music suitable for congregational singing. Today it is a great joy to participate in so many of our parish and diocesan celebrations. The prayerfulness, solemnity, attentiveness and participation move one's heart and become prayer. Many people have taken very seriously the renewal of the liturgy and many parishes and dioceses celebrate wonderfully!

The Decree on Ecumenism has been embraced with enthusiasm. What a sea change we have experienced. While many are disappointed that we have not yet reached the point of intercommunion, we must all recognize a profound change of atmosphere and attitude. Reflecting the call of the council, the code reminds bishops of their need to foster ecumenical dialogue.[9] We recognize that we are all part of the Body of Christ: "There is one Lord, one faith, and one baptism and one God who is Father of all, over all, through and within all" (Ephesians 4:6). We dialogue and discuss, we work together and we pray together. We still have a long way to go, but we have also come a very long way.

The life of many parishes has been transformed. Many of the laity bring their powerful gifts to the service of the community. Many parishes have active, empowered parish councils and other working committees.[10] Committed and trained lay women and men assume roles of ministry and leadership. One parish in our diocese has four hundred families and three hundred and fifty of them are involved in ministry! Many people have responded to the call of *Gaudium et spes*. Marriage enrichment programs and family life programs offer countless people the opportunity to discover the call to holiness in their daily lives. Outreach to the aged, the poor, and the marginalized, at home or abroad, is generous and many individuals and communities work hard at reforming structures which perpetuate injustice and dehumanization in the world.

In many dioceses and parishes one sees serious attempts at providing faith education and programs of spirituality for the laity. These programs can demand a serious commitment of time and resources, but they are responded to with enthusiasm. Many people express a profound desire for a personal spirituality, a relationship with Christ. Study groups, bible study, and faith sharing groups are not uncommon in many of the parish communities. Christian faith communities, new movements, charismatic communities, associates of religious communities are but a few of the many ways in which lay Catholics come together to pray, support each other and reach out to others.

Besides many brilliant flashes of light, there are also shadows in the story of the reception of the council's teachings on the role of the laity. It is important to underline again the monumental paradigm shift found in the council's vision as to how the Church sees itself, how the Church should be renewed internally, and how the Church relates to the world. In the Church of communion, all are gifted,

---

[9] See canon 383 §3.

[10] The Code of Canon Law leaves it to the discretion of individual dioceses to establish parish pastoral councils, see canon 536 §1.

all are mandated, and all are responsible. Some of us can recall the excitement and enthusiasm of the early post-conciliar years.

How easy and tempting it was to mandate external change, but how challenging it is to see the inner meaning of this new vision and allow it to change hearts and communities. The profound and on-going formation of the whole Church remains an enormous task. The council invitation demands a deep, on-going conversion which is both personal and communal, theological and juridical. The Code of Canon Law has an important task to play because it is concerned with the patterns of practice within the community.

Have we kept the vision alive? Many in the Church at every level began the task with amazing energy and resources. The work, however, is very much ongoing, and requires commitment for the long haul. Many bishops who enthusiastically embraced the council's vision were replaced by others who didn't share their experiences. Leaders, at all levels, must worry about the institution committed to their care and leadership is often measured by institutional concerns, so energies lagged were focused on other issues. The priorities of the council could be overshadowed by the practical needs of the institution I am reminded of couples who are renewed by participation in Marriage Encounter. Many sincere resolutions are valiantly made, only to be slowly eroded by the everyday demands of marriage, parenting, and work. New wine must find new wineskins!

It is important to keep in mind that the Second Vatican Council was celebrated in the 1960's, an extremely significant era in the western world's cultural history. The enthusiastic reception of the council responded to the *zeitgeist* of the 60's. The cultural and political forces unleashed in these times created considerable social upheaval which radically affected everything and everyone. Some movements seeking to renew the Church owed more to the spirit of the times than to the vision of the council. These years and their inevitable backlash profoundly changed all sectors of our society, including the people who make up the Church. It is difficult, but important, to try to distinguish the influence of the council teachings from social and political movements occurring in these years.

Christ's faithful live out their lives at the level of the parish and hence the leadership of pastors is crucial. Pastors play an irreplaceable role in church leadership and canons 528 and 529 present a challenging program in respect to the responsibilities of the pastor. Pastors, future bishops, are formed in seminaries. Have seminaries adjusted their role sufficiently so as to produce the leaders envisioned by the fathers of the council? Seminaries, I am sure, are subject to constant and changing hopes, expectations and pressures. The laity, however, will never find their place in the Church unless the seminary provides its students with a concrete, comprehensive, and integrated teaching and formation based on the council's vision.

In *Sacrosanctum concilium* we read: "Mother Church earnestly desires that all the faithful should be led to that full, conscious, and active participation in liturgical celebrations which is demanded by the very nature of the liturgy. … In the restoration and promotion of the sacred liturgy, this full and active participation by all the people is the aim to be considered *before all else*; for it is the primary and indispensable source from which the faithful are to derive their true Christian spirit; and therefore pastors of souls must zealously strive to achieve it, by means of the necessary instruction, in all their pastoral work."[11] I am sure that this is a great challenge for seminary formators, but the code reminds us that the laity need faith-filled preaching, guidance, and solid teaching if they are to take their place in the Church.[12]

The years following the council have seen a dramatic diminution in the number of priests. Introducing the laity into their new place in the Church requires more, not less professionally trained leaders. A deeper understanding and spirituality, new roles in the parish community, and new challenges in outreach requires serious teaching, mentoring, and spiritual direction. This becomes almost impossible if one is the only priest in a large urban parish or the pastor of three or four smaller communities without the assistance of a team trained for ministry. Many dioceses have invited international priests to make up for local decline. While providing many blessings, these priests can come from very different social and ecclesial cultures where the laity, and women in particular, are not in roles of leadership.

Clericalism, a culture of privilege and entitlement of the ordained, maintains a firm grasp on so much of the Church. Clericalism transforms authority into superiority and makes co-responsibility difficult, if not impossible. In order to preserve its hegemony, clericalism needs to be acquiesced to by the laity; this permits the laity to eschew their own leadership and call to responsibility. How common is it to find communities in which priest and people relate to each other as adult to adult? There are different ministries within the Church; the ordained are ontologically different from the laity. This difference, however, should not lead to a two-tiered system of membership and responsibility. In the Church of communion there are not some who are professionals and others amateurs; some adults and most, children. The priesthood of the ordained and the priesthood of the baptized are interdependent and together build up the Body of Christ. To quote St. Paul: "If we live by the truth and in love, we shall grow in all ways into Christ, who is the head by whom the whole body is fitted and joined together, every joint adding its own strength, for each separate part to work according to its function. So the body grows until it has built itself up, in love" (Ephesians 2:21).

While many of the laity have flourished, growing spiritually and contributing generously to Church and world, many have been bewildered by

---

[11] Vatican II, constitution *Sacrosanctum concilium* (Vatican City: Libreria Editrice Vaticana, December 4, 1963; http://www.vatican.va/archive/hist_councils/ii_vatican_council/documents/vat-ii_const_19631204_sacrosanctum-concilium_en.html) 14.

[12] See for example canons 213, 217, and 229 §1.

the change required. The rapid erosion of traditional culture in the western world, especially in respect to community and family, undermined the foundation of much religious practice. Church membership, particularly in ethnic communities, included many whose allegiance responded more to cultural or family expectation and identity than to a personal faith. Many people simply continue their participation, perhaps with irritation about the changes, but without much understanding, or in any way responding to the call for a more personal understanding or engagement.

Two groupings have been particularly hurt in respect to the implementation of the council's vision for the laity within the church: those who were never invited to hear the message and those who heard, desired to respond, but were rebuffed. Once again it is important to remind ourselves as to the radical change of mind, heart, and attitude called for by the council. Many of the laity never heard the good news because some pastors did not understand the vision themselves or were too preoccupied with other things, or perhaps were opposed to any new direction. Much education and formation were required. The challenge of implementation is difficult enough in the green wood, but what happens in the dry?

The regular rotation of pastors can also become a great challenge. Inviting the laity to take ownership of their faith and their community infers that a kind of "parish personality" will develop. A pastor might labor hard to help the parish embrace the council's vision and the people respond with enthusiasm. A new pastor arrives with a new style of leadership and a whole different set of priorities. Tension develops. What recourse do the people have? What recourse does the parish staff have? In times past the faithful hung in, no matter what. People today seem quite prepared to walk away if their spiritual needs are not met.

The council teaches that the Holy Spirit dwells within and speaks through the experience of each of the baptized. The Spirit working in the heart and lives of the baptized enables them to "cling without fail to the faith once delivered to the saints (Jude, 3) penetrate it more deeply by accurate insights, and apply it more thoroughly to life."[13] What role in the life of the Church is given to this lived experience of the faithful? Many local churches are made up of different cultures, each with its unique history, experiences and aspirations. Different points of view, different hopes can be seen as gift or as danger. Dialogue, Paul VI tells us, is the way for evangelization. Where can the laity find the welcome and the space needed to express their experiences and hopes? Is there any space where the laity are invited into healthy debate and dialogue?

The reception of the council's vision of a Church of communion has been, quite understandably, uneven. This is particularly true in respect to the empowerment of the laity and the encouragement of the laity to take their God-given place within the Body of Christ. The Catholic Church is a very big tent with ample room for different ways of living out the faith. Not everyone will

---

[13] *Lumen gentium* 12.

march to the same drummer! The preaching and teaching of the Church must, however, always be inspired and guided by the teachings of the council, rooted, as it is, in the theology of communion. We cannot substitute a different vision. The Church, at all levels, must continue to work tirelessly to enable the laity to see that they are not the objects of the life and ministry of the Church, but its subjects. We cannot try to construct church life in a manner different from the vision developed by the fathers of the council.

And so, as a pastor, I come to you, esteemed canonists of the Church, with a question. You are considering an issue important to all of us, the renewal of the law. I do not have a program of concrete suggestions about particular canons. This, I believe, is the purview of those versed in the science of the law. I am aware that the 1983 code is imbued with much of the teaching of Vatican II. That being said, there are norms in which a Church of communion could be more strongly encouraged and supported. For example, canon 495 §1 *mandates* the establishment of a council of priests, while canon 511 *suggests* a diocesan pastoral council comprising representatives of all the members of Christ's faithful. Does this really reflect a Church of communion where all are gifted, all are mandated, and all are responsible? I am sure there are many other examples of an uneven application of conciliar teaching. And so my question is this: How can we make the law a better servant of the vision given to the Church by God's Spirit through the Second Vatican Council? And in particular, how can the law be modified and developed so that the laity might be more welcomed, more encouraged, and more enabled to enrich the Body of Christ with the manifold gifts they received in baptism? In other words, how could the Code of Canon Law better insert the theology of communion into the juridical language of the Church? The law is concerned with patterns of practice and for us these patterns find life in the Church of communion.

All are gifted, all are mandated, all are responsible!

MAJOR ADDRESS

THE CANON LAW OF MARRIAGE: EVER OLD, EVER NEW

Reverend Monsignor John A. Alesandro

In *Sacrae disciplinae leges*, Pope John Paul II noted that "what constitutes the substantial *newness* of the Second Vatican Council, in line with the legislative tradition of the Church ... constitutes the *newness* of the new code... If, therefore the Second Vatican Council has drawn both new and old from the treasury of tradition ... then it is clear that the Code should also reflect the same note of fidelity in newness and of newness in fidelity"[1]

Fidelity to the "treasure" of the "old" and acceptance of the "treasure" of the "new" in regard to the canon law of marriage is the theme of this presentation.[2] The question, of course, is what qualifies, whether old or new, as "treasure" in our canonical tradition – and what is "dross"? To which are we to be faithful – the specific canonical words and ideas or the sacramental reality itself of marriage, revealed to us by God in Jesus Christ, a gift that is, at the same time, both old and new?[3]

A. Canonical Construct

It is not as if we can separate the reality from the words. There is no bright line between the sacramental reality and the canonical propositions that express it in a juridical framework.[4] In fact, the very purpose of canon law, in its original articulation and its periodic renewal, is to be faithful to the sacramental reality by guiding practice and behavior in a way that will facilitate the grace of the sacrament in redeeming individuals, the Church and the world. This is quite a challenge, for, while revelation and the sacraments of salvation are infinite mystery, our poor canonical attempts at implementation are frustratingly finite. That is, in fact, the lifeblood of an Incarnational Church, expressing the divine in human terms, taking what Christ won for us on the cross and gave to us freely,

---

[1] Pope John Paul II, apostolic constitution *Sacrae disciplinae leges*, in *Code of Canon Law: Latin-English Edition* (Washington, D.C.: Canon Law Society of America, 1989) xxx-xxxi.

[2] Despite the fact that most canon lawyers are immersed primarily in the substance and procedure affecting marriage cases in Books IV and VII, the apostolic constitution of promulgation dwells almost exclusively on ecclesiology. The word "marriage" is not uttered once; there is only a single implied reference when the Pope talks about the need for a visible Church to organize "the functions divinely entrusted to it, especially that of sacred power and of the administration of the sacraments." Ibid, xxxi.

[3] On the balance of newness and fidelity in canon law, see Lawrence Wrenn, "A Balanced Procedural Law," *The Jurist* 46 (1986) 602-623.

[4] As John Paul II put it, "in its own subject matter and in its own particular manner of expression." *Sacrae disciplinae leges*, xxxi.

and rediscovering it in our own way in our own time.

If we collect the juridical propositions about marriage into a unified whole, we might refer to this summary as a "canonical construct of marriage." It is a "construct" not because the Church has invented it, but in the sense that it concretizes and delimits the elements of the sacramental gift of marriage that are relevant to juridical practice. This finite set of propositions is meant to guide us in making decisions about how Christians marry, what rights and duties ensue from their commitment, and how the Church should address failed marriages and the parties' desire to marry again.

Juridical constructs are not new. The Church has been at this task for two millennia – in every aspect of Christian life. The problem is that, in the arena of marriage, this particular construct has not been dusted off for eight-hundred years. Except for minor housekeeping, it has not been reformed in a way that allows the sacrament of marriage to be, in this post-modern world of ours, what Christ intended it to be in every generation.

Unlike other areas of Christian thought, marriage, despite its beauty and centrality for the Church, has had to settle, like Cinderella, for "hand me downs." If truth be told, the ecclesial community became complacent, even fascinated, with its own canonical construct and failed to mine the richness of divine revelation about marriage itself. We have not returned again and again to its source, Jesus Christ, and we have not rediscovered in changing times the radical *newness* that the Son of God brought to all of us, including married couples, by becoming indissolubly "one flesh" with humanity as the son of Mary.

Edward Schillebeeckx knew this quite well. In his seminal work, *Marriage: Human Reality and Saving Mystery*, published during the Vatican Council, he laments the theological and doctrinal abdication that occurred once the ferment of the twelfth century subsided.[5]

A partial explanation for this neglect is the fact that marriage is a natural reality to begin with, an already-existing relationship incorporated by the Christ-event into the new covenant of grace. In the title to his book Schillebeeckx emphasizes this duplex uniqueness – that marriage is "without qualification a secular reality" and, simultaneously, a reality that, because it has been taken up

[5] "The theologians of the later period of scholasticism, however, did not always fully appreciate the medieval background which had occasioned this juridical formalisation, with the result that the 'treatise on marriage' became a study of the juridically formalised constitution of marriage rather than a dogmatic study of the whole reality of marriage. In this way, the theology of marriage developed into a theology of a juridical abstraction which was legitimate in itself, but which led to the neglect of the study of marriage as an anthropological datum – as what Aquinas called the *officium civilitatis*. The theology of marriage was thus able to help the canonists, but it was of scarcely any help in pastoral matters." Edward Schillebeeckx, *Marriage: Human Reality and Saving Mystery*, trans. N.D. Smith (New York: Sheed & Ward, 1965) 392.

into salvation, "has itself become sacramental in the technical sense." [6] Regrettably, theologizing about the sacramental meaning of marriage has been, at best, "sparse" – a conclusion shared by Karl Rahner.[7]

What is this "canonical construct of marriage (or what Schillebeeckx calls its "juridical formalisation")? While one could debate which canonical aspects should be included, the following seven statements are an arguable attempt to capture the essence of the canonical propositions that rule our marital practice:

1. The valid marriage of a validly baptized man and a validly baptized woman is by that very fact a sacrament (c. 1055 §2).
2. All valid marriages, including those in which one or both parties are not validly baptized, are intrinsically indissoluble: the parties themselves cannot dissolve them (c. 1056).
3. All valid marriages are extrinsically indissoluble in the sense that no power on earth other than the vicarious power of the Roman pontiff can dissolve them (c. 1056). Civil divorces do not dissolve the marriage bond; they simply adjudicate civil effects such as maintenance, support and child custody (c. 1059).
4. A valid marriage in which neither party is validly baptized, even if juridically consummated, may be dissolved through the Pauline privilege when the proper conditions, including conversion and baptism, are present (cc. 1143-1147).
5. A valid marriage in which at least one of the parties is not validly baptized, even if juridically consummated, can be dissolved for sufficient reason by the Roman pontiff in favor of the faith (CDF Norms, April 30, 2001; cc.1148-1150).
6. A valid marriage, sacramental or not, can be dissolved by the Roman pontiff if it is not yet physically consummated in a human fashion (c. 1142).[8]

---

[6] Ibid., 396-397.

[7] Schillebeeckx ironically ends his two-volume work as follows: "Later on in this work these two basic assertions will be considered in the light of the concrete problems which marriage raises. First, we shall consider what tradition has to tell us about the relationship between the interpersonal aspect of marriage and the founding of a family, and between married love and sexuality. Then we shall direct our attention to the urgent problems of marriage today." Ibid., 397. Sadly, he never wrote that critical third volume. Rahner's subsequent comment in *Theological Investigations* resonates with Schillebeeckx's conclusion when he opines that, with all the discussion about marriage, little attention has been paid to the crucial sacramental dimension. Karl Rahner, *Theological Investigations*, vol. 10, (Baltimore: Helicon Press, 1973) 199.

[8] Left unanswered is the question of the pope's power to dissolve an unconsummated marriage of *two unbaptized* persons where neither is seeking a favor of the faith dissolution to marry a Catholic. While the Latin code (c. 1142) refers to baptized parties or a baptized and a non-baptized spouse, canon 862 of the Eastern code on the

7. A sacramental marriage, once it has been juridically consummated, cannot be dissolved for any reason whatsoever, even by the exercise of the pope's power as Vicar of Christ (c. 1141). A person bound by such a marriage cannot validly marry another during the lifetime of his or her spouse (c. 1085 §1).

These seven propositions, each of which implicates other theological and juridical assertions, are the building blocks of the juridical construct within which the Church functions and chancery and tribunal officials work. Except for some logical development in regard to the Church's power over non-sacramental or non-consummated unions, the construct is essentially the same as that finalized in the middle ages. It served the Church well for many years, particularly in regard to sacramentality and indissolubility. The last century, however, has tested the construct and, while certain aspects of it remain vibrant and true to revelation, other propositions have begun to let their "finiteness" show. Holding to them is holding back the sacrament of marriage given to us by Christ.

The problem, as with any canonical construct, is that juridical formulations are historically conditioned: in the case of marriage much of the construct was forged mainly in the crucible of the twelfth-century consent-copula controversy. Framed by the juridical questions of that age, the propositions incorporated a certain imbalance, a rather crucial lack of equilibrium. This imbalance is not about indissolubility itself. It is about the inter-relationship of various kinds of marriage and even about stages within the formation of marriage. To dissect this imbalance more precisely, one must submit certain of these canonical propositions to cross-examination, reforming the "old" in a way that is faithful to the "newness" that marriage received from Christ.

Let us start with the last proposition, the absolute indissolubility of the consummated sacramental marriage, by examining briefly each of the three aspects of marriage it references: indissolubility, sacramentality, and consummation.

---

dissolution of non-consummated marriages does not refer at all to the spouses' baptismal status, suggesting by later omission that canon law does not preclude such an extraordinary dissolution by the pope. Actually, at least one canonist has argued, within the context of the "perfect society" theory, that civil authorities have the power to dissolve such non-consummated marriages: "[I]t would seem certain that the civil authority of a perfect society has the power, for just reasons, to dissolve the bond of a marriage not yet formed to the point where the spouses have consummated it with the marriage act whereby they become 'two in one flesh.' ... There are two public authorities which have power over the formation of the matrimonial bond, the Sovereign Pontiff for the baptized and the civil authority for the non-baptized. These two authorities have the power of dissolving the bond of a contracted but not yet consummated marriage when a just reason is present." Luigi Civisca, S.J., *The Dissolution of the Marriage Bond* (Naples: M. D'Auria Publisher to the Apostolic See, 1965) 84-85.

B. Indissolubility

Although divorce and the divorce mentality can today be legitimately termed "rampant," its prevalence is, relatively speaking, a rather recent phenomenon. It emerged in European circles mainly at the time of the French Revolution and the upheavals of the social order that followed.[9] Today, the phenomenon is so matter-of-fact and the natural law property of permanence is so little esteemed, no less respected, that tribunals are encountering cases of nullity not only on the ground of exclusion but on the ground of a party's *error* about the *bonum sacramenti*.[10] In this climate, the attempt to teach permanence as an essential property of marriage simply does not "compute" with the younger generation (some of whom, it is reported, are actually purchasing "divorce insurance"!)[11]

Should the Church raise the white flag, give up the ghost of indissolubility?

---

[9] In England, the first divorce law was not passed until 1857, and the practice did not really become widespread in Europe and North America until nearly a hundred years later. Theodore Mackin identifies the overall secularization of marriage and legalization of divorce as coming to completion in Christian Europe "during the last quarter of the eighteenth century ... mainly during the eleven years from 1781 to 1792." Theodore Mackin, *Divorce and Remarriage* (New York/Ramsey: Paulist Press, 1984) 414-415. The possibility of civil divorce in the French Constitution of 1791 was retained in Article 191 of the Napoleonic *Code Civil*, issued between 1801 and 1803, and most of the other nations of Europe "fell into line during the nineteenth century" (ibid., 416). In England, divorce was the prerogative of the rich, requiring a bill of the House of Lords, but in 1857, in response to, as the story goes, a pauper being jailed for remarrying after his wife deserted him; an act of Parliament established the *Court for Divorce and Matrimonial Causes* and abolished the divorce jurisdiction of the Church courts.

[10] "Since the middle of the twentieth century the strength of the traditional presumption that all people intend to enter marriage as it was designed by the Creator has waned considerably. It has become painfully clear that deeply rooted convictions about the acceptability of divorce and at least serial polygamy are endemic – and often epidemic... By the time the Second Vatican Council ended...there was broad consensus among Rotal judges that the human faculties of intellect and will were not hermetically sealed off from each other but that errors about the indissolubility of marriage, especially deeply entrenched errors or *error pervicax*, in the intellect inevitably had reverberations in the will." John Beal, "Determining Error: Hot New Ground of Nullity or Recycled Old Ground?" *CLSA Proceedings 2009* (Washington, D.C.: Canon Law Society of America, 2010) 62-89, 63. Beal offers summaries of several Rotal cases in this area: *coram* Monier (June 21, 1996) 68; *coram* McKay (February 4, 2005) 71; *coram* Bottone (November 27, 2007) 75; *coram* Stankiewicz (November 26, 1990) 77.

[11] "WedLock, as it's coyly named, is a new type of casualty insurance that gives the unhappily married policyholder a payout after he or she is unhitched." The policyholder must ante up for four years before collecting, and the premium increases 20% for each year of successful marriage. Some purchasers of the protection have been paying as much as $1,000 a month – which makes a divorce look quite lucrative! The article notes that such insurance might even be purchased for a newly-married couple "by relatives concerned about their loved one's choice of loved one." "Marriage: Making Divorce Pay," *Time* 176:11 (9/13/10) 56.

In his book *Divorce and Remarriage*, Theodore Mackin, after 546 intricately reasoned pages, offers the following carefully guarded suggestion: "It seems evident that the pastoral charity of the Church demands that these questions be now reopened and the evidence re-examined."[12] Such guardedness is well founded. Indissolubility is deeply rooted in the revelation of Christ, inextricably intertwined with that great *μυστήριον* of the Incarnation.[13] In the New Testament Jesus proclaims a newness about the permanence of marriage that is startling: it certainly shook his disciples. Opposing both Rabbinic interpretations of the time (the more lenient *Hillel* and stricter *Shammai* schools), he does not mince words: "Whoever divorces his wife and marries another commits adultery against her"[14] and "He who marries a woman divorced from her husband commits adultery."[15] This rejection of the specific provision of an orderly bill of divorce found in Deuteronomic law (the *anwar dabat*) was profound.[16]

The oral tradition that gave rise to the New Testament accounts of Jesus' teaching is extraordinarily solid. The pericopes on marriage in the three synoptic accounts and the references in Paul's writings are close in consistency, and their provenance has been called "the most securely attested saying by Jesus."[17]

It is true that Trent was very careful, when speaking about indissolubility, to phrase canon 7 in a way that would show sensitivity to the Eastern Christians.[18]

---

[12] Ibid., 547.
[13] Eph. 5:32.
[14] Mark 10:11-12.
[15] Luke 16:18.
[16] Deut. 24:1-4. As Schillebeeckx put it, "Christ – and, following his teaching, the early apostolic church – allowed no scope whatever for divorce. This was in complete contrast to the teaching of the Old Testament and in express opposition to the Law of Moses. ... It also ran directly against the practice of the whole ancient world" Schillebeeckx, 142-143.
[17] "Anyone who reads the New Testament with an open mind must surely admit that the tradition of Jesus' having uttered a statement on divorce is well attested. It appears in four different books of the New Testament, in five different versions, and in a variety of literary forms, specifically a conflict story, an isolated saying, and a letter. No matter what one's approach to the criterion of multiple attestation, one must acknowledge that the tradition satisfies the requirements of this criterion for an authentic saying of Jesus. ... [T]he diversity of expression given to this saying by the various New Testament authors shows that it was not a saying created by the early church in order to satisfy its internal needs. Rather it is clear that a traditional saying has been variously adapted by these different writers in order to make the tradition conformable to the real-life situation of the communities for which they were writing. ... The tradition of Jesus' teaching on divorce seems to enjoy as much claim to authenticity as does any other part of his teaching. Indeed, E.P. Sanders has called it 'the most securely attested saying by Jesus.'" Raymond F. Collins, *Divorce in the New Testament* (Collegeville, MN: The Liturgical Press, 1992) 214-215.
[18] Regarding indissolubility: "If someone should say that the Church errs when it has taught and teaches, in accordance with scriptural and apostolic doctrine..." Denziger-Schönmetzer, *Enchiridion Symbolorum Definitionum et Declarationum De Rebus Fidei et Morum, Decretum de sacramento matrimonii*, Can. 7, (Freiberg: Herder, 1963)

Nonetheless, if one critically re-examines the tradition from the scriptures – Jewish, Greek and Christian – through the fathers and medievalists, right up to modern and post-modern times, could one really argue convincingly for the abandonment of the indissolubility of Christian marriage? One could not – and should not.[19]

The sacramental role of indissoluble marriage is essential to the Church's life. It is not some peripheral aspect of ecclesial life; it is intimately connected with the very presence of the God-man among us, never to leave us, indissolubly joined to us, the central Christ-event, inserted into the fabric of society and the Church, the family. If anything, rather than maintaining it beyond its usefulness, perhaps our canonical construct has failed to plumb its depths and, over time, has ended up giving it short shrift.

C. Sacramentality

Trent listed marriage among the seven true and proper sacraments of the new Law instituted by Christ, but it did not offer much of an explanation about its sacramental nature.[20] Nonetheless, the council did affirm the substantial "newness" that Christ gave to all seven sacraments, distinguishing them from the "sacraments" of the old Law as more than simply revised ceremonies and external rites.[21]

Two who become "one flesh" symbolize the incarnational union of the Son of God with humanity and, like all the sacraments, bring about that which they symbolize. Although marriage as a symbol of Christ and the Church traces its roots back to the scriptures, the idea that this is a form of sacramentality in the strict sense arises rather late in the Church's history. Almost all the elements of the canonical construct of marriage, including absolute indissolubility, were in place by the twelfth century – but not strict sacramentality. Symbolism? – Yes. Sacramentality? – No. Even though sacramentality logically underlies and explains indissolubility, it was not put forward juridically as an essential element of indissolubility until afterwards. This may be one of the reasons that sacramentality, although the bedrock of the "newness" of marriage in Christ, has received little theological and canonical development.

Reflect on the fact that, in the first proposition of our canonical construct, sacramentality is, for all practical purposes, reduced to the fact of two valid baptisms: *The valid marriage of a validly baptized man and a validly baptized*

---

n. 1807, 416.

[19] Marriage was already a symbol of God's covenant with humanity in Genesis and the prophets and its role was energized by the establishment of the new covenant in Christ. Marriage represents and participates sacramentally in the great mystery of God's love for his people culminating in Christ's incarnation, death and resurrection, as is so often heard in the reading of the Letter to the Ephesians at wedding ceremonies.

[20] Ibid., *Decretum de sacramentis in genere*, Can. 1, n. 1601, 382. See also *Decretum de sacramento matrimonii*, Can. 1, n. 1801, 416.

[21] Ibid., *Decretum de sacramentis in genere*, Can. 2, n. 1602, 382.

woman is by that very fact a sacrament.[22]

1. The Revision of the Code

This reduction to valid baptism not only avoids the question of the relation of faith and sacrament but even forces conclusions about the validity of marriage that are strained, to say the least. During the revision of the code, the commission relied heavily on this proposition to justify certain canons. Here are two examples:

- The first deals with canon 1095 §3, the incapacity to assume the essential obligations of marriage, a ground of nullity well established by the Roman Rota prior to the promulgation of the revised code. The wording implies that there is nothing unique about sacramental marriages: the essential obligations are identical for all marriages, flowing, as they do, from the natural law.[23] The commission deleted language that might even *suggest* sacramentality, *viz.* the phrase "the communion of life," insofar as it could be interpreted as broadening the "essence" of marriage. The underlying assumption is that essential matrimonial obligations are univocal; they are the same for all, whether baptized or not.[24]

---

[22] As canon 1055 stresses, because "marriage has been raised by Christ the Lord to the dignity of a sacrament between the baptized" (§1), "a valid matrimonial contract cannot exist between the baptized without it being by that fact a sacrament" (§2). This assertion repeats word-for-word canon 1012 §2 of the 1917 code, an unfortunate example of the code commission's tendency to avoid – or, one might suggest, truncate – theological debate: it simply forced into the old wineskin of paragraph 2 the new wine of paragraph 1's deeply theological description of marriage as covenant, drawn verbatim from *Gaudium et spes* 48.

[23] The commission limited the ground by introducing phrases such as *gravis anomalia* and *obligationes essentiales*. In the 1980 schema, which brought all proposed canons together for the first time in the revision process, the wording that eventually developed into canon 1095 §3 was contained in a separate canon, canon 1049. At least two members of the commission considered the norm "dangerous" and likely to open the door to "abuses and undue extensions." They felt that the whole matter should be left to jurisprudential development in a case-by-case approach. Despite such objections, the *relatio* retained the canon, attaching it as the third paragraph of what would be promulgated as canon 1095. The rationale for its retention is interesting: it was defended as *a simple codification of natural law* that "establishes certain limits (grave anomaly, essential obligations). Ecclesiastical tribunals must indeed judge in individual cases, but they need a legal norm to avoid arbitrariness and so that there will be a certain essential uniformity in jurisprudence." *Communicationes* 15 (1983) 231. In fact, however, that precise language did not prevail. The promulgated version deleted the reference to "anomalies" (a term that includes disturbances that are less permanent than disorders and may in fact be curable) and settled, instead, on a more generic description of causality as psychic in nature (*causas naturae psychicae*).

[24] The commission removed from what is now canon 1101 the phrase "the right to those things that essentially constitute the communion of life" (*ius ad ea quae vitae communionem essentialiter constituunt*). *Communicationes* 9 (1977) 374-375. One of the members of the commission had objected in a written *votum* that the phrase "the

- A second example can be seen in regard to the phrase "sacramental dignity," added to what would become canons 1099 and 1101 §2 of the 1983 code. Both additions were approved by the full code commission in October 1981 and sent to the pope in the *schema novissimum*. The promulgated version, however, deleted the phrase from canon 1101 §2 on the basis that any *exclusion of the sacramental dignity* of marriage is *equivalent* to *total simulation.* The rationale? – Every marriage of two baptized persons is *by that very fact* a sacrament (c. 1055 §2). In other words, there is no need to identify marital sacramentality as an element whose exclusion vitiates consent; its exclusion is the exclusion of marriage itself. The *only* difference is that both parties *happen* to be validly baptized; their baptismal status has nothing to do with the nature or object of their consent, only with the result of that consent.[25]

These two examples, and decisions like it, assert such a radical identity of contract and sacrament that words like "sacrament" or "communion" are superfluous: they do nothing more regarding the juridical elements of validity than to point out that the parties positing marital consent are validly baptized. Their consent does not differ from the marital consent of those who are not baptized: what they intend are the essentials of every marriage, sacramental or natural.[26] This reasoning, however, does not seem to be in harmony with other, newer aspects of sacramental law found in the code.

A pervasive theme of the code is that sacraments cannot be reduced to impersonal, *ex opere operato* "things"; they are "celebrations" of properly disposed persons of faith. Canon 840, based on *Sacrosanctum concilium* 59,

---

right to those things that essentially constitute the communion of life" would be "dangerous for the stability of the matrimonial bond." The *relatio* agreed to delete it, replacing it with the generic phrase "some essential element of marriage." The commission stated that such details are not to be settled by inclusion in the revision process; they must be left to determinations by doctrine and jurisprudence. *Communicationes* 15 (1983) 233-234.

[25] The Congregation for the Doctrine of the Faith recommended on January 14, 1981, that the phrase be added to the properties of unity and indissolubility in proposed canon 1053 (which would eventually become canon 1099 of the 1983 code) as an element in which error "does not vitiate matrimonial consent provided that it does not determine the will." The *relatio*, preparing the text and agenda for the final *plenarium* of the code commission, dutifully added the phrase to the proposed canon and, somewhat logically, also included it in a revised version of canon 1055 §2 (eventually canon 1101 §2 of the 1983 code) which stated that that a positive act of the will on the part of one or both parties about marriage or its essential elements, including sacramental dignity, invalidates consent: "*At si alterutra vel utraque pars positivo voluntatis actu excludat matrimonium ipsum aut matrimonii essentiale aliquod elementum vel essentialem proprietatem vel sacramentalem dignitatem, invalide contrahit*." This was the version approved by the commission at the *plenarium* of October 1981. Canon 1101 §2 of the 1983 code retained most of the wording, but deleted the phrase "*vel sacramentalem dignitatem*." *Communicationes* 15 (1983) 233.

[26] See, e.g., *coram* Pompedda, May 9, 1970: *RRDec* 62:476; *coram* Pasquazi, July 28, 1960: *RRDec* 53:429; *coram* Masala, November 20, 1969: *RRDec* 61:1034.

stresses this dynamic notion of all sacraments: "As actions of Christ and the Church, they are signs and means which express and strengthen the faith, render worship to God, and effect the sanctification of humanity and thus contribute in the greatest way to establish, strengthen, and manifest ecclesiastical communion. Accordingly, in the celebration of the sacraments the sacred ministers and the other members of the Christian faithful must use the greatest veneration and necessary diligence."

Yet, canon law holds that the sacramentality of marriage is operative even if the parties do not know that they were baptized. How can two people whose "faith" is limited to the theological virtue infused by valid baptism and who have no awareness, no less practice, of that faith participate in the "celebration" of a marriage – i.e., minister the sacrament by giving and receiving each other (c. 1057 §2)? How are they, in canon 840's words, to "use the greatest veneration and necessary diligence" in doing so?

Even further, what about those who, though aware of their baptism, consciously and purposely *reject* that faith, perhaps even profess atheism? Do they enter a sacramental marriage when they exchange marital consent with another baptized person? Or to put it negatively, if the contracting parties are clearly opposed to the very idea that a marriage is sacramental, are they, in fact, unable to marry validly because they are not properly disposed to posit the consent that is necessary for a sacramental *matrimonium in fieri*?[27]

This kind of reasoning raises a nagging question: Has the right to marry

---

[27] This dilemma was one of the inconsistencies that resulted from the ill-fated inclusion in the code of the "formal act" exemptions and led eventually to their recent abrogation. If a formally departed, exempted, Catholic should marry another baptized person in a civil ceremony, the two of them would still be viewed as "celebrating" the *sacrament* of matrimony. Or would they? Their formal decision to depart the Church might very well indicate their formal rejection of all sacraments. Insofar as the corollary of canon 1055 §2 seems to be "If the marriage is valid, it is a sacrament; but if the marriage fails to be a sacrament, it is invalid," their consent would end up being invalid in any case. The ambivalence inherent in this canonical "dilemma" could be seen in the discussions of the *coetus* during the revision process. Some actually suggested that, instead of creating exemptions for such persons to facilitate their valid marriage, one's act of abandoning the Catholic faith, even if it were not accompanied with ascription to a non-Catholic community, should be the basis of a diriment impediment. The *coetus* rejected this suggestion specifically because such a person does not abandon the right to marry and, inasmuch as the contract and the sacrament are inseparable, the marriage will still be a Christian union. The *coetus* considered, however, that this could constitute a prohibiting (non-invalidating) impediment. Upon a vote, the majority did not wish to introduce such as even a prohibiting impediment (*Communicationes* 9 [1977] 144). The derogations last year of the marriage exemptions based on formal act (including the exemption from the obligation of canonical form) may simply have been a response to the impracticality that emerged since their introduction in the 1983 code. Yet, such derogations could also be interpreted as a symbolic distancing of the code from the concept of religious liberty and from any role for personal faith in regard to marital sacramentality.

(stated so clearly in canon 1058) and the Vatican Council's teaching on religious liberty been abolished in these cases? Has the code taken the position that two baptized persons who, maliciously or even innocently, decline to celebrate marriage as a sacrament will either have their wishes ignored, settling them, perhaps unknowingly, in a sacramental marriage, or be prevented from marrying validly since they lack the minimum right intention required of the sacrament? Many, including the International Theological Commission, the Synod of Bishops, John Paul II, and the prelate auditors of the Roman Rota, have struggled with this quandary.

2. The International Theological Commission (1978)

In 1978 the International Theological Commission (ITC) issued *Propositions on the Doctrine of Christian Marriage*, articulating the horns of the dilemma: [28]

1. Sacramentality and indissolubility are in a "reciprocal, constitutive relationship."[29]
2. Anyone who enters the sacrament of marriage must have the minimum intention to carry out "what Christ and the church desire," leading the ITC to conclude: "Where there is no trace of faith (in the sense of 'belief' – being disposed to believe), and no desire for grace or salvation is found, then a real doubt arises as to whether there is the ... general and truly sacramental intention and whether the contracted marriage is validly contracted or not." The absence of personal faith "compromises the validity of the sacrament."[30]
3. The ITC was hesitant to contradict the canonical identification of the contract of baptized persons with the sacrament (n. 3.3). It was therefore forced to conclude that non-believing baptized persons enter a relationship that, "even if it resembles marriage, cannot in

[28] Richard Malone and John R. Connery, eds., *Contemporary Perspectives on Christian Marriage: Propositions and Papers from the International Theological Commission* (Chicago, Illinois: Loyola University Press, 1984) [hereafter ITC] 3-36.

[29] The proposition adds: "Indissolubility makes it easier to understand the sacramental nature of Christian marriage; from the theological point of view, its sacramental nature constitutes the preeminent, although not the only, grounds for its indissolubility" ITC, n. 2.2. The inclusion of the phrase "the preeminent, although not the only, grounds" is a very cautious and careful foray into the fundamental question of what components are necessary for absolute indissolubility. For example, if physical consummation is necessary, does such an act partake of sacramentality? Is such a marriage "more sacramental" than an unconsummated marriage of two baptized persons?

[30] The ITC goes on to point out: "This gives rise to new problems for which a satisfactory answer has yet to be found, and it imposes new pastoral responsibilities regarding Christian matrimony. 'Priests should first of all strengthen and nourish the faith of those about to be married, for the sacrament of matrimony presupposes and demands faith' (*Ordo Celebrandi Matrimonium Praenotanda, n. 7*)." ITC, n. 2.3.

any way be recognized by the church as a non-sacramental conjugal society. For the church, no natural marriage separated from the sacrament exists for baptized persons, but only natural marriage elevated to the dignity of a sacrament" (n. 3.5).

4. In one of its most important statements, the ITC leaves room for doctrinal and juridical development by asserting that the Church "can further define the concepts of sacramentality and consummation, by explaining them even better, so that the whole doctrine on the indissolubility of marriage can be put forward in a deeper and more precise presentation" (n. 4.4).

3. The Synod of Bishops on the Christian Family (1980)

The ITC propositions clearly influenced the deliberations of the 1980 Synod of Bishops on the Christian Family, which raised the same question without resolving it. Two of the interventions at the synod illustrate the conflict of the canonical construct. Cardinal James Knox, prefect of the Congregation for the Sacraments and Divine Worship, restated the strict identity of contract and sacrament: "For the baptized, a valid matrimonial contract is always necessarily a sacrament. All the baptized who validly enter marriage receive the sacrament of matrimony whether they intend to or not. If they exclude the sacrament as a condition, the marriage is invalid." [31] Conversely, Archbishop Henri Legare of Grouard-McLennan, Alberta, articulated the opinion of many of the members that such a linkage has proved to be inadequate, offering the following state of the question: "First of all, what is the relationship between the marriage sacrament and the human institution of marriage? And, then, what of the relationship between baptism, faith, intention, and the marriage sacrament? In other words, would it not be timely to push forward the present questioning of the teaching which links the marriage contract and the sacrament in the case of baptized non-believers?"[32]

Among the forty-three resolutions and proposals transmitted to Pope John Paul II on October 24, 1980, was the following: "We must further investigate whether the statement that a valid marriage between baptized persons is always a sacrament is also applicable for those who have lost the faith. This will then entail juridical and pastoral consequences. Above all it must be investigated what the pastoral criteria might be for discerning the faith of the engaged couple and how much their intention of doing what the Church does more or less should include the minimal intention of believing with the Church as well."[33]

---

[31] *Origins* 10:18 (October 16, 1980) 281.

[32] Ibid.

[33] Proposition 12d. Jan Grootaers and Joseph Selling, *The 1980 Synod of Bishops "On the Role of the Family": An Exposition of the Event and An Analysis of its Texts* (Leuven: Leuven University Press, 1983) 270, n. 145. "Section 6 (Prop. 12) takes on the problematic of 'Faith and the Sacrament'. The very fact that this is a separate section testifies to the bishops' concern for a real pastoral problem. The *Lin[eamenta]*

4. John Paul II and *Familiaris consortio*

In 1981 John Paul encountered the same dilemma in the document that followed up the synod, *Familiaris consortio*: "When in spite of all efforts engaged couples show that they reject explicitly and formally what the Church intends to do when the marriage of baptized persons is celebrated, the pastor of souls cannot admit them to the celebration of marriage." [34] The implication of this statement is that, if they were admitted, their consent would be invalid, although *Familiaris consortio* refrains from stating that explicitly. This reticence avoided an ecumenical problem, for to say so explicitly would suggest to validly baptized Protestants (many of whom do not in any way whatsoever accept the sacramentality of marriage) that, if their faith were deficient, they would lack the minimum intention to marry validly their Protestant spouse in their own Protestant ceremony.

Pope John Paul II retained an intense interest in this topic. In his 2001 address to the Rota he underscored the caution that should be exercised when relating subjective faith to marital consent. He recalled the 1980 synod and his own reflections in *Familiaris consortio*, noting that, while the Church proposes "a *new* estimation of [marriage's] natural dimension," it is proposing *nothing more* than what existed "according to God's plan from the 'beginning.'"[35] This is another way of stating the same dilemma: how are we supposed to develop the "newness" that Christ brought to Christian marriage without denying its

had nothing to say about the issue and *IL [Instrumentum Laboris], 34* had brought it up, probably at the episcopal insistence. Now the bishops themselves turned their attention to the problem, not with the idea of giving a solution, but with the intention of exposing the issue in its complexity. It does this in five parts. The first paragraph begins with the reference to *Sacrosanctum concilium*, 59 (cf. IL, 34). Then, whereas the original had simply stated that faith is necessary for validity, the bishops added, 'That is why we must investigate to what extent the validity of the sacrament requires faith...'." Ibid., 268-269.

Grootaers and Selling point out in paragraphs 12b and 12c that, although the request for marriage may be a sign of faith, it also may be just a matter of custom having little or nothing to do with faith. In addition, there are different levels of maturity in couples (referring back to Proposition 7), something that can affect the need for a minimal intention. They then clarify the importance of the process that led to the final version of 12d: "Prop. 12, d is almost entirely the result of revision. The original said 'more deeply to be investigated is the statement according to which for baptized persons (even those) who have lost the faith the matrimonial contract is totally identified with the sacrament of marriage. This will have juridical and pastoral consequences' (parentheses added). The final version is much more explicit in its intention." Ibid., 269-270.

[34] John Paul II, apostolic exhortation *Familiaris consortio* (Vatican City: Libreria Editrice Vaticana, November 22, 1981; http://www.vatican.va/holy_father/john_paul_ii/apost_exhortations/documents/hf_jp-ii_exh_19811122_familiaris-consortio_en.html) 68.

[35] Pope John Paul II, "The Natural Dimension of Marriage," *Origins* 30:36 (February 22, 2001) 583 n. 8.

identity with natural marriage? Is marriage "old" or is it "new"? Is it "really new" or is it "nothing more" than ever before?

5. "Dissoluble-izing" or "Indissoluble-izing"?

"Dissoluble-izing" or "Indissoluble-izing"? – that is the question. Which way has the identity of natural marriage and sacramental marriage pushed canonical practice? Do canon lawyers, particularly in nullity cases, really treat sacramental marriages as if they in no way differ from a marriage in which at least one party is unbaptized? Is the same exact criterion used for both kinds of cases – making moot the question of whether both were baptized insofar as the answer has no juridical consequence for the court's standard of judgment? Or have tribunals, in fact, adopted the highest standard of the requisites for validity, those that correspond to the teaching of the Church about the sacrament, and then applied that standard equally to all marriages brought before them, sacramental or not? Theoretically, apart from the fact of the two baptisms, the canonical construct posits no sacramental difference in the areas of capacity, knowledge, freedom, and intention – or does it?

Yet, those immersed in tribunal work are quite aware that severely non-psychotic behavioral disorders destroy the capacity to enter a true marital covenant that is radically interpersonal – as canon 1057 §2 so rightly states, an act of consent in which the spouses "mutually give and accept *each other*" (italics added).

On the heels of psychology's insights, "traditional grounds" have re-emerged from the adjudicatory shadows in some tribunals. Is this simply an attempt to correct an overuse of canon 1095 §§2-3? Or is it recognition of what the above-mentioned authorities have been warning in regard to the minimum of right intention? Is it so unreasonable to suggest that the skewed vision of marriage in our post-modernist "non-culture" – which sees no problem in labeling homosexual unions as "marital"[36] – has resulted in many situations, particularly among those who do not share the Church's vision of marriage, in which the parties truly intend something other than what canon law asserts to be the very essence of marriage – and, in doing so, fail to marry validly?

Such adjudicatory developments in the areas of capacity, error and exclusion are not attacking indissolubility. If anything, they are doing the opposite: such judicial reasoning accepts so radically the canonical doctrine of the identity of natural marriage and sacramental marriage that it is "sacramental-izing" and "indissoluble-izing" *all* marriages – by applying the same standard to one and all.

To a certain extent, the canonical construct of marriage supports such a judgment – canon 1055 §2 *requires* a single standard about validity of consent

---

[36] It is interesting that *GS* 48 and canon 1055 §1 explicitly state "a man and a woman" when speaking about the parties to the marriage covenant, a clarification of the 1917 code's use of "*pars*" in *CIC* 1081 §2's description of matrimonial consent.

– i.e., there should not be any juridical difference in the essential requirements for the valid marriage of (a) those who are committed, baptized Christians, (b) those who are baptized but know nothing of the Christian faith, (c) those who are baptized but have left the Church and/or are opposed to the very idea of a sacrament and (d) those who are unbaptized and have no desire to be baptized.

6. Exclusion of Sacramentality or Total Simulation?

Actually, the canonical construct, despite the wording of canons 1055 §2 and 1102 §2, may admit of some differentiation in tribunal cases between sacramental and non-sacramental marriages. One example is the attempt to categorize as a separate ground the exclusion of the sacramental dignity of marriage, a ground that is applicable only if both parties are baptized. The Rotal auditor Msgr. Jose M. Serrano Ruiz has been a proponent of this legal theory. Rather than identify exclusion of the sacramental dignity of marriage with total exclusion of the marriage itself, he has tried in some cases to isolate the positive act of the will against sacramentality as such. The result is that the nullifying exclusion arises not from some sort of total simulation (in sacramental clothing) but from the specific lack of faith and, even more convincingly, from the party's animosity to faith and to any notion of the divine.[37]

Serrano has no difficulty in reconciling the party's invalidating intention about sacramentality with the same party's sense of sincerely assuming a set of

[37] In such cases, one is not required to find a positive act of the will against the marriage itself (total simulation) nor a partial simulation of one of the three traditional *bona* (children, fidelity, permanence); the ground of nullity is specifically a simulation of one's consent to a marriage that is endowed with sacramental dignity. See, e.g., the two decisions *coram Serrano* published in *Sacramentalità e Validità del Matrimonio nella Giurisprudenza del Tribunale della Rota Romana* (Città del Vaticano: Libreria Editrice Vaticana, 1995): *Romana* (April 18, 1986) 203-215; *Compobassen* (June 1, 1990) 269-284. Serrano lays the groundwork for his rationale in the meaning of marriage as set forth by *Gaudium et spes*, the propositions of the International Theological Commission, and the implications of religious liberty in *Dignitatis humanae*. (See Serrano's own work, *Ispirazione conciliare nei principli generali del matrimonio canonico*, Bologna, 1985, 43-44.) He specifically identifies sacramental dignity as one of the "essential elements" of canon 1101 §2 and uses as one of his arguments the fact that the phrase "sacramental dignity" was intentionally included in the prescripts of canon 1099 on error. Naturally, the rationale for such an exclusion of sacramentality must be deep-seated. The kind of evidence needed will not be found in a person who simply exhibits a certain levity in regard to faith and the sacraments. The simulator must be someone who publicly attacks the faith and is clearly alienated from religion (*coram* Serrano, *Romanum*, n. 7). Two of the cases in which Serrano as *ponens* gives an affirmative decision on the exclusion of sacramentality involve atheists who have had a long history of anti-Church and anti-God sentiments. They went through the religious rite of marriage to please spouse and family but they clearly considered the religious aspect of it to be just a formality and to have little, if any meaning (*coram* Serrano, *Romanum*, n. 9).

interpersonal obligations that all would recognize as "marital."[38] The real question, for him, is whether, by obliging oneself to "marriage," one thereby *obliges* oneself, at least implicitly, to the "sacred" or, alternatively, so entirely *repudiates* "sacredness" that any obligation that was sincerely undertaken would fail to be "conjugal."

In the end, however, he cannot escape the strictures of the canonical construct. He explicitly underscores the canonical problem as follows: "The traditional treatment of the exclusion of sacramentality, i.e., of the sacramental dignity of matrimony, seems to have stressed too much the identity of the covenant and the sacrament, so that 'sacramentality' would not be a property or an essential element of matrimony but would be matrimony itself ('*to esse*', essence)."[39] It is difficult to maneuver within the canonical construct.[40]

---

[38] *Coram* Serrano, *Romanum*, n. 8. Serrano also addresses the subtlety that a judge must have in determining the essence of the "positive act of the will" of canon 1101 §2. He notes that the Church has long recognized sins "by omission," to which he analogizes such positive acts of the will of sacramental exclusion. Citing a 1957 decision of Mattioli, he notes that the nullity arises not from some sort of explicitly formulated internal act of the person but from a "total deficiency of consent." The marriage may be just a "means to an end" rather than the true object of one's consent, even though the excluder does not explicitly reject marriage as such. His reasoning is based on an epistemological analysis of conjugal consent as "personal and interpersonal," an *actus humanus* rather than merely an *actio hominis* (*coram* Serrano, *Campobassen*, n. 5).

[39] *Coram* Serrano, *Campobassen*, n. 10.

[40] Other Rotal auditors reject Serrano Ruiz's approach. A recent example can be seen in *coram* Boccafola (P.N. 19.526, June 25, 2009; unpublished, translated by author). Msgr. Boccafola, citing M. Pompedda ("Fede e sacramento del matrimonio," *Quaderni Studio Rotale II*, Roma [1987] 450), calls the matrimonial contract and the matrimonial sacrament "forms (*modi*) – the one natural, the other supernatural – of the very same reality" (n. 6). For Boccafola, the sacramental dignity of a marriage is "nothing other than the natural bond itself between baptized spouses... It is the '*res*' of matrimony that becomes '*res et sacramentum*' among the baptized.... Sacramentality then adds nothing to the natural covenant" (n. 7).

With this complete identity as a premise, juridical consequences are inevitable: "It follows that the validity or invalidity of sacramental marriage is determined by the same arguments and principles that demonstrate the existence or non-existence of the natural covenant or human contract...the only thing necessary is to posit true matrimonial consent. It follows then that faith is not necessary, only consent" (n. 8). "[T]he validity or not of the matrimonial consent is determined by the same principles and proof as that of total simulation of consent...judicial and extrajudicial confession of the simulator, corroborated by witnesses beyond any exception: the existence of a reason for simulating greater than that for contracting: confirmation by circumstances prior to, during, and after the marriage" (n. 11).

Boccafola categorizes the International Theological Commission's 1979 propositions as raising solely "a doubt of fact in the individual case, which is then to be determined in a judicial process, but in no way any true doubt of law or general presumption against the validity of consent" (ibid.). He admits that more recent Rotal decisions have adopted a different stance in this matter, namely a direct exclusion of sacramentality as a kind of partial simulation of "one of the properties or one of the essential elements of matrimony (*c*. Bruno, February 26, 1988: *RRDec* 80: 168, n. 3; *c*.

7. Directly-and-Principally-Intended Error or Simulation Caused by Error?

Tribunals also encounter cases in which a party's views about unity, indissolubility or sacramental dignity vitiate matrimonial consent either as error or, at least, as the cause of partial simulation. If the invalidity is to result from error, the error's prevalence and intensity, although not a conscious exclusion by a positive act of the will in the traditional sense, must have clearly "determined the will."[41] The rationale is that the parties are so programmed in their thinking that, although they do not suffer from a psychic disorder that disrupts consensual capacity, their value system causes them to intend "directly and principally" something other than true marriage, a union that is essentially erroneous.[42]

Sometimes, however, the distinction between an error that is directly and principally intended and a partial exclusion is difficult to fathom. This is especially so when the argument for "exclusion" is based almost entirely on the excluder's erroneous value system. One example can be seen in a case by Rotal auditor Msgr. Giuseppe Sciacca decided in 2007.[43] While remaining within the

---

Fiore, July 17, 1973: *RRDec* 65: 592-593)," but such analysis is merely "from a psychological perspective, although not at all in an ontological sense since sacramental dignity is identical with the nuptial pact itself" (n. 10). He therefore rejects this approach, aligning himself with a decision "*coram* Burke, May 18, 1995: *RRDec* 87: 297, n. 14: 'Sacramentality does not constitute a kind of supernatural "super-structure" attached to the natural reality of matrimony; and it is erroneously considered an essential "property" or constitutive "element" of Christian marriage.... Sacramentality is not a property or matrimonial element, but coincides with the matrimony itself as it exists for those whose souls have been impressed with the baptismal character" (ibid.).

In the particular case, the petitioner had stated in the context of the couple's pre-nuptial investigation: "I think as the Catholic Church wishes." Boccafola sees this affirmation as expressing "the minimal intention needed to celebrate a valid sacrament" (n. 15). Although the petitioner underwent a Catholic ceremony "reluctantly" and maintained "that he did not at all will to confect and receive the sacramental dignity of matrimony, ... at the same time he also did not will to desist from entering a true natural matrimonial covenant" and therefore had the necessary "vestige of faith" (nn. 15-16). The petitioner's prevailing will was to enter a valid, natural marriage and that will is sufficient for baptized persons: "Because of the inseparability, however, for the baptized between the natural matrimonial contract and the sacrament, the will of the party seeking a true marriage also comprehends and effects the sacrament. In no way do the acts or testimonies prove that the intention of the man was so much against the sacrament that it would constitute an absolute and prevailing will by which he would, if need be, also exclude marriage itself... there is no serious doubt that the petitioner wished to contract matrimony with the respondent, while for him the rite by which he would contract that matrimony was of lesser import" (n. 17).

[41] Canon 1099.

[42] Canon 1097. See John Beal, "Determining Error: Hot New Ground of Nullity or Recycled Old ground?" cited above in footnote 5.

[43] *Coram* Sciacca, Prot. N. 19.369 (June 1, 2007) [unpublished; English translation by this author to be published in the near future in CLSA's *Rotal Jurisprudence*]. Sciacca starts his *in iure* on partial simulation in a traditional manner: "Based on the natural

ground of partial exclusion, Sciacca makes a distinction between an "absolute" act of the will and a "hypothetical" act of the will, which seems to shift him much closer to nullity on the ground of error about indissolubility that is directly and principally intended.[44] Sciacca concludes that *error* based on cultural forces, although not directly the cause of the nullity, is the *cause* of the hypothetical *simulation* that causes the nullity: "Such an exclusion ... can be either absolute, when the contractant excludes the indissoluble bond entirely and in every way whatsoever, or hypothetical, when, e.g., the contractant, because of excessive anxiety about the eventual outcome of his marriage, rejects the perpetuity of the marriage at the very moment of forming consent if the situation should occur, namely, if things turn out badly, always keeping for himself an open door: in this regard, however, it is very important to note that the exclusion, which is clearly present at the origin of the consent and renders it invalid, is not hypothetical; the only thing that is hypothetical is the concrete event of the breakup of the invalidly-entered pseudo-marriage."[45]

---

law... one must presume that the internal consent of the mind is in conformity with the words and signs used in celebrating marriage (c. 1101 §1); nonetheless, the Law foresees cases in which the contractant, even by a positive act of the will, excludes 'marriage itself or some essential element of marriage, or some essential property,' by which the consent is rendered invalid (c. 1101 §2)." *Coram* Sciacca (June 1, 2007) n. 9.

[44] Sciacca makes an interesting point in paragraph 13: Invalidating consent through a hypothetical exclusion is possible in regard to the *bonum sacramenti* because "there is no distinction – as occurs in regard to the goods of children and fidelity – between the right and the exercise of the right, insofar as marriage cannot exist without inseparability, as we are taught by the Angelic Doctor: 'Indissolubility, which the sacrament brings about, pertains to marriage itself according to itself; for from the fact that, through their conjugal agreement, the spouses hand over to each other perpetual power over themselves, it follows that they cannot be separated, and thus it is that there can be no marriage without inseparability... (*IV Sent.*, D. 31, q. 1, a. 3)'."

[45] *Coram* Sciacca (June 1, 2007) n. 13. "'In western society divorce is widely accepted and certainly such acceptance exercises a great influence on the way that people today view marriage. The contractant who reserves to himself the right to terminate the matrimonial pact and to be free to contract a new marriage, if his union does not in fact turn out well, excludes an essential property of marriage' (J. Hendriks, "Dir. Matrim.," [Milano: 1999] 206-207) ... Immersed in false ways of thinking and relativistic doctrine that lead him to promote divorce openly and view it, should the situation arise, as a practical solution, the contractant considers the bond dissolvable. This 'divorce mentality' validly presents a very appropriate cause of simulating." *Coram* Sciacca (June 1, 2007) nn. 14-15.

Sciacca goes on to state: "[O]ne should not in any way deny the fact that – especially these days, as is universally known – a mind that persistently favors divorce and takes it for granted, even though such error must necessarily move from the intellect to a positive act of the will, can constitute a suitable cause of simulating" (n. 15); and, citing Heard, he concludes his *in iure* section as follows: "'If indeed there is a law admitting divorce, and the contractant does nothing, but simply remains silent about the law, content to be subject to it, he is acting out of mere error. However, if he is not only silent about the law, submitting to the law's permissiveness, but also makes the law his own through a positive act of the will, his consent is undoubtedly vitiated

8. Due Discretion and Capacity to Assume "Sacramental" Obligations

Do not these Rotal attempts to distinguish, if ever so slightly, the will acts of sacramental and non-sacramental marriages in regard to sacramental dignity and indissolubility suggest that one should logically expect a *greater capacity to consent* on the part of two baptized persons entering a sacramental marriage, as stated by canon 1095 §§2-3? In analyzing due discretion and capacity to assume essential obligations, many judges, including prelate auditors of the Rota, have relied on the Thomistic rationale that one needs greater discretion to contract matrimony than to commit a mortal sin insofar as the decision to marry consents to a whole host of unknown contingencies.[46] As the old adage goes, "Marry in haste, repent in leisure"! This conclusion has served as the start of many an *in iure* section supporting an affirmative sentence of nullity.

Taking the argument one step further, is it not reasonable, then, to require those who enter an absolutely indissoluble (i.e., sacramental) marriage must have *greater* deliberative capacity and a *higher* degree of freedom to will such an irreversible chain of events than one would require of a couple who are entering a non-sacramental marriage that is not absolutely indissoluble? Perhaps the "right intention" required of baptized persons is different, after all, from that required of non-baptized persons. Even our canonical construct introduces some room to assert a higher standard of judgment for marriage in the new covenant if only because absolute indissolubility traditionally flows totally from sacramentality.

9. Sacramentality and Newness

All of this, however, begs the question. Contrary to the constrictions of the canonical construct, is it not true that *everything* about a sacramental marriage, the marriage of the *new* covenant, is supposed to be "elevated," "greater," "radically new" – to use Pope John Paul II's words? Consider this portion of his 1979 address that he quotes in *Familiaris consortio* 13 (italics added): "In a

---

by his contracting with a true intention of taking advantage of it.' (SRRD., v. XXXIV, p. 167, n. 2)" (n. 16).

To keep his decision one of exclusion rather than error, Sciacca posits a classic distinction: he identifies the defendant's divorce mentality as his "remote" cause of simulating (he was a dedicated proponent of the passage and retention of the divorce law in Italy prior to and at the time of the wedding). Combined with pre-marital doubts about his fiancée's psychological stability and conflicts about finances (which Sciacca terms the "proximate" cause of simulating), the *turnus* answers the doubt in the affirmative: *constat de nullitate* because of the exclusion of the *bonum sacramenti*. *Coram* Sciacca (June 1, 2007) nn. 29-31.

[46] "*Et ideo dicendum est quod ad peccatum mortale sufficit etiam consensus in praesens. Sed in sponsalibus est consensus in futurum. Maior autem discretio rationis requiritur ad providendum in futurum quam ad consentiendum in actum unum praesentem. Et ideo ante potest homo peccare mortaliter quam possit se obligare ad aliquid futurum.*" *ST Suppl.*, qu. 43, art. 2, ad 2.

word, it is a question of the normal characteristics of all natural conjugal love, *but* with a *new significance* which not only purifies and strengthens them, but *raises* them to the extent of making them the expression of *specifically Christian* values."[47] Notice his struggle to identify some sort of "newness." Why does that "new significance" not call for a "new" standard of judgment about *all* essential aspects of the matrimonial covenant – in other words, newness in the *matrimonium in fieri*, not merely in the *matrimonium in facto esse*? One obvious reason is the fact that the canonical construct of marriage does not easily support such "newness."[48]

All of these canonical examples point to a lack of balance, an "in-equilibrium" that is becoming more and more obvious and neuralgic. Sacramentality and indissolubility are being stifled in today's world by the Church's age-old canonical construct. These revealed truths are struggling to be

---

[47] *FC* 19 (italics added): "This conjugal communion sinks its roots in the natural complementarity that exists between man and woman, and is nurtured through the personal willingness of the spouses to share their entire life-project, what they have and what they are: for this reason such communion is the fruit and the sign of a profoundly human need. But in the Lord Christ God takes up this human need, *confirms* it, *purifies* it and *elevates* it, leading it to *perfection* through the sacrament of matrimony: the Holy Spirit who is poured out in the sacramental celebration offers Christian couples the gift of a *new* communion of love that is the living and real image of that unique unity which makes of the Church the indivisible Mystical Body of the Lord Jesus.

"The gift of the Spirit is a commandment of life for Christian spouses and at the same time a stimulating impulse so that every day they may progress towards an *ever richer* union with each other on all levels-of the body, of the character, of the heart, of the intelligence and will, of the soul-revealing in this way to the Church and to the world the *new* communion of love, given by the grace of Christ."

[48] Consider the following statement of the dean of the Roman Rota, citing Pope John Paul's *2001 Allocution to the Rota*: "At times, however, the matrimonial norms of the Code come under criticism insofar as the sacramentality of Christian marriage is based solely on a 'quasi sacramental causality,' i.e. on the fact of the baptism of the spouses (can. 1055 §§1-2). But the emphasis on the exclusive dependence of the sacramentality of marriage on the personal faith of the spouses and their openness to ecclesial communion seems to lose sight of the fact that matrimony is a natural reality, 'evinced by reason for the good of the couple and of society, and confirmed by the revelation of Our Lord, who closely and explicitly relates the marital union to the "beginning" (*Mt* 19, 4-8) spoken of in the Book of Genesis: "male and female he created them" (*Gn* 1, 27), and "the two shall become one flesh" (*Gn* 2, 24).'" Antoni Stankiewicz, "Il Diritto Matrimoniale Canonico nel Momento Presente: Valutazione e Prospettive," *Ius Ecclesiae* 21:1 (2009) 49-61, 59. Immediately following the cited section, Pope John Paul II specifically adds the following: "The fact, however, that the natural datum is authoritatively confirmed and raised by Our Lord to a sacrament in no way justifies the tendency, unfortunately widespread today, to ideologize the idea of marriage - nature, essential properties and ends - by claiming a different valid conception for a believer or a non-believer, for a Catholic or a non-Catholic, as though the sacrament were a subsequent and extrinsic reality to the natural datum and not the natural datum itself evinced by reason, taken up and raised by Christ to a sign and means of salvation." Pope John Paul II, *Allocution to the Roman Rota* (February 1, 2001) n. 4.

set free, to be given some breathing room, so that they will indeed be part of Christ's new covenant, signifying it and, at the same time, bringing it about, not in theory but in the real world of married couples who are baptized people of faith, hope and love and who are called to form with their children an interpersonal ministry of life and love. Unless one is willing to separate absolute indissolubility from sacramentality, to reduce it simply to a juridical add-on, it will be increasingly difficult for a *canonical* construct to hold in check the *mystery* of indissoluble Christian marriage. Viewing a marriage covenant that has been immersed in the incarnation, death and resurrection of Christ as juridically identical to a union that is not part of the sacramental life of the Church is simply going to become more and more untenable.[49]

D. Consummation

1. The Twelfth-century Compromise

The consummation of marriage presents another lack of balance in regard to marriage, one whose explanation is much clearer and whose provenance extends back to the twelfth century. The International Theological Commission explicitly noted further development must take place in regard to the assertion that the valid marriage of two validly baptized spouses does not become absolutely indissoluble unless and until they engage in an act of sexual intercourse.[50] This building block of the canonical construct of marriage dates back to Alexander III's compromise resolution of the consent-copula controversy, epitomized by the debate between Peter Lombard in Paris and Gratian in Bologna. Alexander III retained elements from both theories and, in doing so, created a problem.

Gratian held a mitigated copula theory: Marriage only "begins" with consent or with multiple consents of varying types – some espousal, some marital – but it is not "completed" until the spouses seal their consent by *copula carnalis.*[51] Peter Lombard, on the other hand, gave little, if any, meaning to *copula carnalis* – perhaps a heightened sense of symbolism but no juridic effects, even as to indissolubility.[52] Central to both theories was the protection of the validity of

---

[49] In this kind of tension, age-old philosophical debates emerge. Thinkers like Richard of Middleton and Panormitanus have held that absolute indissolubility is simply a result of the positive law of God, a voluntaristic approach. For them it is an exclusively juridical property and can be cordoned off from the other elements of marriage, including sacramentality. George H., Joyce, *Christian Marriage: An Historical and Doctrinal Study*, 2nd ed. (London: Sheed & Ward, 1948) 386. If, however, one connects the obligation of indissolubility with the meaning of sacramentality, as the International Theological Commission did (ever so tentatively), the tension and some resolution of it are inevitable (ITC 2.2 and footnote 29 above).

[50] ITC 4.4.

[51] Cf. especially C. 27, 2 of the *Decretum Gratiani*.

[52] For him and his followers, an unconsummated marriage represents the union of Christ and the Church by will and by charity; physical consummation adds only the

the *Gottesmutterehe*, the marriage of Mary and Joseph: something that was much easier for Lombard than for Gratian.[53]

Alexander III settled the divergent practice of tribunals by opting fundamentally for the Parisian solution but pragmatically adding a compromise element from Bologna. As Father Coriden put it, "Alexander attributed to consummation a new position in the formation of the bond. It was neither all-important as Gratian claimed, nor inconsequential as Lombard taught, but enjoyed a perfective or complementary function which rendered the marriage indissoluble."[54] The compromise nature of this settlement lacked a certain consistency and theoretical balance. Esmein noted that it introduced "a certain lack of equilibrium that will be felt in all subsequent ages."[55]

In this matter, the foundational discrepancy and lack of equilibrium arises from the age-old contest between the spiritual and the physical. Clearly, a marital relationship is not purely spiritual: it involves sexuality in the fullest sense. Human beings are "fleshed souls," not bodiless spirits.[56] Even the consent that they exchange is not purely spiritual: it had no juridic effect, even in clandestine marriages, without being physically expressed by words or other signs (even by sexual intercourse itself if accompanied by *affectus maritalis*).

Why does consent, the very essence of *matrimonium in fieri*, require something more? If a sacramental marriage is *fully* a marriage with the exchange of consent, how does a single act of physical intercourse render it "more indissoluble"? And if it is "more indissoluble," is it also "more sacramental" (recall that Alexander III's resolution *preceded* the Church's affirmation of marriage's strict sacramentality)? It is clearly not "another" act of consent even though, according to canon 1061 §1, it must be completed "in a human fashion." Nor do modern theologians suggest that the consummated marriage participates more fully in the mystery of the union of Christ and his Church, as the medievalists taught about its symbolic function.

---

representation of Christ's union with the Church in the Incarnation. Of juridical interest to Lombard, instead, was the critical distinction among the various kinds of consent (the distinction to which Gratian paid much less attention): *consensus per verba de futuro* (the promise to marry) in contrast to *consensus per verba de praesenti* (the act of consenting to marriage). Once the latter words are exchanged, with or without formalities and/or blessings (recall that this is the age of "clandestine marriages" without any requirement of canonical form for validity), the marriage that is brought into being is absolutely indissoluble. Petrus Lombardus, *Libri IV Sententiarum*, 2nd ed. (Ad Claras Aquas: Patres Collegii S. Bonaventurae, 1916) l. 4, d. 27, cap. 2, 3, 4.

[53] Cf. C. 27, 2, d.p. c. 39 of the *Decretum Gratiani.*

[54] James Coriden, *The Indissolubility Added to Christian Marriage by Consummation* [excerpts] (Rome: Catholic Book Agency, 1961) 26.

[55] "...un certain manque d'équilibre qui se fera sentir dans toute la suite du temps." Esmein, vol. 1, 139.

[56] The French philosopher, Jean Mouroux, purposely used the term "fleshed soul" or "embodied spirit" (rather than "rational animal") to describe the oneness of the human person, inseparably body-spirit. See Jean Mouroux, *The Meaning of Man* (Garden City Doubleday/Image Books, 1961).

2. Stages of Formation

At the very least, one must explain how the Church has distinguished, in juridic terms, the formation of the marriage bond by consent and the completion of the bond's absolute indissolubility by consummation, for the canonical construct asserts that the *ratum sed non consummatum* marriage is susceptible to dissolution.

An explanation that resolves somewhat the inconsistency of Alexander III's solution is to conclude that there are *stages* in the formation of Christian marriage. For Peter Lombard the stages were words *de futuro* and words *de praesenti*; for Gratian the stages were various kinds of consent, accompanied by or followed by, *copula carnalis*. For neither of them, however, did the early acts produce a "real" marriage; they were only preliminary to it. With Alexander III's compromise, however, one is required to conclude that there are stages *within* the formation of *indissoluble marriage itself*. Marriage is already present with consent and yet becomes qualitatively different when a second stage is reached, when it is "completed" (i.e., "consummated").

Despite its longevity in canonical theory, reliance on a single physical act as the moment of completion must be abandoned; it is a cultural element, introduced in the early middle ages, that no longer fulfills its function. For centuries it proved convenient both juridically and symbolically, but it does not come to our canonical construct from revelation. It finds no basis in scripture unless one is willing to misinterpret the Genesis notion of *una caro* and the teaching of Paul in Ephesians. Nor can it be ascribed to tradition, for to do so, is to ignore the legitimate development by the fathers and medievalists of marriage as indissoluble and sacramental (symbolic) apart from sexual acts.

The cultural origin of the sexual act as the juridical completion of the indissoluble marriage bond leads inexorably to the suggestion that, in today's highly different culture and with a changing view of the object of marital consent, the Church should be open to the notion that marriages pass through varied stages before absolute indissolubility emerges. In other words, using Gratian's terminology, the Church can still require that a process be "consummated" before the absolutely indissoluble marriage is "completed," but this "consummation" may not in every case be fulfilled simply by a sexual act. Such a modification makes sense when one re-examines the intentional shift in the revision of the Code away from the *ius in corpus* to the *persons themselves* as the *proper object of marital consent*.[57] Just as it was legitimate for centuries to consider the first exercise of the *ius in corpus* as the completion of the absolutely indissoluble bond (as a canonized form of *traditio rei*), so also might it not be appropriate to require the actuality of the interpersonal self-giving to be executed before one can say that the spouses' mutual consent is

[57] Compare canon 1057 §2 in the 1983 code with its predecessor, *CIC* 1081 §2 in the 1917 code.

consummated (even though consent is sufficient for validity)?[58]

3. Justiciability: Judging Invalidity or Dissolubility?

Some might object that such a proposition, by moving away from the physical, offers no juridical moment or provable fact to warrant a judgment. At least, physical consummation or the lack of it has been, within reason, justiciable. Such an objection would make sense if applied to consent rather than consummation insofar as there must be a clear moment for the *initiation* of a valid sacramental marriage (one of the juridical rationales of mandatory canonical form). But when it comes to consummation, one is not speaking about validity – neither of the marriage itself, nor of the sacrament with which it is identified. One is speaking, rather, of the *completion* of the *indissolubility* (and, one might suggest, also the sacramentality) of that marriage.

Perhaps the accomplishment of that consummation or its failure to take place could be judged by the 20/20 vision of hindsight. While one might be hard pressed to describe prospectively what would go into the actualization of an interpersonal relationship, it may not be that difficult to determine that, looking back in light of the canonical principles regarding the interpersonal nature of marriage, it just never happened. After all, is this not the retrospective path that judges currently travel to track incapacity or invalidating intentions back to the exchange of consent?

What if the tribunal's task were not, at first, to judge the validity of consent, but rather to examine initially whether the couple *ever* really became "one flesh" in the scriptural sense (i.e. "one life"). For sacramental marriages, the joinder of issues would then be sacramental rather than purely juridical: namely, whether the spouses truly rose to the level of mirroring the union of Christ and the Church in the Incarnation. In such a process, the marriage that was never brought to completion would, according to our canonical tradition, be valid but susceptible to dissolution – by the current practice of papal dispensation,[59] or by

---

[58] In *The Meaning of Man,* Jean Mouroux analyzes marital love in a way that demonstrates how the interpersonal relationship essential to marriage implicates a dynamic complexity of body and spirit; he identifies three components: "The *call of instinct* ... the carnal aspect of love – opaque, hungry, violent ... The *act of the spirit*, the definitive choice that excludes all others ... the spiritual aspect of love – radiant, infinite, creative ... [The] *intoxication of the affectivity,* a whole world of specific feelings, sensible and spiritual together ... like "music awakened" in the soul ... The three components ... integrate a sole reality, which is that of nuptial love; a sole act, the act of loving; and a sole state which is a kind of experience of the infinite." Ibid., 194.

[59] While the *ipso iure* dissolution of non-consummated marriages by the unilateral decision of one of the parties to enter religious life was a very ancient tradition, the use of papal power to do the same under other circumstances developed rather slowly. Some date it back to Martin V (1417-1431) or, at least theoretically, even Alexander III (1159-1181). Commenting on Martin V, Noonan suggests that "the practice was established and had a history predating his pontificate... The routine way these petitions were handled and the easy delegations of power scarcely indicated an

episcopal exercise of such a faculty as was argued in the process of revision,[60] or even by a subsequent valid marriage by analogy with canon 1149's special arrangement for favor cases involving captivity or persecution.[61]

---

awareness that an extraordinary power was being exercised. But these documents were not available to theologians until five centuries later... Two leading sixteenth-century theologians, Cajetan and Navarrus, claimed the Pope had the power without further theological elaboration; they pressed the fact that at least two Popes had exercised it. Another leading sixteenth-century theologian, Domingo de Soto, dismissed the power as a 'dream,' put forward 'without a shadow of probability.' The controversy was warm; no theological consensus existed. When, on November 11, 1563, the Council of Trent enacted its canons on marriage, it asserted, against the denial of Luther, that religious profession dissolved an unconsummated marriage; the rule of Alexander III was put forward as a solemn truth to deny which was to incur anathema. But nothing at all was taught about papal power to dissolve. The silence of the Council...neither condemned nor counseled." Finally, in 1741 Pope Benedict XIV (Prospero Lambertini), in *Dei miseratione*, exposed the marvelous power to the world at large. He kept the curial language which avoided shock: the Pope 'dispensed,' he did not 'dissolve.'...The cases which came to the Curia were 'frequent.' He had handled them himself more than once in the S.C.C....That in passing he gave full publicity to a practice over a century old probably did not seem to him the most significant aspect of his action."

Noonan incisively concludes: "Seeking to centralize responsibility in the Pope, *Dei miseratione* in effect confirmed the treatment of non-consummation cases in the Curia. Incidentally, almost accidentally, nonetheless deliberately, it acknowledged at the highest level that a discretion existed and was employed to terminate one class of Christian marriage." John T. Noonan, Jr., *Power to Dissolve: Lawyers and Marriages in the Courts of the Roman Curia* (Cambridge, Massachusetts: The Belknap Press of Harvard University Press, 1972) 130-136.

[60] In the revision of the code it was agreed that with non-consummated unions the current practice should be retained, namely, that only the pope can dissolve a non-consummated marriage. Some consultors had argued that the dissolution of a non-consummated marriage, as described in the 1917 code, *CIC* 1119, was an act of the "Apostolic See" whereas the revised version of the canon (which would eventually become canon 1142 of the 1983 code) limited it to the "Roman Pontiff." They recommended that the phrase be modified to allow bishops to exercise such a faculty or at least to state more generically "by ecclesiastical authority" so as not to forestall theological discussion about vicarious power and the possibility of its delegation. Others thought that the same power actually belongs to bishops even though they agreed with other members of the *coetus* that its exercise should still be reserved to the Roman Pontiff (*Communicationes* 10 [1978] 108).

[61] The canons arising from missionary quandaries (cc. 1148-1149) are viewed as extensions of the Pauline privilege rather than favor of the faith dissolutions. Accordingly they do not require a dissolution by the Holy Father *in favorem fidei.* Canonically, however, the case described in canon 1149 differs from the others insofar as the law allows the subsequent marriage to cause the dissolution of a marriage that was never consummated after it became sacramental. Canon 1149 permits a convert, who is baptized, to marry again even if his spouse, separated irrevocably by captivity or persecution, has already been baptized. In such a case it is not the pope, acting individually by vicarious power, but the new marriage that *ipso iure* dissolves the first marriage, which is, at that moment, properly termed *ratum sed non consummatum.*

E. Tribunal Procedures

While the major portion of this presentation has been dedicated to the substantive law of marriage, there is much to be considered in the area of procedure, a need experienced by tribunal personnel for decades. It is a need that was not properly addressed by the 1983 revision. The fifth principle of revision instructed the drafters to take subsidiarity seriously: "Procedural law should be uniform throughout the universal Church but can be given a more general and universal form, leaving to regional authorities the faculty to enact rules to be observed in their respective tribunals."[62] The revised code has not done so. The law in this area is universal to the point of stultifying uniformity.

A procedure should be specially crafted for matrimonial cases. Such cases should be "ecclesiastical" in the best sense of the term. They should not imitate civil law nor strive to be juridical in some sort of abstract sense. Their sole *dubium* should be whether the marriage is, within the meaning of the Church's doctrine and law, invalid from the beginning and, if an expanded concept of consummation is accepted, whether the marriage in question, if it was valid, ever became absolutely indissoluble.

Accordingly, this procedure should not be a species of the ordinary contentious process, which, although improved by the 1983 code, is cumbersome, unnecessary, and, generally speaking, inappropriate.[63] The process must begin from the fact that marriage is uniquely sacred, and sometimes sacramental. In such cases, any "contentious" party v. party dynamic is invariably about issues that have nothing to do with validity and indissolubility.[64] It is usually about who "wins." The tribunal should not be an enabler of such antagonism nor should its procedure appear in any way similar to what has often occurred between the parties in a secular divorce proceeding. Instead, the tribunal should follow a theologically nuanced and pastoral process that allows the judge simply to examine the concrete facts and make a judgment

---

[62] "General Introduction," in *The Code of Canon Law: A Text and Commentary*, ed. James A. Coriden et al (New York: Paulist Press, 1985) 6.

[63] Canon 1691: "In other procedural matters, the canons on trials in general and on the ordinary contentious trial must be applied unless the nature of the matter precludes it; the special norms for cases concerning the status of persons and cases pertaining to the public good are to be observed."

[64] *Dignitas connubii* art. 102 recognizes the fact that, in certain cases, the spouses are not at all "opposing" parties: "If both parties are seeking a declaration of the nullity of the marriage, they can name for themselves a common procurator or advocate." In their commentary on this canon Lüdicke and Jenkins note: "This reasonable norm recognizes that the spouses as parties to the process...play a different role than they would in an ordinary contentious trial. The procedural means for the realization of their request (the declaration of the nullity of their marriage) serves to secure their legal rights, rights which are best safeguarded through the formalized process of the trial and the investigation of the truth that occurs there." Klaus Lüdicke and Ronny Jenkins, Dignitas Connubii*: Norms and Commentary* (Washington, D.C.: Canon Law Society of America, 2006) 183-184.

about freedom to marry within the meaning of Church teaching. In such a process a defender of the bond should be required solely in cases where the case is decided by a single judge so that there is a reasonable discussion prior to the final determination.

For centuries, controversies and questions were adjudicated in very informal and local synodal gatherings and by bishops with the help of canonical advisers. Over seven centuries ago, Clement V approved a streamlined procedure called by Italian jurists "the summary process," which was applicable in almost all cases, including marriage cases.[65]

The 1917 code merged the summary and ordinary contentious procedures into a new procedure that was the worst of both worlds, at least for marriage cases. The Instruction *Provida Mater Ecclesia* was issued nineteen years later to try to tailor the process to marriage cases since, as the document underwhelmingly states, "the judges of diocesan curiae...sometimes encounter many difficulties."[66]

The *American Procedural Norms* in 1970 and Paul VI's *Causas matrimoniales* the following year made changes that certainly facilitated marriage proceedings, most of which were incorporated in a systematic manner into the 1983 code. Nonetheless, there was still a felt need for tailoring, which, paralleling what happened with the first code, led to the inter-dicasterial instruction *Dignitas connubii* twenty-two years later. As helpful as certain norms of *Dignitas connubii* have been for tribunal personnel, the instruction does little more than did *Provida*, namely, as Doheny opined at that time, offer "a coordinated restatement of the ruling of the code on matrimonial procedure."[67]

As Msgr. Lawrence Wrenn stated so clearly in a 1986 article entitled *A Balanced Procedural Law*, "the problem is that the whole tone of a contentious

---

[65] *Dispendiosam* (a. 1311). The following gives the flavor of the Clementine procedural reform: "It often happens that we delegate lower courts to hear cases and in some of those cases we order those courts to proceed simply and easily and without the pomp and circumstance of a judicial proceeding. ... We, by this decree, hereby declare as sacred and perpetual that a judge to whom we commit cases of this kind: need not necessarily demand a formal libellus or a joinder of issues; ... may shorten deadlines; may...shorten the trial by denying exceptions and dilatory and unnecessary appeals, and by restricting the contentions and disputes of the parties, advocates and procurators, and by limiting the number of witnesses.
A judge may not, however, abbreviate a trial by curtailing necessary proofs or legitimate defenses. Lest the truth remain concealed...neither the citation nor the taking of the usual oaths of good faith and intent and to tell the truth may ever be omitted." *Saepe contingit* (a. 1306).

[66] Sacred Congregation for the Sacraments, instruction *Provida Mater Ecclesia*, *AAS* 28 (1936) 313. English translation in *Canon Law Digest* (Milwaukee: Bruce, 1956) 2:471.

[67] William Doheny, *Canonical Procedure in Matrimonial Cases: Formal Judicial Procedure* (Milwaukee: Bruce, 1938) 3.

process is wrong for a marriage case, especially an open-and-shut one that is completely uncontested, and all the tinkering in the world is not going to correct that problem. True balance is never achieved that way."[68] (The *Appendix* lists specific changes that might serve as the basis for a truly "matrimonial" procedure.)

F. Conclusion

In summary, our canonical construct of marriage and our procedure for enforcing it both need radical surgery. We are losing the battle for marriage as a sacrament of the New Covenant both in the parish and in the tribunal. Fewer couples, Catholic or non-Catholic, are choosing marriage to begin with, and many fewer couples are approaching the Church to be married according to canonical form. Since the promulgation of the code there has been a 35% decrease in the number of Catholic marriages in the United States in contrast to a 36% increase in the Catholic population.[69]

While many of these couples may be fortunate to be able to receive a declaration of freedom to marry because of lack of form, there are thousands of Catholics every year who, though divorced, are still bound to a presumably valid marriage. Yet, the number of cases being adjudicated by Catholic tribunals in the United States has, in the last quarter of a century, dropped drastically, perhaps by half.[70] Couples are voting with their feet.

Marriage is a sacramental gift Christ has given to our Church to build up the people of God not merely by procreating children but by fostering Christian families in their ministry of living a life of love for God and each other. This sacrificial life should be marked not only by the cross but by daily resurrection to new life. It should be life-giving and life-affirming. For too long canon law has unnecessarily juridicized marriage, stripping it of its truly sacred and sacramental character and reducing it to the secular. It is time to liberate the sacrament of marriage from its suffocating identity with natural marriage and, at the same time, to free our tribunals from slavish imitation of civil law.

---

[68] Lawrence A. Wrenn, "A Balanced Procedural Law," *The Jurist* 46 (1986) 621. The idea of a unique process rather than simply a few special matrimonial canons had been considered by the *De Processibus* coetus during the revision process but without success. The coetus chose to stay with the procedural format of the 1917 code. *Communicationes* 6 (1974) 39-41; 10 (1978) 209-212.

[69] According to the statistics published by *The Official Catholic Directory* for the years in question, 345,521 Catholic marriages were celebrated in 1980 whereas, twenty-five years later, only 223,862 took place.

[70] The author conducted a brief sampling of eleven tribunals in various regions of the U.S. based on figures collected by the Canon Law Society of America in 1984 and 2009. The results were startling. Every one of the eleven tribunals completed many fewer formal declarations of nullity after twenty-five years: the smallest reduction was 31%, the largest 76%; most were in the 50-70% range. Their formal declarations of nullity in 1984 totaled 7,391 while in 2009 they amounted to only 3,192, a decrease of 4,199 (57%).

The revision of canon law cannot on its own turn things around, but it can help. We should remove from the code whatever constrains the sacrament and, at the same time, allow our jurisprudence to find the newness of Christ in today's experiences. The sacrament of marriage should be a celebration of faith and judged as such. It should be recognized as a deep inter-personal encounter, as mysterious as that of Christ's incarnation, one that, through faith and love, becomes indissoluble in the best sense of our Christian tradition. Our procedures for helping those in failed marriages should be sacramental in character and pastoral in application. We should stop worrying about how many declarations of nullity are granted and turn our attention and concern to how few Catholics we are helping to be reconciled with the people of God and to enjoy being active members of the body of Christ.

> In promulgating the 1983 code, Pope John Paul II stated that the purpose of canon law is "to create such an order in ecclesial society that, while assigning the *primacy to love, grace and charisms*, it at the same time renders their organic development easier in the life of both the ecclesial society and the individual persons who belong to it."[71] It is quite a challenge to combine God's revealed mercy and love with legality. The legal tends to confine the love and to reduce the divine to the purely human. That is what has happened to Christian marriage. Yet, if canonical equity and the principle of *salus animarum* teach us anything, it is that the juridical must *facilitate* the pastoral. Human law is at the service of and must cede to divine law, not vice versa; "love, grace and charisms" remain *primary*. That is, of course, what Shakespeare had Portia argue in Venice four-hundred and four years ago:
>
> The quality of mercy is not strain'd,
> It droppeth as the gentle rain from heaven
> Upon the place beneath: it is twice blest;
> It blesseth him that gives and him that takes:
> 'Tis mightiest in the mightiest: it becomes
> The throned monarch better than his crown;
> His sceptre shows the force of temporal power,
> The attribute to awe and majesty,
> Wherein doth sit the dread and fear of kings;
> But mercy is above this sceptred sway;
> It is enthroned in the hearts of kings,
> It is an attribute to God himself;
> And earthly power doth then show likest God's
> When mercy seasons justice.[72]

If we have too rigidly "strain'd" the gentle gift from heaven that we call the

[71] Pope John Paul II, *Sacrae disciplinae leges*, xxix-xxx (italics added).
[72] William Shakespeare, *The Merchant of Venice* (1596) 4:1.

Sacrament of Matrimony, let it be our happy task to release it in every way possible so that we may see it flower as Christ intended for his new covenant. Then marriage, which is ever old, will indeed be, as God designed it, ever new.

Appendix: Selected Canons for Future Revision

A. Substantive Marriage Law

The Code cannot *resolve* theological debates, but, in the same vein, it should not retain as juridical elements propositions that *hinder* theological development. Accordingly, the following recommendations should be given consideration:

1. *Canon 1055*: Delete paragraph 2. The reference to the dignity of the sacrament in paragraph 1 and the "special firmness" in canon 1056 are sufficient to connect baptism and marital sacramentality. This would also remove one of the few paragraphs in which marriage is referred to as a "contract" rather than a "covenant."

2. *Canon 1061 §1*: If the law continues to restrict consummation to the physical act, the inaccurate reference to the scriptural notion of "una caro" should be deleted from the canon. When an expanded understanding of consummation is accepted, this canon and all those affecting consummation should be radically amended.

3. *Canons 1058*, *1085 §2*, and *1098*: Greater consistency of thought can be achieved concerning marriage as covenant by changing the word "contract" to "enter" in these canons.

4. *Canon 1101*: Add the phrase "the sacramental dignity of marriage" to paragraph 2 in order to clarify the fact that a party invalidates his or her consent by specifically excluding sacramentality.

5. *Canon 1102*: As in the Eastern code, no marriage should be permitted if consent is in any way conditioned; such consent is incongruous with the personalist understanding of marriage flowing from *Gaudium et spes*.

6. *Canon 1142*: Diocesan bishops should be authorized to dissolve marriages that are not absolutely indissoluble – both *ratum sed non consummatum* and *non ratum* marriages.

B. Procedural Marriage Law

Combining Wrenn's pointed questions[73] with some of my own might help to offer a brief sketch of what a special matrimonial procedure might look like:

1. Canon 1691 should be abrogated. A completely unique matrimonial process should then be developed to replace canons 1671-1691. The new process need not be universal in every detail; local circumstances should prevail in certain areas. Episcopal conferences should be commissioned to concretize tribunal practice

[73] Wrenn, "A Balanced Procedural Law," 622.

for their people and in accordance with their ecclesiastical resources.

2. A respondent who refuses to cooperate out of spite in order to deprive the petitioner of the sacraments should have few if any rights. Any "right of defense" should simply be the defense by all concerned of the Church's teaching about marriage and the right of all persons to marry if not prohibited by law.

3. The defender of the bond should not always be required to argue for the bond but solely *pro rei veritate*. His or her task should be to assist the judge in making an authentic decision about the right to marry on the part of the two parties in light of Church teaching. In a sense, the roles of defender (cc. 1432-1436; *DC* 52-56 & 59-60) and assessor (c. 1424 and *DC* 52) should be merged.

4. A judge should have the flexibility to change the ground of nullity (or lack of consummation) at appropriate points in the process whenever the evidence supports it.

5. The Rota has been a champion of marriage law. (For example, there would be no canon 1095 §§2-3 in today's code without the Rotal decisions that long preceded its formulation.) It is counter-productive for prelate auditors to be embroiled in cases of second instance, often enough brought to them simply because a disgruntled respondent has the resources to appeal directly to the Rota. The Rota should, instead, act as a supreme court, judging in third instance cases that involve differing sentences in the lower tribunals in order to give sound guidance on deep-seated theological and canonical issues. In unusual circumstances there still could be a procedure similar to a writ of certiorari for the Rota to take a particular case to itself or for the Signatura to arrange such a referral.

6. Canon 1673, 3° should allow the tribunal of the petitioner's non-precarious residence to be an ordinary forum without the need for special permissions. This would respect the fact that a matrimonial case is not a dispute between parties about staying together or not. It would reinforce the central purpose of the procedure: to decide about the petitioner's (and often the respondent's) request to marry someone else "in the Lord," to be reconciled with God and the Church and to participate regularly in the mystery of the Eucharist. The process should not be about marital rights and duties but about the sacramental lives of individual members of the people of God.

7. First instance matrimonial cases should ordinarily be judged by a single qualified judge with a defender; if judged by a collegiate tribunal, the intervention of the defender should be optional.

8. Lay men and women who are qualified should be able to serve as a

single judge; the role should not be limited to priests and deacons. Training and expertise and the recognition of such qualifications by an episcopal appointment are what matter, not whether one happens to be a member of the clerical state.

9. Appeal of a first instance affirmative decision by the defender should be optional and based on weighty reasons. If the defender sees no reason to appeal, he should state this in writing and the judgment should then be executed. If the defender is of the opinion that the judgment must be reviewed, he should state his rationale in writing for review by the appellate tribunal.

10. The current review process for affirmative first instance sentences wastes resources by requiring an appellate defender and a college of three judges in order to issue a simple confirmatory decree of an affirmative sentence (c. 1682 §2). Any review should be conducted and the decree issued by a single judge, lay or cleric, taking into consideration the first instance animadversions of the defender who has called for the review and/or any dissenting judicial opinion in a collegiate tribunal (c. 1609 §4). The appellate defender should have the option of offering animadversions prior to completion of the review to assist in situating all such final decisions within the context of the Church teaching on marriage.

11. When remanded for review, the acts that must be submitted should, as stated in *Causas matrimoniales* 8:2, be the sentence of first instance along with the animadversions of the first instance defender and the observations, if there are any, of the parties, without prejudice to the appellate tribunal's right to demand additional information in individual cases if needed for its review.

12. If the sentence is not confirmed but is, instead, remanded to an appellate trial, the same rules should exist at second instance for the constitution of the tribunal: a single judge with a defender or a collegiate tribunal with an optional defender.

Seminar

Confidential Communications and the Law

Reverend Phillip J. Brown, SS

I. Introduction

One of the results of the clergy sexual abuse crisis is the increased attention it has required be devoted to the question of confidential communications and records on the part of canonists, Church officials, civil attorneys and legislators and other public officials. The Canon Law Society of America published a legal and canonical study of confidentiality in the United States in 1988.[1] Public awareness of the issue of the sexual abuse of minors began to grow during the 1970s as a result of greater efforts to address all forms of child abuse that had begun in the 1960s. However, it was not until the 1980s that discussion of sexual abuse by Roman Catholic clerics began to be covered as a phenomenon in the news media of the United States. According to the Catholic News Service public awareness of the sexual abuse of children in the United States and Canada emerged in the late 1970s and the 1980s as an outgrowth of the growing awareness of physical abuse of children. In 1981 the guilty plea of Father Donald Roemer of the Archdiocese of Los Angeles to the felonious sexual abuse of a minor received widespread media coverage and in September of 1983 the *National Catholic Reporter* published an article on the topic.[2] Awareness of the problem continued to grow in October 1985 when Louisiana priest Gilbert Gauthe pleaded guilty to 11 counts of molesting young boys. Thus, the CLSA study was published just at the time when public awareness of the sexual abuse of minors by Catholic priests was coming about. No one could have predicted the proportions that such scandals would eventually take, but some did warn of a potential crisis surrounding the problem. The CLSA study, given its timing, may be evidence that canonists were aware of the potential effects of the issue on the whole question of the confidentiality of Church-related communications and records.

The 1988 CLSA study includes an article on the implications for the Church of the civil law of confidentiality with an appendix of statutes and court decisions from the fifty states by Donna Krier Ioppolo; an examination of the canonical tradition of the confidentiality of oral communications by Marie Breitenbeck, O.P.; a consideration of the confidentiality of written documents in canon law by Elissa A. Rinere, C.P.; a review of the basis of the "priest-penitent privilege"[3] in American law by Ronald Stake; and an addendum on

---

[1] D. Ioppolo et al., *Confidentiality in the United States: A Legal and Canonical Study* (Washington, D.C.: CLSA, 1988).

[2] "Sex Abuse Crisis: Sex abuse sparks program," Natcath.org., 2002-04-05, http://www.natcath. org/crisis/092383.htm. Retrieved November 18, 2010.

[3] For convenience we will refer to all legal provisions which allow a privilege against the

policymaking by Brietenbeck.

The CLSA study appears to have tried to be as comprehensive as possible, from a canonical point of view, in the context of the times in which it was written. Since then significant developments have warranted further efforts to parse the full implications of the canon and civil law of confidential communications. In particular, the continuing evolution of "mandatory reporting" laws demand that the topic be addressed with greater insight and precision. It is now clear that there is a fundamental difference between the "priest-penitent" evidentiary privilege and the implications of "mandatory reporting laws" requiring a more accurate and precise understanding of the manner in which the law treats religiously-based confidential communications and records in these two different contexts (evidentiary privilege vs. mandatory reporting).

This article will not try to be comprehensive. We will only concern ourselves with the confidentiality of religiously-based oral communications made in pastoral settings, not the confidentiality of Church documents and records, or confidentiality related to ecclesiastical judicial or administrative proceedings.[4]

---

compelled disclosure of communications between a clergy person or other representative of religion and one making such communications as the "priest-penitent privilege" although that denomination cannot be considered adequate or accurate with respect to all of the kinds of communications covered by this evidentiary privilege. While the privilege clearly had its origins in communications made to Catholic priests in a penitential context, for legal and historical reasons the privilege is now much broader than that. Also, various laws and commentators refer not just to the "priest-penitent" privilege but also to the "clergy-penitent" privilege, "clergy-communicant" privilege, "clergy spiritual-counselee" privilege, etc. Our use of "priest-penitent" privilege is intended to refer to all evidentiary privileges in civil law based on communications to a representative of religious faith or some sort of spiritual practice or counseling that are considered privileged under the law of evidence for that reason, regardless of the actual terminology used in any given law or by any given commentator. One must bear in mind also that this expression and the evidentiary privilege it refers to is limited to the evidentiary privilege alone and does not refer to, nor does it necessarily have any relevance to "mandatory reporting" laws, unless the specific law in question has explicitly incorporated the clergy-penitent privilege into its operation in some fashion. In other words, a clergyperson is not exempt from mandatory reporting if identified in the law as a mandatory reporting by virtue of the "priest-penitent" privilege unless the mandatory reporting specifically relieves him or her of the duty to report in virtue of the privilege in identified circumstances.

[4] Indeed, canonical proscriptions against the disclosure of Church records, at least to the extent they prohibit disclosure to civil authorities, may have to be considered a canonical dead letter in the United States today. Efforts to avoid the disclosure of such records and documents based upon canonical prohibitions, relying on First Amendment freedom of religion arguments, have been uniformly rejected by American civil courts. No doubt on the advice of civil attorneys and in order to avoid civil penalties, dioceses have uniformly turned over all Church records requested in connection with the prosecution of lawsuits involving the sexual abuse of minors, even records that canon law prohibits from being disclosed. Some efforts were made to protect records from disclosure, but in the face of court decisions rejecting arguments in favor of non-disclosure the records have been

The topic is complicated enough that it is necessary for now to address specific aspects of confidentiality in individual articles until it is possible to undertake a more detailed and comprehensive study of the entire subject. As such, in this article we will be concerned primarily with the confidentiality of penitential communications and "spiritual direction" as understood and practiced in the Roman Catholic religion, with only passing references to other kinds of pastoral communications.

It will be necessary to consider some more general aspects of the canon and civil law of confidential communications first in order to be able to identify and highlight the central issues of concern for the Church with respect to confidentiality today which are:

1. What is meant by a "confidential communication"?
2. What different categories of religiously-based confidential communications are there?
3. What are the bases for acknowledging and/or requiring confidentiality in moral theology, ethics, and canon law?
4. To what extent and in what way does canon law address each category of confidential communication?
5. What degree of confidentiality does canon law allow or require for each category of confidential communication?
    a. Does it recognize or require the same degree of confidentiality for each category as is recognized or required by moral theology or ethical concerns?
    b. Does canon law recognize or require the same degree of confidentiality as is often assumed in pastoral practice?
6. To what extent will civil law provide the same degree of protection for confidential communications as allowed or required by canon law?
    a. With respect to the "priest-penitent" privilege.
    b. In relation to "mandatory reporting" laws.

II. General Considerations

---

turned over. See, for instance, "Church tries to block public access to files," by Michael Rezendes and Walter V. Robinson (Boston Globe 11/23/2002); "Judge finds records, Law at odds: Lack of care seen in assigning priests," by Walter V. Robinson (Boston Globe, 11/26/2002); "Archdiocese [of Los Angeles] Loses Case to Keep Former Priests' Records Secret" by Archibold, Randal C. (The New York Times 04/18/06); "San Diego Diocese releases priests' records in sex abuse cases," by Tony Perry and Paloma Esquivel (Los Angeles Times, 10/25/10).

1. Meaning of "Confidential Communications"

What is a "confidential communication"? Understanding what is meant by a confidential communication can be approached from several perspectives. It is helpful to distinguish confidential "communications" from confidential information and confidential records (even though confidential communications often result in a documentary record of what has been communicated).

What is meant by the difference between a confidential communication and confidential information is that a confidential "communication" is intended and understood by the one making the communication and/or the one receiving it to be kept confidential. Confidential information, on the other hand, is information that is required to be kept confidential irrespective of the intentions or understanding of the one making or receiving the communication. In this article we are primarily concerned with communications intended and understood to be kept confidential by the one making them and/or the one receiving them, in addition to the effects of any prescriptions of law or ethical responsibilities that also require the information to be kept confidential. We are concerned with three basic kinds of religiously-based confidential communications: communications made to a priest or other religious minister during the sacrament of penance, during "spiritual direction", or in other pastoral situations.

One could say that a confidential communication is any communication by one person to another that is intended by the one making it to be kept confidential and not disclosed to any other person by the one communicated to. However, it could also be such a communication as so considered by the one communicated to, regardless of the intentions or understanding of the one making the communication (for instance, communications during a sacramental confession regardless of the intention or understanding of the penitent; see canons 983 and 984 of the 1983 Code of Canon Law).

Or, a confidential communication could be considered any communication that principles of moral theology, ethics, or canon law and/or civil law recognize as confidential and which are either allowed or required to be kept confidential on that basis regardless of the express or implied intentions of the parties to the communication. This would apply, for instance, to the spousal privilege, or the doctor-patient privilege, in civil law (although these privileges can be waived by the one who holds the privilege if the one communicated to does not have his or her own independent privilege against disclosure). Thus, a "confidential communication" is any communication that principles of moral theology or ethics consider confidential giving rise to a duty not to disclose to any third party on the part of the one communicated to, unless exceptions are recognized under certain circumstances. However, a confidential communication is also any communication that the law recognizes as confidential giving rise to a duty of non-disclosure which is therefore privileged against disclosure when the privilege is invoked in response to a question or request that would result in disclosure. Furthermore, if a legal duty of non-disclosure exists, violation of that obligation might be able to result in some form of legal action by the one who is entitled to have the information kept confidential.

2. Categories of Confidential Communications

Civil law recognizes a variety of confidential communications privileged against compulsory disclosure, one of which is the priest-penitent privilege.[5] Although "priest-penitent privilege" calls to mind a privilege against disclosure of communications made during a Roman Catholic sacramental confession or similar practice in some other Christian Church or community, for historical and technical legal and constitutional reasons the actual civil law privilege covers much more. Furthermore, the breadth of the civil law privilege raises questions concerning whether or not it covers more kinds of communications in Roman Catholic practice than just those during a sacramental confession. The question is not a simple one since the civil law privilege is very often tied to the practices of the particular religion or spirituality involved. In many jurisdictions the privilege only applies to communications considered confidential by the religion in question itself and only to the degree that religions holds the communication confidential. It is possible, therefore, that civil law might provide greater protection for different kinds of communications in non-Catholic settings than in the Catholic depending upon what the theology and canon law of the Catholic Church has to say about the particular kind of communication involved. Thus, it's important to look more carefully at what Catholic theology and canon law actually say about different kinds of communications considered confidential by those who make or them.

The 1983 Code of Canon Law mentions only two kinds of confidential communications of the kind we are concerned with in this article: communications made during or related to a sacramental confession, and spiritual direction. The code does not explicitly mention or recognize the confidentiality of other kinds of oral communications (other than testimony given in ecclesiastical judicial or administrative proceedings, and various kinds of advice or other communications made in connection with church administration, which do not concern us here). But there are a whole range of other kinds of communications in pastoral settings that those making or receiving may consider confidential to one degree or another, so it is important to determine just what degree of confidentiality canon law and civil law, and moral theology or ethical considerations, actually may accord to these other kinds of communications.

In addition to the sacrament of reconciliation and spiritual direction, the following categories of confidential communications can be discerned in the

[5] The privileges generally recognized in civil law are: attorney-client; physician-patient; marital privileges (husband/wife); priest/penitent (minister/spiritual counselee); government privileges: state secret; official information; executive privilege; confidential informants (in criminal matters/perhaps some civil proceedings); miscellaneous: required reports to governmental agencies; trade secrets; constitutional privileges: privilege against self-incrimination.

1983 code and ecclesial practice:

a) Sacrament of Penance: cc. 983, 984, 1388

b) Spiritual direction: cc. 239 §2, 246 §4

c) Spiritual counsel: cc. 529 §1, 543, 548 §§1 & 2

d) Pastoral counsel: cc. 529 §1, 543, 548 §§1 & 2

e) Personal advice: cc. 529 §1, 543, 548 §§1 & 2

f) Communications related to ecclesiastical investigations: c. 1719

g) Testimony in ecclesiastical proceedings: cc. 1455, 1457, 1602 and 1609

h) Opinions expressed regarding placement of a juridic act: c. 127 §3

i) *Ternus* of candidates for the episcopate: c. 344 §§3 & 4

j) Communications interdicted by church authority (pontifical secret)

k) Advice, counsel, and other communications related to church administration.

We are concerned only with categories a-e above (essentially, only oral communications related to strictly pastoral situations).

3. Bases of Confidentiality in Moral Theology/Ethics, Canon and Civil Law

a. Moral Theology/Ethics

The allowance and/or requirement of confidentiality has different bases. It has a basis in moral theology rationalized through natural law reasoning. It has a basis in ethics, that is, in the ethical standards and practices of learned professions (which very often are recognized as binding by society in general and protected by the laws of society). And it has a basis in positive law, canon or civil. The basic principle of confidentiality as grounded in moral theology is summarized in §2491 of the Catechism of the Catholic Church (under the rubric "professional secrets"):

> "*Professional secrets* ... must be kept, save in exceptional cases where keeping the secret is bound to cause very grave harm [*damna gravissima*] to the one who confided it, to the one who received it or to a third party, and where the very grave harm can be avoided only by divulging the truth.[6]

The exception mentioned does not apply in all cases. There may be a specific law requiring absolute confidentiality regardless of the potential consequences (as is the case, for instance, with the seal of confession).

---

[6] *Cathechism of the Catholic Church*, §2491 (Citta del Vaticano: Libreria Editrice Vaticana, 1993).

Commentators have theorized three bases for the confidentiality of professional secrets: implied contract, express contract, and legal justice. The implied contract theory holds that there is an implied contract between one who communicates information expected to be kept confidential and the professional to keep the information confidential. Failure to maintain confidentiality, therefore, amounts to a breach of the implied contract and therefore of an ethical obligation on the part of the professional. The express contract theory holds that there is confidentiality when the one making the communication and the professional explicitly agree that the information is to be kept confidential. The legal justice theory holds that confidentiality serves the common good in those situations where it is recognized, and therefore the grounds for any exception to confidentiality must be very weighty. In fact, as evidentiary privileges have developed in the civil law they ordinarily are grounded in some such notion of serving the common good, and require such a justification in order to be maintained. In today's legal world this basis of the privilege is more likely to spoken of as some "public policy" reason for the privilege (for instance, attempting to preserve the stability of marriage for society by not allowing spouses to testify to communications between one another if the other spouse objects), rather than the requirements of serving the common good (which is natural law language). These bases of confidentiality in the moral tradition are not mutually exclusive. The express contract theory would provide a basis for requiring confidentiality where there is no other basis for it, but it could not be used to argue that there is never confidentiality if the parties doe not have such an express contract, for that would exclude confidentiality based on an implied contract in appropriate circumstances and also confidentiality which is considered to serve the common good regardless of the understanding or intentions of the parties to the communication.

b. Kinds and basis of confidentiality in canon law

The bases of the different kinds of confidentiality explicitly allowed or required by canon law differ according to the kind of communication involved. For instance, the absolute confidentiality of penitential communications is considered integral to the sacrament and its nature. However, there are also policy reasons for this absolute confidentiality: if the Church did not require that everything communicated during a sacramental confession be kept absolutely secret, people would be less likely to confess their sins to a priest and would therefore be deprived of the grace and the other benefits of the sacrament.

To the extent that spiritual direction is protected by confidentiality, directees would lack confidence in the practice and either not make use of it or not be forthcoming with their spiritual directors if they were not assured of confidentiality. They would thereby be deprived of the personal benefits of spiritual direction. In the context of seminary formation, however, the Church would also be deprived of an important means of guiding individual candidates either toward or away from presenting themselves for ordination through an honest appraisal of their suitability for holy orders arrived at with the assistance of the spiritual director. Without absolute confidentiality, seminarians are less likely to be completely self-revelatory to their spiritual directors and more likely to conceal things that might cause the spiritual director either to recommend special assistance in their formation or discourage the candidate from moving forward in the formation process.

The basis of the confidentiality of other kinds of pastoral communications is likely to be found in a hybrid of the various theoretical justifications for confidentiality. Thus, in a spiritual or pastoral counseling situation, the communications between the representative of the Church and the one making the communication are more classically like any "professional secret". Confidentiality, therefore, could be grounded in an express agreement of the parties if there is one, an implied contract given the nature of the communications, or for that matter the "public policy" or common good basis: it is good for the individuals involved but also for the society that the Church is, and for society in general, that individuals seek counsel for their spiritual and personal problems. Going without help is likely to be deleterious for the individual, but also for society in that the individual who does not seek counseling and help is more likely to remain debilitated, dependent, unproductive or for that matter to do harm (or greater harm) to himself or herself or others.

Regardless of the "public policy" or "common good" basis of confidentiality, there is also the purely positivistic basis: if canon law (or civil law) allows or requires confidentiality it is available or mandatory simply because the law allows or demands it. In fact, in contemporary society confidentiality in the civil law is much more likely to be viewed as a product of the positive enactments of the law, albeit often with a "public policy" justification or rationalization, than based on fundamental principles.

III. Confidentiality in Canon Law

The 1983 code identifies a number of kinds of communications that are to be kept confidential to one degree or another. They are:

1. Communications made during a sacramental confession (cc. 983, 984 & 1388)
2. Information contained in documents kept in the diocesan secret archive (cc. 489, 490 & 1719)
3. Information communicated during the course of some ecclesiastical investigations (c. 1719)
4. Names of candidates and opinions expressed concerning the *ternus* of candidates for episcopal office sent to the Apostolic See (c. 344 §§ 3 & 4)
5. Official communications by ecclesiastical authority interdicted from disclosure (pontifical secret)

In some instance the required confidentiality is not absolute, depending on the circumstances:

6. Opinions expressed by those required to offer their opinion to a superior in connection with consent or consultation required regarding the placement of a juridic act (c. 127 §3). (Confidentiality is required "[i]f the seriousness of the matter requires it.")

7. Information communicated in some ecclesiastical judicial proceedings (cc. 1455, 1457, 1602 and 1609)

We are focusing on the confidentiality required by canon law for communications made in pastoral contexts and the extent to which the same degree of confidentiality will be recognized and protected in civil law. We are concerned principally, therefore, with sacramental communications (confession), spiritual direction, and the other kinds of pastoral communications mentioned above.

1. The Seal of Confession

The highest degree of confidentiality in canon law attaches to communications made during the sacrament of penance, that is, the so-called "seal of confession." The seal of confession as regulated by canon law is found in canons 983, 984 and 1388 of the 1983 code:

> Canon 983 §1: The sacramental seal is inviolable; therefore it is absolutely forbidden for a confessor to betray in any way a penitent in words or in any manner or for any reason.
> §2: The interpreter, if there is one, and all others who in any way have knowledge of sins from confession are also obliged to observe secrecy.
>
> Canon 984 §1: A confessor is prohibited completely from using knowledge acquired from confession to the detriment of the penitent even when any danger of revelation is excluded.
> §2: A person who has been placed in authority cannot use in any manner for external governance the knowledge about sins which he has received in confession at any time.
>
> Canon 1388 §1: A confessor who directly violates the sacramental seal incurs a *latae sententiae* excommunication reserved to the Apostolic See; one who does so only indirectly is to be punished according to the gravity of the delict.
> §2: An interpreter and the others mentioned in can. 983 §2 who violate the secret are to be punished with a just penalty, not excluding excommunication.

Commentators, based on the language of canon 983, distinguish between the "seal of confession" that binds confessors and the "secret" of confession binding interpreters employed in the celebration of the sacrament and others who in any way come to knowledge of sins from a confession. Practically speaking, the obligation not to disclose what is learned from a confession is same for both confessors and others according to both John McGreavy[7] and Frederick R. McManus,[8] although technically the term "seal of confession" applies only to confessors. However, the penalties for violations of secrecy do differ for the two classes of person. Direct violation of the seal by a confessor incurs a *latae sententiae* excommunication reserved to the Apostolic See.[9] An indirect violation by a confessor is to be punished according to the gravity of the delict. Any violation by others, direct or indirect, is to be punished with a just penalty not excluding excommunication (though not reserved to the Apostolic See).[10]A direct violation occurs when both the penitent and the sin are easily known from a deliberate revelation of such information.[11] An indirect violation occurs when there is only the possibility that the identity of the penitent may be able to be deduced from revelations about something said in confession.

According to McGreavy, use of the word *nefas* in canon 983 §3 makes it clear that a priest "is strictly forbidden to reveal by any means whatever anything the penitent may have disclosed to him. Even the penitent cannot release him from this obligation."[12] McManus commenting on the same canon likewise states that:

> In order to stress the gravity of the violation of the norm … the canon uses the strong word *nefas* (criminal, abominable). Neither the canon nor earlier interpretations admit exceptions to the norm: this is the intent of the emphasis: 'in any way ... in words or in any manner and for any reason.' No distinction

---

[7] J. McGreavy, "Commentary on Canon 983 §1" in *The Canon Law Letter & Spirit: A Practical Guide to the Code of Canon Law*, ed. Gerard Sheehy et al (Collegeville, MN: Liturgical Press, 1995) [hereafter *CLSGBI Comm*] 535.

[8] F. J. McManus, "Chapter III: The Penitent [cc. 987-991]" in *New Commentary on the Code of Canon Law*, ed. John P. Beal, et al (New York/Mahwah, NJ: Paulist Press, 2000) [hereafter *CLSA Comm2*] 1164.

[9] Canon 1388 §1.

[10] Canon 1388 §2.

[11] T. Green, "Penalties for Individual Delicts [cc. 1364-1399]" in *CLSA Comm2*, 1592; J. McGreavy, *CLSGBI Comm*, 799.

[12] J. McGreavy, *CLSGBI Comm*, 535. If McGreavy is correct that even the penitent cannot release a confessor form the obligation to maintain the secrecy of what has been said in confession, this could put the confessor in a very difficult position if a penitent were to "waive" the privilege against disclosure and release the confessor from the obligation as far as the civil law is concerned. See, for instance, the language of the South Carolina privilege statute cited in footnote 24 below. This raises the civil question of whether or not a clergyperson has his or her own independent privilege to maintain the secrecy of matters confided in a sacramental confession or other pastoral settings. The earliest case on the question, the Philips case (cited below) does seem to recognize an independent privilege on the part of the priest or other clergyperson, and many states today would no doubt recognize the minister's own independent privilege. One cannot presume that all states would do so, however, particularly in the light of statutory language such as that of the South Carolina privilege statute.

> is made among the matters confessed, whether the sinful action itself or attendant circumstances, or the acts of satisfaction or penances imposed, etc. The secrecy is to be maintained concerning the penitent and his or her confession of sins is properly described as total.[13]

T. Green seems to agree, stating in his commentary on canon 1388 that "The sacramental seal is the strict and inviolable obligation to keeping secret whatever has been related to the confessor to obtain absolution, the revelation of which would render the sacrament odious and onerous."[14] He goes to distinguish (apparently) between the *obligation* of the seal and *when an ecclesiastical delict has been committed* by violating the seal, stating that, "there is no delict if the confessor honestly believes that such information is available from extra-confessional sources."[15] He further states in a footnote that "If the penitent is not betrayed and permits the confessor to reveal certain confessional information, there is no delict."[16]

McManus is less clear about admitting the possibility of exceptions to absolute non-disclosability, stating that canon 983 is concerned with "any kind of betrayal of a penitent … and this even if he or she has not been absolved. It is any betrayal of a person who has simply confessed in the context of the sacrament."[17] Green seems to be parsing the text of canon 983 with respect to the meaning of *prodo, prodere, prodidi, proditus* in the Latin version of the canon, while McManus nuances the text in a manner that may leave the door open to exceptions to absolute secrecy.

Prodo, prodere, prodidi, proditus can be understood in either a moral sense or a communicative sense. In the moral sense, it means any "betrayal" of the penitent (in the sense of causing detriment). In the communicative sense, it means any revelation of information whatsoever. Two online searches of the meaning of *prodo, prodere, prodidi, proditus* yielded the following possible meanings: 1) deliver, transmit, hand over; publish, bring forth, appoint/abandon, betray;[18] 2) project, thrust forward; bring forth, produce, give birth to; create; nominate; institute; extend, prolong; hand down (lore); publish/record, reveal, uncover; put out; assert; betray; give up, abandon, forsake.[19] It is apparent that the Latin word *prodere* in the text of canon 983 is susceptible of either sense, with attendant consequences for the degree of secrecy required by the sacramental seal. While not necessarily dispositive, it is at least worth

---

[13] F. McManus, *CLSA Comm2*, 1164.
[14] T. Green, *CLSA Comm2*, 1592.
[15] Ibid.
[16] Ibid., footnote 257, citing D. Brewer, "The Right of a Penitent to Release the Confessor from the Seal: Considerations in Canon Law and in American Law," *The Jurist* 54 (1994) 424-476.
[17] F. McManus, *CLSA Comm2*, 1163-64.
[18] http://www.freedict.com/onldict/lat.html: prodo.
[19] http://www.stars21.com/translator/latin_to_english.html: *prodo, prodere, prodidi, proditus*.

mentioning that a 1915 instruction of the Holy Office addressing violations of the seal states that:

> the Holy Office deems it its duty to give to all Ordinaries … and Superiors … of all religious institutes a command of the Lord, gravely binding in conscience, … that in the future, not only in theological classes but also in conferences on moral "cases" … they carefully see to it that the priests subject to them be taught never to dare mention anything which pertains to the matter of sacramental confession in any form or under any pretext, … directly or indirectly, in public or private speech (except the case of necessary consultation … according to the rules laid down by approved authors).[20]

It is not possible or necessary to resolve here which reading of the obligation of the seal is the best or required one, but this is a question that would benefit from more detailed treatment, and perhaps an authoritative interpretation by the appropriate dicastery of the Holy See. Based on the discussion in the commentaries, there are two questions involved: 1) How absolute is the seal? Is the confessor (and are others) absolutely forbidden from ever revealing anything whatsoever that has been communicated in relation to a sacramental confession, or are there exceptions if doing so will not "betray" the penitent (and especially if the penitent has authorized disclosure); 2) when and under what circumstances does the disclosure, "direct" or "indirect", of something communicated in connection with a sacramental confession constitute a delict?

Finally, it is also worth noting that the *Rite of Penance*, the ritual text describing and regulating how the sacrament of penance is to be celebrated, also address the seal: "Conscious that he has come to know the secret of another's conscience only because he is God's minister, the confessor is bound by the obligation of preserving the seal of confession absolutely unbroken."[21] It would be hard to imagine language more absolute than this. Nothing in the *Ritual* acknowledges any exceptions under any circumstances whatsoever to this absolute non-disclosability. It is worth noting also that the *Ritual* constitutes liturgical law the code recognizes as independent and binding unless contrary to the canons of the code.[22]

For our purposes we will simply conclude that the seal of confession represents the strictest and most absolute requirement of confidentiality for oral communications in canon law, and that the protection that it will be afforded in civil law will depend at least minimally on the degree of confidentiality required of it in canon law.

2. Spiritual Direction

---

[20] *Instruction of the Holy Office*, June 9, 1915, in *Canon Law Digest* 1:413-414.
[21] *Rite of Penance* 10d, in *Documents on the Liturgy 1963-1979, Conciliar Papal and Curial Texts* (Collegeville: Liturgical pres, 1982), 3075.
[22] Canon 2.

"Spiritual direction" is mentioned in only two places in the 1983 code, both in connection with the seminary formation of candidates for the priesthood:

> Canon 239 §2: Every seminary is to have at least one spiritual director, though the students remain free to approach other priests who have been designated for this function by the bishop.
>
> Canon 246 §4: Students are to become accustomed to approach the sacrament of penance frequently; it is also recommended that each have a director of his spiritual life whom he has freely chosen and to whom he can confidently open his conscience.

It is notable that at least as far as canon law is concerned only one form of spiritual direction is recognized: the director of the spiritual life of seminarians as part of the seminary formation process. It is also notable that this director of spiritual life is mentioned in the same canon in relation to the admonition that seminary students approach the sacrament of penance frequently. This reflects the tradition of seminary formation that a student's spiritual director also serves as his confessor. This traditional practice makes sense of the traditional understanding that the seal of confession covers more than just what is said during a ritual celebration of the sacrament of penance, for the tradition, certainly among seminary spiritual directors, has been that the seal covers everything "leading up to" a sacramental confession. In the tradition of seminary spiritual directors, everything said during spiritual direction, in one way or another, eventually leads to a celebration of the sacrament of reconciliation. Therefore, the tradition has been that everything communicated during spiritual direction is "under the seal of confession" to the same extent as anything communicated during an actual celebration of the sacrament in any other context. The author can attest that this has undoubtedly been the tradition for members of the Society of St. Sulpice which specializes in seminary formation, and it is in fact the existing policy of the Society for spiritual directors in its seminaries.

However much this may be the tradition in Sulpician seminaries and other seminaries, there is nothing explicit in canon law which ascribes this degree of confidentiality to seminary spiritual direction, much less to any other kind of spiritual direction in the tradition and practices of the Catholic faith. Indeed, there is nothing explicit in the *Constitutions* or proper law of the Society of St. Sulpice that acknowledges or requires this degree of confidentiality for spiritual direction. The only explicit mention of spiritual direction in the *Constitutions* of the Society is in one of the "Orientations and Rules of Application" (O.R.A.) appended to Article 25 of the *Constitutions*. A *Note* in the published version of the *Constitutions* explains the nature of an O.R.A.:

> The text which has been approved in its French-language version and confirmed by the Congregation for Institutes of Consecrated Life and Societies of Apostolic Life is that of the Introduction and articles. The approval does not include the

> O.R.A. and the Appendices.
> The approved text cannot be modified without the approbation of the Congregation for Institutes of Consecrated Life and Societies of Apostolic Life. The O.R.A. and the Appendices, on the other hand, can be modified by a General Assembly.[23]

The O.R.A. following Article 25 of the Constitutions (in Chapter III, The Ministries of the Society: Ministries to Future Priests) says:

> O.R.A. In consideration for others and in order to preserve an atmosphere of trust in the community, everyone should maintain *a suitable discretion*, particularly in group work and even more so in spiritual direction.[24]

However well-founded and constant, the tradition of treating the confidentiality of that which is communicated during spiritual direction in seminaries as equivalent to the confidentiality of the seal of confession is at best an oral tradition with no explicit approbation in canon law. Once again, however, this may be understandable in the context of the tradition and past practice that a spiritual director always, or almost always, also served as the seminarian's confessor. In line with that tradition and practice, since the spiritual director was the seminarian's confessor, canonically the seal of confession would cover at least whatever would be covered by the seal in relation to sacramental confessions made by the seminarian. Here, then, one would have to take into consideration the canonical understanding that the seal covers more than simply what is communicated within the boundaries of ritualistic practices which seem to define when the celebration of the sacrament begins and ends, for as already noted the seal has always been understood as covering as well whatever "leads up to" celebration the sacrament.

The fact that the seal covers more than just what is communicated during the ritual of the sacrament is reflected at least as long ago as the thirteenth century in the theology of St. Thomas Aquinas:

> I answer that, The seal of confession does not extend directly to other matters than those which have reference to sacramental confession, yet indirectly matters also which are not connected with sacramental confession are affected by the seal of confession, those, for instance, which might lead to the discovery of a sinner or of his sin. Nevertheless these matters also must be most carefully hidden, both on account of scandal, and to avoid leading others into sin through their becoming familiar with it. [25]

For the purpose of determining (or making an argument regarding) the

---

[23] *Constitutions of the Society of the Priests of Saint Sulpice* (Paris, Société de Saint Sulpice, 2003 French Edition, 2005 English Translation), vi.
[24] Ibid., 23 (emphasis added).
[25] *Summa Theologica*, Supp. Quest. 11.

degree of confidentiality (non-disclosability) the civil law ought to accord to spiritual direction, it is essential to ascertain the degree of non-disclosability that attaches as a result of canon law, but also as a result of the established theology, understanding and practices of the Catholic faith. Ascertaining the degree of non-disclosability that canon law ought to ascribe to spiritual direction cannot really be arrived at without considering the relationship between spiritual direction and the sacrament of penance in the tradition and as spiritual direction is practiced in seminaries today. None of that, of course, answers questions about other kinds of spiritual direction (that is, other than in seminaries) practiced by Catholics (not to mention adherents of other faiths) or newer forms of spiritual direction, nor the advent of spiritual direction in seminaries that has no relationship to the sacrament of penance, even if the spiritual director is a priest (but especially if he or she is not). More recently the Holy See has made it clear that all spiritual direction in seminaries is to be done by priests, which may obviate some of the uncertainty with respect to the status of seminary spiritual direction, but it still does not answer questions about other kinds of spiritual direction that are practiced.

Without going into a detailed explanation why, American civil law would likely protect from disclosure communications during all forms of spiritual direction by non-Catholic ministers and spiritual advisors. Because the protection of civil law is normally tied to the degree of confidentiality accorded to communications by the religious body or religious faith or spirituality involved, it is necessary to ask exactly what degree of confidentiality is accorded to a given kind of communication by the Catholic Church, the Catholic faith and Catholic practices.[26] It might seem anomalous, but American civil law might afford greater protection to religiously-based confidential communications than the canon law of the Catholic Church does, perhaps even in a Catholic context, and perhaps greater protection for the same kind of communication for non-Catholics than if made in a Catholic context.

3. *Effects of New PPF*

Finally, the most recent edition of the *Program of Priestly Formation* for the United States may impact the degree of confidentiality accorded to communications made during spiritual direction in seminaries, perhaps lessening the degree of confidentiality that seminarians and their spiritual directors can expect to be accorded such communications by the Church (and, consequently, very likely by civil authorities as well).

---

[26] See, for example: South Carolina Code, Section 19-11-90. Priest-penitent privilege: In any legal or quasi-legal trial, hearing or proceeding before any court, commission or committee no regular or duly ordained minister, priest or rabbi shall be required, in giving testimony, to disclose any confidential communication properly entrusted to him in his professional capacity and necessary and proper to enable him to discharge the functions of his office *according to the usual course of practice or discipline of his church or religious body*. This prohibition shall not apply to cases where the party in whose favor it is made waives the rights conferred.

Canon 242 contains the basic norm regarding programs of priestly formation:

> Canon 242 §1: Each nation is to have a program of priestly formation which is to be established by the conference of bishops … which … is to define the main principles of the instruction to be given in the seminary and general norms adapted to the pastoral needs of each region or province.
> §2: All seminaries, both diocesan and inter-diocesan, are to observe the norms of the program mentioned in §1.

The *Program of Priestly Formation* established by the United States Conference of Catholic Bishops is in its fifth edition. The relevant provisions are ¶¶134 and 128:

> ¶134: the spiritual director is held to the strictest confidentiality concerning information received in spiritual direction. He may neither reveal it nor use it. *The only possible exception to this standard of confidentiality would be the case of grave, immediate, or mortal danger involving the directee or another person* (emphasis added)
> … If what is revealed in spiritual direction coincides with the celebration of the Sacrament of Penance (in other words, what is revealed is revealed *ad ordinem absolutionis*), that is, the exchange not only takes place in the internal forum but also the sacramental forum, then the absolute strictures of the seal of confession hold, and no information may be revealed or used.
> ¶128: Seminarians should confide their personal history, personal relationships, prayer experiences, their cultivation of virtues, their temptations, and other significant topics to their spiritual director.

The italicized language in the first paragraph of ¶134 was added in the fifth edition of the *PPF*. All prior versions simply stated that "the spiritual director is held to the strictest confidentiality concerning information received in spiritual direction. He may neither reveal it nor use it." This language reflected the tradition in seminaries regarding the confidentiality of spiritual direction noted above. The language of the prior versions of the *PPF* is easily equated with the same degree of confidentiality accorded a sacramental confession by the language of the relevant canons of the code and commentaries thereon. The language added to the fifth edition, however, seems to equate the confidentiality that attaches to spiritual direction more with that accorded to "professional secrets" in the moral tradition, admitting of the possibility of exceptions to confidentiality. Thus, according to the fifth edition, if a spiritual director discerns the possibility of grave, immediate, or mortal danger involving the directee or another person from something related in spiritual direction, the *PPF* seems to acknowledge the possibility that the director could disclose the information. But how is the language of the fifth edition to be interpreted and understood?

The language of ¶134 does not *require* spiritual directors to disclose anything. Rather, it states that the only *possible* exception to the standard of absolute confidentiality *would be* the case of grave, immediate or mortal danger involving the directee or another person. This is inherently, one must presume intentionally, ambiguous language. One has to wonder why the wording of this addition to ¶134 was crafted in such an oblique manner. The word "possible" here is ambiguous: does the *PPF* mean to say that it's possible that there is an exception to absolute confidentiality, but it is not certain? Or does it mean that an exception is possible in the kind of case identified? Furthermore, it doesn't say the only possible exception *is* the case of grave, immediate or mortal danger to the directee or another, but only that it *would be*. It is hard to imagine a weaker statement regarding whether or not the confidentiality of spiritual direction is absolute. ¶134 appears to be saying that *if* there were an exception to the absolute confidentiality of spiritual direction it *would be* in the case of grave, immediate or mortal danger—but we're not sure if there really is such an exception. Where does this leave spiritual directors?

Under prior versions of the *PPF* a spiritual director could confidently raise the "priest-penitent" privilege in civil law proceedings, or claim a right not to report under a mandatory reporting statute, in relation to communications during spiritual direction based on a well-established religious principle and practice that considered communications during spiritual direction to be absolutely confidential. He could then point to ¶134 as evidence that this is in fact the understanding of how spiritual direction is to be treated under the theology and practices of the Roman Catholic religion and furthermore that it is mandated by the *PPF*. Since the *PPF* has the force of law in light of canon 242, the confidentiality mandated for spiritual direction by the *PPF* is the confidentiality mandated by the canon law of the Church.

Under the new version of ¶134 in the fifth edition of the *PPF*, however, this authoritative document now acknowledges the possibility of an exception to absolute confidentiality, even though it does not affirmatively state that there is such an exception. The USCCB appears to have become agnostic regarding the question, leaving spiritual directors to sort it out for themselves. That is not necessarily bad, since it gives spiritual directors who are truly conflicted about whether they should reveal something a basis upon which to soothe their consciences if they feel that they should disclose information for preventative purposes. Might this be counter-productive, however? Awareness of the revised standard is not likely to enhance the willingness of seminarians to be completely open and transparent in spiritual direction, one of the principal objectives of spiritual direction in the seminary or anywhere.

¶134 does not require spiritual directors to reveal anything, but appears to leave it to the conscience and discretion of individual spiritual directors to determine whether they *can* reveal something and whether they *should*. It may also constitute a trap for the unwary, however. Since this authoritative document of the USCCB acknowledges at least the possibility of an exception to confidentiality, it could be interpreted as removing discretion from spiritual directors when it can be shown that there *was* a danger of grave immediate or mortal danger. If a spiritual director could have revealed information that later proves to have evidenced the possibility of grave immediate or mortal danger and that danger is realized causing harm to another, the language of ¶134 could be used to argue that the spiritual director should have revealed the information and his failure to do so constituted negligence rendering him personally liable for any harm done. This is not likely to enhance the willingness of priests, or others if and when possible, to serve as spiritual directors. On the other hand, if they do choose to serve it may make them risk-aversive and willing to reveal anything and everything that could possibly be interpreted as presenting a grave risk of immediate or mortal danger to the spiritual director or another, effectively compromising the confidentiality of spiritual direction almost entirely. This may be especially true in the face of "mandatory reporting laws" which sometimes contain relatively vague standards regarding what must be reported. ¶134 provides spiritual directors with very little to rely on in defending themselves against a claim that they should have revealed something that they did not reveal under a mandatory reporting law or in the face of a demand for testimony regarding things communicated during spiritual direction in a civil law proceeding where the spiritual director wants to assert the priest-penitent privilege. In other words, it appears that seminary spiritual directors are on their own, with very little to back them up canonically or legally in the civil arena regarding the confidentiality of spiritual direction, as far as some of the more serious matters that may be related in spiritual direction are concerned. Since spiritual direction is only addressed in the seminary context in canon law, it appears that other Roman Catholic spiritual directors have nothing to rely on canonically or civilly whatsoever.

4. Other Pastoral Communications

All of the other kinds of communications in pastoral settings alluded to present two easy questions which are, however, equally difficult to answer: 1) What degree of confidentiality does canon law afford such communications, and 2) what degree of confidentiality will civil law afford them in the different contexts of a) situations where the priest-penitent privilege would be available to non-Catholic ministers and b) in the face of "mandatory reporting" laws? The difficulty of answering these questions rests on the fact that, as mentioned, most priest-penitent privilege statutes base the availability of the privilege on the degree of confidentiality accorded the communication under the law, policies and/or practices of the religion in question. If there are no explicit rules in the religion, the presumption tends to be in favor of the availability of the privilege. However, if the rules regarding confidentiality are spelled out with specificity, as appears to be the case in the Catholic faith, it is possible that a civil court would rule that these other kinds of pastoral communications do not enjoy the same level of confidentiality as confession, but only that accorded them by the rules of the Catholic Church.

IV. Civil Law

We turn now to a consideration of the extent to which civil law provides protection for religiously-based confidential communications, whether through the priest-penitent privilege or as an exception to mandatory reporting requirements.

1. General Rule of Evidence

The general rule of evidence law in the United States is that a court (or other official body) is entitled to *all relevant information* concerning the truth of issues raised in official proceedings regardless of the source. Coupled with this principle is that a court has the power to compel the production of testimony or other evidence through coercive means (primarily fines and/or incarceration). Therefore, one may withhold information requested as evidence by a court or other official body *only if there is a recognized privilege against disclosure.* Every state has its own rules of evidence and the federal courts additionally have their own rules of evidence. Therefore, the existence and nature of any privilege against disclosure will depend entirely upon the jurisdiction one is in and the court or other official body or agency of the state or federal government involved and the rules of evidence that apply in that venue.

For illustrative purposes the general evidentiary rules of three representative states are as follows:

> Hawaii: Rule 402. Relevant evidence generally admissible: irrelevant evidence not admissible. All relevant evidence is admissible, except as otherwise provided by the Constitutions of the United States and the State of Hawaii, by statute, by these rules, or by other rules adopted by the supreme court.

Evidence which is not relevant is not admissible.
Rule 401. Definition of "relevant evidence." "Relevant evidence" means evidence having any tendency to make the existence of any fact that is of consequence to the determination of the action more probable or less probable than it would be without the evidence.

Nevada: 48.025. Relevant evidence generally admissible; irrelevant evidence inadmissible.
1. All relevant evidence is admissible, except:
(a) As otherwise provided by this Title;
(b) As limited by the Constitution of the United States or of the State of Nevada; or
(c) Where a statute limits the review of an administrative determination to the record made or evidence offered before that tribunal.
2. Evidence which is not relevant is not admissible.[27]

California: §911. Refusal to be or have another as witness, or disclose or produce any matter
Except as otherwise provided by statute:
(a) No person has a privilege to refuse to be a witness.
(b) No person has a privilege to refuse to disclose any matter or to refuse to produce any writing, object, or other thing.
(c) No person has a privilege that another shall not be a witness, shall not disclose any matter or shall not produce any writing, object, or other thing.

The starting point is that as far as the civil law is concerned no one can withhold any information whatsoever requested by an authorized official of the government that is relevant to an issue under investigation or in controversy, unless there is a specific principle of law, rule or privilege that permits withholding the information. Is there such a principle, rule or privilege that permits religious ministers to withhold religiously-based confidential communications from civil authorities who request it or mandate that it be disclosed? If so, what limitations are there to it, if any? And once again we have to distinguish between the priest-penitent privilege and circumstances under which the law requires that certain information be disclosed under "mandatory reporting" laws.

2. Priest-Penitent Privilege

---

[27] The Nevada statute was chosen in particular because, in conjunction with the Nevada mandatory reporting statute which will be referred to later, it presents the clearest example of a state in which under certain circumstances a priest might theoretically (and legally) be required to report even something which he comes to know of through hearing a sacramental confession.

Every state has some form of priest-penitent evidentiary privilege, and the privilege is also recognized under federal law. The manner in which the privilege made its way into American law is complicated and technical. There are three possible bases for the privilege: a privilege that exists as a constitutional right; a Common Law evidentiary privilege; a statutory (or rule of court) evidentiary privilege.

Although the first court case recognizing the priest-penitent privilege appears to have seen it as required by a constitutional provision guaranteeing freedom of religion, the decision was in a state court and the court was referring to the state, not the federal, constitution freedom of religion clause (even though the clause was virtually identical to the that in the First Amendment to the United States Constitution).[28] There has been no other court decision, state or federal, that has clearly recognized a constitutionally mandated privilege for religiously-based confidential communications and, therefore, other than possibly in the particular state of that first decision (New York), there is no firmly established constitutional right to claim the priest-penitent privilege by either the penitent or the clergyperson.

After *Philips* every state including New York began to treat the priest-penitent privilege as a statutory or evidence rule privilege and so the presumption must be that in American law the privilege will be treated as such. One cannot rely on the possibility that a court might recognize a constitutional basis for the privilege. The significance of this is that the authoritative body creating the privilege (usually the state legislature, but it could also be a court, and in the case of the federal evidentiary privilege it is a court-made or court-recognized privilege not one created by Congress) can alter the privilege or abolish it altogether. That would not be the case if it were the product of a firmly-established constitutional right under the First Amendment.

Notwithstanding the fact that every state currently has some form of priest-penitent privilege, one cannot presume that will always be the case. There have been significant efforts in recent years, especially in the aftermath of the clergy sexual abuse of minors scandals, to limit severely or abolish altogether the priest-penitent privilege in certain jurisdictions, and these efforts continue almost every legislative session in some states. It is therefore important that the Church be especially vigilant regarding efforts to make inroads in the civil law into the confidentiality of pastoral communications, especially efforts to lessen civil law protection for the seal of confession.[29]

---

[28] The first case is People v. Philips (N.Y. Ct. Gen. Sess. 1813), an unreported case; the decision was abstracted in 1 Western L.J. 109 (1843, is available in public records in the Court of General Sessions of the County of New York, and has been referred to in several historical works and journal articles). See: "Privileged Communications to Clergymen," 1 Cath. Law. 199 (1955); M. H. Mitchell, "Must Clergy Tell? Child Abuse Reporting Requirements Versus the Clergy Privilege and Free Exercise of Religion," 71 Minnesota Law Review 723 (1987).

[29] For instance, efforts have been made in Maryland and other states to weaken or abolish the priest-penitent evidentiary privilege and to remove the exemption from mandatory

There is a possibility that one could argue in favor of a Common Law priest-penitent privilege, but is unlikely that this would succeed.[30] English Common Law rules received into American law are as they existed at the time of the ratification of the United States Constitution (adopted by the states so there would not be a void in the rules of law before new laws were enacted on every subject necessary for the adjudication of controversies). While it is all but certain that there was a priest-penitent privilege, or something akin to it, in English Common Law at some point, by the time of the American Revolution and the American Constitution whatever privilege may have existed had been abolished in English law (at some time following the Protestant Reformation). Therefore, there is not much basis to claim any Common Law priest-penitent privilege in American law.

Most state priest-penitent privileges are based on a model rule of evidence proposed by a commission constituted to propose model rules of evidence for the states many years ago. The model rule states:

> Communications to Clergymen
>
> a) Definitions. As used in this rule:
>
> 1) A "*clergyman*" is a minister, priest, rabbi, or other similar functionary of a religious organization, or an individual reasonably believed so to be by the person consulting him.
>
> 2) A communication is "confidential" if made privately and not intended for further disclosure except to other persons present in furtherance of the purpose of the communication.
>
> b) General rule of privilege. A person has a privilege to refuse to disclose and to prevent another from disclosing a confidential communication by the person to a clergyman in his professional character as a spiritual adviser.
>
> c) Who may claim the privilege: The privilege may be claimed by the person, by his guardian or conservator or by

---

reporting for sacramental and other similar kinds of communications. See: C. E. L. Miller, "Comment: Holding Clergy Accountable: Maryland should require Clergy to Report Suspected Child," 34 U. Balt. L. Rev. 337 (2005); C. Wolf, "Ky. Bill to Repeal Clergy "Silent Right," Associated Press, January 10, 2003, 5:50 PM EST.

[30] Although the federal privilege may be a product of the federal courts recognizing a kind of Common Law priest-penitent privilege in federal practice pursuant to the peculiar approach adopted by the Federal Rules of Evidence respecting evidentiary privileges:

> Federal Rule of Evidence 501. General Rule: Except as otherwise required by the Constitution of the United States or provided by Act of Congress or in rules prescribed by the Supreme Court pursuant to statutory authority, the privilege of a witness, person, government, State, or political subdivision thereof shall be governed by the principles of the common law as they may be interpreted by the courts of the United States in the light of reason and experience. However, in civil actions and proceedings, with respect to an element of a claim or defense as to which State law supplies the rule of decision, the privilege of a witness, person, government, State, or political subdivision thereof shall be determined in accordance with State law.

> his personal representative if he is deceased. The clergyman may claim the privilege on behalf of the person. His authority to do so is presumed in the absence of evidence to the contrary.

It must first of all be born in mind that this is only a model rule, and that each state has its own controlling rules of evidence. Thus, one must consult the particular rule of the particular state in question to know whether that state's privilege rule conforms to the model rule or not, and in what ways it may differ. For instance, some states alter the definition of clergyman in various ways making it either more or less inclusive. Some states limit the privilege to ministers of "a recognized religious denomination" or attempt to limit its availability in other similar ways. For instance, the Georgia Code only makes the privilege available to certain kinds of ministers of certain recognized religious denominations:

> O.C.G.A §24-9-22. Communications to clergyman privileged. Every communication made by any person professing religious faith, seeking spiritual comfort, or seeking counseling to any Protestant minister of the Gospel, any priest of the Roman Catholic faith, any priest of the Greek Orthodox Catholic faith, any Jewish rabbi, or to any Christian or Jewish minister, by whatever name called, shall be deemed privileged. No such minister, priest, or rabbi shall disclose any communications made to him by any such person professing religious faith, seeking spiritual guidance, or seeking counseling, nor shall such minister, priest, or rabbi be competent or compellable to testify with reference to any such communication in any court.

At least by the terms of the statute, the Georgia evidentiary privilege would not be available for communications made to a Muslim Imam, or a Buddhist monk, etc. Whether this aspect of the statute would survive constitutional scrutiny if challenged is open to question. Compare this with the model rule which makes the privilege available for communications to "a minister, priest, rabbi, *or other similar functionary of a religious organization*, or an individual reasonably believed so to be by the person consulting him." Even limiting the privilege to functionaries of a religious organization might present constitutional questions if challenged. However, these examples are offered only to make the point that in order to understand what the privilege protects in any given jurisdiction one must consult the statute or rule in force in that jurisdiction. The fact of the matter is that the kind of communications we are concerned with regard to Catholic clergy are definitely privileged to one degree or another in most if not all jurisdictions (as are similar exemptions from mandatory reporting). The more important question for Catholic clergy and ministers is to know exactly what kinds of communications are protected in civil law and to what extent. That is, do the privilege and mandatory reporting exemptions cover anything other than communications during a sacramental confession, and if so what and to what degree. This addresses our concern with the degree to which communications made during spiritual direction will or will not be protected from disclosure under civil law, not to mention all of the other kinds of pastoral communications one can think of.

For the purposes of this article we can assume that the model rule fairly well represents the basic priest-penitent privilege as it exists in most if not all of the states. However, one must remember that the priest-penitent privilege applies only in the case of official proceedings when one has been called upon to give testimony or otherwise provide information which one might claim is privileged from disclosure by the priest-penitent privilege. The evidentiary privilege does not exist with respect to a statute that requires certain information be reported to the authorities by identified persons as soon as they have the information ("mandatory reporting" laws) unless it has been explicitly incorporated as an exception to the reporting law by the reporting law itself.

3. Mandatory Reporting Laws

Do mandatory reporting laws include exemptions from reporting for religiously-based confidential communications? Do they exempt from mandatory reporting information gained during a sacramental confession? Do they exempt reporting based on information gained from communications during other kinds of pastoral encounters (such as spiritual direction, spiritual counseling, pastoral counseling, etc.)? Most if not all of these laws do exempt at least some of these kinds of communications. Disturbingly for Catholics and Catholic priests and ministers, at least one or two of these laws on their face do require that certain kinds of information received even in confession would have to be reported. For instance, §432B.220 of the Nevada Revised Statutes only exempts clergy from reporting the sexual abuse of a minor that he learns of "from the offender" during confession. The exact language of the statute is:

> NRS 432B.220 Persons required to make report; when and to whom reports are required; any person may make report; report and written findings if reasonable cause to believe death of child caused by abuse or neglect.
>
> 1. Any person who is described in subsection 4 and who, in his or her professional or occupational capacity, knows or has reasonable cause to believe that a child has been abused or neglected shall:
>
> (a) Except as otherwise provided in subsection 2, report the abuse or neglect of the child to an agency which provides child welfare services or to a law enforcement agency; and
>
> (b) Make such a report as soon as reasonably practicable but not later than 24 hours after the person knows or has reasonable cause to believe that the child has been abused or neglected.
>
> 2. If a person who is required to make a report pursuant to subsection 1 knows or has reasonable cause to believe that the

> abuse or neglect of the child involves an act or omission of:
> (a) A person directly responsible or serving as a volunteer for or an employee of a public or private home, institution or facility where the child is receiving child care outside of the home for a portion of the day, the person shall make the report to a law enforcement agency.
> 4. A report must be made pursuant to subsection 1 by the following persons:
> (d) A member of the clergy, practitioner of Christian Science or religious healer, unless the person has acquired the knowledge of the abuse or neglect *from the offender* during a confession.[31]

Thus, under the language of this statute if a child victim of sexual abuse mentions that he or she had been abused during a sacramental confession the priest is required to report it to the authorities. This is the clearest example of a state where the seal of confession is not recognized as exempting from mandatory reporting, although it is not known if a priest has ever been prosecuted for failure to report under this statute in Nevada. Nevertheless, it is cause for concern that this is the actual state of the law.

V. Conclusion

Many challenges lie ahead respecting religiously-based confidential communications. To conclude this article I would like to outline the most important challenges I see in relation to the priest-penitent privilege, mandatory reporting laws, spiritual direction and other kinds of pastoral communications, meriting and regaining the trust of society with respect to confidentiality, alluding along the way to what is really at stake in all of this.

1. Priest-penitent privilege

The first and foremost challenge respecting the priest-penitent privilege is vigilance in the face of efforts to lessen the legal protection given communications connected with the sacrament of penance. As noted, there have been efforts in state legislatures to weaken the privilege or abolish the privilege altogether in recent years.[32] However vigilant the Church may be, it must also be born in mind that maintenance of the priest-penitent privilege only protects communications in the context of formal proceedings where testimony or other information is requested. It does not with certainty protect such communications in relation to mandatory reporting laws. Thus, efforts to diminish confidentiality in the context of mandatory reporting laws must be addressed in relation to those laws on a case-by-case basis.

There should also be analysis of what pastoral communications, other than those made in relation to the sacrament of penance, the priest-privilege as it

---

[31] Nevada Revised Statutes (NRS) 432B.220 (emphasis added).

[32] See footnote 30 above.

currently exists protects in Roman Catholic contexts. If it is concluded that the privilege does not protect all the kinds of communications that it is felt it should protected, consideration should be given to making efforts to the have the law amended to assure that the privilege will be understood in civil law as protecting the confidentiality all of the kinds of communications that it is felt should be protected. Such efforts may be difficult in the current climate, but should be undertaken nonetheless in order to do everything possible to assure the protection of communications that should be protected.

2. Mandatory reporting laws

The challenges respecting mandatory reporting laws include those that apply to the priest-penitent privilege, although in the specific context of the nature of these laws. Efforts should be made to assure that every mandatory reporting law includes an exemption from reporting for all communications covered by the seal of confession. It should also be determined whether other kinds of pastoral communications should be exempt from reporting. Not everything covered by the seal of confession is exempt from mandatory reporting in every jurisdiction today. Therefore efforts should be undertaken in those states where adequate exemptions do not exist to have the laws amended so that they do, also with respect to other kinds of pastoral communications if advisable.

There is widespread support for the idea of mandatory reporting of known or suspected child abuse today in the effort to address, prevent or remedy child abuse as completely as possible. Translating these objectives into effective legislation is not as easy as it might seem, however. When mandatory reporting carries a criminal penalty for failure to report, as in many states, principles of criminal law require that statutory language clearly identify and describe the conduct which is required or prohibited in order to avoid criminal liability. Those subject to the law must be able to understand what is required or prohibited in a manner that adequately puts them on notice regarding the standard of conduct to which they are being held. This is a basic principle justifying the imposition of criminal liability in our system. Furthermore, offenders must have had the requisite criminal state of mind, known as *mens rea*, in order to be subjected to criminal liability and punished for a violation of the law. The law in question must therefore be written in such a way that it is possible to discern clearly the behavior that is prohibited or required to avoid criminal penalties and the *mens rea* required for a successful prosecution of the offense.

Some existing mandatory reporting laws may be open to question with respect to these requirements. For instance, Nevada's mandatory reporting law provides in relevant part:

> NRS 432B.220 Persons required to make report;
> 1. Any person who is described in subsection 4 and who, in his or her professional or occupational capacity, knows or has reasonable cause to believe that a child has been abused or neglected shall:

(a) Except as otherwise provided in subsection 2, report the abuse or neglect of the child to an agency which provides child welfare services or to a law enforcement agency; and
(b) Make such a report as soon as reasonably practicable but not later than 24 hours after the person knows or has reasonable cause to believe that the child has been abused or neglected.

NRS 432B.121 Definition of when person has "reasonable cause to believe" and when person acts "as soon as reasonably practicable." For the purposes of this chapter, a person:
Has "reasonable cause to believe" if, in light of all the surrounding facts and circumstances which are known or which reasonably should be known to the person at the time, a reasonable person would believe, under those facts and circumstances, that an act, transaction, event, situation or condition exists, is occurring or has occurred.

Ordinarily one can only be prosecuted and punished for his or her own behavior based on her or his own state of mind. The Nevada law is somewhat unusual in that it subjects one to potential criminal liability for not doing something based not on what he or she knows or believes but, rather, on what some theoretical "reasonable person" should know or believe under the circumstances. Does this law abolish all defenses based on the state of mind of the accused (such as insanity, etc.) since the standard of culpability may be the state of mind of a theoretical "reasonable person" not that of the actual accused person? The law could be challenged on two grounds: first of all, that it holds one potentially criminally liable for conduct based not on his or her own state of mind at the time of the offense but that of a theoretical "reasonable person"; secondly, the standard one is held to by the law is not necessarily clear enough to support criminal liability. In order to avoid criminal liability one must discern not what he or she knows or believes but what some "reasonable person" would know or believe.

Not to be facetious, but how is an unreasonable person to know what a reasonable person would know or believe? By definition the requisite knowledge or belief would be beyond his or her capacity. Even an unreasonable person can understand a law which says "you must do this" or "you may not do that." However, not everyone, in fact perhaps no one, is capable of understanding what a *theoretical* "reasonable person" would know or believe. Just how reasonable does this theoretical reasonable person have to be? Are we talking about someone with perfect reason? Only limited reason? A somewhat defective reasonableness? What is the standard? The actual standard of this law is, in fact, rather vague.

Criminal statutes which lack sufficient definiteness or specificity can be held "void for vagueness." The basic doctrine was stated in the case of Cantwell v.

Connecticut:[33] such legislation "may run afoul of the Due Process Clause because it fails to give adequate guidance to those who would be law-abiding, to advise defendants of the nature of the offense with which they are charged, or to guide courts in trying those who are accused."[34] "Men of common intelligence cannot be required to guess at the meaning of [an] enactment."[35]

Statutes like Nevada's may work well in relation to their intended objective when they induce someone who believes a child may have been abused to report the suspected abuse. However, if there has been no report and a person is prosecuted on the grounds that he or she *believed* that the child may have been abused, how is a jury to judge what a criminal defendant did or did not believe (as opposed to what he or she "knew" (which can be deduced from objective evidence)? Or how is a jury to determine what a "reasonable person" would have believed? And even if that can be determined, does it comport with our constitutional standards to hold someone criminally responsible for what another person, a theoretical reasonable person, would have believed as determined by twelve jurors? It just seems that the standard for determining criminal responsibility of at least some child abuse reporting statutes may be

---

33 *Cantwell v. Connecticut*, 310 U.S. 296, 308 (1940).

34 *Musser v. Utah*, 333 U.S. 95, 97 (1948): "The vagueness may be from uncertainty in regard to persons within the scope of the act ...or in regard to the applicable tests to ascertain guilt." Id. at 97. "Vague laws offend several important values. First, because we assume that man is free to steer between lawful and unlawful conduct, we insist that laws give the person of ordinary intelligence a reasonable opportunity to know what is prohibited, so that he may act accordingly. Vague laws may trap the innocent by not providing fair warnings. Second, if arbitrary and discriminatory enforcement is to be prevented, laws must provide explicit standards for those who apply them. A vague law impermissibly delegates basic policy matters to policemen, judges, and juries for resolution on an *ad hoc* and subjective basis, with the attendant dangers of arbitrary and discriminatory applications." *Grayned v. City of Rockford*, 408 U.S. 104, 108-09 (1972), quoted in *Village of Hoffman Estates v. The Flipside*, 455 U.S. 489, 498 (1982).

35 *Winters v. New York*, 333 U.S. 507, 515-16 (1948). "The vagueness may be from uncertainty in regard to persons within the scope of the act ...or in regard to the applicable test to ascertain guilt." Id. *Cf. Colten v. Kentucky*, 407 U.S. 104, 110 (1972). A statute may be so vague or so threatening to constitutionally-protected activity that it can be pronounced wholly unconstitutional; in other words, it is "unconstitutional on its face." Thus, for instance, a unanimous Court in *Papachristou v. City of Jacksonville*, 405 U.S. 156 (1972) struck down as invalid on its face a vagrancy ordinance which punished "dissolute persons who go about begging, ...common night walkers, ...common railers and brawlers, persons wandering or strolling around from place to place without any lawful purpose or object, habitual loafers, ...persons neglecting all lawful business and habitually spending their time by frequenting houses of ill fame, gaming houses, or places where alcoholic beverages are sold or served, persons able to work but habitually living upon the earnings of their wives or minor children ...." The ordinance was found to be facially invalid, according to Justice Douglas for the Court, because it did not give fair notice, it did not require specific intent to commit an unlawful act, it permitted and encouraged arbitrary and erratic arrests and convictions, it committed too much discretion to policemen, and it criminalized activities which by modern standards are normally innocent.

open to question in relation to these considerations.

Mandatory reporting laws should be analyzed to determine if they meet constitutional standards for criminal laws, and amended where necessary to assure that they are in conformity with applicable constitutional and criminal law standards. They should also be studied and amendments proposed where necessary to assure that they all contain exemptions from the reporting requirement under all of the same circumstances that are covered by the seal of confession in canon law, and perhaps other kinds of religiously-based confidential communications as well where that seems desirable.

Finally, at least some consideration should be given to whether mandatory reporting laws may be, at least in some instances, counter-productive. Mandating the reporting of child abuse as soon as it is known or suspected is designed to stop such behavior at the earliest moment, thereby protecting victims from further abuse, a worthy objective. Where knowledge or suspicion of abuse comes from voluntary disclosures to a trusted person or professional in a putatively confidential exchange, however, mandating an immediate report may counteract other values and the possible benefits of non-disclosure. If awareness of the actual or possible abuse comes from the possible victim, mandatory reporting may cause a sense of betrayal on the part of the victim. Once it becomes widely known that reporting is mandatory, victims who are uncertain or afraid may easily be less likely to confide in others regarding behaviors of others that may be abusive, either out of fear of the consequences to themselves, uncertainty about what they are experiencing, or simply a desire not to "get into trouble" or get someone else into trouble. If this is the result of mandatory reporting, it will increase not decrease the amount of abuse suffered by victims.

Counselors and pastors have often felt that it is more productive to work with victims over time and bring them to explicitly report abuse to the authorities themselves when they are ready. Of course, when it is known, as it is now known, that some of those who victims did or might have confided in were themselves perpetrators of such abuse, who sometimes used the cloak of confidentiality to mask their offenses or protect themselves, it is much more difficult to expect society to reside this kind of confidence in those who are in a position to receive confidential communications and assist victims.

From another perspective, the instinct of the Church and the counseling professions has always been that when perpetrators of these kinds of behavior have no one to turn to for counsel and assistance the behavior tends to become worse. Empirical research may now suggest an objective basis for this conclusion.[36] And it does make a certain amount of sense that this may be the case. Why would anyone want to discuss such behavior with a priest, other minister or a counselor, if he or she were not struggling with it and did not know that there was something wrong with it; if she or he did not want to stop? If such

---

[36] See: P. J. Pagan, *Sexual Disorders Sexual Disorders: Perspectives on Diagnosis and Treatment* (Baltimore, MD: Johns Hopkins University Press, 2004).

troubled persons have no one to turn to for counseling and assistance, their consciousness of the inappropriateness and wrongness of the behavior is much more likely to become dulled and the behavior to continue, if not worsen. Counseling with an authority figure or therapeutic helper will reinforce social norms that condemn such behavior and will reinforce the perpetrator's own sense and awareness of its wrongness and that it should stop. Without that reinforcement the behavior is all the more likely to become routine and habitual, with no internal or external incentives to stop. Once again, however, since counselors and priests are known to have been perpetrators of abuse, it will be all the more difficult to convince society to give them the necessary discretion to serve in this role again, however much it might benefit society by lessening the amount of abuse that occurs and helping at least some perpetrators seek effective help that leads them to cease the harmful behavior. To say anything of the benefit to perpetrators themselves, who may sincerely want to stop but who are trapped in a psychological and behavioral web that few, perhaps no one, is really able to understand. But how many will avail themselves of psychological, therapeutic and/or spiritual counseling if they know the result will be a mandated reporting to the civil authorities and possible, if not likely, criminal prosecution? Who will such trouble persons turn to if there is no privileged forum in which they can bring their behavior out into the open with a trusted professional and try to deal with it?

3. Spiritual Direction

Confidentiality with respect to spiritual direction presents a host of issues in need of serious study. Seminary spiritual directors can no longer assume they can treat what is communicated in spiritual direction the same as what they hear in sacramental confession in view of the new language of ¶134 of the fifth edition of the *PPF*. There is a need to clarify, therefore, the meaning and consequences of this new language for seminary spiritual direction. There is also a need to consider whether canon law should address other forms of spiritual direction that have become common in Catholic practice and give greater guidance regarding the degree of confidentiality that can be expected by directees, and the degree directors are expected and required to maintain.

More than study is needed, however, for spiritual directors now practicing in the field who have to be able to understand exactly what degree of confidentiality is expected and required in the work they do now, and what they have to rely on if they are either asked to reveal something learned in spiritual direction or what the standards are for revealing something learned in spiritual direction. Or, must they resign themselves to bearing full responsibility for judgments made about whether or not something can or should be revealed. Does ¶134 state a rule that directors can fall back on to justify judgments they make, or does it simply relegate questions concerning the confidentiality of spiritual direction completely to the discretion and judgment of spiritual directors themselves?

In addition to the above, there needs to be greater clarity regarding what constitutes a *grave* danger as referred to in ¶134 of the *PPF*, what constitutes an *immediate* danger, whether an immediate danger must also be grave in order to be relieved of the duty to maintain confidentiality, and what constitutes mortal danger to the directee or another. Furthermore, will the possibility that information relayed in spiritual direction might be able to be revealed deter directees from being completely open and transparent with their directors? Will it compel directors to become more defensive and risk-aversive in the way they carry out their role as spiritual directors? Will directors feel caught between the possibility that they might have to betray a directee on the one hand and legal serious consequences if they don't on the other? Will fewer priests and others be willing to serve as spiritual directors because of the risks involved? All of these are serious questions and serious challenges for the future in relation to the confidentiality of spiritual direction.

4. Summary

Developments since the publication of the CLSA's study *Confidentiality in the United States: A Legal and Canonical Study* in 1988, most notably the ongoing evolution of mandatory reporting laws and the clergy sexual abuse crisis in the United States, have brought to the fore questions regarding confidentiality that may not have occurred to the authors of that study. The need to address questions of confidentiality has become more critical than ever. The purpose of this article has been to raise awareness of the need to address the issues alluded to herein, many of which will require profound study and some new approaches. This article asks questions that have been on the table for a long time, and is attempting to re-start and continue the discussion of confidentiality that the CLSA began in the current context. It is hoped that others will take an interest in this subject, so that through joint efforts the Church and society in general will be well served by adjustments to both canon and civil law, refining the way the dignity of individuals is respected through the maintenance of appropriate levels of confidentiality without sacrificing the equally important objectives of preventing and remedying child abuse and other harmful behaviors, and bringing those who do harm to others, especially those who do harm to children, to justice.

SEMINAR

DIGNITAS CONNUBII: FIVE YEARS LATER

Reverend Paul D. Counce

Dignitas connubii[1] has been the subject of lots of study over the past five years. It has been the principal subject of consideration at numerous canonical seminars and study days since its publication in 2005. A number of symposia immediately were organized, with proceedings published.[2] The Lüdicke-Jenkins *Commentary*[3] and numerous articles in canonical journals have appeared.[4] Excepting only the 1983 *Code of Canon Law* itself, it could arguably

---

[1] Pontifical Council for Legislative Texts, *Dignitas Connubii: Instruction to be Observed by Diocesan and Interdiocesan Tribunals in Handling Causes of the Nullity of Marriage, Official Latin Text with English Translation* (Rome: Libreria Editrice Vaticana [hereafter LEV]) 2005.

[2] See for example: XI Colloquium Juris Canonici della Facoltà di Diritto Canonico della Pontificia Università Gregoriana, June 8, 2005, published in *Periodica* 94 (2005) 417-452; XXIV Curso de Actualización en Derecho Canónico, Titulado "La Instrucción *Dignitas connubii* sobre los procesos de nulidad matrimonial," Universidad di Navarra, October 24-26, 2005, published in *Jus canonicum* 91 (2006) 33-206; Study Day held at the Pontifical University of the Holy Cross in Rome, January 19, 2006, published in *Studies on the Instruction Dignitas Connubii*, ed. Patricia Dugan (Montréal, QC: Wilson & Lafleur, Ltée., 2006); and Spring Canonical Seminar of the School of Canon Law at The Catholic University of America in Washington, DC, March 23-24, 2007, "*Dignitas Connubii*: Two Years Later."

[3] K. Lüdicke and R. E. Jenkins, *Dignitas Connubii: Norms and Commentary*, Washington, DC: Canon Law Society of America (2006) xiii-557. This is an expanded, revised English translation of K. Lüdicke, *Die Eheprozeßordnung der katholischen Kirche. Text (Latein und Deutsch) und Kommentar. Münsterischen Kommentar zum Codex Iuris Canonici*, vol. 42 (Münster: Polylein Verlag, 2005).

[4] See for example: Il Giudizio di nullità matrimoniale dopo l'istruzione "*Dignitas connubii*" (a cura di P. A. Bonnet e C. Gullo), Parte Prima: I principi, *Studi Giuridici* 75 (LEV, 2007); Parte Seconda: la parte statica del processo, *Studi Giuridici* 76 (LEV, 2007); and Parte Terza: La parte dinamica del processo, *Studi Giuridici* 77 (LEV, 2008); *Ius Ecclesiae* 18/2 (2006), with articles by: F. Daneels, "Una introduzione generale all'istruzione '*Dignitas connubii*,'" 317-343, English translation in "A General Introduction to the Instruction *Dignitas Connubii*," *Forum* 17 (2006) 361-384; J. Llobell Tuset, "La natura giuridica e la recezione ecclesiale dell'istr. '*Dignitas connubii*,'" 343-370; A. Stankiewicz, "Indicazioni circa il can. 1095 nell'Istruzione '*Dignitas connubii*,'" 371-386; M. Angel Ortiz, "Le dichiarazioni delle parti e la certezza morale," 387-416; P. Moneta, "La determinazione della formula del dubbio e la conformittà della sentenza nell'istr. '*Dignitas connubii*,'" 417-438; G. Erlebach, "L'impugnazione della sentenza e l'invio 'ex officio' della causa al tribunale di appello nell'istr. '*Dignitas connubii*,'" 439-466. See also P. Biandi, "L'Istruzione *Dignitas Connubii* e il can. 1095," *Periodica* 94 (2005) 509-542; J. Kowal, "L'Istruzione *Dignitas Connubii* e la competenza della Chiesa circa il matrimonio dei battezatti," ibid., 477-507; G. Paolo, "Alcune questioni processuali intorno alla Decretazione di

be stated that it has been the single most studied canonical document related to Tribunal ministry since the promulgation of that foundational law.

This seminar will focus upon the use of *Dignitas connubii*, not a re-exposition of its content or interpretation thereof.

The approach was to survey personnel in every diocesan tribunal in the USA by means of questionnaire; a wholly random sampling of eleven Canadian and four British/Irish tribunals was also surveyed in this manner. A copy of the questionnaire sent is appended to the text of this presentation. Thirty-four written responses were received in response to this (one from Canada and one from England, the rest being from the USA), a statistically good albeit non-scientific sampling. Additionally, "followup conversations" were held with about fourteen persons, each representing one of the tribunals which responded in writing. Personnel of another eight tribunals which did not respond in writing were interviewed. Confidentiality was promised to those responding.

After these and just a few additional preliminary remarks, I shall attempt to expose in an organized way the findings of my survey. The use of *Dignitas connubii* over the past five years in general, and then more specifically the reported implementation or not of its emphases and novelties will be considered. What appear to be the still-undiscovered or underused aspects of the law which *Dignitas connubii* exposed will then be mentioned briefly, before going on to note the ways in which *Dignitas connubii* has been used, was not used or remains underutilized. These shall be followed by some concluding remarks.

In all of this I admit that the responses from the various tribunals surveyed were surprisingly broad in their content. I had expected more commonality to be reported regarding the ways in which *Dignitas connubii* was received and used; instead, what was described were different uses given the document by various tribunal offices, clearly in response to the unique situation in which each found itself.

First, before examining individual issues or topics within the instruction, it is helpful to note that *Dignitas connubii* itself was utilized in several broad ways. These, in fact, are the almost universal way in which *Dignitas connubii* has impacted tribunal work.

The first aspect in which almost every tribunal has made use of *Dignitas connubii* is in its training. Every responding tribunal head reported that upon its publication the text of the instruction was obtained swiftly, immediately made the subject of internal examination, and indeed has become a ready reference on virtually every staff person's desk.

Conformità Equivalente," *Periodica* 95 (2006) 483-551; L. Robitaille, "Through the Lens of *Dignitas Connubii*: the Judge's Active Role in Marriage Nullity Cases," *Studia canonica* 40 (2006) 137-182; A. Mendonça, "What is New? A Brief Analysis of Selected Themes Found in *Dignitas Connubii*," *Proceedings of the Canon Law Society of Great Britain and Ireland Annual Conference – 2006*, 41-49; R. Pagé, "L'Instruction Dignitas Connubii – Questions choisies," *Studia canonica* 41 (2007) 309-343, etc.

As mentioned above, numerous national and regional canon law conferences and presentations have focused on *Dignitas connubii*; in the first few years exposing its content and especially its emphases and novelties was a priority for national canonical societies such as our own, and regional and diocesan meetings of canon lawyers.

In addition to the training offered to tribunals' staff personnel, *Dignitas connubii* has also been utilized by individual tribunal personnel in offering training to others (*e.g.*, to parish clergy and lay ministers who seek to assist the faithful in filing tribunal cases). In fact, four judicial vicars reported that in providing instruction to non-canonists, they found the more orderly presentation of the matrimonial process contained in the instruction to be more useful than the text of the *Code of Canon Law* itself. This – the provision of a more unified presentation of the various norms contained in the sections of the code relative to Trials in General (cc. 1400-1500), the Contentious Trial (cc. 1501-1655), and Special Matrimonial Processes (cc. 1671-1691) – is one of the stated purposes of *Dignitas connubii* after all.

Every judicial vicar and tribunal director with whom I spoke made specific mention of Lüdicke-Jenkins' *Dignitas Connubii: Norms and Commentary* as now being a standard reference work within their offices. I suspect that this volume enjoys almost universal presence in English-speaking tribunals.

Another virtually universal application of *Dignitas connubii* has been its integration by reference into formularies. These include the various form letters and document templates used by tribunals in the processing of cases, but also in the informational materials (brochures, website expositions, etc.) published for the general public. In the former it is simply additional references to article number that typically have been added to citations of canon numbers. But in the latter *Dignitas connubii* is often utilized by reference to its purposes, stated in its *Proemium* (and in that of its predecessor, *Provida Mater Ecclesia* of 1936),[5] "to provide for these causes to be instructed and decided more quickly and more surely."

Other modifications to form letters went beyond the mere addition of references to the instruction. For example, two judicial vicars specifically mentioned modifications made to the standard letters sent notifying parties of the acceptance of the *libellus*, now to include identification of all the persons appointed to the court for the case, including the defender of the bond and auditor, in case any objection might be posed against one or more of these (art. 68).

One tribunal reported that it disseminates copies of *Dignitas connubii* as a reference to inquirers and those others objecting or needing clarification regarding tribunal process and practice. While the instruction's technical canonical terminology admittedly may be too mysterious for many readers,

[5] SCDS, instruction *Provida Mater Ecclesia*, August 15, 1936: *AAS* 28 (1936) 313-361; English translation in *Canon Law Digest* 2:471-530.

some have found that the straightforward publication by the Church of its procedural norms in *Dignitas connubii* reassured them that it is not an arbitrary process.

Every tribunal minister who provided a response noted that the publication of *Dignitas connubii* occasioned the office's revisiting its entire praxis. In most cases, judicial vicars and doubtless their bishops were heartened to discover that a comparison of their standard procedures with the instruction revealed little if any need for modification of the former. This was, however, not always the case. One new judicial vicar noted that despite the 1983 code, the numerous papal allocutions to the Roman Rota down through the years, occasional directive correspondence from the Supreme Tribunal of the Apostolic Signatura, and now *Dignitas connubii*, the largest number of cases being adjudicated by his office were still being done "as if it was still 1970"! Another noted that the publication of *Dignitas connubii* occasioned at long last the revamping of their documentary case process (*e.g.,* establishing competence, citing the respondent and formulating the doubt as in a standard or formal case) which heretofore had been entirely misunderstood.

But the bulk of the responses from the tribunals surveyed consisted of mention of individual norms of *Dignitas connubii* which led to some change to, or at least a strong reconsideration of some prior practice(s) within their offices. Compilation of these responses provides something of a litany of the emphases and "novelties" of *Dignitas connubii.*

The mention in articles 2 and 4 that the "proper law" of non-Catholic churches and ecclesial groups, including secular law, must be considered binding upon parties otherwise not subject to Catholic procedural law, has certainly occasioned much discussion; seven responding judicial vicars noted that their tribunals have begun to consider possibilities under this rubric as being able to lead to affirmative judgments relative to cases between non-Catholic parties. Even more in conversation acknowledged that full implementation of this directive remains too difficult to pursue in practice.

The heads of three tribunals reported that *Dignitas connubii* occasioned for them a renewed effort to insist that documentation of efforts made to locate a respondent whose whereabouts are unknown be generated and maintained in the acts (art. 13 §6).

Four judicial vicars noted that the instruction opened up the possibilities of personnel of one tribunal serving by special appointment *ad actum* – although never stably – in assisting other tribunals, even hierarchically related ones (art. 36 §1).

One judicial vicar reported a major change in his tribunal which was implemented due to the clear preference of *Dignitas connubii*: "All courts became collegiate with the implementation of *Dignitas Connubii*," he said (arts. 30 §1 and 48 §1). He went on to note that "the judicial vicar is the presiding judge in all cases (art. 46 §1). The *ponens* may be a lay judge (art. 47 §1). The responsibility of the *ponens* per *Dignitas connubii* as opposed (*sic*) to those of the presiding judge have been identified" (arts. 46 §2, esp. nn. 8-16, 18 and 21, and art. 47 §2).

Two judicial vicars reported that the role of auditor, which had heretofore been rarely used, has become more common (arts. 50-51); it was an institute which had not been noticed or utilized much prior to the "discovery" of this in the instruction!

One judicial vicar reported that *Dignitas connubii* inspired his tribunal to begin citing the defender of the bond in writing at more stages of the process, *e.g.*, acceptance, joinder, publication, appointment of the expert, and *conclusio in causa*, in addition to the constitution of the court, at the citation of the parties for their declarations, and at publication (which had been its previous practice) (arts. 56 §§1-2 and 59 §1).

Four tribunal heads mentioned their renewed emphasis, *per* article 71 of *Dignitas connubii*, on the provision that the judge "supply for the parties' negligence in presenting proofs" – one phrased it as "accommodating for the inadequacies of the parties" – "...in order to avoid an unjust sentence." It cannot be expected that parties to tribunal cases are well-versed in canon law, and often the judge or auditor in a case knows more precisely the sort of proofs which likely can be advanced successfully by a party: while remaining objective the judge can explore the possibilities of such likely proofs.

The possibility of the judge in a case appointing a procurator and not just an advocate for a party who has refused to appoint one (art. 101 §1), for exceptional reasons, was mentioned by three judicial vicars as being a change in their court's usual perspective. One had actually had this figure arise already within his court on one occasion.

Dignitas connubii was reported to have led to a number of changes in the manner of citation of the respondent. One judicial vicar says now he provides the standard option to the respondent "to remain uninvolved, with no contact from the tribunal, of course we will continue to transmit to them the final decision and how they may appeal," in accord with the prescriptions and tenor of article 134.

One judicial vicar made special mention of the increased specificity of arguments and observations now sought from and proposed by the defender of the bond within his court, in accord with *Dignitas connubii*, especially in cases wherein incapacity for marriage is alleged (art. 56 §§3-4).

One judicial vicar reported that the requisites of *Dignitas connubii*'s article 136 regarding any valid change in the formulation of the doubt(s) prompted his court to insist that these communications be made in writing. Further, he stated, he and his judicial colleagues came to realize that while the defender of the bond can request a modification in the formulation of the doubt, she or he cannot request the addition of a ground (art. 56 §5).

One judicial vicar mentioned that his tribunal has utilized articles 179-181 of the instruction as an aid to reaching moral certainty principally from the declarations/confessions of the parties, when strong affirmations of their credibility are also offered and their assertions are not contradicted by known, certain facts.

One tribunal reported increased consideration and use of the procedures to suspend a cause seeking marital nullity, changing it instead to a process seeking a dissolution *super rato* (arts. 153-154).

One judicial vicar reported that *Dignitas connubii* prompted his diocese to train and provide a stable corps of advocates, both clerical and lay (art. 112), these now publicized as such and available to the public on the tribunal's website.

Five judicial vicars made reference to the specific "new" figures of the "head of the tribunal chancery" (art. 61) and the canonical "adviser" which a tribunal is to make available to inquirers (art. 113 §1). Regarding the former office, two of the judicial vicars responding noted that this is not necessarily an office requiring a licensed canonist, but is principally an administrative position. In this vein, both noted that this figure is *not* the "director of the tribunal" in any sense. Two judicial vicars noted that, regarding the latter figure, it is difficult in a small tribunal for the needed advice not to be given by the canon lawyers who are most knowledgeable about procedure and jurisprudence, sometimes leading to awkward situations in which the canonist who has answered a party's honest questions later must recuse himself or herself from participation at trial (art. 113 §2).

One judicial vicar mentioned that the advent of *Dignitas connubii* finally led his tribunal to establish as standard procedure the deposing of the petitioner, respondent, and witnesses after the formulation of the doubt (art. 160), whereas before this it had been common for the tribunal not to join the issues until after declarations from both petitioner and respondent had been received.

Sixteen judicial vicars noted that their courts eagerly embraced the norms of *Dignitas connubii* permitting the non-publication of acts to respondents who are declared absent from the trial (art. 134 §§3-4 and 141-142) or who refuse to take an oath of confidentiality (art. 232 §1). In fact, all of these responders to the survey expressed appreciation for the instruction's giving greater clarity about the procedures to be followed when a respondent's whereabouts are unknown (arts. 13 §6 and 132). They also expressed greater satisfaction with *Dignitas connubii*'s greater clarity about the process to be followed when a respondent indicates she or he wishes no further notice about the case (*e.g.*, waiving the right to be notified, even of a copy of the sentence [art. 258 §3]).

Eighteen judicial vicars (the largest number regarding any single point) referenced their courts' paying much closer attention to expert input, noting the requirements that specific questions be addressed by *periti* in incapacity cases (art. 209), and the explication of the defender of the bond's role in evaluating expert intervention; one noted in particular that this had led to his tribunal "largely eliminating the use of minor psychological disturbances as grounds for incapacity."

Thirteen responders to the survey noted that the requirements of *Dignitas connubii* for "mandatory" prohibitions in cases of incapacity and simulation – with the added specifications of who is competent to lift these – occasioned changes to prior standard procedures within their courts (art. 251).

All nine judicial vicars of tribunals which acted in second instance noted that the more clear understanding of conformity of sentences in *Dignitas connubii* (art. 291) has been greatly appreciated. The instruction's guidance in this regard has made terminological differences regarding grounds to be far less problematic, and made the pursuit of justice without undue formalism easier.

This just-mentioned long list of various reported changes to tribunal praxis perhaps has a contrary listing. This list would consist of the undiscovered or underused aspects of the law which the publication of *Dignitas connubii* revealed or brought to light again:

In fact, one figure in this regard has been uncovered, one in fact which arose before *Dignitas connubii* but not directly addressed therein. It has been motivated by practicality but also can be seen as consonant with *Dignitas connubii* and its insistence on the judicial vicar as being the one responsible to the bishop moderator of the operations of the tribunal (*cf.* arts. 38-42 and 46 §1). Inasmuch as it is often impossible for the judicial vicar or his adjutant(s) to oversee personally all of the operations of a tribunal office and the docket of every case, an unnamed but often-appointed assistant to the judicial vicar has arisen. This "delegate of the judicial vicar" – often a canonist, perhaps with the title of "tribunal director" – functions with the broadest of mandates as auditor, sometimes as collegiate judge, and often as administrative superior of the other ministers of the tribunal. This is not a new kind of tribunal minister (in fact proscribed by article 37 of *Dignitas connubii*) but rather a far-ranging application of utilitarian possibilities. In such an office, judicial power is only delegated "for the purpose of carrying out acts preparatory to some decree or sentence" (art. 32 §1), but administrative authority connected to the office of the judicial vicar is more broadly shared.

Fourth, it must be noted that in many tribunals *Dignitas connubii* has not been used or has been under-used. Conversations with those responding on behalf of their tribunal offices have helped to explain this phenomenon.

From one perspective, this is not strange. Where a tribunal was using the procedural canon law correctly, the advent of *Dignitas connubii* meant that no change was needed. Indeed, fully half of the persons responding to the tribunal survey indicated no or only very minor modifications in their standard practices came about as a result of the 2005 instruction. One observed that the instruction "did not make a great deal of difference for us since our procedures were in line with the code"; another said "personnel roles did not change as we were already following the code slavishly" (*sic*)! In this regard most judicial vicars found *Dignitas connubii* helpful in that it provided a set of procedural standards against which a tribunal's operations could be fairly – and in timely manner – measured.

One major reason for the lack of significant impact is the different situation in law. When *Provida Mater Ecclesia* of 1936 was issued, the 1917 *Codex iuris canonici*[6]– the first such code of its kind – existed only in Latin, and in fact could not be translated into the vernacular; commentaries on its text, given the seminary setting which gave rise to them, also were more generally in Latin. These factors heightened the need for a vernacular *vade mecum* in order for the code's provisions to be more swiftly and surely implemented. In the modern setting in which *Dignitas connubii* finds itself, there is less of a need for this sort of aid because the revised *Code of Canon Law* of 1983[7] is available in the vernacular. The revised code itself has been exposed more comprehensively not only by recent, new commentaries – with much classic commentary also retaining its value – but also in the now more numerous canonical journals and other occasions of canonical study.

Let me be clear. In no case did I encounter any direct rejection of or express antipathy toward *Dignitas connubii*. Yes, in a few conversations one or another canonist did state a wish for some other provision which was not included in the final text of the instruction, and hardly can it be assumed that the present text of the law and ecclesiastical polity in implementing same can be perfect in every time and place. Tribunals in less developed parts of the world surely still have more difficulty in carrying out all of the prescriptions of the law, just as was the case prior to the publication of *Dignitas connubii* in 2005.

In fact and in closing, I note that a number of those responding used the opportunity of my questionnaire or interview to identify areas in which further procedural clarification or change may be needed.

One judicial vicar asked if the norm of *Dignitas connubii*'s article 2 could be "taken a step further," so that Orthodox law which is more restrictive than Catholic law could be used to find for invalidity due to defect of canonical form (*e.g.*, when an Orthodox marries before a non-Orthodox priest?).

No fewer than seven judicial vicars expressed longing for some eventual relaxation of the law requiring the parties to reside within the territory of the same conference of bishops in order for the tribunal where the petitioner has domicile to obtain permission to exercise its competence (art. 10 §1, 3° and c.

---

[6] *Codex Iuris Canonici Pii X Pontificis Maximi iussu digestus Benedicti Papae XV auctoritate promulgates* (Rome: Typis Polyglottis Vaticanis, 1917) *AAS* 9 (1917) 3-521; English translation in E. N. Peters, *The 1917 or Pio-Benedictine Code of Canon Law in English Translation with Extensive Scholarly Apparatus* (San Francisco: Ignatius Press, 2001).

[7] *Codex Iuris Canonici auctoritate Ioannis Pauli PP. II promulgates* (LEV, 1983) *AAS* 75 (1983) 1-320; English translation in *Code of Canon Law, Latin-English Edition, New English Translation* (Washington, DC: Canon Law Society of America, 1999).

1673, 3°). One area in which *Dignitas connubii* remains largely silent is in offering insight as to when malicious or frivolous activity on the part of a party (usually a respondent) exists, and how such a finding might affect the process (*e.g.*, could an appeal against an affirmative decision by a Catholic already remarried again "outside of the Church" give rise to a presumption of enmity toward the former spouse, if not malice).

A "national formulary book" was advised and requested by one judicial vicar. On the point of common forms *Dignitas connubii* is silent, but this does not mean such a project could not have value.

One judicial vicar complained that "occasionally we have found other tribunals unwilling or reluctant to fulfill rogatory requests" (art. 29), but the recourse a tribunal might have against this kind of recalcitrance is not specified in law.

Again, I wish to express my thanks to those busy tribunal personnel who took time away from their work to write and speak with me about the impact which *Dignitas connubii* had within their courts. I found in every place a commitment to implementing the law of the Church properly, and no little gratitude that *Dignitas connubii* has facilitated this.

Exemplars of the Survey Cover Letter and Questionnaire

June 3, 2010

Dear Judicial Vicar or Tribunal Director:

I am writing in the hopes that you could assist me with your experience and expertise.

At this fall's convention of the Canon Law Society of America in Buffalo, NY, I have been asked to present a seminar focusing on the impact of "the 2005 Instruction *Dignitas connubii* – Five Years After."

Dignitas connubii certainly has attracted a great deal of canonical attention since it was issued in 2005. Most of this has been careful analysis of its content. As an Instruction it has clarified canon law prescriptions, and developed and further specified how these are to be implemented (see can. 34, §1).

I was thinking of focusing, however, not so much on its content but on its actual application. What difference has it made? Has it proven useful to Tribunal ministers? What among its novelties have been implemented or ignored in actual praxis? In other words, my approach to this seminar will try to identify not so much the content but the impact of the Instruction in the Church today.

Accordingly, I am hoping that you could help provide some insights into this. The enclosed brief questionnaire may serve as a guide. You will note that it is very general: please feel free to offer other ideas you might have from your experience and Tribunal situation. And please share this request with others in your Tribunal whose knowledge and reflections would be helpful, particularly if your office deals with cases in more than one instance.

Neither your name nor that of your (arch)diocese or Tribunal will appear in my spoken or written remarks. I will be back in touch with you if something you share needs to be better understood by me or if it seems advisable if an item or idea from you needs some kind of special consideration.

Please send your ideas to me via mail at 412 North Street, Baton Rouge, LA 70802-5496, USA, via fax to 225-287-5929, or by email at pcounce@diobr.org (and of course if you would like a copy of the seminar presentation, I will be happy to send you one).

With my thanks already for your help, I remain

Sincerely yours,

Dignitas connubii – Five Years After

(Please indicate if your answers refer to your Tribunal's work in Second Instance, if any; otherwise it will be presumed that only First Instance work is meant.)

1. How were personnel of your Tribunal – as well as parish ministers who assist with Tribunal work – informed about *Dignitas connubii* when it was published in 2005, and how did these persons become familiar with its provisions?

2. Within your Tribunal, please describe any modifications to your standard or prior practices which were made due to the provisions of *Dignitas connubii*?

   a. Regarding personnel: Has *Dignitas Connubii* led to any changes in the way personnel and roles within the Tribunal are identified and carried out?

   b. Regarding materials: Have any new formularies or forms been created as a result of *Dignitas Connubii*? Have any of your formularies or forms been modified to correspond with its provisions? Please indicate what these changes were (attaching sample formularies would be helpful).

   c. Regarding procedure: Has *Dignitas Connubii* resulted in any additional steps being added to your standard process? Have there been any modifications in the way your typical course of action in a marriage nullity trial proceeds? Are there things you now specifically look for or consider which were not previously? (*E.g.*, relative to venue, incidental questions, etc.)

   d. Regarding jurisprudence: Have the provisions of *Dignitas Connubii* occasioned any change in your application of the law to the facts, or to your Court's evaluation of evidence? (*E.g.*, jurisprudential standards mentioned in the Instruction, etc.) Has the manner and contribution of the psychological expert changed in any way?

   e. Regarding follow up to trials: Have post-trial activities or institutes been changed or affected in any way by the provisions of *Dignitas Connubii*? (*E.g.*, relative to transmittal of cases to higher Instance, prohibitions imposed at the conclusion of the trial, etc.)

3. Were there any changes made in the above areas as a result of *Dignitas Connubii*, but which have now been rescinded or changes again in light of your Tribunal's experience?

4. Are any more modifications foreseen in your Tribunal as a result of

Dignitas Connubii? Have any of its provisions proven to be inadvisable, too unwieldy, or even impossible for your Court to adopt?

5. Is there anything further regarding *Dignitas Connubii* and its implementation in your Tribunal that you think is relevant? You may, if you wish, indicate areas in which you still think more direction or specification from the Holy See is warranted regarding Tribunal ministry.

And thank you for taking the time to help!!

SEMINAR

NAVIGATING THE VACANT SEE

Doctor Barbara Anne Cusack

I. Introduction

My own personal experience over the last eight years informs part of this seminar. My diocese experienced one vacant see as a result of a canon 401 §1 resignation with the bishop reaching age seventy-five. We were able to anticipate and prepare for this three-month vacancy. Six and a half years later we experienced a vacant see as a result of a transfer of the diocesan bishop. This vacancy was unanticipated and lasted eight months. Neither vacancy was as long as some dioceses have experienced but many of the same issues are relevant regardless of the length of the vacancy.

This seminar is not intended as an historical overview; it is not a brilliant canonical analysis; it is not a study of controverted issues (with one exception as we will see later). It is simply a practical review from a practitioner who welcomes various perspectives from others' experiences. We will be bringing together relevant canons from various parts of the code.

II. Circumstances Leading to a Vacant See

We begin with canon 416:

> The episcopal see is vacant upon the death of the diocesan bishop, resignation accepted by the Roman Pontiff, transfer, or privation made known to the bishop.

Let us examine each scenario:

A. Death

While it is clear when that actually happens, it may be unanticipated and sudden. So the diocese and its staff are left not only with the need to plan a proper funeral for their diocesan bishop and deal with the attendant grief, but also with the need to put in place the mechanics to handle the vacancy of the see. Therefore, it is not a bad idea to have some outlines in advance regarding how the process will unfold in every chancery or canonical affairs office.

B. Resignation

1) There is the expected resignation of canon 401 §1:

> A diocesan bishop who has completed the seventy-fifth year of age is requested to present his resignation from office to the Supreme Pontiff, who will make provision after he has examined all the circumstances.

Obviously we know the ages of our diocesan bishops! Therefore, we should be able to anticipate in advance when a seventy-fifth birthday is approaching. What we do not know is the length of time between the submission of the letter of resignation and notification of its acceptance. There does not seem to be a formula for calculating that time frame. However, advance preparation for a vacancy is still appropriate. How much advance preparation can be done may be dependant on the mindset and attitude of the diocesan bishop toward his own resignation.

What is some of the advance preparation that can be completed?

Diocesan Profile for the Nuncio:

When a vacancy is anticipated, the nuncio may request from the current bishop of a diocese a report on the conditions and needs of the diocese. Broad consultation within the diocese is encouraged with regard to the needs of the diocese. There can be group consultations about the profile of the diocese but not a discussion of the names of candidates. The profile will include response to specific questions and analysis of areas of diocesan life that are provided by the nuncio. The profile outline is quite similar to the quinquennial report topics.

For example:

Mass attendance and sacramental reception – included here could be any trends that have developed, evangelization efforts that are underway, as well as any areas of concern such as declining numbers of marriages celebrated in the Church.

Spiritual life of priests and religious, their numbers and morale – it would be important to highlight the presence of major superiors of institutes of consecrated life and effective working relationships with religious based on *Mutuae relationes.*

Continuing formation for clergy – institutions in accord with canon 384 that are provided for clergy ongoing formation, any special concerns about care for senior priests could be included here.

Higher education – included here would be not only any Catholic institutions of higher learning and the applications of *Ex corde ecclesiae*, but also the means of pastoral care provided at secular and state educational institutions.

Permanent deacons – their presence and role in the diocese as well as the means of formation provided.

Vocations – trends with regard to numbers and age of applicants.

Diocesan seminary (if applicable) – the size and viability of the diocesan seminary along with any special concerns should be highlighted. (If there is no diocesan seminary, information about where seminarians are sent for priestly formation would be included.)

Pastoral life – statistics and analysis of the current situation and projections for the future, parish pastoral and finance councils and other lay involvement in parish life.

Charity and social work – not only diocesan sponsored outreach such as Catholic Charities, but other social ministry needs of the diocese such as prisons or juvenile facilities should be mentioned along with the role of the diocese in providing pastoral care there.

Liturgy – any special liturgical situations should be included, such as the scope of use of the extraordinary form within the diocese or catechetical formation for the use of the revised missal.

Needs of any ethnic groups(s) – special language skills that would be useful could be mentioned along with the use of the services of international priests.

Education (schools and religious education) – any special challenges or initiatives such as school funding should be noted.

Diocesan administration – summary information about the size and structure of the diocesan curia, special commissions, or other administrative support systems such as an autonomous pious foundation would be useful information.

Presbyteral council and pastoral council – as assessment regarding the use that has been made of these advisory bodies should be included.

State of the tribunal – not only statistics about matrimonial cases, but also information about any penal trials that are underway or pending with the Congregation for the Doctrine of the Faith would be important.

Finances – included here should be not only the financial stability of the diocese but also any significant issues on the horizon as well as the activity of the finance council.

The preparation of the profile can be accomplished in a variety of ways. For example, a survey on the state of the diocese can be prepared to obtain input from the presbyteral council and pastoral council as well as diocesan staff and other leadership personnel. (See sample in appendix A.) When preparing the profile, its purpose in providing the nuncio with a clear and accurate picture of the state of the diocese should shape its preparation.

2) Voluntary Resignation

In addition to the resignation asked of the diocesan bishop when he reaches age seventy-five, the code also provides for a voluntary resignation for other reasons in canon 401 §2:

> A diocesan bishop who has become less able to fulfill his office because of ill health or some other grave cause is earnestly requested to present his resignation from office.

Such a voluntary resignation may be one that is anticipated after a period of declining health or it may be unexpected as in the case of recent resignations in cases of sexual abuse of minors. Again, the resignation does not take effect until it is accepted and notification made, but the circumstances may dictate a more expeditious response. These situations may be ones where an apostolic administrator is appropriate and one is appointed by the pope or a new diocesan bishop is named immediately.

C. Transfer

When a diocesan bishop is being transferred there are two stages:

First there is the notice of the transfer and then the taking possession of the new diocese. These are two different events with different effects.

The announcement is made of the transfer but this notice does not result in the vacancy of the see. Rather, there is a change in the status of the diocesan bishop in his current diocese. It is with the taking possession of the new diocese that there is a significant impact on the former diocese. Canon 418 §1 provides the timeframe:

> Upon certain notice of transfer, a bishop must claim the diocese to which he has been transferred and take canonical possession of it within two months;

The canon also states the effect:

> On the day that he takes possession of the new diocese, however, the diocese from which he has been transferred (*a qua*) is vacant.

With the transfer of a diocesan bishop we need to look at what happens during this interval between notice and taking possession. For the diocese, it is not a vacant see. Therefore, even if there is a coadjutor bishop in place, he does not yet assume the office of diocesan bishop. For the diocesan bishop, there is a change in his status as stated in canon 418 §2:

> Upon certain notice of transfer until the canonical possession of the new diocese, a transferred bishop in the diocese from which he has been transferred:
>
> > 1° obtains the power of a diocesan administrator and is bound by the obligations of the same; . . .
> >
> > 2° receives the entire remuneration proper to this office.

The restrictions on the governance of a diocese by a diocesan administrator, which we will see in a moment, also affect the diocesan bishop during this interim period.

D. Deprivation

The final way a see may become vacant is through deprivation. Deprivation is an expiatory penalty as defined in canon 1336, 2° – in this case, it involves removal from power and office and, as a penal action, it must involve some criminal act that calls for punishment.

Canon 1338 §1 (citing the applicable parts) notes:

> The privations and prohibitions listed in can. 1336 §1, n. 2 never affect powers or offices which are not subject to the power of the superior who establishes the penalty.

Therefore, the deprivation of the power and office of the diocesan bishop must be done by the pope as he controls the office. Again, deprivation is penal in nature as noted in canon 196:

> §2 Privation from office, namely, a penalty for a delict, can be done only according to the norm of law.
> §2 Privation takes effect according to the prescripts of the canons on penal law.

The code cites the following delicts as punishable by privation:

- Solicitation in the confessional (c. 1387)
- Abuse of ecclesiastical power or function (c. 1389)
- Attempted marriage by a cleric (c. 1394)
- Grave violation of the obligation of residence (c. 1396)
- Homicide, or forceful or fraudulent abduction, imprisonment, mutilation or gravely wounding a person (c. 1397)

So, if we are in the arena of deprivation from the office of diocesan bishop, the Apostolic See will be the primary agent.

III. Governance Models *sede vacante*

A. Extraordinary situation

Appointment of Apostolic Administrator

The norms on the vacant see do not anticipate a situation in which an administrator is appointed to a diocese by the Apostolic See. The term "apostolic administrator" in the code refers to the situation in canon 371:

> §2 An apostolic administration is a certain portion of the people of God which is not yet erected as a diocese by the Supreme Pontiff due to special and particularly grave reasons and whose pastoral care is entrusted to an apostolic administrator who governs it in the name of the Supreme Pontiff.

During a vacancy a diocese does not cease to be a diocese. It is not an apostolic administration.

Therefore, the appointment by the Apostolic See of someone to govern the diocese *sede vacante*, using the title "apostolic administrator" would have to be seen as extraordinary in nature. There may be circumstances as noted before when, with a sudden resignation of a diocesan bishop, or a time of internal turmoil in a diocese, that the Holy Father may make the decision to appoint someone directly and use the title: "apostolic administrator."

In my opinion such an action should be rare and exceptional. We have no explanation why the decision to circumvent the ordinary process of handling a vacant see is made absent unusual and grave circumstances.

B. Ordinary situation

Election of Diocesan Administrator – Timing and Process

As soon as the see is vacant, and until the diocesan administrator is named, the auxiliary bishop assumes governance of the diocese; if there is more than one auxiliary, the one who is senior by promotion does so; if there are no auxiliary bishops, the college of consultors assumes governance. Within eight days of the see becoming vacant, the election of the diocesan administrator by the college of consultors must take place.

Failure of a college of consultors to fulfill this obligation results in the appointment of the diocesan administrator by the metropolitan. If the metropolitan see is vacant or both a suffragan see and the metropolitan see are vacant, this appointment of the diocesan administrator falls to the senior suffragan bishop.

The auxiliary bishop or senior auxiliary bishop, as the interim diocesan leader, has the responsibility to convene the consultors within this time period. There should be written documentation that he has given notice of this meeting (See sample in appendix B).

In those situations where there are no auxiliary bishops, the college itself assumes the governance of the diocese. The section of the code dealing with the vacant see does not specify how they are to be convened and who has the responsibility to do so. However, in the norms on the college itself, canon 502 §2 gives us guidance:

> The diocesan Bishop presides over the college of consultors. When a see is impeded or vacant, however, the one who temporarily takes the place of the bishop or, if he has not yet been appointed, the priest who is senior in ordination in the college of consultors presides.

This provision may be one that should be restated in the diocesan statutes on the college of consultors noting this priest's responsibility to convene the college for the election of the diocesan administrator and preside over that election.

We move then to the election itself. It must be conducted as a canonical election or the results are invalid. Canons 165-178 are to be observed (See appendix C).

Prior to the election the qualifications required for election as diocesan administrator (canon 425) should be reviewed:

- Priest
- Completed his thirty-fifth year of age
- Outstanding for doctrine and prudence

One cannot serve as both the diocesan finance officer and the diocesan administrator at the same time (canon 423 §2). Therefore, if the diocesan finance officer meets the qualifications and is elected, he has two choices (although only one seems explicit in the code) – he may refuse to accept the election or he must resign as diocesan finance officer. If he resigns as diocesan finance officer the finance council is to elect a temporary diocesan finance officer (canon 423 §2).

Once the diocesan administrator is elected and accepts, he makes the profession of faith and takes the oath of fidelity in the presence of the college of consultors in accord with canon 833, 4°.

Notification of the election is made to the nuncio by the one elected.

IV. Exercise of Governance *Sede Vacante*

A. Effect on office-holders /councils /other bodies

Various tables and outlines have been prepared to demonstrate the impact of a vacant see on various individual office holders and canonical bodies (See appendix D). These outlines may also be useful as briefing resources for communication purposes as well.

B. Permitted /forbidden /conditioned acts

The diocesan administrator does not have full governance authority over the diocese during the vacancy. Some acts are permitted but others are forbidden or conditioned. They may be conditioned either by the requirement of consultation or consent or may be restricted until the passage of a certain time period. Again charts and outlines have been provided to demonstrate the role of the diocesan administrator (See appendices E and F).

C. Controversial Issue

I promised we would have at least one controverted issue. Question: May diaconal ordinations occur *sede vacante*?

What is the source of the controversy? Ordination to the diaconate results in incardination.

We can look at one opinion first:

Incardination can occur *sede vacante* only if the see has been vacant for a year and the college of consultors gives consent. Therefore, since incardination results from diaconal ordination, absent some prior authorization, deacon ordinations cannot be celebrated when the see is vacant.

Now we can turn to another opinion:

The *sede vacante* incardination that is forbidden (until one year and with consent) is the administrative act of incardination found in canon 267. The incardination that arises from diaconal ordination is an *ipso iure* incardination. Nowhere among the acts forbidden *sede vacante* do we find diaconal ordination. The issuance of dimissorial letters is addressed *sede vacante* – they can be issued by the diocesan administrator with the consent of the college of consultors (c. 1018 §1, 2°). Since the issuance of dimissorial letters is related to ordination to the diaconate, it only seems reasonable that these letters are issued if there is an ordination anticipated.

V. Post *Sede Vacante*

After the new diocesan bishop has taken possession of the diocese, a number of actions are needed to bring the diocese back to its fully functional state. Vicars general and episcopal vicars need to be appointed to office (and issued episcopal mandates if applicable). The judicial vicar needs to be confirmed in office. The presbyteral council must be established within one year by means of the issuance of a decree of establishment and promulgation of its statutes. The pastoral council, while established at the discretion of new bishop, because of the important role it plays in pastoral planning and vision for the diocese would ordinarily also be established by the issuance of a decree of establishment and promulgation of its statutes.

If pastoral administrators were appointed *sede vacante* the diocesan bishop should consider the timing of their appointment as pastors since their terms of office, if applicable, begin with the new appointment.

VI. Concluding Remarks

We navigate best, in choppy waters or calm, when we chart the course in advance, coordinate the work of an able crew, and keep our eyes firmly fixed on the horizon ahead. Perhaps these remarks and materials may be of some assistance should you need to embark on the voyage of navigating a vacant see.

APPENDIX A

DIOCESE OF METROPOLIS

1. List three (3) strengths in each of the following aspects of the Diocese of Metropolis:

- diocesan organization/structures

  ____

  ____

- parish organization/structures

  ____

  ____

- ministry of the bishop

  ____

  ____

- liturgical and sacramental life

  ____

  ____

- education

  ____

  ____

- clergy

  ____

  ____

- response to societal needs

  ____

  ____

2. List any current challenges /opportunities or ones you see on the horizon in each of these same aspects of diocesan life.

- diocesan organization/structures

  ____

  ____

- parish organization/structures

- ministry of the bishop

- liturgical and sacramental life

- education

- clergy

- response to societal needs

3. If you had to describe the Diocese of Metropolis to someone from another part of the U.S., what would you say? (Please confine your response to 25-50 words.)

4. If that person came to visit, what would you want them to see or experience of the Diocese of Metropolis?

For additional comments, please attach a separate page.

Name (optional)

APPENDIX B

College of Consultors

Notice of Meeting

Most Reverend Auxiliary Bishop
Most Reverend Auxiliary Bishop
Reverend
Reverend
Reverend
Reverend
Reverend
Very Reverend
Very Reverend
Reverend
Very Reverend

On [DATE], the above-listed members of the College of Consultors were notified of a meeting to be held on [DATE] at the Diocesan Pastoral Center at 1:30 p.m. This notification was made by Bishop [NAME], senior auxiliary bishop.

With the installation of Bishop [NAME] to the See of Metropolis on [DATE], the Diocese of City will be a vacant see and the meeting of the Consultors will include the canonical election of the diocesan administrator.

____
Chancellor

____
Date

APPENDIX C

ELECTION OF DIOCESAN ADMINISTRATOR

Election conducted according to canonical norms [cc. 165-178]:

- all those eligible to vote in the election, i.e. all Consultors, must be notified of meeting date, time, and place (SAMPLE NOTICE)
- the senior Auxiliary Bishop presides over the election
- a majority of those eligible to vote must be present for the election
- voting by proxy is not permitted
- there may be only one vote per elector; an abstention counts as a valid vote
- two tellers from among the Consultors are designated prior to the election
- the ballots are to be secret
- the tellers are to collect the ballots and examine them before the senior Auxiliary Bishop to determine that the number of ballots corresponds to the number of electors, to count the votes, and to announce the number of votes each person has received
- the one receiving an absolute majority of votes (i.e., one more than half the votes cast) is declared elected by pronouncement of the senior Auxiliary Bishop [c. 119]
- after two indecisive ballots, a vote is taken between the two individuals with the most votes, or if there are more than two, the two senior in age; the one receiving the most votes is declared elected by pronouncement of the senior Auxiliary Bishop [c. 119]
- after a third ballot, if a tie remains, the one who is senior in age is considered elected and so pronounced by the Auxiliary Bishop [c. 119]
- the entire electoral process is to be committed to writing by the one acting as secretary at the election, signed by that same secretary and the Auxiliary Bishop along with the two tellers; these minutes are to be transmitted to the diocesan archives

Auxiliary Bishop immediately notifies the one elected and informs him that he has eight days within which to communicate back whether or not he accepts the election; if the Auxiliary Bishop is elected he declares immediately or within eight days his acceptance of the election; if the one elected does not accept, the Auxiliary Bishop is to reconvene the College of Consultors within one month of notification of non-acceptance and repeat the electoral process [c. 177].

Diocesan Administrator immediately informs the Apostolic See of his election [c. 422].

APPENDIX D

STATUS OF DIOCESAN OFFICE HOLDERS / ADVISORY BODIES

SEDE VACANTE

OFFICE / ADVISORY BODY	STATUS
Vicar(s) General	Cease from office; auxiliary bishop ceases from office of Vicar but retains powers and faculties attached to the office
Judicial Vicar	Remains in office; needs confirmation in office by new bishop
Finance Officer	Remains in office for full five-year term with removal only for grave cause and having heard consultors and finance council
Chancellor	Remains in office; removal only with consent of consultors
Deans (Vicars Forane)	Remain in office for duration of terms
College of Consultors	Remains in place and assumes additional governance responsibilities
Finance Council	Remains in place
Presbyteral Council	Ceases to exist; its functions are assumed by the College of Consultors; must be reestablished within a year by new bishop
Pastoral Council	Ceases to exist; reestablished at discretion of new bishop

APPENDIX E

ROLE OF DIOCESAN ADMINISTRATOR

SEDE VACANTE

I. Canonical norm

Canon 427 §1: A diocesan administrator is bound by the obligations and possesses the power of a diocesan bishop, excluding those matters which are excepted by their nature or by the law itself.

> §2: When he has accepted election, the diocesan administrator obtains power and no other configuration is required, without prejudice to the obligation mentioned in canon 833, 4° [Profession of Faith in the presence of the College of Consultors].

II. General Principle

Upon election, the diocesan administrator acts in the stead of a diocesan bishop unless the law or the nature of the act provides otherwise. [Nature of the act: if the diocesan administrator is not a bishop, he cannot perform any sanctifying functions flowing from episcopal orders.]

III. Acts Excluded Completely (*Ipso Iure*)

1. approval of diocesan associations of the faithful
2. entrusting a parish to a clerical religious institute or society of apostolic life
3. removal of judicial vicar or adjutant judicial vicar(s)
4. issuance of dimissorial letters to anyone denied orders by the diocesan bishop
5. removal, destruction, or alteration of any curial documents
6. access to the secret archives (except out of true necessity)

IV. Acts Requiring Consent of College of Consultors

1. issuance of dimissorial letters for ordination
2. removal of chancellor or other notaries

V. Acts After One Year of Vacancy with Consent of Consultors

1. excardination, incardination, or temporary transfer of priest/deacon to another diocese

VI. Acts After One Year of Vacancy

1. appointment of pastors

APPENDIX F

GOVERNANCE OF A DIOCESE BY A DIOCESAN ADMINISTRATOR

FORBIDDEN ACTS

- Approval of diocesan associations of the faithful
- Entrusting a parish to a clerical religious institute or society of apostolic life
- Removal of judicial vicar or adjutant judicial vicar(s)
- Issuance of dimissorial letters to anyone denied orders by the diocesan bishop
- Removal, destruction, or alteration of any curial documents
- Access to the secret archives (except out of true necessity)

ACTS REQUIRING CONSENT OF COLLEGE OF CONSULTORS

- Issuance of dimissorial letters for ordination
- Removal of chancellor or other notaries

ACTS REQUIRING CONSENT OF CONSULTORS AFTER ONE YEAR

- Excardination, incardination, or temporary transfer of cleric to another diocese

ACTS PERMITTED AFTER ONE YEAR

- Appointment of pastors

NIHIL INNOVETUR

- No parish mergers
- No new building projects unless in process
- No alienation of property unless in process
- Other major projects / initiatives

VACATED OFFICES

- Vicar General / Episcopal Vicar

ADVISORY BODIES

- Presbyteral Council ceases to exist
    - Acts requiring consultation / consent are referred to College of Consultors
- Pastoral Council ceases to exist
- Finance Council continues in place
- College of Consultors continues in place

SEMINAR

THE NOTION OF MORAL CERTITUDE WITH PARTICULAR APPLICATION TO THE ACTS MENTIONED IN CANON 1682 §2 (*CCEO*, C. 1368 §2)

Mister William L. Daniel

I am honored to have been asked to speak about the notion of moral certitude at this convention. This is a topic of great significance to all canonists—since it is a general concept of the canonical science—and to tribunal officials in particular since it sets the tone for the entire judicial process in canon law. I am preceded by Fathers Arthur Caron, OMI and Dennis Burns, who discussed moral certitude at the CLSA conventions of 1958 and 1975, respectively.[1] The present seminar paper is the first to treat the topic of moral certitude subsequent to the promulgation of the 1983 Code at the convention of the CLSA and, as far as I know, the CCLS.

The present seminar is for me an occasion to propose a few reflections on the notion of moral certitude, both in an historical and theoretical way and in a concrete and practical way. In the short time allotted us, we will recall the notion of judicial moral certitude, briefly illustrate the manner in which it informs the whole process, and finally explain the nature of the certitude that judges must reach when they are in a position to confirm an affirmative sentence that first declares the nullity of marriage.

While the standard of moral certitude applies to every kind of trial in the Church, we will use examples from marriage nullity trials, since these constitute the majority in diocesan tribunals and since the second part of this paper deals exclusively with the allege nullity of marriage.

I. Moral Certitude in General

A. The History of Canonical Moral Certitude—in Brief

Under the influence of ancient Roman and Germanic procedural law, the canonical tradition has demanded of the judge the standard of certitude before issuing a judicial sentence in favor of the allegation. This is detected as early as the middle of the first millennium; for example, Pope St. Gregory the Great (590-604) wrote: "It is quite serious and unbecoming that a certain decision (*certa sententia*) be issued about a dubious matter."[2] Neither the precise

---

[1] Arthur Caron, "The Concept of Moral Certitude in Canonical Decisions," *The Jurist* 19 (1959) 12-28; Dennis J. Burns, "Moral Certitude," *CLSA Proceedings* 37 (1975) 38-47.

[2] "Gravis satis est et indecens, ut in re dubia certa detur sententia" (C. XI, q. 3, c. 74). See also the *dictum Gratiani* at C. XXX, q. 5, c. 11. All translations (except those of

character of this judicial certitude nor even the term "moral certitude" can be found in the *Corpus iuris canonici*. Instead of articulating principles about the conviction and mind of the judge, the *Corpus iuris canonici* concentrated on the weight of different kinds of proof, and it presumed that judges knew that they would be accountable before God for any lack of truth or justice in their decisions.[3] Moral certitude began to be discussed by moralists and canonists in the 16th and 17th centuries, and it was finally mentioned in some procedural law from the late 19th century. In two Instructions of the Roman Curia dealing with the discipline of clerics, it was stated that "moral certitude" was required before imposing a penalty, "with every reasonable doubt to the contrary being removed."[4]

During the era of Decretalists, it was commonly accepted that different kinds of causes demanded different degrees of certitude. In contentious causes of minor importance, it was not necessary that there be full proof (*plena probatio*) in order for the judge to decide in favor of the petitioner; partial proof (*semi-plena probatio*) was sufficient. In other words, for these causes the judge could decide on the basis of probability. Nevertheless, in criminal causes and contentious causes of greater importance, the judge could only decide in favor of the petitioner if full proof was obtained. And full proof has always been required in order to declare a marriage null.[5]

With the promulgation of the 1917 code, it was established that moral certitude was required for every kind of cause (c. 1869, §1).[6]

B. The Notion of Moral Certitude

The basic notion of moral certitude has been most eloquently and authoritatively articulated in the Servant of God Pius XII's 1942 allocution to the Tribunal of the Roman Rota; he made similar, abbreviated remarks in his 1941 allocution to the Rota and in his 1954 message to the association of Catholic Italian Jurists.[7] His teaching was emphasized and elaborated upon by

---

Dignitas connubii) are the author's.

[3] Edward A. McCarthy, *De certitudine morali quæ in judicis animo ad sententiæ pronuntiationem requiritur* (Rome: Catholic Book Agency, 1948) 9, 13, 16-17, 19, 21-23, 27-28, 30-31; Zenon Grocholewski, "La certezza morale come chiave di lettura delle norme processuali," *Ius Ecclesiæ* 9 (1997) 423-424.

[4] Sacred Congregation of Bishops and Regulars, Instructio *Sacra hæc*, June 11, 1880, no. 16, *Codicis iuris canonici fontes*, ed. Pietro Gasparri, vol. 4 (Rome: Typis polyglottis Vaticanis, 1926) 1023; Sacred Congregation for the Propagation of the Faith, Instructio *Cum magnopere*, 1883, no. 16, ibid., vol. 7 (1935) 477. Moral certitude was also mentioned in an 1883 Instruction of the Sacred Congregation of the Holy Office, Instructio ad Episcopos rituum orientalium *Quemadmodum matrimonii foedus*, 1883, no. 42, ibid., vol. 4 (1926) 406, 407.

[5] McCarthy, *De certitudine morali*, 43-47.

[6] Péter Erdö, "La certezza morale nella pronuncia del giudice. Problemi attuali," *Periodica* 87 (1998) 91, note 30.

[7] Pius XII, allocutio, October 3, 1941, *AAS* 33 (1941) 421-426 [hereafter "Pius XII, 1941 allocutio"]; idem, allocutio ad Prælatos Auditores ceterosque officiales et

the Servant of God John Paul II in his 1980 allocution to the Roman Rota.[8] Based on these speeches, as well as jurisprudence and canonical doctrine, moral certitude can be explained in terms of doubt and in terms of the fear of erring (*formido errandi*). Let us consider the notion from these two perspectives.[9]

A judge is not to declare that the petitioner's claim is proven if objective doubt remains about the matter. Pius XII thus defines moral certitude in terms of doubt; consolidating all of his definitory statements, moral certitude can be defined as *the adhesion of the judge's mind to the petitioner's claim, excluding every founded and prudent positive doubt that the claim is true*. He distinguishes

---

administros Tribunalis S. Romanæ Rotæ necnon eiusdem advocatos et procuratores, October 1, 1942: *AAS* 34 (1942) 338-343 [hereafter "Pius XII, 1942 allocutio"]; Nuntius, December 5, 1954: *AAS* 47 (1955) 60-71.

[8] John Paul II, allocutio ad Tribunalis Sacræ Romanæ Rotæ Decanum, Prælatos Auditores, Officiales et Advocatos, novo Litibus iudicandis ineunte anno: de vertitate iustitiæ matre, February 4, 1980: *AAS* 72 (1980) 172-178 [hereafter "John Paul II, 1980 allocutio"].

[9] On the notions which follow, see the following in the pontifical Magisterium: Pius XII, 1941 allocutio, nn. 1-2, 422-424; idem, 1942 allocutio, nn. 1 and 3, 339-340; John Paul II, 1980 allocutio, nn. 4-6, 174-176. In jurisprudence, see, e.g., Tribunal of the Roman Rota (TRR), Definitive Sentence *c.* Bruno, May 30, 1986, no. 9, *RRT Decisiones* 78 (1986) 356; idem, Definitive Sentence *c.* Pompedda, November 30, 1990, no. 2, unpublished, cited in *RRT Decisiones* 88 (1996) 633; idem, Definitive Sentence *c.* Civili, March 22, 1995, no. 12, *RRT Decisiones* 87 (1995) 214; idem, Definitive Sentence *c.* Faltin, March 20, 1996, no. 14, *RRT Decisiones* 88 (1996) 286-287. In canonical doctrine, see, e.g., Felix Capello, *Summa iuris canonici in usum scholarum concinnata*, vol. 3 (Rome: Universitas Gregoriana, 1948) 255, no. 307; Caron, "The Concept of Moral Certitude," 15, 18-21, 25; Carmelo de Diego-Lora, "Title VII. The Pronouncements of the Judge," *Exegetical Commentary on the Code of Canon Law*, Gratianus Series, vol. IV/2 (Montréal: Wilson & Lafleur, 2004) 1460-1462; Orio Giacchi, "La certezza morale nella pronuncia del giudice ecclesiastico," *Ius Populi Dei. Miscellanea in honorem Raymundi Bidagor*, vol. 2 (Rome: Università Gregoriana Editrice, 1972) 607-611; Tommaso Giussani, *Discrezionalità del giudice nella valutazione delle prove,* [Studi Giuridici 1] (Vatican City: LEV, 1977) 130; Franz Hürth, "Allocutio S. Pontificis ad S. R. Rotam. De certitudine morali in processibus iudicialibus," *Periodica* 31 (1942) 360-363, nn. 3-7; Michele Lega and Vittorio Bartoccetti, *Commentarius in iudicia ecclesiastica iuxta Codicem iuris canonici*, vol. 2 (Rome: Anonima Libraria Cattolica Italiana, 1939) 934, no. 2; Joaquín Llobell, "La certezza morale nel processo canonico matrimoniale," *Il diritto ecclesiastico* 109 (1998-I) 758-765; idem, "Oggettività e soggettività nella valutazione giudiziaria delle prove," *Quaderni di diritto ecclesiale* 14 (2001) 396-398; McCarthy, *De certitudine morali*, 66-68, 86; Mario F. Pompedda, "Decision-Sentence in Marriage Trials: of the Concept and Principles for Rendering an Ecclesiastical Sentence," *Quaderno Studio Rotale* 5 (1990) 87-88; Giovanni Torre, *Processus matrimonialis*, 3rd ed. (Naples: M. d'Auria, 1956) 344, citing a February 3, 1949 Rotal sentence *c.* Staffa. For a particularly philosophical approach, see María del Mar Martín García, "Aproximación al concepto de 'moralis certitudo' del canon 1608 del *CIC* en relación con las sentencias declarativas de nulidad de vínculo matrimonial," *Escritos en honor de Javier Hervada. Ius Canonicum: Revista del Instituto Martín de Azpilcueta*, special volume (Pamplona: Universdad de Navarra, 1999) 474-478.

this certitude from two other kinds of judicial convictions: absolute certitude and probability (quasi-certitude). Absolute certitude is that conviction of the mind which excludes any *possible* doubt; if one had the capacity to have all knowledge of a given matter (which is usually not the case), absolute certitude would allow one to be 100% certain that the matter is true to the exclusion of any possible alternative conclusion. Probability is a conviction which is uncertain since it coexists with doubt. Absolute certitude is not required (and, as we said, frequently not possible), and probability is insufficient.

Authors recognize that there are two principal kinds of prudent doubt.[10] First, doubt could arise from a positive argument at odds with the conclusion toward which the judge is tending. This argument could be proposed by a public or private party or an advocate, or it could be proposed simply by the judge's own reflection on the law and the facts. For example, while a party seems to have entered marriage being in error about a quality that was directly and principally intended (c. 1097, §2), the *criterium reactionis* was not fulfilled, since the allegedly erring party remained in the common life. In one cause judged before the Rota, the woman-petitioner not only remained in the marriage after discovering the missing quality (viz., that her husband had a doctorate) but she helped him obtain this quality.[11] Second, doubt could arise from an identifiable lack of some significant evidence which the judge reasonably thinks could contradict the conclusion indicated by the majority of the evidence. For example, in one cause of marriage nullity, the evidence was limited to the statements of the man-petitioner and his witnesses. It may be true that he tried his best to prove that the respondent was incapable of assuming the essential obligations of marriage, but prudent doubts remained in the mind of the judge—especially since the absent respondent's personality structure could not be analyzed, and there was no documentary evidence of her mental disorder.[12]

In addition to the presence or absence of doubt, a declaration of truth can also be described in terms of its freedom (or not) from error—understanding error as a mistaken judgment about what is true. While judges must be free of doubt when issuing a definitive sentence, they need not be free of error. For, when issuing the sentence, judges do so with the firm conviction that they are pronouncing what is the truth; but "to err is human," so the decision may be wrong. Judges know this. Does this mean that they should never claim to be morally certain, knowing their own human limitations? No. While we do err, we are capable of knowing what is true. Therefore, we are enjoined to set aside our fears, and proceed with conviction. Moral certitude therefore allows for the

[10] See Klaus Lüdicke and Ronny E. Jenkins, Dignitas connubii. *Norms and Commentary* (Alexandria, VA: CLSA, 2006) 398, no. 11; McCarthy, *De certitudine morali*, 86; Antoni Stankiewicz, "La certezza morale e la motivazione della sentenza," eds. Héctor Franceschi, Joaquín Llobell, and Miguel Á. Ortiz, *La nullità del matrimonio: temi processuali e sostantivi in occasione della* Dignitas connubii, Subsidia Canonica (Rome: Edizioni Università della Santa Croce, 2005) 240.

[11] TRR, Decree *c.* Civili, May 12, 1993, no. 7, *RRT Decreta* 11 (1993) 110.

[12] TRR, Decree *c.* Boccafola, January 19, 1995, no. 4a, *RRT Decreta* 13 (1995) 2.

fear about whether the sentence is possibly erroneous (*formido errandi*)—fear of hypothetical, unfounded contradictions. However, it does not allow for fear when there are concrete, positive reasons to think one may be in error;[13] judges who think they may be in error are not morally certain. And obviously, judges who know they are in error are not morally certain.

We have seen how there are different degrees of certitude—absolute, moral, quasi-; and the judge can neither insist on absolute certitude nor be satisfied with quasi-certitude. It is also true that there are degrees or moral certitude itself. These are not defined precisely; rather, they correspond to the gravity of the object of the trial. Pius XII said that "prudence can sometimes advise that, although there is not an express disposition of the law, in causes of graver significance the judge not be content with a low degree of certitude."[14] There is no universally recognized spectrum of the degrees of moral certitude; it is left to the prudence of the judge to decide what degree of moral certitude is sufficient in light of the gravity of the matter. I would suggest that the gravity of the matter corresponds to the objective intensity of the questions that pertain to the object of the trial—e.g., how complex or subtle the matter is, how serious the ecclesial and personal implications of the issues are, etc. All these questions must be resolved before judges can deem themselves to be morally certain.

We may all agree that the imposition of the most serious penalties are clearly among the most grave matters - such as dismissal from the clerical state, excommunication, or dismissal from a religious institute. Let there be no doubt, however, that the nullity of marriage is commonly recognized in doctrine and jurisprudence as a very grave matter (cf. c. 1425 §1, 1º).[15] It is a grave matter for two reasons. First, it pertains to the public good of the Church since it deals

---

[13] "With regard to the meaning of *formido* …, it is observed that 'the intellect in itself cannot properly have this fear: nevertheless, it can know the possibility of error, or the possibility of the opposite, and in this sense it is said to have the fear of the opposite, or knowledge of the opposite as being possibly true'" (Stankiewicz, "La certezza morale," 233, note 12, citing F. Morandini's *Critica*).

[14] Pius XII, 1942 allocutio, no. 5, 342.

[15] "… matters of the maximum gravity are causes concerning the validity of the matrimonial bond, in which the maximum public and private good, the spiritual and temporal good, are called into question" (TRR, Definitive Sentence *c.* Staffa, June 3, 1949, no. 3, cited in Grocholewski, "La certezza morale," 437, note 67). See also Piero Antonio Bonnet, "De iudicis sententia ac de certitudine morali," *Periodica* 75 (1986) 97; William L. Daniel, "The Ethical Dimension of the Role of the Ecclesiastical Judge in the Rotal Allocutions of John Paul II," *Studia canonica* 40 (2006) 78-79, 90-92; Henricus Flatten, "Qua libertate iudex ecclesiasticus probationes appretiare possit et debeat," *Apollinaris* 33 (1960) 202-204; Juan José García Faílde, "Garantías procesales para el hallazgo de la verdad en el proceso canónico," *Cuestiones básicas de derecho procesal canónico*, XII Jornadas de la Asociación Española de Canonistas (Madrid, 22-24 abril 1992), ed. Julio Manzanares (Salamanca: Universidad Pontificia, 1993) 55; Giacchi, "La certezza morale," 615; Ignacio Gordon, "De nimia processuum matrimonialium duratione. Factum – Causæ – Remedia," *Periodica* 58 (1969) 719, no. 274 and 722, no. 284; McCarthy, *De certitudine morali*, 89-93; Mario F. Pompedda, "Il giudice ecclesiastico," *Quaderni dello Studio Rotale* 13 (2003) 32.

with the validity of a sacrament and the stability of marriage and the family—the fundamental cell of the ecclesial society. And second, in causes dealing with a defect of consent, it is objectively very difficult to prove that a person's consent is null. I find this to be illustrated by Fr. Wojciech Kowal, OMI in his very interesting study on the use of logical reasoning in the process of reaching moral certitude. He writes:

> The question of validity of a marriage ... is placed in the realm of interpretive reality. As far as facts are concerned, one can say that, for instance, a person's external behavior shows some symptoms of a psychic disorder. There is, however, no direct way of proceeding from stating the fact of the presence of symptoms of a disorder to concluding that the marriage is invalid. For one can pronounce directly on the existence of symptoms of the disorder on the basis of some external evidence, but proving the effect of the disorder on the act of marriage consent ... requires a structured process of reasoning. For the fact of validity of marriage cannot be accessed directly, as it is not an observable fact ....[16]

Those of us who deal regularly with causes of marriage nullity can become desensitized to the seriousness of the alleged nullity of marriage—both with regard to the substance of the claim and the challenge of proving it.

C. *The Object of Moral Certitude*

The current legislation—which simply received c. 1869, §1 of the 1917 Code—has been imprecisely drafted since it says that moral certitude is needed in order to pronounce any sentence whatsoever.[17] This is not accurate, though, for the object of the judge's certitude is in part the petitioner's allegation attached to the *libellus* (e.g., the delict was freely and deliberately committed; the property was illicitly acquired; the marriage consent was invalidly placed). Therefore, reaching moral certitude is not a prerequisite for issuing a sentence. Rather, moral certitude is or is not reached depending on whether the allegation has been proven such that every positive, reasonable doubt is excluded. In causes of marriage nullity, the question is whether the judge is morally certain that the alleged nullity of the marriage has been proven: affirmative (the judge is morally certain), negative (the judge is not morally certain).[18]

---

[16] "Moral Certainty and Truth Justification," *The Jurist* 65 (2005) 151. See also Martín García, "Aproximación al concepto de 'moralis certitudo,'" 479, and Stankiewicz, "La certezza morale," 239.

[17] *CIC*/1983, c. 1608, §1; *CCEO*, c. 1291, §1. On this point, see Grocholewski, "La certezza morale," 418. See also Stankiewicz, "La certezza morale," 240. Since it has been promulgated in this manner, though, it is necessary to interpret it in light of §4 (Martín García, "Aproximación al concepto de 'moralis certitudo,'" 473).

[18] This more precise articulation recently received normative expression. See Pontifical Council for Legislative Texts, Instructio servanda a Tribunalibus diœcesanis et interdiœcesanis in pertractandis causis nullitatis matrimonii *Dignitas connubii*, January 25, 2005 (Vatican City: LEV, 2005): "In order to declare the nullity of a marriage,

D. The Source of Moral Certitude (ex actis et probatis)

Canon 1608 §2 (*CCEO*, c. 1291 §2) establishes the sources of the judge's moral certitude: "The judge must draw this certitude from what has been carried out and proven." Perhaps the reader expected this to say "from the acts and the proofs"; this is what it says in all the English translations of these canons that I have seen. Notice, though: the Latin says *ex actis et probatis*, not *ex actis et probationibus*. The use of the word "proofs" is actually quite problematic. For "the proofs" (*probationes*) are all the kinds of evidence mentioned in the law: declarations of parties, documentation, testimony of witnesses, experts, and presumptions. If judges draw certitude from these, they may very well neglect the most pressing issue: what is truly *proven* by the evidence advanced in the process? What has been certainly demonstrated?[19] The correct translation of *probatis*, even if it is a bit wordy, is "from what has been proven" or "from the proven facts"—the perfect passive participle of *probare*. Judges have not reached moral certitude if they can only support their subjective conviction with a few pieces of evidence found in the acts of the cause; they may not pick and choose from the evidence. Moral certitude is only reached when the judge is certain that specific phenomena are truly proven after a thorough study of all of the acts. The judge who is morally certain is able to draw *full proof* of the allegation from the acts of the cause.[20]

In this regard, the Servant of God John Paul II declared:

> ... the judge cannot limit himself[21] to giving credence to affirmations alone; on the contrary, he must keep in mind the possibility that, during the instruction, the objective truth may have been obscured by shadows brought about by different causes, such as forgetfulness of certain facts, a subjective interpretation of them, carelessness, and sometimes malice

---

there is required in the mind of the judge moral certainty of its nullity" (art. 247 §1) [hereafter *DC*].

[19] For a published example of the confusion caused by this misunderstanding of the meaning of the term *probata*, see Martin E. Lavin, "Canonical Equity Applied to Moral Certainty and to the Worth of Expert Testimony," *The Jurist* 35 (1975) 316.

[20] "If ... the judge is able to deduce the moral certitude on the justice of the request of the petitioner, this will signify that in favour of such a solution the acts of the process offer the 'full proof.' In fact, the concept of full proof is symmetric with that of moral certitude, the former constituting the fundamental basis of the latter: full proof is that which furnished the moral certitude because it 'excludes every founded or reasonable doubt' in favour of the position argued by the other party (public or private). Moreover, full proof can be a single proof or, normally, a collection of proofs from which moral certitude arises'" (Joaquín Llobell, "The Contentious Trial [cc. 1185-1356]," *A Guide to the Eastern Code. A Commentary on the Code of Canons of the Eastern Churches*, ed. George Nedungatt, Kanonika 10 [Rome: Pontificio Istituto Orientale, 2002] 759).

[21] The appointment of women as judges was not permitted until the 1983 Code came into effect. For this reason, only masculine pronouns are used here, as well as in other pre-1983 texts.

> and fraud. It is necessary that the judge act with a critical sense. This is a difficult task, because there may be many errors, while on the contrary the truth is only one. It is necessary, therefore, to search in the acts for proof of the alleged facts, and then to proceed to a critique of each of these proofs and to compare one piece of evidence with the others.[22]

One common offense that is rebuked in causes judged before the Roman Rota is when the judge reaches an affirmative decision on the basis of the assertions of the petitioner and his or her witnesses, while the assertions of the respondent, who denies the allegations, are ignored or improperly weighed.[23] In these cases, the assertions the petitioner and his or her witnesses were among the "proofs," in the sense of *probationes*, but they were yet among that which was "proven," in the sense of *probata*. Therefore, they could not constitute *plena probatio* and thus could not lead the judge to moral certitude.

In light of all of this, the English translation of this norm provided by the Holy See in *Dignitas connubii* is most welcome: "The judge must derive this certainty from those things which have been carried out and proven in the process (*ex actis et probatis*) (can. 1608 §2)" (art. 247 §3). Here *acta* is translated "those things which have been carried out," because it refers not precisely to the judicial acts but also all of the actions and exceptions, objections, assertions and denials made by the parties (including the Defender of the Bond), the claims of the witnesses and the experts, and the acts of the judge.[24]

---

[22] John Paul II, 1980 Allocutio, no. 5, 175.

[23] See, e.g., TRR, Decrees *c.* Pompedda, March 27, 1984, no. 9, *RRT Decreta* 2 (1984) 42; *c.* Colagiovanni, May 9, 1984, no. 7, ibid. 60; *c.* Agustoni, June 5, 1984, no. 3, ibid. 84; *c.* Agustoni, December 4, 1984, ibid. 133-136; *c.* Giannecchini, December 18, 1984, ibid. 146; *c.* Ferraro, December 18, 1984, nn. 5-6, ibid. 149; *c.* Masala, January 15, 1985, no. 5, *RRT Decreta* 3 (1985) 2; *c.* Colagiovanni, January 29, 1985, no. 7, ibid. 25; *c.* Fiore, January 29, 1985, no. 5a, ibid. 28; *c.* Giannecchini, October 18, 1985, nn. 1-2, 4, ibid. 232; *c.* Ragni, March 11, 1986, no. 3b, *RRT Decreta* 4 (1986) 32; *c.* Masala, October 14, 1986, no. 9, ibid. 140; *c.* Pinto, March 27, 1987, *RRT Decreta* 5 (1987) 57-59; *c.* Doran, July 26, 1988, no. 8, *RRT Decreta* 6 (1988) 180; *c.* Colagiovanni, April 25, 1989, no. 12, *RRT Decreta* 7 (1989) 75; *c.* Ragni, February 12, 1992, no. 2, *RRT Decreta* 10 (1992) 12; *c.* de Lanversin, April 24, 1996, no. 9, *RRT Decreta* 14 (1996) 78; *c.* Serrano Ruiz, June 7, 1996, no. 4, ibid. 103; *c.* Pompedda, July 31, 1997, nn. 6-7, *RRT Decreta* 15 (1997) 179; *c.* Defilippi, October 23, 1997, no. 5a, ibid. 221-222; *c.* Giannecchini, October 24, 1997, no. 5, ibid. 241.

[24] See, e.g., Gianpaolo Bianchi, "La certezza morale e il libero convincimento del giudice," *Il giudizio di nullità matrimoniale dopo l'Istruzione* Dignitas connubii. *Parte Prima: I principi*, eds. P.A. Bonnet and Carlo Gullo, Studi Giuridici 75 (Vatican City: LEV, 2007) 389-390; de Diego-Lora, "Title VII. The Pronouncements of the Judge," 1460; Giussani, *Discrezionalità del giudice*, 128-129; Grocholewski, "La certezza morale," 430-431; Lüdicke- Jenkins, Dignitas connubii. *Norms and Commentary*, 397, no. 8; McCarthy, *De certitudine morali*, 80, notes 1-2; TRR, Definitive Sentence *c.* Pompedda, October 30, 1978, no. 4, *RRT Decisiones* 70 (1978) 470.

E. The Manner of Reaching Moral Certitude

The law also establishes the manner in which moral certitude is reached (*CIC*, c. 1608 §3; *CCEO*, c. 1291 §3). It states that the judge is "to evaluate the evidence in his or her own conscience, without prejudice to prescripts of law concerning the efficacy of certain proofs." Here the legislator establishes that the normal way for reaching certitude is what canonical tradition calls the free evaluation of evidence (*libera æstimatio probationum*). As a rule, the judge is to be free to examine each piece of evidence within the context of the all the evidence, and thus reach a reasonable conclusion about the objective weight of each piece of evidence. Quite rarely, the law itself will tell the judge how much weight a piece of evidence has—the clearest example is that public documents are to be trusted as to what they directly and principally assert (*CIC*, c. 1541; *CCEO*, c. 1222); these are called legal proofs (*probationes legales*).[25]

The principle of the free evaluation of proofs does not give the judge total discretion in evaluating the evidence. The judge cannot arbitrarily determine what weight a piece of evidence has. For instance, the judge cannot determine that a witness statement provides full proof when the source of the witness's knowledge remains in doubt (c. 1563); or the judge cannot uncritically accept the conclusions of an expert, when they are based on pure speculation (c. 1579, §1). To do so would be an abuse of the free evaluation of evidence. In the words of Pius XII, the judge is not to decide what weight the evidence has on the basis of a "sentiment or only a merely subjective opinion about this or that," nor "on personal belief, thoughtlessness, or inexperience."[26]

When evaluating evidence freely, in order to prevent arbitrariness, judges must rely on the guidance that is available to them in canonical sources. They must follow these and apply them to each case placed before them. This guidance is fourfold: legal principles which explain how a piece of evidence is to be evaluated (without assigning a certain weight to the evidence), jurisprudence (especially of the Roman Rota and the Apostolic Signatura), the insights of proven authors, and the judge's own experience.[27]

---

[25] On the principle of the free evaluation of evidence, see Pius XII, 1942 allocutio, nn. 3-4, 340-342; TRR, Definitive Sentence *c.* Civili, March 22, 1995, nn. 8-12, *RRT Decisiones* 87 (1995) 212-214; Marcelino Cabreros de Anta, *Nuevos estudios canónicos* (Vitoria: Editorial Eset, 1966) 742; Manuel Arroba Conde, *Diritto processuale canonico*, 5th ed. (Rome: EDIURCLA, 2006) 406-410; Bonnet, "De iudicis sententia," 84-85; de Diego-Lora, "Title VII. The Pronouncements of the Judge," 1462-1466; Fernando della Rocca, "De morali certitudine in sententia canonica," *Apollinaris* 33 (1960) 211-212; Erdö, "La certezza morale," 92-93; Henricus Flatten, "Qua libertate," 185-210; Giussani, *Discrezionalità del giudice*, 131-136; Joaquín Llobell, "La certezza morale," 769-777, 783-78; McCarthy, *De certitudine morali*, 97-98; Mario F. Pompedda, *Studi di diritto processuale canonico*, Ateneo Romano della Santa Croce, Monografie Giuridiche 9 (Milan: Giuffrè Editore, 1995) 145-148; Antoni Stankiewicz, "Le caratteristiche del sistema probatorio canonico," *Apollinaris* 67 (1994) 107-117.

[26] 1942 allocutio, no. 3, 340.

[27] See Pericle Felici, "Juridical Formalities and Evaluation of Evidence in the

F. Implications of Moral Certitude for the Judicial Process—2 Examples

The standard of moral certitude informs the whole judicial process since the definitive declaration of its realization (or not) is the focal point of each phase of each trial.[28] Much could be said about the particular implications of the notion of moral certitude for the whole process. We limit ourselves here to perhaps the two most significant: namely, 1) the judge's obligation to take an active part in the collection of evidence, and 2) the motivation of the definitive sentence.

1. The Judge's Active Part in the Instruction of the Cause

Distinct from many secular legal systems, the canonical judge is to pursue evidence that is known to exist but which has not been introduced by the parties, especially in causes of marriage nullity. This is an area of judicial praxis which seems underused in North America. It is an application of c. 1452 (*CCEO*, c. 1110 §1), in which the judge is exhorted to search for and strive to obtain evidence which exists but which has not been brought forward by the parties. In §1 of that canon we read, in part: "... once a cause has been legitimately introduced, the judge can *and must* proceed even *ex officio* in causes ... which concern the public good of the Church or the salvation of souls" (emphasis added).[29] This was emphasized in the allocution of the Servant of God John Paul II to the Roman Rota on January 26, 1989, in which he presented this dimension as an aspect of protecting the parties' right of defense: "Even if one of the parties has renounced the exercise of defense, there remains for the judge in causes [of marriage nullity] the grave obligation of making serious attempts to obtain the judicial deposition of the party and also of the witnesses which he or she could introduce." The judge is moved to do this "in order to avoid a partial judgment in a matter so grave."[30] This is further emphasized in *Dignitas connubii*, which urges the judge to make sure not to conclude the cause if "something else is still to be sought in order that the cause might be sufficiently instructed" (art. 238), and which says that the college of judges should refrain from issuing a decision if it perceives that that the instruction still needs to be completed (artt. 247 §5; 248 §5).

The judge's obligation to instruct the cause as thoroughly as possible does not cause the judge to take any personal interest in the final decision itself. Rather, it ensures that the judge's moral certitude or lack thereof is well founded

---

Canonical Process," *The Jurist* 38 (1978) 154-155; Giacchi, "La certezza morale," 617-618; Eduardo Labandeira, "Las maximas de experiencia en los procesos canónicos," *Ius Canonicum* 29-57 (1989) 245-273; McCarthy, *De certitudine morali*, 84-85. In one respect, then, it can be said that evidence is rarely left to the fully free evaluation of the judge (Stankiewicz, "La caratteristiche," 110-111).

[28] Grocholewski, "La certezza morale," 449; McCarthy, *De certitudine morali*, 3.

[29] [...] Causa ... legitime introducta, iudex procedere potest et debet etiam ex officio in causis ... quæ publicum Ecclesiæ bonum aut animarum salutem respiciunt.

[30] John Paul II, Allocutio ad Romanæ Rotæ Auditores, officiales et advocatos coram admissos, no. 5, January 26, 1989: *AAS* 81 (1989) 923.

and corresponds to the truth. Judges should only declare that moral certitude has or has not been reached if they are certain that all the relevant, available evidence is before them. The judge's only "interest" in the final decision is that it be in conformity with the objective truth about what is proven.

2. The Motivation of the Definitive Sentence (cc. 1611, 3°; 1612 §3)

The definitive sentence is a public ecclesiastical document which not only creates obligations for parties or declares facts; it also stands as the pre-eminent witness of the judge's moral certitude. We know that the sentence does not merely provide the judge's ultimate disposition (affirmative or negative); it must also be motivated, that is, it must explain the juridical principles at play in the cause (*in iure*) and demonstrate how these apply to the proven facts of the cause (*in facto*) (cc. 1611, 3°; 1612 §3).

With regard to moral certitude, the sentence has a twofold function: the manifestation and the objectivization of the moral certitude. In order words, the sentence must demonstrate why the judges reached the conclusion that they did, and it must be a convincing, logical explanation of why the judges hold their conclusion to correspond with the objective truth. The sentence must do this because the judge is obliged to explain and illustrate for others why moral certitude was or was not reached. The others to whom the judge is accountable in this regard are the private parties and the public parties (the Defender of the Bond and the Promoter of Justice), to whom the judge must give a full copy of the sentence (*DC*, art. 258 §§1-2) as well as the superior tribunals before whom the decision may be challenged.

Said otherwise, the motivation of the sentence is the means by which the parties and hierarchical authorities gain access to the rationale for the judge's moral certitude. Through logical argumentation, the sentence should convince them that the judge's certitude is based on objective fact and that it is not arbitrary.[31]

---

[31] See Stankiewicz, "La certezza morale e la motivazione della sentenza," 231-245, esp. 241-245. See also della Rocca, "De morali certitudine," 212; Giacchi, "La certezza morale," 618-619; Joaquín Llobell, "La certezza morale," 795-796, 798; idem, "The Contentious Trial," 759; Martín García, "Aproximación al concepto de 'moralis certitudo,'" 481-482; Miguel Ortiz, "The Declarations of the Parties and Moral Certitude," *Studies on the Instruction* Dignitas connubii, eds. Patricia M. Dugan and Luis Navarro, Gratianus Series (Montréal: Wilson & Lafleur, 2006) 79-80 [hereafter "*Studies on the Instruction* Dignitas connubii"]; Pompedda, "Decision-Sentence in Marriage Trials," 89, 95-97. On the pastoral function (*pastoralidad*) of the motivation of the sentence, see Joaquín Llobell, "El valor jurídico de la Instr. *Dignitas connubii*, su recepción, el objeto y la conformidad de la sentencia, y la certeza moral," *Procesos de nulidad matrimonial. La Instrucción* Dignitas connubii, Actas del XXIV Curso de Actualización en Derecho Canónico de la Facultad de Derecho Canónico (Pamplona, 24-26 octubre de 2005), eds. Rafael Rodríguez-Ocaña and Joaquín Sedano (Pamplona: EUNSA, 2006) 286-287.

G. The Crisis of Moral Certitude

In the mid-late 1960s, there was an aspiration in North America and elsewhere to remove the judicial standard of moral certitude, especially for causes of marriage nullity. Obviously this aspiration was never realized, but it is important to acknowledge and understand it since it has had lasting effects on how the standard of moral certitude is applied in contemporary judicial praxis.

The most prominent proponent of the derogation of moral certitude in North America was Msgr. Stephen Kelleher of New York, chairman of the special committee of the CLSA entrusted with the drafting of what are commonly called the American Procedural Norms.[32] Among his many proposals for an improvement in the administration of justice, he suggested that moral certitude be replaced with the civil law standard of a preponderance of evidence ("more probable arguments"). This was also proposed in general by the CLSA.[33] The basis for this proposal was an augmentation of the *favor libertatis* and a diminishment of the *favor matrmonii*—that is, the freedom of parties to abandon their marriage and enter a new one over the presumption of the validity of every marriage (*CIC*/1917, c. 1014).[34] In effect, this gave pride of place to the private interests of spouses (or at least one of the spouses) over the public good of the Church.[35]

---

[32] See Thomas J. Green, "The American Procedural Norms – An Assessment," *Studia canonica* 8 (1974) 319-320.

[33] See Gordon, "De nimia processuum matrimonialium duratione," 702-703, nn. 237-238.

[34] See, e.g., the following three essays by Kelleher: "The Dignity of Persons in a Marriage and the Dignity of Their Marriage," *The Jurist* 26 (1966) 244, no. 6; "Canon 1014 and American Culture," *The Jurist* 28 (1968) 7-8; "A Suggested Method of Procedure in the *Recognitio* of the Fourth Book of the Code," *The Jurist* 29 (1969) 81 and 84.

[35] It is not that Kelleher did not seek the public good of the Church; rather, he maintained that the public good of the Church was not achieved when a negative decision was issued, since the parties frequently abandon the practice of the Catholic faith and attempt a new marriage regardless. Scarcely, if ever, do negative decisions prompt the parties to seek reconciliation with each other. The public good of the Church which the presumption of law allegedly protected was merely an ill perceived good, he argued ("Canon 1014 and American Culture," 6-7). This, of course, was an unbalanced, overly pragmatic understanding of the public good of the Church. For the public good of the Church in a cause of marriage nullity is the declaration of the truth about a sacrament. To declare invalid a marriage that is either valid or at least not proven to be invalid is, in a sense, blasphemous since it asserts that the Holy Spirit did not act when he truly did or may have; it insults the dignity of persons since it falsely declares that they were impaired from consenting to marriage, that they were dishonest when marrying, that one of them deceived the other, etc.; and it disturbs the whole Church since the faithful often (perhaps rightly) perceive that marriages are declared null when they were once held in honor and esteem in the community of faith. So what is at stake in a marriage nullity trial is not ultimately the public good as realized in a particular marriage but the public good of the sanctity of marriage in the Church.

For a thorough and thoughtful rebuke of Kelleher's position by a great expert of

During the revision of the code, one consultor of the *Cœtus studii "De processibus"* proposed that the words *certitudo moralis* of c. 1869 §1 be replaced with the words *fortiores et graviores probationes*: "The sentence will make a pronouncement according to the stronger and more serious evidence." At a separate meeting, another consultor asserted that moral certitude was not necessary but that it would be sufficient for there to be "a preponderance of proofs and indications." These proposals were rejected by almost all of the consultors since they constituted a break from the clear Magisterial teaching of Pius XII and since moral certitude, especially in causes of marriage nullity, is "absolutely required."[36]

While the standard of moral certitude was never removed from universal law, it was essentially removed in certain parts of the world via particular procedural law, especially in the United States (in the American Procedural Norms) and Australia. Norm 21 of these two countries' law read: "The judge will render his decision according to moral certitude generated by the prevailing weight of that evidence having a recognized value in law and jurisprudence."[37] Even though the expression "moral certitude" was used here, the norm stood in tension with the traditional notion of moral certitude. For it introduced some ambiguity about moral certitude which appeared to stand in contrast with the teaching of Pius XII, Rotal jurisprudence, and proven authors. For it suggested that moral certitude could be based on a preponderance of evidence rather than

---

procedural law contemporary to him, see Gordon, "De nimia processuum matrimonialium duratione," 694-711. He notes (at 708-711) that Kelleher fails to attend properly to whether and why moral certitude should be derogated and raced forward to explain how it should be derogated. As a result, he erroneously absolutized the dignity and rights of persons at the expense of the public good of the Church, viz., the stability of marriage. He makes no effort to coordinate the good of the spouses and the good of society but just sacrifices the public good of the stability of marriage. In effect, therefore, the insertion of the standard of "greater probability" allows an avenue for Catholic divorce with no recognition of the varying gravity of judicial causes. In the Church there are contentious causes, criminal causes, and causes concerning the status of persons, and his proposal does not appreciate the varying demands of each kind of cause.

For a fair and convincing *apologia pro certitudine morali* contemporary to Kelleher, see Charles P. Koster, "Reaching Certitude in Marriage Cases," *The Jurist* 29 (1969) 305-325.

[36] Pontifical Commission for the Revision of the Code of Canon Law, "Cœtus studii 'De processibus'. Sessio VI[a] (diebus 10-15 februarii 1969 habita), Adunatio II[a] die 10 februarii 1969 vespere habita," *Communicationes* 39 (2007) 91; "Cœtus studii 'De processibus.' Sessio VIII[a] (diebus 20-25 octobris 1969 habita), Adunatio IX[a] die 25 octobris 1969 mane habita," ibid. 309-310.

[37] Council for the Public Affairs of the Church, Rescriptum, April 28, 1970, prot. no. 3320/70, *Documenta recentiora circa rem matrimonialem et processualem cum notis bibliographicis et indicibus*, eds. Ignacio Gordon and Zenon Grocholewski, vol. 1 (Rome: Pontificia Universitas Gregoriana, 1977) 247, no. 1402; *CLD* VII:961. On the approval of use of this norm in Australia in the same year, see *Documenta recentiora*, 259, no. 1456.

a resolution of all prudent doubts.[38]

Together with the American Procedural Norms was published an unofficial commentary, which speaks repeatedly of "adequate proof" or "adequate, prevailing proof." It claimed: "Moral certitude is not something over and above adequate, prevailing proof. It is simply the subjective state which adequate, prevailing proof produces in the mind of the mature judge."[39] It removed all reference to the judge's obligation to resolve positive, prudent doubts. In fact, one author who frequently addressed the CLSA in the 60s and 70s explicitly stated that an affirmative decision in a cause of marriage nullity should be given even if "there are *probable* reasons favoring validity," since "[n]ot *all* doubt need be excluded."[40]

I think it could be said that this confusion has had an ongoing influence on Tribunal praxis in the U.S. This is seen in the not uncommon tendency to declare the nullity of marriage even when prudent doubts remain (or should remain) in the mind of the judge. It was likely this which moved the Servant of God John Paul II to confront this obscured notion of moral certitude in his 1980 allocution to the Roman Rota, where he expressly cites the influence of the American Procedural Norms. He declared:

Consequently, it is not licit for any judge to pronounce a sentence in favor of the nullity of a marriage if there has not first been acquired moral certitude about the existence of that nullity. Probability alone is not sufficient for deciding a cause. One could apply to every compromise of this what was wisely said of other laws related to marriage: each relaxation of them contains an impelling dynamic: "If the practice is permitted, the way is paved in the Church for tolerating divorce, covered by another name."[41]

Most recently the Instruction *Dignitas connubii* explicitly forbade recourse to the standard of a "preponderance of evidence" and reiterated the teaching of

---

[38] "Implicit in the expression 'prevailing weight of evidence' is that, although the evidence may foster one decision, contrary arguments still retain their intrinsic probability. Therefore, the term 'moral certitude' in the context of norm 21 cannot with juridical necessity be identified with the middle classification of Pius XII, the traditional one, but it can be extended even to quasi-certitude" (Francis Harman, "Certitudo moralis præsupposita in normis processualibus Tribunalibus Statuum Fœderatorum Americæ necnon Australiæ concessis," *Periodica* 61 [1972] 385). This author's commentary is most thoughtful; especially to be noted are his critiques of this obfuscation of the notion of moral certitude at page 393. See also M.B. Ahern, "The Interpretation of Norm 21," *The Jurist* 32 (1972) 531-535 (at 532, no. 3: "Something cannot be at the same time *both* morally certain and merely probable"); Bianchi, "La certezza morale," 395; Miguel Á. Ortiz, "The Declarations of the Parties and Moral Certitude," *Studies on the Instruction* Dignitas connubii, 83-84; Peter A. Pijnappels, "Sufficiency of Evidence in Formal Trials," *Studia canonica* 8 (1974) 167-171; Stankiewicz, "La certezza morale," 235-237.

[39] *CLD* VII: 962.

[40] Burns, "Moral Certitude," 44, emphasis in original.

[41] John Paul II, 1980 Allocutio, no. 6, 176.

Pius XII. Article 247 §2 of the Instruction reads: "In order to have the moral certitude necessary by law, a preponderance (*prævalens momentum*) of the proofs and indications is not sufficient, but it is required that any prudent positive doubt of making an error, in law or in fact, is excluded, even if the mere possibility of the contrary remains."

These general statements—both morally and juridically binding—need to be supplemented by authoritative practical guidance on how moral certitude is reached in particular cases. And this guidance is found especially in the jurisprudence of the Tribunal of the Roman Rota.[42] And it is to that which we now turn.

II. Application of Moral Certitude to the Acts of the Judge Mentioned in c. 1682 §2

Now that we have explored the concept of judicial moral certitude, which applies to the definitive decisions of ecclesiastical judges in every kind of judicial cause, let us analyze the specific manner in which moral certitude is demanded of judges when they place the acts mentioned in c. 1682 §2—that is, the decree confirming a definitive sentence that first declares the nullity of a marriage in the ordinary contentious process or admitting the cause to an ordinary examination in second instance. (For the sake of simplicity, we will speak only with reference to first and second instance tribunals, excluding any possible third instance scenarios.) Readers might only be involved in causes of marriage nullity during the stage of first instance and therefore think that this has little relevance for them. However, this is not so. For, as we will see, the whole first instance process, from start to finish is under the jurisdictional oversight and judgment of the second instance judges; and so anyone who is involved in the process in first instance must understand with what criteria the second instance judges will (or should) judge their activities in first instance.

A. The Processus brevior

Let us first recall the basic elements of *CIC*, c. 1682 and *CCEO*, c. 1368 (*DC*, art. 265). When a marriage is first declared invalid in the ordinary contentious process by a first instance tribunal, the acts and sentence must be transmitted to the ordinary second instance tribunal (or to the Roman Rota) within 20 days of the publication of the definitive sentence. Within this 20 day period, the parties and the defender of the bond (and promoter of justice if he is involved at this stage) have a right to appeal the sentence, either wholly or partially; they enjoy the right to appeal for fifteen days (*CIC*, c. 1630; *CCEO*, c. 1311 §1). Once the second instance tribunal has received the acts (both the acts of the cause and the acts of the process), the sentence, and any appeals, they notify the parties and the defender of the bond about the cause and invite them to offer any observations regarding the affirmative sentence and the possible

[42] John Paul II, Constitutio Apostolica de Romana Curia *Pastor bonus*, art. 126, June 28, 1988: *AAS* 80 (1988) 892.

confirmation of it. Typically, the petitioner or his advocate will take this opportunity to urge the college of judges to confirm the affirmative sentence so that the petitioner may be declared free to marry; the defender of the bond is bound (within reason) to urge the college to admit the cause to an ordinary examination in his opinion (*votum*); and the respondent with the help of his or her advocate is free to argue either position. Once all the observations have been received, or the established time limit has passed (*CIC*, c. 1466; *CCEO*, c. 1125), the college of judges convenes to decide whether to confirm the first affirmative sentence or admit it to an ordinary examination.

B. The Object of the Judges' Moral Certitude

How do the judges make this decision? It seems that there is not a little disagreement in North America about what should motivate the judges either to confirm the sentence or admit the cause to an ordinary examination in second instance. The activity of the college of judges at this moment in the process has been commonly called "a review,"[43] but this term is misleading. It may imply that the judges are merely checking to see if the decision is reasonable or if the allegations in the case are convincing. Second instance judges who are merely "reviewing" the decision may be inclined to give the first instance judges the benefit of the doubt or to presume that they decided correctly in the case.[44] No such presumption exists; if the sentence enjoyed the presumption of justice, it would not require any jurisdictional oversight. The supreme legislator himself, though, imposes a jurisdictional control on the first instance decision; this means that the first instance decision in itself is insufficient and cannot be binding.

Indeed, there is a strongly judicial character to what the second instance judges are doing. In a certain respect, there is more at stake than there was in first instance: not only the question of the nullity of the marriage but also the quality of the work carried out by the first instance judges. The second instance college of judges makes a true judgment about the firmness of these elements based on objective criteria. They freely weigh the evidence, but the conclusions they reach are based on their conviction about what is objectively true. For this reason the Roman Rota rightly insists that the decision of whether or not to confirm an affirmative decision is not an act of discretion (*merum iudicum arbitrium*) but one that is reached on the basis of moral certitude about the confirmability of the affirmative decision.[45]

---

[43] See, e.g., Craig A. Cox, "Article 5: The Sentence and the Appeal," *New Commentary on the Code of Canon Law*, eds. John P. Beal, James A. Coriden, and Thomas J. Green (New York/Mahwah, NJ: Paulist Press, 2000) 1775 (this author also wrongly describes the confirmation and admission to ordinary examination as "two options"); Daniel J. Murray, "The Preliminary Experience of Mandatory Review in Diocesan Tribunals," *CLSA Proceedings* 45 (1983) 100-111 (*passim*); Kenneth J. Ruzick, "Competence, Nullity of the Acts and the Appeal Process: A Look at the Procedural Law of the New Code," *CLSA Proceedings* 44 (1982) 114.

[44] See, e.g., Lüdicke-Jenkins, Dignitas connubii. *Norms and Commentary*, 428-429.

[45] See, e.g., TRR, Decree *c.* Stankiewicz, June, 1, 1993, no. 7, *RRT Decreta* 11 (1993) 130; idem, Decree *c.* Colagiovanni, January 20, 1994, no. 3, *RRT Decreta* 12 (1994) 2.

This moral certitude pertains to two aspects of the first instance trial: 1) whether the first instance definitive sentence sufficiently demonstrates the moral certitude of the first instance college of judges, and 2) whether the alleged nullity of the marriage on the specific ground is indeed proven by the acts of the cause.[46] So the second instance judges must scrutinize and critique both the sentence itself and the acts. Msgr. Grzegorz Erlebach—judge of the Roman Rota and renowned scholar of jurisprudence—describes this as the *intrinsic confirmability* and *extrinsic confirmability* of the definitive sentence.[47] The sentence is intrinsically confirmable when it convincingly and logically argues the nullity of the marriage, leaving no reasonable doubts in the minds of the second instance judges as to whether the first instance judges were truly morally certain. And the sentence is extrinsically confirmable when it is evident that the sentence is based on acts that provide conclusive proof of the nullity of the marriage.

Acknowledging that, among practitioners in tribunals, this may not be the common understanding of the role of the second instance judges as they are

---

[46] Some canonists claim that it is not obligatory for the judges to review the acts of the cause; this position, though, cannot be sustained. The majority of authors insist that it is obligatory (see note 45), and, more significantly, the unanimous jurisprudence of the Roman Rota testifies that it is clearly obligatory. It would not be an exaggeration to say that every Rotal decree confirming or admitting to ordinary examination a cause decided in the affirmative at a lower tribunal states that the Rotal judges first examined all the acts. This is a standard expression concluding such decrees.
It has been argued that this is not obligatory on the basis of art. 265 §3 which says that "all the acts are to be available (*præsto*) to the judges before the college issues the decree" of confirmation or admission to an ordinary examination. To say that the acts must merely be "available" is said to imply that, if a given judge wishes to study the acts of the cause, he or she may, but there is no obligation to do so. This is certainly a misreading of the norm, however. The term "available" should not be misunderstood; the Latin *præsto* does not mean available in the sense of "optional for viewing" but "at hand" or "ready" to be inspected. And the judges must examine these acts. See, e.g., Grzegorz Erlebach, "The Challenge of the Sentence and the Transmission of the Cause *Ex Officio* to the Appeal Tribunal," *Studies on the Instruction* Dignitas connubii, 131, note 41.

[47] Grzegorz Erlebach, "I motivi di rinvio ad esame ordinario nella giurisprudenza della Rota Romana," *La procedura matrimoniale abbreviata*, Studi Giuridici 49 (Vatican City: Libreria editrice Vaticana, 1998) 57-58. On the moral certitude needed in order to confirm an affirmative sentence, see also Bianchi, "La certezza morale," 398; Carmelo de Diego Lora, "Art. 5. The Judgement and the Appeal," *Exegetical Commentary*, vol. IV/2, 1851-1852; Augustine Mendonça, "The Structural and Functional Aspects of an Appeal Tribunal in Marriage Nullity Cases," *Studia canonica* 32 (1998) 483-484; Maria Teresa Romano, "La trasmissione della causa al Tribunale d'appello e la sua trattazione (artt. 263-268)," *Il giudizio di nullità matrimoniale dopo l'Istruzione* Dignitas connubii. *Parta terza: La parta dinamica del processo*, Studi Giuridici 77 (Vatican City: Libreria editrice Vaticana, 2008) 588; Bassiano Uggé, *La fase preliminare/abbreviata del processo di nullità del matrimonio in secondo grado di giudizio a norma del can. 1682 §2*, Tesi Gregoriana – Serie Diritto Canonico 60 (Rome: EPUG, 2003) 238-239, 268-275, *et passim*.

deciding whether or not to confirm the affirmative sentence, I refer to the praxis and jurisprudence of the Roman Rota, which consistently and unambiguously insists on both of these elements of moral certitude at this stage of the process. The most recent, clear statement of this that I have seen is found in the Rota's Annual Report from 2007:

> ... in order to confirm the affirmative sentence of marriage nullity, it is not sufficient to verify the intrinsic correctness and not even the adherence to what emerges from the instruction, or the balanced evaluation of the evidence made by the first instance judges. In fact, the judge of the higher instance is not a mere reviewer (*revisore*) of the process that was previously carried out; but ... this judge must autonomously judge whether, on the heels of the first affirmative sentence, it is possible to sustain with moral certitude the nullity of the marriage, at least on the basis of the ground decided in the affirmative.[48]

This is articulated in many particular decrees of the Rota; I discovered this explicitly in no less than 31 decrees issued by the Roman Rota between the years 1983-1997.[49] (As of this lecture, the most recent volume of the decrees of the Rota contains decrees from 1998, which the author has not yet been able to examine.) I will cite a couple of the more notable ones here. A passage used by Bishop Thomas Doran in many of his decrees while he was a Rotal judge is the following:

> The prompt confirmation of the first affirmative sentence can only happen when it is established from what has been carried out and proven that moral certitude was reached. It cannot be thought that this has happened when the appealed sentence is not correctly based on principles of law and on the facts. In other words, when a reasonable or prudent doubt about the contrary remains, the prescribed moral certitude is lacking; therefore the cause must be remitted to an ordinary examination in second instance.[50]

---

48 "Relazione sull'attività della Rota Romana nell'anno giudiziario 2007," *Quaderni dello Studio Rotale* 18 (2008) 75, citing the decree marked B. 11/07.

49 See, e.g., TRR, Decrees *c.* Stankiewicz, June 20, 1985, no. 3, *RRT Decreta* 3 (1985) 168; *c.* Agustoni, October 15, 1985, no. 6, ibid., 227; *c.* Giannecchini, October 18, 1985, no. 10, ibid., 233; *c.* de Lanversin, March 9, 1988, no. 2, *RRT Decreta* 6 (1988) 64; *c.* Corso, May 18, 1988, no. 3, ibid., 119; *c.* Corso, July 6, 1988, no. 4, ibid., 167; *c.* Doran, December 13, 1989, no. 13, *RRT Decreta* 7 (1989) 201; *c.* Stankiewicz, March 22, 1990, no. 2, *RRT Decreta* 8 (1990) 58; *c.* Turnaturi, December 13, 1994, no. 5, *RRT Decreta* 12 (1994) 192; *c.* Turnaturi, December 15, 1995, no. 6, *RRT Decreta* 13 (1995) 174; *c.* Monier, July 24, 1996, no. 8, *RRT Decreta* 14 (1996) 174; *c.* Giannecchini, October 8, 1996, no. 7, ibid., 191; *c.* Turnaturi, October 24, 1996, no. 9, ibid., 194; *c.* Pompedda, October 24, 1997, no. 3, *RRT Decreta* 15 (1997) 236. See also notes 49-51.

50 TRR, Decree *c.* Doran, June 1, 1988, B. 62/88 (unpublished), cited in many of his

The commonly cited Rotal text is that written by the current Dean, Bishop Antoni Stankiewicz, which he has used many times, adding little nuances here and there:

> In this brief judicial procedure, the appellate judges in a preliminary judgment about the sentence issued in first instance in favor of the nullity of marriage according to c. 1682 §2 can confirm it immediately by decree if, from the firmness of the arguments on which the dispositive part of the sentence is based, they can reach moral certitude concerning the declaration of the nullity of the marriage (cf. c. 1608 §1). For otherwise, especially when the first instance sentence is established on faulty arguments or unproven facts, the same judges are bound to admit the cause itself to an ordinary examination in second instance.[51]

Finally, it is very concisely put in another Rotal decree in this way: "[The judges] must arrive at a resolution of the question after weighing all the acts of the cause and after diligently and prudently examining the law and the facts of the first [affirmative] sentence."[52]

Defect of Moral Certitude Preventing Confirmation

Now that we have seen the object of the judges' moral certitude on the occasion of deciding whether or not to confirm an affirmative sentence, let us highlight the concrete ways in which this moral certitude is lacking. In other words, let us see the kinds of problems that require the second instance judges to admit a cause to ordinary examination. It is impossible to be exhaustive here—not only because there is so much to draw from Rotal jurisprudence on this matter that time would not allow a complete discussion, but also because each concrete case presents its own concerns which each judge must detect in his or her own detailed examination of the first instance acts and sentence. I have attempted a comprehensive study of all the published decrees of the Tribunal of the Roman Rota available to me which admit a cause to an ordinary examination in order to discover more about the nature of the moral certitude which the judge must reach before confirming an affirmative sentence. For in each of these decrees, the Rota explains clearly why it could not reach the

---

published decrees: see those issued on July 26, 1988 (no. 6, *RRT Decreta* 6 [1988] 178), December 15, 1988 (no. 2, ibid. 236), May 11, 1989 (no. 7, *RRT Decreta* 7 [1989] 84), July 12, 1990 (no. 8, *RRT Decreta* 8 [1990] 138), June 27, 1991 (no. 6, *RRT Decreta* 9 [1991] 85), July 11, 1991 (no. 6, ibid. 99), and April 29, 1993 (no. 5, *RRT Decreta* 11 [1993] 96).

[51] TRR, Decree *c.* Stankiewicz, May 28, 1991, no. 6, *RRT Decreta* 9 (1991) 77; see the same text (with some adaptations) in the decrees of the same *ponens* dated February 23, 1988 (no. 3, *RRT Decreta* 6 [1988] 43), February 27, 1992 (no. 3, *RRT Decreta* 10 [1992] 19), April 3, 1992 (no. 4, ibid. 63); June 1, 1993 (no. 7, *RRT Decreta* 11 [1993] 130), February 28, 1997 (no. 5, *RRT Decreta* 15 [1997] 57), April 25, 1997 (no. 4, ibid. 80), and June 19, 1997 (no. 4, ibid. 105).

[52] TRR, Decree *c.* Colagiovanni, January 20, 1994, no. 3, *RRT Decreta* 12 (1994) 2.

requisite moral certitude.

It should be said that, even if the second instance judges are morally certain of the proven nullity of the marriage and the firmness of the argumentation in the definitive sentence, they will also admit the cause to an ordinary examination if there are notable procedural irregularities.[53] These are given abundant attention in Rotal jurisprudence, and they could be the object of another paper. We limit ourselves to the two areas discussed above: 1) when the affirmative sentence itself contains reasonable doubts about the nullity of the marriage, and 2) when the first instance acts cause reasonable doubts about the nullity of the marriage to arise.

1. Manifest defect of moral certitude in the definitive sentence (lack of intrinsic confirmability)

Some affirmative sentences cannot be confirmed because they manifestly display a defect of moral certitude in the first instance judges; this induces reasonable doubts about the nullity of the marriage and about whether the sentence is a just act. This occurs when the affirmative sentence itself undermines the affirmative conclusion, especially by highlighting defects of evidence which have not been surmounted in the instruction.

Some sentences admit that there is a great lack of evidence.[54] One sentence that was examined before the Rota stated the following: "Concerning the merits of the present cause, it is observed preliminarily that the evidence is not entirely clear, also because the voluntary absence of the respondent has not permitted an objective comparison. Nevertheless, in its totality the evidence seems sufficiently suitable for establishing the necessary moral certitude for accepting the petitioner's claims." The Rotal *turnus* concluded: "With the current state of things, there is no one who doubts that it is necessary that a supplementation of the instruction be solicitously and very diligently carried out in order to remove doubts and difficulties, to fill lacunæ, and to discover the objective truth of things."[55] Other sentences admit that there was a lack of corroboration of the confession,[56] that the confession is uncertain and doubtful,[57] that there is a lack of consistency in the testimony offered by the witnesses,[58] that the testimony of the witnesses is insufficient,[59] and that which parties and witnesses merit

---

[53] Erlebach, "I motivi di rinvio ad esame ordinario nella giurisprudenza della Rota Romana," 38-41, 51-53.

[54] See, e.g., TRR, Decrees *c.* Bruno, October 26, 1984, no. 2a, *RRT Decreta* 2 (1984) 120; *c.* Jarawan, November 27, 1985, no. 7, *RRT Decreta* 3 (1985) 259.

[55] TRR, Decree *c.* Neuhaus, March 14, 1988, nn. 4 and 5, *RRT Decreta* 6 (1988) 76 and 77.

[56] TRR, Decree *c.* Funghini, February 20, 1985, no. 5, *RRT Decreta* 3 (1985) 49.

[57] TRR, Decree *c.* Giannecchini, January 17, 1986, *RRT Decreta* 4 (1986) 3.

[58] TRR, Decree *c.* Colagiovanni, March 26, 1985, no. 10, *RRT Decreta* 3 (1985) 104.

[59] One admitted that it was "a little bit weak" (TRR, Decree *c.* Jarawan, November 27, 1985, no. 5, *RRT Decreta* 3 [1985] 259); Another stated, "There is very little but allegation in this case. Whatever witnesses have been cited had little or nothing of value

credibility is still unknown.[60]

Some sentences admit that there are objective difficulties with the case.[61] One sentence admitted to an ordinary examination by a Rotal *turnus* stated this (the man-petitioner was the alleged simulator): "… there are points which can make one think that, although the petitioner had preferred not to marry, he did so willingly. … other indications can contradict the alleged simulation."[62] Another sentence which the Rota could not confirm admitted a host of difficulties and nevertheless issued an affirmative decision; that sentence "very often speaks of 'some divergences,' 'a certain contradiction,' a 'discordant deposition,' 'not a few divergences,' 'witnesses who express only their own ignorance,' or witnesses who 'in their depositions clearly go beyond what was said by the respondent,' and so on."[63]

In a cause of incapacity because of a grave defect of discretion of judgment (c. 1095, 2°), the first instance sentence admits that the three expert reports obtained in the instruction are not wholly conclusive and that perhaps another report is needed.[64] And so the judges displayed that they remained uncertain about the existence, nature, and gravity of the psychic anomaly and nevertheless issued an affirmative sentence. In another cause on the same ground decided by a sole clerical judge, the judge's own reasoning betrays his orientation toward an affirmative decision despite a lack of necessary evidence and in contradiction to the evidence advanced. The sentence admits that the parties appeared to have an "ideal relationship," and even the witnesses said that "they seemed like the ideal couple." The sentence emphasized the parties' "unmet needs for affection and security," but it in effect demonstrated that there was not a psychic anomaly causing incapacity.[65]

Many elements found in affirmative sentences addressing simulation prevent the second instance judges from reaching moral certitude. One affirmative sentence said that the *causa simulandi* was "possible,"[66] while in fact the judge must be certain of the *causa simulandi* before issuing an affirmative sentence. Another affirmative sentence neglected the fact that the acts contained no confessions, no *causa simulandi*, and even no evidence of

---

to add by way of actual testimony" (idem, Decree *c.* Doran, July 12, 1990, no. 11, *RRT Decreta* 8 [1990] 138). See also Decree *c.* de Lanversin, March 16, 1994, no. 6, *RRT Decreta* 12 (1994) 27.

[60] TRR, Decrees. *c.* Jarawan, October 26, 1985, no. 2, *RRT Decreta* 3 (1985) 235; *c.* de Lanversin, April 30, 1986, no. 2, *RRT Decreta* 4 (1986) 54; *c.* Corso, May 18, 1988, no. 4, *RRT Decreta* 6 (1988) 119-120.

[61] See, e.g., TRR, Decree *c.* Ferraro, January 25, 1983, no. 7, *RRT Decreta* 1 (1983) 11.

[62] TRR, Decree *c.* Funghini, April 20, 1988, no. 3, *RRT Decreta* 6 (1988) 90-91.

[63] TRR, Decree *c.* Giannecchini, March 11, 1988, no. 6, *RRT Decreta* 6 (1988) 73.

[64] TRR, Decree *c.* Boccafola, October 29, 1987, no. 4, *RRT Decreta* 5 (1987) 114.

[65] TRR, Decree *c.* Stankiewicz, February 27, 1992, nn. 4 and 6, *RRT Decreta* 10 (1992) 19, 20-21.

[66] TRR, Decree *c.* Ragni, July 18, 1985, no. 4, *RRT Decreta* 3 (1985) 209.

simulation at all.[67]

The reasoning found within the affirmative sentence may be so poor that the second instance judges firmly doubt that the first instance judges were truly morally certain, thus necessitating that the cause be admitting to an ordinary examination. It is not uncommon for the Rota to admit a cause to an ordinary examination due, in part, to obscurities and contradictions detected within the affirmative sentence.[68] For example, in one cause, while the first instance judge rejected the party's credibility when issuing a negative decision on one ground, the same presumed that the party was credible when issuing an affirmative decision on the other ground.[69] In another cause, the affirmative sentence drew conclusions that were clearly contrary to what the petitioner openly asserted and the respondent confirmed, and the judge at the same time did not deem them to lack credibility.[70] In another cause, the woman-respondent's decision not to offer her declarations before the Tribunal were taken as proof of her alleged simulation, which was rightly deemed to be unreasonable.[71]

A most frequent offense against properly judicial reasoning in an affirmative definitive sentence is the acritical acceptance of the statements found in an expert report. That is, quite frequently a sentence on a ground of incapacity will heavily base its affirmative decision on the expert report, and it will merely quote the expert's statements without any analysis.[72] This analysis, though, is

---

[67] TRR, Decree *c.* de Lanversin, March 18, 1986, *RRT Decreta* 4 (1986) 38.

[68] "... he confusingly mixed everything up ... that is, substantial elements and accidental elements, the efficient cause and the consequences flowing from the efficient cause, principal effects and secondary effects, effects or facts distributed directly or indirectly once the marriage was brought into being ...." (TRR, Decree *c.* Ragni, June 20, 1995, no. 4f, *RRT Decreta* 13 [1995] 70-71). See also Decrees *c.* Boccafola, January 19, 1995, no. 4, ibid. 2; *c.* Faltin, May 3, 1995, no. 9, ibid. 58. Regarding a problem of understanding and interpreting the law, see Decree *c.* Turnaturi, December 15, 1995, no. 7, ibid. 174.

[69] TRR, Decree *c.* Pompedda, January 31, 1983, no. 3, *RRT Decreta* 1 (1983) 17-18. Similarly, in another cause, while two grounds on simulation were based on the same *causa simulandi* and the same direct evidence, one was decided in the negative and the other in the affirmative (Decree *c.* Defilippi, November 13, 1996, no. 8, *RRT Decreta* 14 [1996] 233).

[70] TRR, Decree *c.* Faltin, November 13, 1991, no. 13, *RRT Decreta* 9 (1991) 144.

[71] TRR, Decree *c.* Sable, January 19, 1996, no. 8d, *RRT Decreta* 14 (1996) 9.

[72] See, e.g., TRR, Decrees *c.* Faltin, December 5, 1989, no. 13, *RRT Decreta* 7 (1989) 188; *c.* de Lanversin, March 16, 1994, no. 6, *RRT Decreta* 12 (1994) 27; *c.* Boccafola, February 23, 1995, no. 5, *RRT Decreta* 13 (1995) 12; *c.* Pinto, February 23, 1996, no. 5, *RRT Decreta* 14 (1996) 29; *c.* Turnaturi, October 24, 1996, no. 15, ibid. 195-196; B. 85/99 ("Relazione sull'attività della Rota Romana nell'anno giudiziario 2000," *Quaderni dello Studio Rotale* 11 [2001] 186); B. 75/00 ("Relazione sull'attività della Rota Romana nell'anno giudiziario 2001," *Quaderni dello Studio Rotale* 12 [2002] 193); *c.* Turnaturi, March 6, 2003, B. 22/03 (Maria Teresa Romano, "Rassenga ragionata della giurisprudenza di rito della Rota Romana. Anno 2003," *Quaderni dello Studio Rotale* 14 [2004] 91); *c.* Serrano Ruiz, June 22, 2002, B. 54/02; *c.* Sciacca, February 5, 2004, B. 13/04; *c.* Monier, February 20, 2004, B. 21/04; *c.* Monier,

required by the law itself in c. 1579 §2 (*CCEO*, c. 1260 §2).

With regard to each ground of nullity, there are certain elements that an affirmative definitive sentence must address in order to demonstrate moral certitude adequately. When these are lacking (and lacking in the acts), the second instance college of judges must admit the cause to an ordinary examination to ensure that the allegation is not simply accepted without being proven. We could dwell on each ground of marriage nullity here, but because of time constraints let us limit ourselves to the grounds of grave defect of discretion of judgment (c. 1095, 2°) and the incapacity to assume the essential obligations of marriage due to causes of a psychic nature (c. 1095, 3°).

When the ground of grave defect of discretion of judgment is used (c. 1095, 2°), the second instance judges should remain in doubt about the nullity of marriage and the certitude of the first instance judges when there is no evidence of a *psychic* cause of the alleged incapacity (a psychic anomaly).[73] As the Rota frequently points out, there must be a psychic anomaly or pathology that gravely affects the person at the time of consent, not merely hesitations, doubts, pressures, or imprudence.[74]

November 5, 2004, B. 111/04; *c.* Turnaturi, November 25, 2004, B. 123/04 (all cited by Maria Teresa Romano, "Rassenga ragionata della giurisprudenza di rito della Rota Romana. Anno 2004," *Quaderni dello Studio Rotale* 15 [2005] 168); B. 115/03, B. 11/04, B. 21/04 ("Relazione sull'attività della Rota Romana nell'anno giudiziario 2004," *Quaderni dello Studio Rotale* 15 [2005] 48); *c.* Pinto, February 18, 2005, B. 13/05 and *c.* De Angelis, December 2, 2005, B. 121/05 (Maria Teresa Romano, "Rassenga ragionata della giurisprudenza di rito della Rota Romana. Anno 2005," *Quaderni dello Studio Rotale* 16 [2006] 180); B. 79/06, B. 86/06 ("Relazione sull'attività della Rota Romana nell'anno giudiziario 2007," *Quaderni dello Studio Rotale* 18 [2008] 76).

[73] See, e.g., TRR, Decrees *c.* Corso, May 3, 1989, no. 5, *RRT Decreta* 7 (1989) 81-82; *c.* Pompedda, May 29, 1989, ibid. 109; *c.* Doran, December 13, 1989, no. 13, ibid. 200; *c.* Boccafola, May 3, 1990, no. 8, *RRT Decreta* 8 (1990) 87-88; *c.* Stankiewicz, May 28, 1991, no. 7, *RRT Decreta* 9 (1991) 78; *c.* Doran, June 27, 1991, no. 10, ibid. 87; *c.* Faltin, November 13, 1991, no. 15a, ibid. 145; *c.* Stankiewicz, February 27, 1992, no. 5, *RRT Decreta* 10 (1992) 20; *c.* Serrano Ruiz, February 28, 1992, no. 5, ibid. 30; *c.* Doran, April 29, 1993, no. 10, *RRT Decreta* 11 (1993) 98; *c.* Colagiovanni, January 20, 1994, no. 9, *RRT Decreta* 12 (1994) 2; *c.* Funghini, June 22, 1994, no. 2, ibid. 136; *c.* Boccafola, February 23, 1995, no. 5, *RRT Decreta* 13 (1995) 11; *c.* Pinto, February 23, 1996, no. 3, *RRT Decreta* 14 (1996) 28; *c.* Sable, March 18, 1997, no. 7, *RRT Decreta* 15 (1997) 69-70; *c.* López-Illana, December 16, 1997, no. 9, ibid. 297-298; *c.* Erlebach, January 24, 2003, B. 3/03; *c.* Ciani, July 23, 2003, B. 81/03; *c.* Verginelli, November 14, 2003, B. 110/03; *c.* Erlebach, November 21, 2003, B. 116/03 (all cited in Maria Teresa Romano, "Rassenga ragionata della giurisprudenza di rito della Rota Romana. Anno 2003," *Quaderni dello Studio Rotale* 14 [2004] 91); B. 90/04 ("Relazione sull'attività della Rota Romana nell'anno giudiziario 2004," *Quaderni dello Studio Rotale* 15 [2005] 47); B. 118/04 ("Relazione sull'attività della Rota Romana nell'anno giudiziario 2005," *Quaderni dello Studio Rotale* 16 [2006] 68).

[74] "Indeed, John Paul II admonishes that a true psychic incapacity to make valid consent can arise *only from a grave anomaly or pathology*, which must affect the capacity to understand and to will, and not merely one which causes difficulty in the

With regard to the ground of incapacity to assume the essential obligations of marriage (c. 1095, 3º), an affirmative sentence on this ground does not adequately demonstrate moral certitude when the essential obligation that could not be assumed is not specified;[75] for this leaves the second instance judges in doubt as to whether the first instance judges adequately understood the ground. Quite often, moral certitude of the alleged incapacity is lacking because there is no proven psychic anomaly rendering the assumption of an essential obligation of marriage impossible.[76] Often the affirmative sentence claims to have identified an incapacitating cause, but the cause is not truly of a *psychic* nature (c. 1095, 3°) but of another nature: for example, a conflict of character,[77] one party's poor character,[78] the breakdown of the marital relationship,[79] so-called "immaturity,"[80] immoral behavior,[81] incompatibility,[82] social and professional difficulties,[83] a vague condition such as "chronic mood disturbance,"[84] so-called

---

conjugal life (Allocution to the Auditors of the Roman Rota in the presence of those admitted, February 5, 1987, no. 7, *AAS* 79 [1987] 1457)" (TRR, Decree *c.* Stankiewicz, May 28, 1991, no. 7, *RRT Decreta* 9 [1991] 78). "In order for a defect of discretion of judgment to vitiate consent, it must provoke not a mere difficulty but a true incapacity which induces a state of impossibility of making consent. This excludes certain ill-advised acts that there may be, which cannot be explained by pathological, serious, or permanent causes" (TRR, Decree *c.* Giannecchini, April 28, 1992, no. 2, *RRT Decreta* 10 [1992] 73-74).

[75] See, e.g., TRR, Decrees *c.* Doran, July 11, 1991, no. 9a, *RRT Decreta* 9 (1991) 100; *c.* Boccafola, April 10, 2003, B. 43/03 and *c.* Ciani, November November 26, 2003, B. 118/03 (Maria Teresa Romano, "Rassenga ragionata della giurisprudenza di rito della Rota Romana. Anno 2003," *Quaderni dello Studio Rotale* 14 [2004] 91); B. 54/04, B. 84/04 ("Relazione sull'attività della Rota Romana nell'anno giudiziario 2004," *Quaderni dello Studio Rotale* 15 [2005] 48); *c.* Pinto, February 18, 2005, B. 13/05 and *c.* Yaacoub, November 9, 2005, B. 108/05 (Maria Teresa Romano, "Rassenga ragionata della giurisprudenza di rito della Rota Romana. Anno 2005," *Quaderni dello Studio Rotale* 16 [2006] 179).

[76] See, e.g., TRR, Decrees *c.* Doran, July 11, 1991, no. 9a, *RRT Decreta* 9 (1991) 100; *c.* Sable, March 18, 1997, no. 9, *RRT Decreta* 15 (1997) 70; *c.* Pompedda, October 24, 1997, nn. 4-5, ibid. 237.

[77] TRR, Decrees *c.* Ferraro, May 29, 1984, no. 10, *RRT Decreta* 2 (1984) 81; *c.* Colagiovanni, December 6, 1988, no. 3, *RRT Decreta* 6 (1988) 229.

[78] TRR, Decree *c.* Doran, July 12, 1990, no. 11, *RRT Decreta* 8 (1990) 138.

[79] TRR, Decrees *c.* Colagiovanni, November 27, 1985, no. 4, *RRT Decreta* 3 (1985) 256; *c.* Palestro, May 22, 1991, no. 6, *RRT Decreta* 9 (1991) 74; *c.* Stankiewicz, May 28, 1991, no. 7, ibid. 78; *c.* Turnaturi, December 13, 1994, no. 13, *RRT Decreta* 12 (1994) 194.

[80] TRR, Decree *c.* Doran, June 27, 1991, no. 10, *RRT Decreta* 9 (1991) 87.

[81] TRR, Decree *c.* Stankiewicz, April 3, 1992, no. 8, *RRT Decreta* 10 (1992) 65.

[82] TRR, Decree *c.* Turnaturi, December 13, 1994, nn. 9-10, *RRT Decreta* 12 (1994) 193.

[83] TRR, Decree *c.* de Lanversin, March 16, 1994, no. 9, *RRT Decreta* 12 (1994) 28.

[84] TRR, Decree B. 90/00, "Relazione sull'attività della Rota Romana nell'anno giudiziario 2000," *Quaderni dello Studio Rotale* 11 (2001) 187.

"relative" incapacity,[85] attachment to one's mother [*mammismo*],[86] or a lack of positive examples of marriage.[87]

Finally, it is conceivable that a given affirmative sentence would insufficiently demonstrate the moral certitude of the first instance judge, while, in the judgment of the second instance college of judges, the *acta et probata* themselves contain conclusive evidence of the alleged nullity of marriage. In such a case, is the second instance college free to confirm the affirmative sentence nevertheless? In principle, they are not, since the sentence cannot be confirmed if it fails to manifest an objectively reached moral certitude due to defects such as those described above. A sentence that manifestly betrays a lack of moral certitude is unjust since it has the appearance of an arbitrary act of judicial power, being based not on what is truly proven (*probata*) but merely on pieces of evidence (*probationes*); and the confirmation of an unjust act is itself an unjust act. Nevertheless, the gravity of the defects in the affirmative sentence must be carefully weighed by the second instance college of judges; for the matter is subject to the latter's free evaluation (cf. *CIC*, c. 1608 §3; *CCEO*, c. 1291 §3). It is therefore possible that the college may decide that the defects are not so significant as to induce founded doubt about the moral certitude of the first instance judge.

2. Defect of moral certitude arising from an examination of the acts (lack of extrinsic confirmability)

After examining the acts of the cause, the second instance college of judges is obliged to admit the cause to an ordinary examination if it is evident that serious errors or omissions pertaining to the evidence are detected. The predominant categories of such errors or omissions are two: when 1) there was a clear defect in how the first instance judge evaluated the evidence; and 2) there are significant lacunæ in the instruction of the cause. The second instance judges must weigh the gravity of these and the degree to which they obscure the truth or cause injustice.[88] Let us highlight some the most common and serious defects, which typically merit that the cause be admitted to an ordinary examination.

a. Evaluation of Evidence

As we mentioned earlier, reaching moral certitude is the result of the judge's

---

[85] TRR, Decree B. 44/00, "Relazione sull'attività della Rota Romana nell'anno giudiziario 2001," *Quaderni dello Studio Rotale* 12 (2002) 193.
[86] TRR, Decree B. 80/00, "Relazione sull'attività della Rota Romana nell'anno giudiziario 2001," *Quaderni dello Studio Rotale* 12 (2002) 193-194.
[87] TRR, Decree B. 19/07, "Relazione sull'attività della Rota Romana nell'anno giudiziario 2007," *Quaderni dello Studio Rotale* 18 (2008) 76.
[88] Depending on its nature and gravity, an individual deficiency may not itself demand that the judge admit the cause to an ordinary examination. Some by their nature may absolutely require it, while others may not; these latter are to be carefully weighed by the judge before a decision is made. See Erlebach, "I motivi di rinvio ad esame ordinario nella giurisprudenza della Rota Romana," 56.

free evaluation of the evidence. The judge is to evaluate the evidence freely but not arbitrarily; that is, the judge does not dictate the probative weight of the evidence but draws it out. While the judge does this freely, it is possible for the judge to err. When making a thorough examination of the acts, the second instance judges may realize that the first instance judges seriously erred in their evaluation of the evidence; they are thus bound to admit the cause to an ordinary examination so that the evidence may be evaluated correctly in the external forum. We note here defects of the first instance judges in evaluating the declarations of the parties, the testimony of witnesses, the credibility of the parties and witnesses, expert reports, the observations of the defender of the bond, and indications of valid consent.

i. The declarations of the parties

The acts sometimes reveal that there are significant contradictory statements between parties or within a party's own statements, and these contradictions are not resolved before an affirmative decision is issued. For example, in a cause of simulation against the *bonum sacramenti*, the man-petitioner says the parties never discussed his alleged simulation before consent, while the respondent writes that he told her of his non-belief in the indissolubility of marriage before consent.[89] In a cause of simulation against the *bonum sacramenti* and the *bonum prolis* on the part of the woman-petitioner—in which the lower tribunal decided the grounds in the affirmative and in the negative, respectively—the party condemned the possibility of terminating her pre-marriage pregnancy because of her religious principles, and yet these same principles would have also precluded the alleged simulation of the *bonum sacramenti*.[90] In a cause of force or grave fear, the woman-petitioner stated that her parents forced her to marry the respondent, and yet she admits that they were opposed to the relationship.[91]

ii. Testimony

There are many ways in which the first instance judges' examination of the witness testimony is defective. For example, this occurs when the judges fail to appreciate the fact that the witnesses did not know the parties until some time after consent or even after their separation.[92] Sometimes it is discovered that the direct witnesses significantly differ from the declarations of the petitioner.[93] Other times, there is a founded suspicion of collusion among the witnesses.[94]

---

[89] TRR, Decree *c.* Giannecchini, January 17, 1986, *RRT Decreta* 4 (1986) 3.

[90] TRR, Decree *c.* Ragni, March 11, 1986, no. 3a, *RRT Decreta* 4 (1986) 32.

[91] TRR, Decree *c.* Ragni, March 11, 1986, no. 4, *RRT Decreta* 4 (1986) 32.

[92] See, e.g., TRR, Decrees *c.* Colagiovanni, May 9, 1984, no. 6, *RRT Decreta* 2 (1984) 60; *c.* Colagiovanni, July 14, 1987, no. 10, *RRT Decreta* 5 (1987) 86; *c.* Giannecchini, October 8, 1996, no. 4, *RRT Decreta* 14 (1996) 190.

[93] See, e.g., TRR, Decrees *c.* de Lanversin, January 16, 1991, no. 8, *RRT Decreta* 9 (1991) 7; *c.* Huber, February 3, 1994, no. 4c, *RRT Decreta* 12 (1994) 12; *c.* Giannecchini, April 4, 1995, no. 8, *RRT Decreta* 13 (1995) 43; *c.* Ragni, June 20, 1995, no. 4a, ibid. 70.

[94] See, e.g., TRR, Decrees *c.* Pompedda, January 24, 1984, *RRT Decreta* 2 (1984) 11; *c.* Stankiewicz, June 20, 1985, no. 5, *RRT Decreta* 3 (1985) 168; *c.* Ferraro, April 20,

Quite frequently, the witnesses are too general and not objective or vague, either because of ignorance[95] or because they are clearly trying to oppose the other party[96] or to favor the party to whom they are associated.[97]

iii. Credibility

Despite the fact that most statements are acquired under oath, credibility cannot be presumed; the judge must become certain of the credibility of statements before deeming them probative.[98] Second instance judges must admit to an ordinary examination, for example, causes in which the credibility of the petitioner remains in doubt; this is very frequently done by the Rota.[99] The judge remains in doubt about the credibility of the petitioner in circumstances such as the following, when they persist unresolved: when it is proven that the woman-petitioner lied to the priest preparing her for marriage as well as to her spouse;[100] when the man-petitioner allegedly lied both to his parents and the Church by allegedly committing total simulation;[101] when, in an effort to prove that the woman-respondent simulated, the man says that before the wedding she was concerned only about having documents in order, when in fact he ordered her to take care of the documents;[102] when a man-petitioner said that he married the respondent on the basis of a mere sexual impulse without any affection, while the respondent and the rest of the evidence indicates that he married for love;[103] when the priest-witness doubts the petitioner's credibility.[104]

1985, no. 7, ibid. 108.

95 See, e.g., TRR, Decrees *c.* Colagiovanni, January 29, 1985, nn. 7-8, *RRT Decreta* 3 (1985) 25-26; *c.* Colagiovanni, March 26, 1985, no. 5, ibid. 103; *c.* Giannecchini, January 17, 1986, *RRT Decreta* 4 (1986) 2; *c.* Pompedda, February 27, 1989, *RRT Decreta* 7 (1989) 38; *c.* Serrano Ruiz, June 7, 1996, no. 4, *RRT Decreta* 14 (1996) 104.

96 See, e.g., TRR, Decrees *c.* Serrano Ruiz, February 24, 1984, no. 3b, *RRT Decreta* 2 (1984) 21; *c.* Colagiovanni, May 8, 1984, no. 7, ibid. 57; *c.* Giannecchini, January 17, 1986, *RRT Decreta* 4 (1986) 2-3.

97 See, e.g., TRR, Decree *c.* de Lanversin, April 30, 1986, no. 4, *RRT Decreta* 4 (1986) 55.

98 See Gero P. Weishaupt, "De necessitate credibilitatis partium intrinsecæ ad certitudinem moralem in causis matrimonialibus adipiscendam," *Periodica* 95 (2006) 647-674.

99 See, e.g., TRR, Decrees *c.* Agustoni, October 9, 1984, nn. 3-4, *RRT Decreta* 2 (1984) 111; *c.* Agustoni, January 29, 1985, no. 7, *RRT Decreta* 3 (1985) 15-16; *c.* Colagiovanni, January 29, 1985, no. 6, ibid. 25; *c.* Doran, May 11, 1989, no. 9, *RRT Decreta* 7 (1989) 85; *c.* Doran, December 13, 1989, no. 13, ibid. 200; *c.* Giannecchini, July 23, 1996, no. 8a, *RRT Decreta* 14 (1996) 157; B. 55/07 ("Relazione sull'attività della Rota Romana nell'anno giudiziario 2007," *Quaderni dello Studio Rotale* 18 [2008] 77).

100 TRR, Decree *c.* Masala, March 5, 1985, no. 6, *RRT Decreta* 3 (1985) 80.

101 TRR, Decree *c.* Serrano Ruiz, November 22, 1985, *RRT Decreta* 3 (1985) 253.

102 TRR, Decree *c.* de Lanversin, June 18, 1986, no. 4, *RRT Decreta* 4 (1986) 91.

103 TRR, Decree *c.* de Lanversin, March 9, 1988, no. 3, *RRT Decreta* 6 (1988) 64.

104 TRR, Decree *c.* Huber, February 3, 1994, no. 4b, *RRT Decreta* 12 (1994) 12.

iv. Expert reports

The defective evaluation of an expert report also merits that a cause be admitted to an ordinary examination when the report in fact leaves room for reasonable doubts about the alleged incapacity. This occurs, for example, when the report lacks certainty, stating that there is only a possibility of a psychic disturbance.[105] Or even if it is certain, the report is filled with conjecture.[106] Other times, the report consists merely of a psychological description of the party, lacking any conclusions about the presence of a psychic anomaly.[107] The first instance judge wrongly reaches moral certitude when the experts themselves admit that they are in doubt about the authenticity and veracity of certain acts.[108]

v. Observations of the Defender of the Bond

Another area in which the judge's evaluation of the acts is proven to be defective is when the observations of the defender of the bond *adversus nullitatem* are completely ignored in the sentence.[109] While the law itself does not explicitly demand that these each be addressed in the sentence, failure to do so causes the sentence to inadequately display the first instance judge's moral certitude. For the defender's observations is a public act that is to be given to the advocates and the parties during the discussion phase of the process (c. 1603). A sentence that does not address such arguments leaves one in doubt as to whether the judge has truly resolved the doubts raised by the defender before issuing an affirmative decision. Such a sentence must therefore be admitted to an ordinary examination in second instance.

vi. Indications of Valid Consent

While the sentence may contain strong arguments in favor of the nullity of marriage, a thorough analysis of the acts discloses the fact that the first instance judge ignored significant indications of the validity of consent—indications in favor of the presumption of law (c. 1060). For example, with respect to the ground of grave lack of discretion of judgment, the allegedly incapable party, who was said to be gravely immature, may show signs of maturity and good judgment, and these are not addressed in the sentence. Examples of this are the following acts of the allegedly incapable party: rescuing and caring for siblings when in danger due to the character of their mother's new boyfriend;[110] the

---

[105] See, e.g., TRR, Decrees *c.* Stankiewicz, April 3, 1992, no. 6, *RRT Decreta* 10 (1992) 64; *c.* Funghini, June 22, 1994, no. 7, *RRT Decreta* 12 (1994) 137; *c.* Faltin, May 3, 1995, no. 10f, *RRT Decreta* 13 (1995) 59.

[106] See, e.g., TRR, Decrees B. 102/02, B. 51/04, B. 79/05 ("Relazione sull'attività della Rota Romana nell'anno giudiziario 2005," *Quaderni dello Studio Rotale* 16 [2006] 69).

[107] See, e.g., TRR, Decrees *c.* Funghini, June 22, 1994, no. 8, *RRT Decreta* 12 (1994) 137; *c.* Sable, October 24, 1995, 13 (1995) 120.

[108] See, e.g., TRR, Decree *c.* Ragni, April 29, 1986, no. 3b, *RRT Decreta* 4 (1986) 52.

[109] See, e.g., TRR, Decree *c.* Faltin, May 26, 1988, no. 6b, *RRT Decreta* 6 (1988) 136.

[110] TRR, Decree *c.* Stankiewicz, October 10, 1985, no. 3b, *RRT Decreta* 3 (1985) 222.

successful carrying out of his private life;[111] freedom in many areas of life, including in relationships;[112] the ability to carry out a "normal" two year pre-nuptial relationship with the other party;[113] and exhibiting a good character and a demonstrated understanding of the *bona matrimonialia.*[114]

b. Instruction

When the second instance judges are examining the acts of the cause from first instance, they are also observing whether there are any notable lacunæ in the instruction. If there are, the cause should be admitted to an ordinary examination since the existence of significant outstanding evidence should leave the judge in doubt about the object of the trial. This is not to say that the cause must be perfectly instructed; but the acts must show that serious efforts were made to obtain all significant evidence, and an affirmative sentence should explain why it could not be obtained and why its absence does not amount to a prudent doubt. For, depending on the nature of the evidence, the judge might find it impossible to reach moral certitude when some evidence is lacking.

For example, when an expert report in causes of psychic incapacity is lacking, whether it is due to a grave defect of discretion of judgment (c. 1095, 2°) or incapacity to assume the essential obligations of marriage (c. 1095, 3°), the second instance judges should almost always admit the cause to an ordinary examination. This is among the most frequently recurring motives for admitting a cause to an ordinary examination by the Roman Rota; dozens of examples could be cited.[115] As a rule, an expert report is required whenever the allegation

---

[111] TRR, Decree *c.* Ragni, April 29, 1986, no. 3d, *RRT Decreta* 4 (1986) 52.
[112] TRR, Decree *c.* Colagiovanni, July 14, 1987, no. 6, *RRT Decreta* 5 (1987) 85-86.
[113] TRR, Decree *c.* Funghini, June 22, 1994, no. 3, *RRT Decreta* 12 (1994) 136.
[114] TRR, Decree *c.* Pinto, February 23, 1996, no. 6, *RRT Decreta* 14 (1996) 29.
[115] See the many decrees cited in the recent Annual Reports of the Roman Rota on this point, as printed in the annual journal *Quaderni dello Studio Rotale*: seven decrees are cited at 18 (2008) 76, twelve at 17 (2007) 97, eight at 16 (2006) 69, and three at 15 (2005) 47-48. More specifically:
For causes involving c. 1095, 2°, see, e.g., the following Rotal decrees: *c.* Agustoni, December 4, 1984, *RRT Decreta* 2 (1984) 137; *c.* Pompedda, January 29, 1985, *RRT Decreta* 3 (1985) 22; *c.* Jarawan, October 26, 1985, no. 2, ibid. 235; *c.* Giannecchini, April 28, 1992, no. 3.E, *RRT Decreta* 10 (1992) 74; *c.* Doran, April 29, 1993, no. 11, *RRT Decreta* 11 (1993) 98; *c.* de Lanversin, November 17, 1993, no. 9, ibid. 204; B. 22/04, B. 56/04, B. 84/04, B. 90/04 ("Relazione sull'attività della Rota Romana nell'anno giudiziario 2004," *Quaderni dello Studio Rotale* 15 [2005] 47); *c.* López-Illana, 11.XI.2004, B. 112/04 and *c.* Defilippi, March 16, 2006, B. 24/06 (Maria Teresa Romano, "Rassenga ragionata della giurisprudenza di rito della Rota Romana. Anno 2005," *Quaderni dello Studio Rotale* 16 [2006] 174).
For causes involving c. 1095, 3°, see, e.g., the following Rotal decrees: *c.* Ragni, February 19, 1985, no. 4, *RRT Decreta* 3 (1985) 47; *c.* Colagiovanni, November 27, 1985, no. 4, ibid. 256; *c.* Doran, July 12, 1990, no. 14, *RRT Decreta* 8 (1990) 139-140; *c.* Palestro, May 22, 1991, no. 5, *RRT Decreta* 9 (1991) 73; *c.* Ragni, June 19, 1994, no. 2, *RRT Decreta* 12 (1994) 58; *c.* Huber, June 25, 2003, B. 69/03 (Maria Teresa

of incapacity is at issue in a trial; the exception of c. 1680 (*CCEO*, c. 1366) is to be read strictly (c. 18). This is because a psychic anomaly alone can render a person incapable; and if the anomaly is truly psychic in nature, typically only a psychological expert can provide conclusive evidence of its existence. The Supreme Tribunal of the Apostolic Signatura has identified two exceptions: namely, when medical documentation or qualified testimony in the acts already establishes the incapacity of the person or when the incapacity is otherwise evident in the proven facts and circumstances. Following the example of jurisprudence, the judge should consider these exceptions to be rare. Outside of these exceptions, the judge cannot reach moral certitude without an expert report that provides a firm basis for concluding that a psychic anomaly rendered the person incapable at the time of consent.[116]

Another recurring lacuna in the acts that the Rota draws attention to is a lack of *ex officio* witnesses, when it is clear that they exist and have valuable testimony to offer.[117] Among those witnesses who should be cited *ex officio* are those who are presumed to know about the alleged defect of consent because of their public function (c. 1573), especially the priest who prepared the couple for marriage or received their consent,[118] other priests who have been close to or ministered to the parties,[119] and witnesses of the act of consent itself (*testes*

Romano, "Rassenga ragionata della giurisprudenza di rito della Rota Romana. Anno 2003," *Quaderni dello Studio Rotale* 14 [2004] 92).

[116] Supreme Tribunal of the Apostolic Signatura, Response, June 16, 1998, prot. no. 28252/97 VT, *Periodica* 87 (1998) 619-622, at no. 5. Another exception found in canonical doctrine is that the judge can decide not to cite an expert when the alleged incapacity is manifestly unfounded and a negative decision is inevitable. See, e.g., Paolo Bianchi, "Le perizie mediche e, in particolare, quelle riguardanti il can. 1095," *La nullità del matrimonio: temi processuali e sostantivi in occasione della* Dignitas connubii, eds. H. Franceschi, J. Llobell, and M.Á. Ortiz, Subsidia canonica (Rome: Università della Santa Croce, 2005) 154-155.

[117] See, e.g., TRR, Decrees *c.* Ferraro, May 29, 1984, no. 6, *RRT Decreta* 2 (1984) 80; *c.* Ferraro, December 18, 1984, no. 5, ibid. 149; *c.* Ferraro, April 20, 1985, no. 7, *RRT Decreta* 3 (1985) 108; *c.* Agustoni, May 21, 1985, no. 3, ibid. 125; *c.* Pinto, May 24, 1985, no. 8, ibid. 143; *c.* Funghini, October 16, 1985, no. 5, ibid. 229; *c.* Pompedda, October 28, 1985, ibid. 241; *c.* de Lanversin, March 20, 1986, no. 7, *RRT Decreta* 4 (1986) 43; *c.* de Lanversin, April 30, 1986, no. 2, ibid. 55; *c.* de Lanversin, June 18, 1986, no. 5, ibid. 92; *c.* Pompedda, June 21, 1986, ibid. 106; *c.* Giannecchini, March 11, 1988, no. 6, *RRT Decreta* 6 (1988) 73; *c.* Faltin, December 5, 1989, no. 11, *RRT Decreta* 7 (1989) 187; *c.* Funghini, January 14, 1997, no. 4, *RRT Decreta* 15 (1997) 5; *c.* Bruno, February 28, 1997, no. 3f, ibid. 55; *c.* Civili, October 15, 1997, no. 7, ibid. 194.

[118] See, e.g., TRR, Decrees *c.* de Lanversin, January 17, 1997, no. 15, *RRT Decreta* 15 (1997) 10; *c.* Faltin, January 29, 1997, no. 9, in ibid. 17; B. 71/04, "Relazione sull'attività della Rota Romana nell'anno giudiziario 2005," *Quaderni dello Studio Rotale* 16 (2006) 69.

[119] See, e.g., TRR, Decrees *c.* Doran, July 26, 1988, no. 8, *RRT Decreta* 6 (1988) 180; *c.* de Lanversin, January 18, 1989, no. 8, *RRT Decreta* 7 (1989) 7; *c.* de Lanversin, January 16, 1991, no. 9, *RRT Decreta* 9 (1991) 7; *c.* Funghini, January 14, 1997, no. 5, *RRT Decreta* 15 (1997) 6; *c.* de Lanversin, January 13, 1997, no. 9, ibid. 24.

sacramentales).[120] Also, the judge should cite the family and friends of the one whose consent is allegedly defective[121] and other close associates of the erring party.[122]

Conclusion

This tour through the jurisprudence of the Roman Rota on the moral certitude to be reached before confirming an affirmative sentence and especially defects in that certitude offer canonists an occasion to come to a new appreciation of the authentic meaning of moral certitude and how serious a standard it truly is. By no means is it to be seen as an insurmountable standard, but it is a standard that is not easily or routinely met. This may call for a *novus habitus mentis* for tribunal practitioners in North American who, for example, may be accustomed to seeing the nullity of marriage as something that is self-evident simply when a petitioner believably relates a few startling facts about his or her upbringing or the parties' courtship, or when the common life lasted only six months. The burden of proof remains with petitioners even in these situations; but it is a burden that the judge shares, following the model of Jesus Christ the Good Shepherd. And the judge can only do this in charity and in truth if his or her judicial labors are animated by prayer.

> O God, who marvelously created the family at the very beginning of the world and willed the conjugal covenant to be elevated to the dignity of a sacrament through Your Son, who commanded that "what God has joined man may not separate" (Matt. 19:6); mercifully regard my lowliness, to whom the Church has entrusted the most lofty responsibility of declaring whether some marriages, while appearing valid, were however null and void from the beginning due to a defect or impediment.
>
> Fill my mind, O Lord, with the light of the Holy Spirit so that, after diligently and carefully collecting and examining the proofs and applying canon law to the factual circumstances with thorough deliberation, I may be able to uncover and

---

[120] See, e.g., TRR, Decrees *c.* Funghini, October 16, 1985, no. 6, *RRT Decreta* 3 (1985) 229; *c.* de Lanversin, June 18, 1986, no. 5, *RRT Decreta* 4 (1986) 92; *c.* Funghini, June 14, 1989, no. 6, *RRT Decreta* 7 (1989) 133; *c.* de Lanversin, January 16, 1991, no. 9, *RRT Decreta* 9 (1991) 7; *c.* Civili, May 12, 1993, no. 9c, *RRT Decreta* 11 (1993) 110; *c.* Ragni, April 19, 1994, no. 2, *RRT Decreta* 12 (1994) 58; *c.* Ragni, February 28, 1995, no. 6, *RRT Decreta* 13 (1995) 18; *c.* de Lanversin, April 24, 1996, no. 8, *RRT Decreta* 14 (1996) 77-78; *c.* de Lanversin, January 13, 1997, no. 9, *RRT Decreta* 15 (1997) 24.

[121] See, e.g., TRR, Decree *c.* Bruno, October 28, 1994, no. 3c, *RRT Decreta* 12 (1994) 182; *c.* de Lanversin, January 13, 1997, no. 9, *RRT Decreta* 15 (1997) 24; *c.* Alwan, May 16, 1997, no. 6, ibid. 84; *c.* Caberletti, November 28, 1997, no. 10, ibid. 272.

[122] See, e.g., TRR, Decree *c.* de Lanversin, April 24, 1996, no. 8, *RRT Decreta* 14 (1996) 78.

clearly observe the objective truth of things, at least as far as humanly possible.

O Lord, permit me not to be led astray by false testimony or fallacious arguments, nor to reject wrongly the legitimate requests of the faithful because of weariness in the deep investigation of the truth. Assist me lest, being deceived by a vain hope of helping the souls of the spouses, I place my own soul in jeopardy, distorting the sacred dignity of so great a sacrament by declaring a marriage null despite the fact that there remain even one prudent doubt about its validity.

O God, who know the hearts of men, although I aim to have only You before my eyes and to foster in my mind an upright intention, nevertheless, deign to liberate me from any disordered inclination or aversion that may be concealed in the hidden places of my spirit, lest I even unknowingly turn aside from the path of truth and justice.

Be present to me and my labors, O sweetest Virgin Mary. Grant, by your maternal protection, that I may not suffer punishment for my decisions from the Supreme Judge; rather, may I obtain the reward of the good and faithful servant. Amen.

Mother of Good Counsel, Seat of Wisdom, pray for me.[123]

---

[123] Vittorio Bartoccetti, *De causis matrimonialibus (Titulus XX). Extractus ex volumine III Commentarii in iudicia ecclesiastica iuxta Codicem iuris canonici* (Rome: Typis publicæ officinæ polygraphicæ, 1951) 344; idem, *De regulis juris canonici* (Rome: Angelo Belardetti Editore, 1955) 260-261.

SEMINAR

ADVOCACY: CIVIL AND CANON LAW ISSUES

Doctor Patricia M. Dugan

Introduction

Professionally, I have worked actively as a lawyer in both civil law and canon law. The first seven years of my *civil* practice were in criminal defense trial work. I suspended that practice to study canon law. When I returned to Philadelphia I took my civil practice into family law, again, a highly litigious field of law. Five years ago my mother came to live with me and during that time I have come to see, first hand, the sad way in which seniors are treated within our U.S. society. So now, I am morphing my civil practice again, this time into elder law. It is less litigious, but more effective on the quality of life for people on a basic level. My *canon* law practice has always been an independent one. I have never worked *at a job*, for the Church. I have always been an independent consultant. It was not until 2002 that I started to work specifically for individuals and these were both accusers and *accused priests* in allegations of sexual abuse of a minor.

This work has been for me, as it has been for many others, something we were not specifically trained for in our canonical studies. Without any identifiable jurisprudence to consult, we have all very much learned *on the job*. I have been greatly influenced by my civil trial work in how I advise or advocate for an accused priest. I have learned *hands on*, that neither civil law nor canon law is superior one to the other. I have, however, dreamed of a system that would take the best of each system and melt them together. My purpose here is to explain on a very basic level, some legal concepts that civil lawyers cannot do without and cannot understand how canon lawyers *do* do without. These concepts can be the bane of the existence of diocesan attorneys, and of civil attorneys who sue the Catholic Church hoping to find deep pockets or perhaps, more importantly, closure for their clients.

When I talk about civil law, it is mostly referring to *federal* rules and law, as opposed to state law. Think of it as the difference between universal law and particular law. Also, there is always some confusion between canon and civil lawyers because among the non-canon lawyers there is actually a differentiation between civil lawyers and criminal lawyers. Think Barristers and Solicitors. So, here too, I will distinguish between those. Finally, this presentation is going to deal on the basic level of civil law, civil law 101. It is not going to delve deeply into nuances of jurisprudence or reversible error. I am just going to deal with the civil law concepts, explain them on a basic level, and then correlate them to canons that may exist for the same concept. Sometimes there is no correlation. So, I am starting here with the basic civil law concept, character.

Character Testimony

In civil law, character testimony is based on the good character of the adult person involved in the litigation. The essence of character is a combination of moral and ethical qualities that are formed in a person throughout their lives. Civil law puts enormous stock in character testimony when it is used in a criminal trial. There is virtually no use of it in civil cases[1] but it can be extremely useful in criminal matters. If a defendant can present character testimony, it alone can determine the verdict in a case. In a criminal trial, a defendant may always introduce evidence as to his or her good character, to prove that he or she did not commit the crime accused.

Character evidence is not merely the presentation of someone to say that the defendant is a good person, or saved a cat from a tree, or helped an old nun across the road. There is a specific line of questioning that must be followed when introducing character testimony into a trial. In Pennsylvania, there is a sequence of questions that include: *how* does the witness know the defendant; who else does the witness know who is acquainted with both this witness and the defendant; when was the last time the witness discussed the defendant with some of these mutual acquaintances; and finally, among those people who know the defendant and whom the witness knows, what is the defendant's reputation for being an honest and law abiding citizen. Usually the prosecutor will have no cross-examination.

This line of questioning can lead to many nuances for the defendant. An example would be if the witness can testify that he knows the defendant from seeing him at Mass every single Sunday and holy day for the last fifty years. Another example of strategy using a character witness would be if the witness could say that among those mutual acquaintances were the Holy Father and Mother Theresa. Who the actual character witness is, can also be a strategic decision. If it is the defendant's mother, than that is usually yawned at by a jury. If it is Bill Gates, the jury would sit-up and take notice. In the end, after these initial attempts to personally ingratiate the defendant to the jury, the aim is to show that the defendant is of good and law abiding character in the eyes of the witness and others who know him.

If the defendant does successfully present un-impeached character testimony, the Judge must instruct the jury as to the weight that testimony may be given. A typical jury instruction on this can read:

> Evidence of good character or reputation of an accused is always competent in the trial of a criminal action, and is to be entitled to be considered by you. You, the jury, should consider all of the relevant testimony, including that relating to the defendant's good character or reputation, and if, on such consideration, there exists a reasonable doubt of his or her guilt, even though that doubt may arise merely from his or her previous good character, then he or she is entitled to an

[1] Cases of defamation and/or slander would be the exceptions in civil law cases.

acquittal.

In criminal law, character testimony alone is sufficient to affect an acquittal for a defendant, no matter what the crime. Think about that. There could be eyewitness testimony, strong motive, and a smoking gun, but if there is even one, un-impeached character witness, the jury has cause to vote not guilty. This harkens back to the "Hail Mary" pass kind of closing argument by the defense, the one where the defense lawyer claims that he is not asking for the jury to find the defendant innocent, just "not guilty" of the crime.

In canon law character is not nurtured or formed, but imprinted by the sacraments of baptism, confirmation and holy orders.[2] These sacraments "imprint in the soul an indelible character, that is, a spiritual sign that distinguishes it from all others." It is this indelible character which makes us like Christ and incorporated in the Church.[3] Baptism is necessary for salvation. The sacrament of confirmation confers a character that enriches one with the gift of the Holy Spirit and links one more closely to the Church.[4] The sacrament of orders marks some with an indelible character constituting them as sacred ministers, consecrated and deputed so that, each according to his grade, fulfills in the person of Christ, the offices of teaching, sanctifying and ruling, to nourish the people of God.[5] Character is a type of anointing or marking, not an aggregate of features and traits, like courage, honesty or perseverance, which form the individual nature of a person.

In canon law, we see the *aggregate* type of character of a person relevant in broader ways. For example, an expert witness must be of good character in canonical cases, in order to serve as an expert. Monsignor Kenneth E. Boccafola in the *Exegetical Commentary of the Code of Canon Law* on canon 1575, comments that when a judge selects an expert, the qualities sought in the expert, above all, should be profound knowledge of the subject, a *good reputation* among his peers, and *personal integrity and honesty*. That is in the expert!

There is no provision for the weight of the character of an accused in a penal matter. When I advocate for an accused priest, the first thing I ask that priest to do is to assemble a list of potential character witnesses, not to approach them, just line them up. This usually gives the accused priest an action that makes him focus on something other than the accusation and the process. But, it also tells me a lot about my client. To my great surprise, I have had priest clients who could not give me the name of any potential character witness, or at least one who would be relevant to the last twenty years. Besides giving the accused priest or cleric some homework to keep him actively involved in the working of the case, it gives the priest an insight into the good he has done during his ministry. I always ask for the opportunity to review the priest's personnel file. This is something very few priests do, even though they can do it at any time.

[2] See canon 845.
[3] See canon 849.
[4] See canon 879.
[5] See canon 1008.

Frequently, a priest is pleasantly surprised to find letters of praise, gratitude and commendation for work and events. More often than not, these types of letters have never been made known to the priest. These are always worth emphasizing in a penal process. Even though they do not hold the same evidentiary weight as in civil law, the ability to make or break a case, it is hard to imagine that evidence of a good character, especially over a long period of time, would not somehow be impressed in the mind of the finder of fact. A civil lawyer who represents an accused priest often cannot understand why that priest's character can be of no relevance to a review board, an ordinary, or *turnus*. This is especially true if the accused is dealing with an accusation from many years before. Do all of the years of ministry in between count for *anything* in the process? Definitely not in the same way it would in a criminal prosecution.

Experts and Their Testimony

The use of experts in cases, both canonical and civil, is very similar. It is probably the one area where the two systems of canon and civil law are most alike in procedure and advocacy.

General witness testimony in civil cases limits itself to facts within the observation of the witness based on his or her own observation, knowledge or recollection. These are gathered by the witness personally using his or her own senses. It is the facts, just the facts, without the witness' impressions, opinions, inferences or conclusions. Witness opinion, based on facts, is not admissible as evidence. What can be discerned from the facts set forth before the fact finder, either a judge or a jury, is the job solely of that fact finder and not of the witness. There are specific exceptions in civil law which allow a witness to provide opinion evidence. These are divided as lay opinion and expert opinion.

A general/lay witness may give his or her opinion when that opinion is (1) rationally based on the perception of the witness; (2) helpful to a clear understanding of the witness' testimony or the determination of a fact in issue; and (3) not based on scientific, technical, or other specialized knowledge. Thus, a lay witness who has had an opportunity to observe a vehicle in motion can usually testify that it was speeding. Giving testimony approximating height or weight or whether someone's voice is raised is technically opinion testimony, but permitted, even though it is not precise.

In civil law, expert testimony is testimony about a scientific, technical, or professional issue given by a person qualified to testify because of his or her familiarity with the subject or special training in the field. In order to give such testimony, the expert witness must *qualify* as an expert. Both sides of a case may ask the court to hear an expert they have selected who supports their case. The Court may also use an expert of its choosing to assist the Court in obtaining certain knowledge. If there were a contest over the mental competency of an individual, the Court may request the testimony of an unbiased medical doctor using hypotheticals of symptoms exhibited by the individual in question and the possible diagnoses that can come from the symptoms attested to factually.

Frequently in civil law, a trial can become a battle of the experts. This becomes expensive and since most lawyers in civil trials in the United States, have a retainer agreement with their clients, they regulate the money spent on expert testimony. The side with the most experts or the most expensive experts can be viewed to have an edge toward success, especially in trials involving huge reimbursement amounts and possible million dollar verdicts.

It is not possible to have a *single* evidentiary rule for qualifying an expert in a civil or criminal trial. Usually, when an expert is proffered by one side of the trial, the Court will hold an in camera hearing to decide if the witness proffered qualifies as an expert. The opposing counsel is given the opportunity to challenge the credentials of the proffered witness to testify before the court as an expert in the field at issue. The Court will hear about the proffered witness' education and background, publications, professional work, and *previous experience as an expert witness in other trials*. Depending on the issue of the contest, other factors can enter into whether or not a witness is qualified as an expert or the broadness of the opinion eventually offered. Courts hearing a workmen's compensation case may be more swayed by the testimony of a treating physician as opposed to a doctor who never treated the person bringing the case.

The testimony of an expert is often the evidence that decides the case for a fact finder. Expert evidence is often the most important part of civil and criminal cases today. Perhaps today's juries, as fact finders, are more attuned to expert evidence with the proliferation of television shows that crack every weekly crime with scientific evidence finessed by handsome actors who display excitement over the most technical of scientific details. In reality, fingerprint examination, blood analysis and DNA are common kinds of expert evidence heard in criminal cases from homicides to drunk driving. In civil cases, the work of accident analysis, varied engineers, and forensic accountants can be critical not only in assessing negligence, but also damages both actual and punitive. In civil trials, expert testimony can equate to big bucks.

The role of the expert in canon law is less about big verdicts and more about being helpful to the integrity of the process. The canons that deal with experts in general are canons 1574 through 1581.[6] Specifically, these general canons deal with the use of experts as a source or means of proof in a canonical trial. A judge is to use an expert when it is prescribed by law, or, when a judge ascertains that such help is needed to reach moral certitude in some fact. A judge can select who will serve as expert, after having consulted with the parties, or at their request. The judge can also accept reports already made by other experts. The expert in a matrimonial case should be professionally qualified in psychiatry and psychology. This is particularly important since the function of some experts is only to help establish a given fact, but in a matrimonial case, the expert is to help the Judge to fully understand the nature of the matter in question and to draw conclusions from the facts presented. Experts can be excluded or

---

[6] There are also canons on specific situations such as valuing fine art in canon 1189.

objected to for the same reasons as a witness.[7] Canon 1577 directs the judge to define precisely the object of the inquiry and the specific task for which the expert is needed. In the *Exegetical Commentary of the Code of Canon Law* on canon 1577, Monsignor Boccafola, the expert on experts, notes that "Judges are often negligent in that they give only a general charge to the Expert without clearly specifying the precise task that they require of him" (1337). This is a complaint heard often in regards to issues in civil law cases as well.

To sum this up, experts are held necessary to process and trial in both civil and canon law. Who serves as an expert must be carefully decided based on qualifications and experience. What the expert may give an opinion on, must be defined before testimony or a report is submitted into the case. Finally, both systems of law require the Judge to not just accept the Expert report, but to actively evaluate it in relation to the facts of the case.

Statute of Limitations

Civil Lawyers tend to think that there is very little similarity between statutes of limitation in their civil system, and the prescription of canon law. In fact, they are very much alike.

In civil law systems a statute of limitations sets forth the maximum time after an event that legal proceedings based on that event may be initiated. Once the time allowed for a case by a statute of limitations runs out, if a party raises it as a defense and that defense is accepted, any further litigation is foreclosed. Most jurisdictions provide that limitations can be tolled or suspended under certain circumstances. Tolling will prevent the time for filing suit from running while the condition exists. For example, if a child is sexually abused at an early age, the statute of limitation on this offense can be suspended until the child reaches majority or to some maximum age after majority is reached. In Pennsylvania, a divorce proceeding will be tolled if, during the divorce proceedings, one of the parties files for personal bankruptcy, until that bankruptcy is completed. Statutes of limitation can be complicated in their variety. Based on legislative acts and laws, there are different time limits for different crimes. Debt collection statutes can vary by state, by type of debt, by amount of debt. Some statutes do not begin to run until a certain event happens. For instance, the discovery of the harm, as in a medical malpractice claim where the fact or the impact of the doctor's mistake is not immediately apparent, starts the statute running. In some jurisdictions the action is said not to have become actionable until the harm is discovered.

Statutes of limitation are enacted to protect persons against claims made after evidence has been lost, memories have faded, or witnesses have disappeared. The periods prescribed for different actions in different jurisdictions vary considerably. If a case involves identification issues, it is even worse. Identification testimony is not the most reliable testimony even when it is done close to the time of the event. Now with the hindsight help of DNA

[7] See canon 1576.

testing, the accuracy of even eyewitness identification is often contradicted. Imagine how faulty it can be years and years later.

In cases involving the abuse of minors, there have been some actions in legislatures to retroactively change the statute of limitation for this crime. It is the retroactive part that has many constitutional scholars opposed. How can one crime or class of people be targeted? In some states proposed legislation may go so far as to specifically target Catholic priests and no one else. The proposed legislations vary in how far back the window should be opened and for how long. Some of these proposals are totally unconstitutional and pander to the emotional hot button issues which are the mantras of the media.

In canon law, this concept is known as prescription, and is the three canon Title X of Book I, canons 197, 198 and 199. Prescription originated as a method of acquiring or losing goods or rights and for being freed of obligations through the passage of time. Canon 197 shows the concept to be more personal in nature in the code than in civil law. In this canon, the Church "canonizes" civil law for the purposes of acquiring or extinguishing property rights, as long as it does not contradict the civil laws which also have some sovereignty over the property.[8]

Canon 198 speaks to the good faith of a prescription: No prescription is valid unless it is based on good faith, not only in its beginning, but throughout the whole time required for the prescription, without prejudice to canon 1362. The emphasis on good faith is not one common to any statute of limitation I could find. Civil law eliminates good faith from its statute of limitations equation. There is a much more practical side which seems to be more on keeping order in the already back logged courts struggling with trial schedules and choking on judicial operating budgets.

Canon 199, like a civil statute often does, specifically lists matters that are not affected by prescription: these include rights and obligations of divine law, apostolic privilege, and the certain and undisputed boundaries of ecclesiastical territories. An example in criminal law of such an exclusion is where the crime of murder has no statute of limitations.

Canon 1344 examines the case of a perceptive penalty, which may be determinate or indeterminate. This is out of the realm of this discussion in any detail, but in civil law, there is no provision for a Judge to delay sentencing for the good of society or the defendant himself. There are circumstances though, such as where a judge may delay sentencing for a first offender who did not make bail on a misdemeanor conviction, if the judge's intention is to sentence him to time served.

So, the reasoning behind prescription and statutes of limitations is very similar when it comes to property. The canonical reference to personal rights is not a priority in civil statutes of limitations. When it comes to criminal aspects, the civil laws are tighter and much more defined. The real difference between

[8] See also canon 1268 in the acquisition of goods.

statutes of limitations and prescription is in the retroactive possibilities in canon law, such as has been perceived by both canonists and civil lawyers in the *graviora delicta* of sexual abuse of minors. But now, with the continual onslaught of lobbying for suspending of statutes of limitations for crimes of sexual abuse of a minor, is there really that much of a difference between the two systems?

Jurisprudence of Courts/Case Law

Jurisprudence can refer to either of two definitions. First, in common law jurisdictions, it means simply "case law", the law that is established through the decisions of the courts and other officials. In the second definition, it means the philosophy of law, or legal theory, which studies not what the law is in a particular jurisdiction, but law in general, and any attributes common to all or certain legal systems. This presentation refers to the definition of jurisprudence as case law.

In the United States, the law is derived from four sources. These four sources are the U.S. Constitution, statutory law (which are the laws enacted by legislative bodies), administrative regulations (which are established by governmental agencies like the IRS, and case law (often cited as a subdivision of common law). Case law is the reported decisions of selected appellate and other courts (called courts of first impression) which make new interpretations of the law and can be cited as precedents in a process known as *stare decisis*. *Stare decisis* is the legal principle by which judges are obligated to respect the precedents established by prior decisions. This doctrine is basically a requirement that a Court must follow the rules established by a Court above it. The purpose of the principle is that a judge should act in a predictable and non-chaotic manner. The Courts are often asked to interpret legislation as well as rule on its constitutionality. This gives society stability in both its legislation and its judiciary.

Case law makes the world go round in civil/criminal law. Law firms spend astronomical amounts of money on West Law and Lexis-Nexis, to "Shepardize" a case; that is, get the latest case law on a particular issue. It is expected that a lawyer will have copies of cases he or she relies on, copied and ready to hand up to the bench or at least a complete citation for looking up later by the law clerk. The stronger your fact situation matches the facts of the precedent case, the more likely you will be in convincing a court to find in your favor. This is true of every type of legal issue from what makes a driver drunk to how disabled one has to be to collect workmen's compensation. This world of case law jurisprudence works best in a system where trials are a matter of public record.

Obviously, this has not been the case in canon law. In canon law we have canon 19 as our guiding light! Or not. It reads:

> If on a particular matter there is not an express provision of either universal or particular law, nor a custom, then provided it is not a penal matter, the question is to be decided by taking

> into account laws enacted in similar matters, the general principles of law observed with canonical equity, the jurisprudence and practice of the Roman Curia, and the common and constant opinion of learned authors.

Canon 19 attempts to provide means for dealing with the silences in the law. A problem with this is that the means outlined in the canon, are very abstract and raise more questions than answers.

For our purposes here, let us focus on "the jurisprudence of the Roman Curia". The first impediment for many canonists is language and the publication of decisions in Latin. This will soon become less of a problem when plans to publish in English as well come into fruition. Making this information more and more easily accessible to canonists universally opens many possible avenues for its use. There is no doubt that the jurisprudence of the central tribunals, in addition to being a resource for supplementation of law (which is the function assigned to it in canon 19), is also a dynamic resource in the interpretation of law and in the modeling of the juridical system. But to what use? With quicker access to the decisions, will canonists use prior decisions and sentences? Will they have more expectations of their weight? There were constant warnings by Pope John Paul II in his Rotal addresses (1980, 1983, 1984, and 1985) to respect the "normative choice" made by the legislator. And, he also made repeated exhortations to judges that they remain faithful to the law. *Pastor bonus* 126 assigns to the Roman Rota the function of ensuring the "unity of jurisprudence" in such a way that "through its own sentences, it is a help to the lower tribunals." Is this a ratification of the existence of the very concept of jurisprudence an invitation from the law for it to be operative?

In summation here I simply posit that the discussion of the future (still) in canon law is jurisprudence, one that in the end will need first to pass through stages of legal theory, before it can accurately value case law within the system that may soon be at our fingertips.

The Sixth Amendment of the U.S. Constitution

This presentation will discuss two of the 6th Amendment rights in relation to canon law. They are the right to confront witnesses against them, and, the right to a trial by a fair and impartial jury.

The Sixth Amendment reads:

> *I*n all criminal prosecutions, the accused shall enjoy the right to a speedy and public trial, by an impartial jury of the State and district wherein the crime shall have been committed, which district shall have been previously ascertained, to be confronted with the witnesses against him, to have compulsory process for obtaining witnesses in his favor, and to have the assistance of counsel for his defense.9

[9] The Seventh Amendment extends many of these same rights to litigants in a civil trial.

Of the five rights addressed in this Amendment, two will be discussed here.

The Confrontation Clause: The Right to Confront Witnesses Against You/Direct Questioning of a Witness

The Confrontation Clause gives the defendant the right to cross-examine witnesses—to test their credibility in front of the judge and jury; to hear what they have to say and how they say it, to view their demeanor, and even to consider their body language. Our criminal judicial process is an adversarial one, so this makes sense in light of that. The U.S. system places its emphasis on individual rights as opposed to a system like France or Spain or Italy, where the most important player is the prosecutor who is less interested in the win-lose count, than in seeking truth and fairness. The U.S. system leads to some closing arguments about smoke screens and the air of truth telling by a witness, rather than the actual facts of a case.

Under the Confrontation Clause, defense lawyers place a high priority on calling witnesses into question before the jury. A successful defense attorney can get the jurors to dislike and perhaps disbelieve prosecution witnesses. Strategies to do this include pointing out even the smallest inconsistencies in prior statements made by the prosecution witnesses. Little things like moving around the courtroom during questioning or changing the rhythm of the questioning can confuse a nervous witness. It is not uncommon for a defense attorney to attack the character of the prosecution witness or even point out to the jury that the witness has a motivation to lie. The key strategy is to make the jury dislike the witness even more than they dislike the defendant.

In canon law, canon 1663 from the oral contentious process assures that a party and his or her advocate can assist at the examination of the other parties, of the witnesses and of the experts. On the other hand, canon 1670 is a very good example of what canon law giveth, canon law can taketh away. It allows for the tribunal (while safeguarding justice) to derogate from procedural norms (which are not prescribed for validity). This gives a great amount of discretion to the judge. Even though he must execute an explanatory decree and act without any detriment to justice, which can leave endless possibilities for abuse of discretion (a phrase that is ingrained in many areas of civil law.) In penal cases involving abuse of a minor, many courts of first instance do not allow the presence of the accused at any level other than to give a statement himself. His advocate is deemed adequate to protect the accused. Presumably this could be to insulate the accuser from additional pain in seeing the accused again, or to safeguard the accuser from any potential intimidation felt by the presence of the accused.

In many jurisdictions, there have been accommodations made for an allegedly abused minor to testify via closed circuit television from another room. This trend has moved in slowly and very carefully due to the sacrosanct place confrontation of witnesses has in the U.S. Criminal justice system.

The Right to a Trial by a Fair and Impartial Jury
Article III, Section 2 (3) The Judicial Branch: The Trial of all crimes, except in cases of impeachment, shall be by jury

The Sixth Amendment reinforces Article Three, which in and of itself, shows the importance of the jury trial system in U.S. law. This concept comes from as far back as the *Magna Carta*. Noblemen insisted on this to make certain that if they were ever tried for any crimes, they would be tried by a jury of their peers, that is, by other, presumably sympathetic, noblemen.

Today the peer part is covered by taking all prospective jurors from the voting register. If you are registered to vote, you could be called to jury duty. At the time the Constitution was drafted, it was thought that an impartial jury system would protect citizens from aggressive prosecutors and incompetent jurists. Bringing in common citizens to do the fact finding kept the prosecutors and judges from having too much authority. Those empanelled in a jury, whether civil or criminal, are not expected to know anything about the law. It is the Judge who administers the law and the jury who determines the facts. This is so important a roll for the jury that on appeal that court may overturn for failure to follow legal procedure, but not for any determination of fact such as identity.

The concept of trial by jury does not exist in canon law, period. The role of judge is extensively covered in the code from canon 1420 through 1426. It is possible that a matter be assigned to a collegiate tribunal of three to five judges, (with a majority vote for a decision). Canon 1425 directs that judges be assigned by the vicar general in order by rotation. Whether the judge or *turnus* is appointed by the vicar general, the ordinary or the CDF, the accused has no part in participating in who passes judgment on him. This completely flies in the face of U.S. Constitutional Law. True, for priests, the current make-up of a panel is other priests and, in that respect, a body of his peers. But this still skirts the civil law issue of the accused participating. In some dioceses, bishops have refused to allow judges or advocates to be from the same diocese as the accused, presumably to guard against any possible conflicts from prior classes at the seminary or parish assignments. There seems to be no official channel for an accused to challenge who sits as fact finder for good cause. It is incumbent on the Judge to act in an abundance of caution if he is not sure of his integrity to sit fairly and impartially towards everyone involved.

Hearsay

The concept of hearsay is strongly related to the Confrontation Clause. Hearsay is actually governed by civil law Rules of Evidence (every state and the federal system have such Rules). Hearsay is an out of court statement, made in court at trial, to prove the truth of the matter asserted. Trial lawyers are programmed to jump up and scream "Objection" the second they hear a witness say "he said that..." or "she told me this..." Hearsay is not admissible into evidence in either civil or criminal trials, because it cannot be cross-examined.

The theory of the rule excluding hearsay is that assertions made by human beings are often unreliable; their statements are often insincere, subject to flaws in memory and perception, or infected with errors in narration at the time they are given. The civil law finds it necessary to subject this form of evidence to "scrutiny or analysis calculated to discover and expose in detail its possible weaknesses, and thus to enable the judge or jury to estimate it at no more than its actual value". Since you have the right to confront any witnesses against you, you cannot confront them if they are not in court.

Canon law has no prohibition of hearsay. I have seen it used in the first, second and third degree. "My brother's girlfriend's cousin told him that…" The most egregious type of use of hearsay has sometimes caused the mere accusation of sexual abuse of a minor, to be acknowledged and acted upon. I am not certain which is worse, the use of it at trial or the use of it to start an initial investigation. My civil law background makes both equally nightmarish. The accused is left with little defense unless some attack can be made on the remoteness of the hearsay witness and the chain of the hearsay. In addition, the admission of hearsay, even if extremely remote, can prejudice the mind of the fact finder against the accused. Take the situation where a priest has been accused and the media coverage is extensive. Frequently in civil cases, when a defendant waives a jury trial in favor of a judge, there is a level of trust in that particular judge that he or she will not allow that objectionable testimony to affect his or her ability to remain impartial. But at that level, the defendant has probably taken a non-jury trial *because* he was offered a lenient judge or one who actually knows how to put the words not and guilty together in a sentence. In canon law, that has no bearing on a penal trial.

Burden of Proof /To a Moral Certitude

Burden of Proof is the level of proof or evidence that a party must meet, to convince the fact finder of his position in a case, *that his version of the facts is true*.

In a civil trial there is a conflict between two or more parties over issues such as property rights, personal injury, and breach of contract. The plaintiff must prove his or her case by a preponderance of evidence, sometimes also named "clear and convincing evidence". This put simply is that the plaintiffs must prove that their case is more likely true than false.

In a criminal trial, because there is much more at stake, namely the defendant's reputation and freedom, the burden is higher. This seriousness is heightened by virtue of the fact that when a person stands trial on a criminal matter, he or she is *presumed innocent* of the charges against him or her. In criminal trials the burden of proof is *proof beyond a reasonable doubt.* This requires that the Prosecution demonstrate the defendant's guilt for each element of each crime charged (act *actus reus* and intention, *mens rea*), beyond a reasonable doubt. Some judges and model jury instructions compare this burden to be synonymous to proof to a "moral certainty". This burden rests solely on the shoulders of the prosecution so that the defendant is not required to prove his innocence. The Fifth Amendment says so. All the defendant has to do is argue that the prosecution has failed to prove its case. No defense witnesses need be called at all.

The standard of proof in canonical matters is *to a moral certainty*. Canon 1608 holds that a judge must have in his mind, moral certainty about the matters to be decided in the judgment. Paragraph 3 sets this standard of proof to be a personal one. It posits that: the judge must weigh the proofs in accordance with his conscience, with due regard for the provisions of law about the efficacy of certain proofs. This concept of a judge using his own *conscience* as part of the standard is purely canonical in relation to our purpose here.

The canonical standard is as difficult to define as the civil law ones: Pope Pius XII in his allocutions (to the Roman Rota 1941 and 1942). In brief he said that moral certainty must not be a subjective certainty, rather, it must be an objective certainty based on objective reasons regarding the reality of the fact(s). The objective concept of moral certainty must always have as its basis a sure judgment, excluding all reasonable doubt.

There is really no comparison between the civil law standard of a preponderance of the evidence, and the canonical standard of moral certainty. There is much to consider in comparing the standard of beyond a reasonable doubt. The challenge to the judge, the requirement to engage his own conscience in the process of making a decision calls on a different level of commitment to justice.

In Conclusion

In this presentation, I have picked out mostly Constitutional concepts in the United States system of law. These are ones that are so ingrained to our system that civil lawyers very seldom remember that they may not be the backbone of any other legal system. U.S. civil lawyers also cannot usually conceive of a *universal* code of law, let alone one that is not emblematic of a democracy. This is the true source of tensions between the U.S. civil system(s) of law and canon law.

What is the purpose of *civil* law? It is a method used by a sovereign for delegating his authority to those under him and for governing and ruling the nation. In democracies, the state makes all the rules and laws with the explicit intention to provide the most complete protection for the citizen's right to life, liberty and property. The problem with the "ensure the rights" approach to law is that it requires and *needs* citizens to be active participants in the exercise of their rights and a respect for the rights of others. The purpose of *canon* law is much simpler. It is for the salvation of souls, which in the Church must always be the supreme law.[10] With this loftier purpose in mind, *systematic* differences become trivial.

---

[10] See canon 1752.

SEMINAR

CANONICAL FORM OF MARRIAGE THROUGHOUT THE CENTURIES: SEEING POPE BENEDICT XVI'S MOTU PROPRIO *OMNIUM IN MENTEM* IN CONTEXT

Reverend Monsignor Frederick C. Easton

On October 26, 2009, Pope Benedict XVI issued an apostolic letter, *Omnium in mentem*, which modified the 1983 code concerning those who are obliged to observe the canonical form of marriage, those who are subject to the impediment of disparity of cult, and the need for the permission to marry a Christian who is not Catholic. This change in the law of canonical form, which went into effect on April 9, 2010,[1] is situated in a lengthy history of marriage law in the Catholic Church. In this presentation, I hope to give a brief survey of the various attempts which have been made to balance the freedom of the individual Catholic to marry with the communitarian or public nature of the marriage and marital state.

It is a well-known fact that Roman law was quite influential in the development of ecclesiastical law. Looking back it is easy to see that as the Roman Empire in the west decreased the Church increased. The Roman Empire in the east survived more or less intact throughout the Middle Ages and even for a thousand years thereafter. In his latest book, *The Medieval Origins of the Legal Profession*, Dr. James Brundage stated the following concerning the survival of the infrastructure of the Roman Empire in the west:

> That so much of Roman administration either survived or adapted successfully to changing circumstances was due in considerable part to the leaders of the Western Church. The church's own organization helped to preserve numerous features of Roman administrative style. Some of its structural elements, such as provinces and dioceses, corresponded to administrative units of the late empire, while its reliance on written documents mirrored the routines of late imperial government and its officials long preserved the habits and practices of late Roman bureaucracy.[2]

The study of Roman law revived just as the twelfth century began. As Dr. Brundage noted, "Bishops and popes, as well as practicing canonists and teachers of canon law, discovered that numerous Roman law concepts,

---

[1] It was ordered by Pope Benedict XVI to be promulgated in the January 8, 2010 issue of the *Acta Apostolicae Sedis*. Therefore, it became effective after a three month *vacatio legis* in accord with canon 8 of the 1983 *Code of Canon Law*.

[2] James Brundage, *The Medieval Origins of the Legal Profession* (Chicago: University of Chicago Press, 2008) 47.

categories, and analytical tools could usefully be applied to canonical problems."[3] For that reason, it would be useful in this paper to consider briefly the mind of Roman law concerning marriage.

Roman law required not only the consent of the two parties but also required the consent of the parents for marriage to be recognized by the community.[4] Justinian's *Institutes* stated clearly that the parties "must first obtain the consent of their parents, in whose power they are. For both natural reason and the law require this consent; so much so, indeed, that it ought to precede the marriage."[5]

This requirement of parental consent was consistent with the position Roman law took on the role of the *pater familias* especially in relation to his children. The preceding section (IX) of the *Institutes* of Justinian dealt with the power of parents. We note the following points found there:

2. Our children, begotten in lawful marriage, are in our power;
3. Marriage, or matrimony, is a binding together of a man and woman to live in an indivisible union;
4. The power which we have over our children is peculiar to the citizens of Rome; for no other people have a power over their children, such as we have over ours;
5. The child born to you and your wife is in your power.

This Roman concept of the role of the parents in determining the marriage of their offspring continued into the Middle Ages where it saw some further development. Feudal overlords would also claim power over the choice of marriage partners.

There was one pope, however, who strove to extricate the choice of marriage partners from the power of parents, families, and overlords and reserve it solely for the contracting parties, namely Alexander III (1159-1181). Although much has been written about his role in development of marriage law, this author finds that the aforementioned medievalist, James Brundage, is a helpful guide in understanding ecclesiastical laws regarding marriage during the Middle Ages in his book, *Law, Sex and Christian Society in Medieval Europe.*[6]

The notion that all that was required for marriage was the consent of the two parties had earlier been considered heretical at least in the case of one Henry of Lausanne in 1135.[7] However, the canonists of mid-twelfth century debated the question of what formed marriage. Many canonists in that time did not feel

---

[3] Ibid., 75.

[4] *Institutes of Justinian*, 1.10 and *Digest* 23.2.2.

[5] *Institutes of Justinian*, 1.10.

[6] See James A. Brundage, *Law, Sex and Christian Society in Medieval Europe* (Chicago: University of Chicago Press, 1987) 331- 337 and notes.

[7] Ibid., 333, n. 38. The issue of his rejection of the public form of marriage was only one of his many rejections of church doctrine and discipline of this twelfth century charismatic monk.

comfortable with the view espoused by Gratian, namely, his primary emphasis on the role of consummation in the formation of marriage even though he acknowledged that consent was also an essential element.[8] It was the well-known view of Peter Lombard, the famous Parisian theologian that solely the consent expressed in the present tense created a marriage. However, he did allow that a marriage could come about by sexual intercourse, if there had been a prior promise of marriage. But if there was consent between the two parties in the present, then there was a marriage even if there was no conjugal intercourse.[9] Customary laws in many European countries required public form and consent of the parents, but canonists did not.[10]

Alexander III certainly came to espouse the free consent doctrine of Peter Lombard. In an undated response, *Veniens ad nos*, made to the Bishop of Norwich in England, Alexander III in effect ruled that a valid marriage could be contracted in one of two ways: free and voluntary consent of two parties who were of the canonical age and free of any impediments, or by the exchange of future consent, i.e., promise to marry, between two parties who were of canonical age and free of impediments who eventually ratified that consent by conjugal intercourse.[11]

It is easy to see that such a determination would lead people to conclude that they could get married legitimately even if no one would know about it except themselves. Thus, in effect, Alexander III's rulings had the unintended consequence of facilitating clandestine marriages. Yet, the pope recognized that some might abuse their freedom and enter marriages clandestinely and so he issued other decrees which decried such marriages. For example, in *Solet Frequenter*[12] he reprobated those who would contract clandestine marriages and said they needed to marry before witnesses but he stopped short of making it a requirement for validity. At the same time, he stated in *Quod nobis*[13] that there might be "a reasonable and legitimate cause" to contract a marriage without

---

[8] C. 27, q. 2.

[9] Cf. Peter Lombard, *Libri IV Sententiarum*, 4.27.2-5, 4.28.3.

[10] Brundage, *Law, Sex and Christian Society in Medieval Europe*, 275.

[11] X 4.1.15: "Veniens ad nos G. lator praesentium sua nobis relatione monstravit, quod in domo sua mulierem quandam recepit, de qua prolem habuit, et cui fidem coram pluribus praestitit, quod eam duceret in uxorem. Interim autem, quum apud domum vicini sui pernoctaverit, eius filia nocte illa secum concubuit, quos pater puellae simul in uno lecto inveniens, ipsum eam per verba de praesenti desponsare coegit. Qui nuper in praesentia nostra constitutus nos consuluit, cui potius adhaerere deberet. Quia vero nequaquam innotuit nobis, utrum post fidem praestitam primam cognoverit, Ideoque mandamus, quatenus rei veritatem diligenter inquiras, et, si inveneris, quod primam post fidem praestitam cognoverit, ipsum cum ea facias remanere; alioquin secundae, nisi metu coactus, qui posset in virum constantem cadere, eam desponsaverit, adhaerere facias ut uxori."

[12] 1 Comp. 4.4.4, in Philip Jaffé, *Regesta pontificum romanorum*, 2nd ed., ed.S. Lowenfeld, F. Kaltenbrunner and P. Ewald, (Leipzig: 1885–88; repr. Graz: 1956).

[13] X 4.3.2.

witnesses. Further, in *Super eovero*[14] he affirmed that a marriage contracted without the priest or witnesses was nevertheless fully binding.

Clearly, the principal difficulty with the clandestine marriage was the issue of proving its existence when someone who allegedly had been married in a clandestine exchange of consent would later marry someone else in a public ceremony. In many cases, the first spouse would petition the bishop or his tribunal to declare that the earlier union was valid. Then the difficulty of proving the existence of that earlier clandestine marriage would arise in the judicial forum.

Sometimes it was not possible to find such proof in the external forum other than from the testimony of the parties themselves. The principle of Roman law was always followed in these situations: "*Actori incumbit probatio.*" If the two parties to the first secret marriage either would deny its existence or one of the parties of that marriage could not be found, there would be serious problems of proof that the marriage had actually taken place. In the *Decretals of Gregory IX* we find the determination that if a couple had married clandestinely and either the woman or the man denied it happened, then, the proof rested with the man.[15] One thirteenth century commentator, Henry of Segusio, but most often known as Hostiensis, interpreted this provision more broadly and said that if the one attempting to prove the existence of the clandestine marriage was really the woman, she, in effect, had taken on the role of the petitioner which would normally be that of the man.[16] Another commentator, Bernard of Papia, disagreed with that interpretation. His views were consistent with the male dominant culture of his day when he argued that in judicial matters the man's word has more dignity and worth.[17] This discussion about proofs reveals the seriousness of the situation for the Church regarding clandestine marriages.

Nevertheless, despite the difficulty of the frequent occurrence of clandestine marriages, the determinations of Alexander III prevailed throughout the Middle Ages. This issue would be one of the points brought up by the reformers of the sixteenth century. James Brundage gives a good summary of the positions of Martin Luther, John Calvin and Ulrich Zwingli on this matter.[18]

Luther insisted that the marriage be public and that the consent of the parents was essential. He argued that disobedience to one's parents was rebellion against God. Marriages contracted without the consent of the parents were to be

---

[14] 1 Comp. 4.4.6(8), in *Regesta pontificum romanorum*.

[15] C. 1, X, De cland. Desp., IV, 3. "Si quis clam desponsaverit aliquam, et mulier vel vir negat hujusmodi desponsationem, viro incumbit probatio."

[16]Hostiensis, *Summa*, 355: "Nam si ver negat matrimonium contractum et mulier asserat, hic mulierbris sexus convertitur in virile, et e contgra; et sic dicitur mulier vir a virtute animi et ver mulier a mollitie cordis."

[17] Bernard Papiensis, 142: "…nec mirum cum vir sit dignior muliere, et dignioribus et honestioribus magis in judicio credatur."

[18] Brundage, *Law, Sex and Christian Society in Medieval Europe*, 552-553.

regarded as invalid.[19] Luther's stance was clearly in opposition to that of Alexander III on the freedom of the parties from the pressure of parents.

Calvin held the same view as Luther. He developed legislation in Geneva according to which marriages contracted by young people without their parents' approval were to be rescinded.[20] Zwingli in Zürich established marriage courts which declared invalid marriages contracted without prior parental consent.[21]

The growing pressures of the reformers about a host of matters led to a call for a general (ecumenical) council to address those many issues in the Church including the difficulties with the clandestine marriages. However, members of the papal curia argued that in time the novelties of these outspoken reformers would disappear and so there would be no need for a council. Actually, they feared that such a council would strip them of their powers. By the time Pope Paul III established a commission of cardinals to survey the needs of the Church and to develop a working document for this council, large sections of Western and Central Europe had renounced allegiance to Rome.[22]

The Council of Trent opened on December 13, 1545. However, it was not until November 11, 1563, after more than fifteen years of discussion and in its twenty-fourth session that this ecumenical council addressed the long-standing problem of clandestine marriages which had been the unintended consequence of the marriage doctrine of Pope Alexander III in the twelfth century. The council fathers determined that in order to have a valid marriage the exchange of consent had to take place in the presence of witnesses and that one of these witnesses had to be the proper pastor of one of the parties. The council further required that these parish priests keep written records of these marriages in their parishes.

This law, known by its incipit, *Tametsi*, would not take effect until it was properly promulgated. Promulgation of this law did not immediately take place all over the world. For example, in many regions of Europe it was neither published nor even explained for many generations after the Council of Trent. We know that it was not received in Normandy until sometime in the seventeeth century. It was not published and received in England until the nineteenth century.[23] Of notable interest is that in 1753 the Anglican Church had legislated for themselves in Hardwicke's Act what the Catholic Church had done in the *Tametsi*.[24]

---

[19] Martin Luther, *Von den Ehesachen* (1530), in *Werke, kritische Gesamtausgabe* (Weimar: Hermann Böhlaus, 1883- ; repr. Graz: Akademische Druck- u. Verlaganstalt, 1966).
[20] John Calvin, Ecclesiastical Ordinances of 1561 as quoted in Eric Fuchs, *Sexual Desire and Love* (Cambridge: J. Clarke, 1983) 143-144.
[21] Ulrich Zwingli, Zurich Marriage Ordinance (1525), in his *Selected Works*, ed. Samuel Macauley Jackson (Philadelphia: University of Pennsylvania Press, 1901; repr. 1972) 121.
[22] Brundage, 562.
[23] Ibid., 565.
[24] Ibid., 572.

The requirement of *Tametsi* that the priest who witnessed the marriage had to be the *proper* pastor of one of the parties created certain difficulties when the parties were not actually living in the place where the proper pastor was living. Also, the proper pastor might have to travel for a wedding outside his own parish. Therefore, responding to the need to make the implementation of the required canonical form simpler and more straight forward, Pope Pius X on August 10, 1907 issued the decree, *Ne Temere*, which determined that any pastor was properly authorized to witness marriages as long as it was celebrated *in the confines of his own parish*. This change in canonical form took effect on Easter, April 19, 1908.

At this point in history, in order to know the laws of the Church a canonist would be dependent upon the various collections of laws which had been put together. Although it was not the first such collection, the *Concordantia Discordantium Canonum* of Joannes Gratian was a preeminent milestone in such collections in that he used the scholastic method in order to harmonize the contradictory laws and come up with more basic principles of law. By the time of the *Ne Temere* decree the collections which followed the so-called Decree of Gratian had been gathered into one *Corpus Iuris Canonici*. Thus, the introduction of a code of canon law in 1917 was truly an innovation in the history of law in the Catholic Church.

The 1917 Code of Canon Law stated that all the baptized who had reached the age of seven were bound by merely ecclesiastical laws unless by that time they had not gained the use of reason. The wording of the law made it clear that the Catholic Church presumed that baptized non-Catholics were, in general, obliged to observe ecclesiastical laws. However, the 1917 code allowed exceptions to the obligation to observe specific laws.[25] The 1917 code specifically exempted baptized non-Catholics from the following: the impediment of mixed religion;[26] the diriment of disparity of worship;[27] and the canonical form of marriage.[28]

Nine years intervened after the *Ne Temere* decree went into effect (April 19, 1908) before the promulgation of the Code of Canon Law. However, the Church had experienced by that time, at least in principle, a required public form of marriage for over 350 years. However, the Pio-Benedictine Code made two

---

[25] Canon 12: Legibus mere ecclesiasticis non tenentur qui baptismum non receperunt, nec baptizati qui sufficienti rationis usu non gaudent, nec qui, licet rationis usum assecuti, septimum aetatis annum nondum expleverunt, *nisi aliud iure expresse caveatur* (emphasis added).

[26] Canon 1060: Severissime Ecclesia ubique prohibet ne matrimonium ineatur inter duas personas baptizatas, quarum altera sit catholica, altera vero sectae haereticae seu schismaticae adscripta; quod si adsit perversionis periculum coniugis catholici et prolis, coniugium ipsa etiam lege divina vetatur.

[27] Canon 1070 §1: Nullum est matrimonium contractum a persona non baptizata cum persona baptizata in Ecclesia catholica vel ad eandem ex haeresia ut schismate conversa.

[28] Canon 1099 (This canon will be discussed later in the text).

notable exceptions to the binding force of canonical form:

First, in canon 1098 the Legislator recognized that there might be situations in which it was not morally possible to observe the canonical form because of a grave inconvenience (*grave incommodum*) for the couple to approach the properly qualified priest as the principal witness. In such a case, a marriage would be recognized by the Church if the marriage consent was exchanged before two witnesses. This canon noted that one such situation of moral impossibility would be when there was danger of death. However, in addition to danger of death, the same form was valid if it was foreseen that it would be morally impossible for the Catholic to approach the properly qualified Catholic priest for at least a month.

Even when the exception of the grave inconvenience was verified, if there was any priest available, he had to be called to assist at the marriage even though the law was clear that there was no doubt that a marriage in this special situation was valid if celebrated only before two witnesses.

The other exception was found in canon 1099. This canon stated that, in general, all Catholics or those converted to the Catholic Church from heresy or schism were bound to observe the form. It is interesting in light of the original provisions of the 1983 code (canon 1117) that the Legislator of the first code expressly provided for no exception to the obligation to the form even if a Catholic had defected from the Church (*licet sive hi sive illi ab eadem postea de fecerint*[29]).

However, the 1917 code did provide that anyone who was baptized a Catholic in infancy but was the child of non-Catholic parents would not be bound to canonical form when marrying a non-Catholic if he or she had been reared from infancy onward in heresy, schism, or as an infidel or without any religion. The Code Commission was later asked whether the persons *ab acatholicis nati* mentioned in canon 1099 § 2 included also those born of a mixed marriage even when the *cautiones* were given in accordance with canon 1061 and canon 1071. On July 20, 1929, the Code Commission replied in the affirmative.[30]

However, the Code Commission determined on April 29, 1940 that these Catholics ("*ab acatholicis nati*") were still bound by the impediment of disparity of cult when they contracted marriage with an unbaptized person even though exempt from canonical form by reason of the exception of canon 1099 §2.[31]

Questions continued to arise about the meaning and application of this exception of canon 1099 §2. Many of these were decided by the Supreme Sacred Congregation of the Holy Office (now the Congregation for the Doctrine of the Faith). These questions arose primarily because canon 19 of the 1917 code directed that an exception to a general principal of law has to be interpreted

---

29 1917 *CIC* c. 1099 §1, 1°.

30 July 20, 1929: *AAS* 21 (1929) 573; *Canon Law Digest* 1:543.

31 April 29, 1940: *AAS* 32 (1940) 212; *CLD* 2:290.

strictly.[32] Thus, almost anything which could indicate some Catholic upbringing would eliminate the application of the exception. Anecdotal evidence suggests that if such a person, who while never formally educated in the Catholic faith, was taught how to pray the rosary, the Holy Office would declare that the person was bound to canonical form.

On August 1, 1948, Pope Pius XII, in a *motu proprio* abrogated the second clause of section 2 of canon 1099 which began with the words, *item ab acatholicis nati.* He explained the reason for this abrogation:

> The experience of thirty years has sufficiently shown that the exemption from observing the canonical form of marriage, which was given to this class of persons baptized in the Catholic Church, has not been conducive to the good of souls, and has moreover very frequently multiplied difficulties in the solution of cases; wherefore We have deemed it expedient that this exemption be revoked.[33]

The 1983 Code of Canon Law introduced its own exception regarding who is bound to observe the canonical form of marriage. Canon 1117 states: "The form established above must be observed if at least one of the parties contracting marriage was baptized in the Catholic Church or received into it and *has not defected from it by a formal act*, without prejudice to the prescripts of can. 1127 §2."

The phrase, "and has not defected from it by a formal act," was the fruit of the discussion in the Code Commission. We can read in *Communicationes* the discussion of this issue which took place on February 10, 1971.[34] The discussion began with a return to the same issue which was behind the clause in the original 1917 code, *ab acatholicis nati*, namely, the concern that those who were not really educated in the Catholic faith even though baptized as infants should not be bound to canonical form of marriage. However, some of the consultors noted that to base the exception to the law of canonical form on whether or not a baptized Catholic received Catholic education might excuse a very large number of Catholics from canonical form. Further, there would be difficulty in determining when there was no Catholic education. As noted above, Pope Pius XII had said that this exception "very frequently multiplied difficulties in the solution of cases" and, moreover, was not conducive to the good of souls.

The discussion then turned to whether or not it would be better to base an exception to canonical form upon a public or a notorious departure from the Catholic Church. As we know, the end result was the determination that a formal act would be the better way to determine whether or not a person should be exempted from the law of canonical form (canon 1108).

---

[32] 1917 *CIC* c. 19: Leges quae poenam statuunt, aut liberum iurium exercitium coarctant, autexceptionem a lege continent, strictae subsunt interpretationi (Note: this is the exact wording of canon 18 in the 1983 Code of Canon Law).

[33]August 1, 1948: *AAS* 40 (1948) 305; *CLD* 3:463-464.

[34] *Communicationes* 8:1 (1976) 58-61.

Thus, the Code Commission for the 1983 code attempted again to respond to the concern and value of the natural right to marry being unduly restricted for those people for whom the laws of the Church were practically meaningless. In the end the Legislator responded on three fronts.

In canon 1117 it was determined that those who have defected from the Church by a formal act would thenceforth not be bound to observe the canonical form when marrying. Similarly, a Catholic who defected from the Church by a formal act would not need the "express permission of the competent authority" to marry a non-Catholic as required by canon 1124. Finally, formal defection from the Catholic Church would thenceforth eliminate the impediment of disparity of worship for such a Catholic marrying an unbaptized person (c. 1086 §1).

Not long after the 1983 code became law it became clear that there was confusion on what constituted departure by a formal act. However, it was only after over twenty-two years that, finally, on March 13, 2006, the Pontifical Council for Legislative Texts issued a clarification about "the so-called *actus formalis defectionis ab Ecclesia catholica* mentioned in canons 1086, §1[35], 1117[36] and 1124[37] of the Code of Canon Law."

The Pontifical Council's explanation was emphatic that formal defection was more than an empty formality. It said:

> The substance of the act of the will must be the rupture of those bonds of communion – faith, sacraments, and pastoral governance – that permit the Faithful to receive the life of grace within the Church. This means that the formal act of defection must have more than a juridical-administrative character (the removal of one's name from a Church membership registry maintained by the government in order to produce certain civil consequences), but be configured as a true separation from the constitutive elements of the life of the Church: it supposes, therefore, an act of apostasy, heresy or schism.[38]

---

[35] Canon 1086 §1: A marriage between two persons, one of whom has been baptized in the Catholic Church or received into it and has not defected from it by a formal act and the other of whom is not baptized, is invalid.

[36] Canon 1117: The form established above must be observed if at least one of the parties contracting marriage was baptized in the Catholic Church or received into it and has not defected from it by a formal act, without prejudice to the prescripts of can. 1127 §2.

[37] Canon 1124: Without express permission of the competent authority, a marriage is prohibited between two baptized persons of whom one is baptized in the Catholic Church or received into it after baptism and has not defected from it by a formal act and the other of whom is enrolled in a Church or ecclesial community not in full communion with the Catholic Church.

[38] Pontifical Council for Legislative Texts, *Actus Formalis Defectionis Ab Ecclesia Catholica* (Vatican City: March 13, 2006) Prot. N. 10279/2006.

This background is helpful for understanding the following three elements required for a formal act of defection:

1. The internal decision to leave the Catholic Church;
2. the realization and external manifestation of that decision; and
3. the reception of that decision by the competent ecclesiastical authority.

Concerning the three types of rupture of the bonds of communion, the Pontifical Council said: "On the other hand, heresy (whether formal or material), schism and apostasy do not in themselves constitute a formal act of defection if they are not externally concretized and manifested to the ecclesiastical authority in the required manner." This sentence explains the nature of the formal act mentioned in canons 1086 § 1, 1117, and 1124. Although four other canons speak of defection from the Church, they do not employ the modifier, *formal*.[39]

Since the formal defection itself is a juridic act, it requires an external manifestation by the interested party in written form and communicated to the competent authority of the Catholic Church. It defines this competent authority as the ordinary or proper pastor. It states that this authority is uniquely qualified to make the judgment concerning the existence or non-existence of the act of the will to break this bond of communion. It is possible that a person could want to formally defect from the Church for one motive but still want for other reasons to remain in the communion of the faith.

Thus, the third essential element, namely, is the "reception by the competent ecclesiastical authority" of this external manifestation. The competent ecclesiastical authority is not merely passive but must make a decision about whether or not there was an authentic decision on the part of the person to leave the Catholic Church and break the bonds of communion. In order to be able to make such a decision, the competent ecclesiastical authority might need some further communication with the person. By its very nature the decision of the competent ecclesiastical authority must itself be externally manifested in some way, such as by making a reply to the person making the request.

In Germany some people were claiming not to be Catholics solely for the purpose of avoiding the payment of a special church tax. German pastors are obliged annually to report to the state who was baptized during the year which information is used by the government in determining who is subject to such a tax. Then, when a Catholic would pay the regular income tax, an additional eight to nine percent of this amount would be deducted and sent to the Church. If someone, in order to avoid paying this additional eight to nine percent, declared to the civil registrar that he or she was no longer Catholic, the civil authorities would report this departure from the Church to the parish church of baptism. If someone claimed to the registrar to have left the Catholic Church, the pastor of the Church of baptism would then make a notation of this departure in the

[39] Cc. 171 §1, 4°; 194 §1, 2°; 316 §1; 694 §1, 1°.

baptismal register.

Thus, in Germany, when someone declared to the government that he or she was no longer a Catholic, this process looked like a departure by a formal act. The point of the clarification by the Pontifical Council was that the notification of departure must be to the competent ecclesiastical authority and not to the state government. Further, and more importantly, in this tax avoidance process, there is real question whether or not the person truly wanted to depart from the Church. In fact, it would easily appear that such a person was not seeking to sever connections with the Catholic Church but just to avoid paying additional taxes. This situation was most likely the rationale for the parenthetical statement of the Pontifical Council: "(the removal of one's name from a Church membership registry maintained by the government in order to produce certain civil consequences)."

Immediately after the Pontifical Council published this clarifying document many wondered if its provisions were retroactive. In this matter of retroactivity, canon 16 §2 must be carefully considered:

> An authentic interpretation put forth in the form of law has the same force as the law itself and must be promulgated. If it only declares the words of the law which are certain in themselves, it is retroactive; if it restricts or extends the law, or if it explains a doubtful law, it is not retroactive.

Applying the norm of this canon to this document of the Pontifical Council, it is easy to see that the substance of this document truly declares the words of the law of the three canons concerned. Therefore, most of what is in the document from the Pontifical Council is retroactive.

In his opinion on this matter found in the 2006 *Advisory Opinions*, John Huels stated that the following provisions are retroactive:

1. The person must freely and knowingly have the intention to leave the Catholic Church;
2. There must be a juridic act that externally manifests and brings about the juridic effects of that intention (recognizing, of course, that no one can truly leave the Catholic Church);
3. The substance of the act is, or is accompanied by, an act of apostasy, heresy, or schism;
4. The act of defection must be received by the competent ecclesiastical authority.40

Fr. Huels argues that the Pontifical Council's specification that the

[40] John M. Huels, JCD, "Retroactivity of Clarification: Defection from the Church by a Formal Act," *Roman Replies and CLSA Advisory Opinions 2006*, ed. F. Stephen Pedone and Paul D. Counce (Canon Law Society of America: Alexandria, Virginia, 2006) 80-81.

competent ecclesiastical authority is either the local ordinary or pastor is something new and, therefore, not retroactive. He said that others who collaborate with the ordinary and pastor, for example, the parochial vicar, parish deacon, pastoral associate, or pastoral administrator would also be competent in this regard. By the same logic, I could see the chancellor or any ecclesiastical notary, the judicial vicar or adjunct judicial vicar qualifying as the competent ecclesiastical authority for this matter. However, given the nature of what is happening by formal defection, I can see that the Legislator could have easily intended to limit this matter to the local ordinary or pastor.

In the light of this clarification by the Pontifical Council, it is the opinion of this author that there were, most likely, very few Catholics who joined other churches or who even became atheists who at the same time actually formally defected from the Catholic Church. A simple internet search using a search engine such as Google will enable one to find many sites dealing with this issue some of which include a link to the clarification by the Pontifical Council. There is at least one site which will help people follow the points of the clarification given by the Pontifical Council in order to formally defect: www.atheistactivist.org.

It seems to this author that a formal defection from the Church should not have been something automatically accepted upon receipt of any application. I believe that some further clarification would almost always have been needed in order to truly know that the person was sincere and knew what he or she was doing. That need to clarify the intent of the person was the reason for the process which the Pontifical Council determined was necessary for a formal defection from the Church.

In the October 26, 2009 apostolic letter, Pope Benedict XVI abrogated this exception of the formal act of defection from the Catholic Church. The key sentence specifying the abrogation reads as follows:

> Auferenda proinde decernimus in eodem *Codice* verba: "neque actu formali ab ea defecerit" canonis 1117, "nec actu formali ab ea defecerit" canonis 1086 §1, et "quaeque nec ab ea actu formali defecerit" canonis 1124.
>
> Therefore I decree that in the same *Code* the following words are to be eliminated: "and has not left it by a formal act" (can. 1117); "and has not left it by means of a formal act" (can. 1086 §1); "and has not left it by a formal act" (can. 1124). (Translation provided by the Holy See on its website at www.vatican.va.)

The apostolic letter explains this phrase was essentially an exception to the provisions of canon 11.[41] The letter goes on to explain that after receiving the

---

[41] Merely ecclesiastical laws bind those who have been baptized in the Catholic Church or received into it, possess the sufficient use of reason, and, unless the law expressly provides otherwise, have completed seven years of age.

opinions from members of the Congregation for the Doctrine of the Faith, the Pontifical Council for Legislative Texts, as well as the various conferences of bishops throughout the world, it was clear that this exception to canon 11 was not really pastorally helpful and useful. [42] Pope Benedict specified the following reasons for abrogating the exception of formal defection from the Catholic Church:

- In individual cases the definition and practical configuration of such a *formal act* of separation from the Church has proved difficult to establish, from both a theological and a canonical standpoint;
- The new law regarding formal defection appeared, at least indirectly, to facilitate and even in some way to encourage apostasy in places where the Catholic faithful are not numerous or where unjust marriage laws discriminate between citizens on the basis of religion;
- The new law also made difficult the return of baptized Catholics who greatly desired to contract a new canonical marriage following the failure of a preceding marriage;
- Many of these marriages in effect became, as far as the Church is concerned, "clandestine" marriages. [43]

As mentioned earlier, we now know that the apostolic letter was promulgated in the January 8, 2010 issue of the *Acta Apostolicae Sedis* and, thus, in accord with the provisions of canon 8, the change in the law went into effect on April 9, 2010. Therefore, from now on in order to determine that a

---

[42] The deliberations of the Commission for the Revision of the Code revealed there was a strongly held opinion of some of the consultors that the provisions of canon 12 of the 1917 code should be maintained because the canon captured the traditional teaching that validly baptized persons constitute the Church of Christ and, therefore, should be bound by merely ecclesiastical laws. In the end, the commission proposed that only Catholics would be bound to merely ecclesiastical laws. It is interesting to note that in the discussions a paragraph was added which stated that the laws apply to those who defect from the Catholic Church unless otherwise provided. Eventually, the text was simplified so that it had only the one paragraph we now have in canon 11. (Cf. MyriamWijlens, *Sharing the Eucharist: A Theological Evaluation of the Post Conciliar Legislation* [Lanham, MD: University Press, 2000] n. 301-302.)

[43] Horum autem annorum experientia ostendit, e contra, novam hanc legem pastoralia problemata haud pauca genuisse.Imprimis difficilis apparuit determinatio et practica configuratio, singulis in casibus, huius *actus formalis defectionis* ab Ecclesia, sive quoad eius substantiam theologicam sive quoad ipsius aspectum canonicum. Multae praeterea exsurrexerunt difficultates cum in actione pastorali tum in tribunalium praxi. Etenim e nova lege oriri videbantur, saltem oblique, commoditas ac veluti adiumentum apostasiae illis in locis ubi fideles catholici exigui sunt numero, vel ubi iniquae vigent leges matrimoniales discrimina statuentes inter cives ratione religionis; difficilis praeterea fiebat reditus horum baptizatorum qui novum contrahere exoptarent matrimonium canonicum, post prioris ruinam; denique, ut alia omittamus, horum matrimoniorum permulta devenerant de facto pro Ecclesia matrimonia sic dicta clandestina.

person is bound to canonical form, the only document needed is a recent copy of that person's Catholic baptismal certificate, a certificate of the marriage to show that it was not a marriage in the Catholic Church, and, of course, a decree of divorce to show civil freedom.

Some Practical Impact

In this paper, I have been dealing with issues of purely ecclesiastical law – the canonical form of marriage. However, the determination of whether or not a person is bound to canonical form and whether or not the Catholic in question has observed that form has a very practical impact on the Catholic's standing in the Church community, including the reception of Sacraments.

The marriage outside the Catholic Church of a Catholic who has followed the norms for departure by a formal act and married prior to April 9, 2010 is recognized by the Catholic Church because the Catholic was not then bound to observe canonical form. Prior to the explanation by the Pontifical Council for Legislative Texts of what is required for formal defection many canonists thought that this defection came about simply by a Catholic joining another church. The tribunal which encountered the situation of such a person then coming back to the Catholic Church and revealing this story of joining another church and then getting married there would easily determine that the only option was a formal nullity trial. In the case with which I am familiar, the petitioning man received an affirmative sentence and then the explanation from the Pontifical Council for Legislative Texts arrived. What to do? In this case, I informed the tribunal of second instance of the facts of the man's case and of our new understanding of the exception contained in canon 1117. It was clear that this case could not be adjudicated in second instance, since the marriage did not have the *species matrimonii*. This Catholic was already free to marry again even before first instance started the case.

It has become increasingly evident that many more Catholics than in decades past have no idea there is a required form of marriage for them. However, along with that fact we also know that more and more people, whether Catholic or not, have mistaken notions about the very nature of marriage and what is naturally required to consent to marriage. Students of matrimonial jurisprudence know of the fact that some people have a deeply rooted error about the indissolubility of marriage. Already in the 1950s the late Rotal judge and later Cardinal Prefect of the Signatura, Pericles Felici wrote in one of his sentences of the existence of *error pervicax* – deeply rooted error concerning indissolubility.[44] In the spring of 2008 our present Holy Father, Pope Benedict XVI, in a question and answer session with priests in northern Italy, said this: "Today, however, this axiom, which holds that man prompted by his nature will make one faithful marriage, has been transformed into a somewhat different axiom. "*Volunt contrahere*

[44]*Coram* Felici, December 17, 1957: *RRDec* 49:844

matrimonium sicut ceteri homines."[45]

The Holy Father went on to say that we simply cannot throw up our hands and do nothing about this situation. At least as far as Catholics who come to the Church for marriages are concerned, our catechesis must attempt to address this situation. On November 17, 2009, the United States Conference of Catholic Bishops issued a pastoral letter on marriage entitled, *Love and Life in the Divine Plan.* This pastoral letter was an effort to address the many cultural phenomena which impact the views of people about marriage, such as the privatization of marriage which is in opposition to the whole idea of canonical form for marriage for Catholics and the notion that the marriage commitment is really not forever. Dioceses are being encouraged to develop a plan to implement the pastoral letter. In my own archdiocese one of the proposed initiatives is to see how the experience of the tribunal with adjudicating marriage cases can be of assistance in identifying the problems in more detail.

Some Concluding Reflections:

As one can see, over the centuries the Church has tried to balance the value of the personal freedom of the parties to marry with the value of certitude of knowing who is married to whom in the eyes of the Church. In most of the world today, marriages are recorded by local governments and so are not as clandestine as they were in the Middle Ages. Yet, the Catholic Church's stance on marriage and divorce diverges notably from that of the secular culture. Therefore, the requirement of the canonical form of marriage is totally consistent with our ethos about marriage. Further, the abrogation of the exception to the law of canonical form by departure by a formal act will not, in practice, hamper the perceived freedom to marry of those who truly have departed from the Church.

This paper has been focused on the law of the form of marriage which is a matter solely of ecclesiastical law. Perhaps, the following paragraph written by the late Stephan Kuttner, noted medieval canonist in a talk he gave at St. Vincent Archabbey in Latrobe, Pennsylvania in 1960, might be a fitting conclusion to this discussion:

> To many of us, clergy or lay, the law of the church appears as no more than a sum of dry technical rules for ecclesiastical administrators and judges, the rubrics, as it were, of ecclesiastical routine or, even worse, a stifling instrument of regimentation. But in fact canon law is something much nobler and greater: it is a living force, giving form to the social body which is the Church; a rational order encompassing her sacramental and pastoral functions; and organized mode of thinking that teaches us the right reason of ecclesiastical life, from the essential principles to practical particulars—in short, a universal system of jurisprudence, composed of divine and human elements, and of no lesser intellectual dignity than the

[45] Zenit News (online Catholic News source).

speculative disciplines of theology and philosophy. The fact that in its details canon law deals with contingencies and practical necessities rather than with timeless truths must not blind us to the grandeur of its purpose, which is the ordering of those contingencies in a coherent whole.[46]

[46] Stephan G. Kuttner, *Harmony from Dissonance: An Interpretation of Medieval Canon Law* (Wimmer Lecture X) (The Archabbey Press: Latrobe, Pennsylvania, 1960).

SEMINAR

CREATING VIBRANT AND DYNAMIC PARISHES

Most Reverend Joseph A. Galante

Beginning in March 2005 I began a commitment that was to last for fifteen months whereby I went to each of our one hundred twenty-four parishes for a minimum of two hours, four nights a week, to listen to our people. In addition, I met with sixteen other groups (more than 8000 men and women) consisting of clergy, religious, diocesan personnel and ethnic groups.

At each meeting people were asked to reply to the question: "Looking to the future, what do you see as the three most important priorities for the Church in South Jersey." The people were very enthusiastic in their replies. After the fifteen months of meeting and collecting all this information we had a diocesan assembly to work on the top priorities. Six pastoral priorities were chosen: *Lifelong Faith Formation*, *Youth and Young Adults*, *Liturgy*, *Lay Ministry*, *Vocations*, and *Compassionate Outreach.*

It soon became apparent that these priorities for the most part had to be met in the parishes. It also became obvious that many of our parishes did not have the resources to carry out these ministries. And so began a period of planning for parish reconfiguration. Each parish had a planning team, however, these teams were to come together to plan in regions not merely for one parish. Then the regions planned for the deanery. The planning teams were given the various canonical possibilities for this reconfiguration: merger, cluster, stand alone. Canon 517 §2 was brought up but was not encouraged since it did not fit the diocesan profile.

The Camden Diocese, which contains the 6 southern counties of New Jersey, has one county with 2000 people per square mile (Camden County) and another county (Salem) with fewer than 60 people per square mile. A major concern from the beginning of the planning process was to try to make the parish reconfigurations reasonable for the people, especially as to distance. I did not want to go in the direction of giving one priest several parishes to pastor. Multiplying meetings and duplicating programs is not the best use of time for a pastor.

The directives for parish planning process followed:

1) *No parish or school can plan for itself alone.* Local considerations must address the common good of the Catholic Church, not just one parish or one school. Human and material resources are limited. Parishes are asked to submit plans for their entire region. Schools will be doing the same for their cluster.

2) *Parishes and schools or any new configurations are to be financed by funds generated through parish income, other income, or tuition collections.*

This financing includes meeting expenses, including a just payroll and diocesan assessments, without incurring indebtedness to the diocese.

The diocese will no longer ignore unpaid parish debts or bail out failing parishes or schools. As we began the planning, 41 of the 124 parishes could not pay their basic bills, e.g. utilities, pensions, and health care. The diocese, which forgave 12 million dollars of that debt in the year 2000 had reached that same amount of unpaid debts by 2008. Thus it was impossible to have vibrant parishes that could not meet necessary payments, let alone provide for the ministries which the people had requested.

3) *Plan for priests and deacons to do the ministries for which they are ordained and expand the role of religious and laity in administration, leadership, decision-making, and lay ministries*. The number of priests will likely decline by fifty percent in the next ten years. Provide for greater collaboration between clergy and laity and between parishes, avoiding duplication of efforts.

4) *Provide for accountability through transparency*. Publish policies, minutes of the Parish Planning Team and other council meetings. Involve councils in decisions about administration and stewardship of Church assets. Keep parishioners, parish leaders, and pastoral staffs informed and involved in the planning process.

5) *Ensure that there is a balance between the efforts in Catholic unity and cultural diversity so that all, especially new immigrants, feel equally welcome and accepted*. Hospitality and inclusion should guide use of human and material resources, allocation of time and space.

6) *Use the steps in our discernment process*: 1) gathering quality data, 2) interpreting the data in the light our religious tradition, and 3) choosing to decide through consensus.

7) *Plans for the region or school cluster are submitted for review, feedback, and dialogue but final decisions regarding approval of plans rests with the Bishop and his advisors*. Among the important documents which formed the basis for our planning were *Lumen gentium*, *Novo millennio ineunte* (January 6, 2001) and Pope John Paul's 2004 *ad limina* address for the bishops of Pennsylvania and New Jersey.

In the Holy Father's talk he pointed out that those who form the local church should be involved in its mission and in decision making:

> Saintly reformers like Gregory the Great, Charles Borromeo and Pius X understood that the Church is only authentically "reformed" when she returns to her origins in a *conscious re-appropriation of the apostolic Tradition* and a purifying re-evaluation of her institutions in the light of the Gospel. In the present circumstances of the Church in America, this will entail a spiritual discernment and critique of certain styles of governance which, even in the name of a legitimate concern

> for good 'administration' and responsible oversight, can run the risk of distancing the pastor from the members of his flock, and obscuring his image as their father and brother in Christ. In this regard, the Synod of Bishops acknowledged the need today for each Bishop to develop 'a pastoral style which is ever more open to collaboration with all' (*Pastores Gregis 44*), grounded in a clear understanding of the relationship between the ministerial priesthood and the common priesthood of the baptized (cf. *Lumen Gentium* 10).
>
> While the Bishop himself remains responsible for the authoritative decisions which he is called to make in the exercise of his pastoral governance, ecclesial communion also 'presupposes the participation of every category of the faithful, inasmuch as they share responsibility for the good of the particular Church which they themselves form' (*Pastores Gregis,* loc.cit.) Within a sound ecclesiology of communion, a commitment to creating better structures of *participation, consultation and shared responsibility* should not be misunderstood as a concession to a secular 'democratic' model of governance, but as *an intrinsic requirement* of the exercise of Episcopal authority and a necessary means of strengthening that authority. Experience shows that when priority is mainly given to outward stability, the impetus to personal conversion, ecclesial renewal and missionary zeal can be lost and a false sense of security can ensue (*Origins* 34:16, September 30, 2004, 254).

As we progressed in the planning, we tried to keep in mind our principles and our goal. Our goal was to form dynamic and vibrant parishes that would have the resources to implement the pastoral priorities and other ministries that were needed.

At the time we began the planning process only about 22 percent of our people were regular participants in Sunday liturgies. We knew from a CARA survey that by 2015 we would have half the number of active diocesan priests and we also were aware that there had been great demographic shifts in the diocese over a 30 year period.

We had large numbers of Hispanic immigrants, many of whom were from Mexico. (We estimate that we have about 150,000 Hispanics in the diocese, both documented and undocumented). We also had an influx of Asian, African, and Caribbean immigrants.

Where we had large farmlands there are now many new housing developments. The northwestern areas of the diocese, near the Delaware River, were mostly suburban bedroom communities. The central part of the diocese still had a large number of farms, but also the above mentioned new housing.

The eastern end of the diocese, from Atlantic City to Cape May, was heavily seashore resorts with a great influx of visitors during the summer months and an increasing number of retirees year round.

All of these realities were factored into the planning and the evaluation of the plans which were presented to the deaneries.

The original submissions called for 66 parishes. After evaluations by the Diocesan Planning Commission we added 2 more parishes bringing it to 68. After these decisions were announced in April 2008, there continued to be some discussions and reflection resulting in further adjustment to bring the total to 72.

At this point we have completed about three-fourths of our mergers. So far they have been well accepted by the people. The merged parishes are experiencing increased Mass attendance and new ministries are being established. The people are responding with acceptance and even enthusiasm as the new parishes are being formed.

SEMINAR

THE *MISSALE ROMANUM, EDITIO TYPICA TERTIA*: ORGANIC CONTINUITY AND GROWTH

Reverend Monsignor James P. Moroney

In the course of the Jubilee of our Redemption Pope John Paul II published the *editio typica tertia* of the *Missale Romanum*. First issued in 1969 and then, in a slightly revised edition in 1975, the *Missale Romanum* was significantly updated in the millennium year in the light of the experience of the first thirty years of its post-conciliar use. In this brief reflection on the relationship of the third edition to its predecessors I will attempt to answer four questions: What is organic continuity and growth? What examples do we see of organicity in the Roman Missal as a whole, the General Instruction of the Roman Missal, and the new principles of translation which have been used to translate the missal?

What is organic continuity and growth?

Gardeners know a lot about organic growth. For them, organic growth is the sign that they have succeeded in nurturing a plant or a tree to its full maturity. The endeavor begins with the establishment of a root system which emerges to form the trunk of the tree. From the trunk sprout branches, which are followed by larger and then increasingly smaller shoots, from which sprout leaves. As the seasons unfold and the shoots become stronger, they take on the role of branches from a growing tree, all the while propagating further shoots from which myriad leaves begin to grow.

A similar sort of process is experienced from age to age in the Church. Tradition, rooted in the teaching of Christ and cultivated by the propagation of the Apostles, comes to form the magisterial trunk which is the source of unity in our ecclesial enterprise. Each local church, each adapted liturgical rite, is a branch off this trunk, grown organically, in continuity with the deepest roots of the Catholic faith.

We experience organic continuity in every dimension of our lives. Many of us typed our first papers on manual typewriters. Recall the wonder of the first Selectric, the boxy little Macintosh, the wondrous portability of our first laptop, and now our new favorite, the iPad. In each instance, this continuity is characterized by certain dimensions:

1. A basic identity is preserved throughout the growth.
2. Such growth evolves in dialogue with changing conditions.
3. Variations are always built on prior conditions.
4. Heritage is recognized and respected throughout.

Such an organic continuity has characterized the Sacred Liturgy from the upper room to the church in which we celebrated Mass this morning. Recall the Mass of your first Communion and the Mass we celebrated today. In the development of one to another, the basic identity of the "holy and living sacrifice" has been preserved. The adaptations and evolutions of texts and rites have occurred in reaction to changing cultural and pastoral conditions. The variations which the Church has admitted to the Liturgy today are built upon prior conditions and experiences, while throughout this development the Catholic heritage has been recognized and respected.

Indeed, we might apply the same observations concerning the organic continuity of the Petrine office in our own time. While preserving a basic identity, each pope has responded to changing conditions in the world and the Church, introducing variations based upon prior conditions with respect for and recognition of our Catholic traditions.

The first words spoken by the Fathers of the Second Vatican Council set forth an impressive agenda "to impart an ever increasing vigor to the Christian life of the faithful; to adapt more suitably to the needs of our own times those institutions which are subject to change; to foster whatever can promote union among all who believe in Christ; to strengthen whatever can help to call the whole of mankind into the household of the Church."[1] Such a vision of reform is the very definition of organic continuity.

In the same Spirit, Pope John Paul II called for a renewal of "that spirit which inspired the Church at the moment when the constitution *Sacrosanctum concilium* was prepared, discussed, voted upon and promulgated, and when the first steps were taken to apply it."[2] He continued with the same arboreal imagery used by my gardening friends: "The seed was sown; it has known the rigors of winter, but the seed has sprouted, and become a tree. It is a matter of the organic growth of a tree becoming ever stronger the deeper it sinks its roots into the "soil" of tradition."[3]

This theme was picked up in 2004 by then Cardinal Joseph Ratzinger:

> "Growth is not possible unless the Liturgy's identity is preserved...[and] proper development is possible only if careful attention is paid to the inner structural logic of this "organism." Just as a gardener cares for a living plant as it develops, with due attention to the power of growth and life within the plant and the rules it obeys, so the Church ought to give reverent care to the Liturgy through the ages, distinguishing actions that are helpful and healing from those

---

[1] Vatican II, constitution *Sacrosanctum concilium* 1, December 14, 1963: *AAS* 56 (1964) 97-134.

[2] John Paul II, apostolic letter *Vicesimus quintus annus* 23, December 4, 1988.

[3] Ibid.

that are violent and destructive."[4]

Pope Benedict XVI's insistence on the organic development of the Liturgy is also evident in the post-synodal apostolic exhortation *Sacramentum caritatis*, in which he expresses admiration for "the orderly development of the ritual forms in which we commemorate the event of our salvation." Noting "the beneficial influence on the Church's life of the liturgical renewal which began with the Second Vatican Ecumenical Council," he nonetheless observes that the full benefits of the conciliar reform are yet to be fully explored, requiring an understanding of the "overall unity of the historical development of the rite itself, without the introduction of artificial discontinuities."[5]

Organicity in the *Missale Romanum, editio typica tertia*

There have been three editions of the *Missale Romanum* in the postconciliar reform. Approximately seven percent of the pages of the 1970 edition were emended by the *editio altera* of 1975. The more extensive emendations of the third edition include changes on approximately twenty-five percent of the pages of the missal involving editorial revisions, updating in the light of subsequent editions and documents, and truly innovative changes.

The origins of the majority of these emendations are clear. *Varietates Legitimae*, the fourth instruction on the implementation of *Sacrosanctum concilium*, had perhaps the most significant impact on the new missal, most notably in the addition of an entirely new ninth chapter to the General Instruction of the Roman Missal. Second typical editions of a number of Latin liturgical books, including the Rite of Ordination of a Bishop, Priests, and Deacons (1989), the Rite for the Dedication of a Church and Altar (1977), the rites for the Pastoral Care of the Sick and Dying (1972), and the Lectionary for Mass *editio typica altera* (1991) were responsible for a large number of the changes, as were the Book of Blessings (1984), the Ceremonial of Bishops (1984), and the new Code of Canon Law (1983). Finally, a number of instructions, circular letters, responses to *dubia*, and other documents, including *Dominicae cenae* (1980) and *Inestimabile donum* (1980), played a significant role in the development of the third edition of the Roman Missal.

An examination of the changes introduced to the General Instruction of the third edition of the Roman Missal (GIRM) demonstrates a certain continuity from the 1970 edition. The general instruction of 1970 contained 341 paragraphs, while the GIRM of the third edition contains 399, while one third of the lines of the general instruction have been amended in one way or another.

What are the sources of these emendations? Forty-seven percent of the changes to the General Instruction of the Roman Missal may be traced directly

---

[4] Cardinal Joseph Ratzinger, foreword to Alcuin Reid OSB, *The Organic Development of the Liturgy* (San Francisco: Ignatius Press, 2005).

[5] Post-synodal apostolic exhortation *Sacramentum caritatis* 2, February 22, 2007: *AAS* 99 (2007) 105-180.

to the instruction *Varietates legitmae*. Thirty-nine percent of the changes stem from the revised second typical editions and other documents we have cited above. Finally, the last fourteen percent of the changes arise from various responses to *dubia* published in the official journal of the Congregation for Divine Worship and the Discipline of the Sacraments, *Notitiae*.

Let us take a closer look at seventeen of the paragraphs of the general instruction inspired by the instruction *Varietates legitimae.* These include the more general references to adaptation found in the general instruction nos. twenty-three through twenty-six, as well as the entirely new chapter nine, entitled "Adaptations Within the Competence of Bishops and Bishops Conferences" (nos. 383-399). The ninth chapter consists of a general introduction, a description of the competencies of the diocesan bishop, the conferences of bishops, the provision for a diocesan calendar and proper Masses, and the process to be followed for more profound variations and adaptations. The ninth chapter concludes with a description of liturgical texts and rites as the sign and instrument of unity of the Roman rite itself.

Forty-nine paragraphs of the general instruction are inspired by the revised liturgical books and other liturgical documents of the Holy See, including seven from the *Ordo Lectionum Missae, editio altera* (nos. 56, 58, 59, 66, 349, and 360-361), two from the *Ceremoniale Episcopoum* (nos. 277, 22), three from the *De Ordinatione, editio altera* (nos. 94, 253, and 108), and four from *De Benedictionibus*. Three paragraphs are revised in the light of *Dominicae cenae* (nos. 314-317) and three by *Inestimabile donum* and *Ecclesia de Eucharistia* (nos. 160-162).

One of the most significant innovations of the third edition of the Roman Missal is in the extension of the faculty for permitting a more general distribution of Holy Communion under both species to all bishops of the Catholic world. I suggest that the gradual development of the insights responsible for this more generous permission provides a good example of organic development in the postconciliar Roman Missal.

Organic Growth and Distribution of Holy Communion Under Both Kinds

The first initiative for a more generous distribution of Holy Communion under both species is found in the conciliar document *Sacrosanctum concilium* itself:

> The dogmatic principles which were laid down by the Council of Trent remaining intact, communion under both kinds may be granted when the bishops think fit, not only to clerics and religious but also to the laity, in cases to be determined by the Apostolic See. For example:
>
> -To the newly ordained in the Mass of their ordination;
>
> -To the newly professed in the Mass of their religious profession;
>
> -To the newly baptized in the Mass which follows their

baptism.[6]

The conciliar mandate was given concrete form in the 1965 Rite for the Distribution of Holy Communion Under Both Kinds, *Ecclesiae Semper*, and then again in the Rite for the Distribution of Holy Communion Under Both Kinds contained in the *Missale Romanum* of 1970. The Roman Missal of 1970 makes provision for the distribution of both species to "specific, well-ordered, and homogeneous," groups, including the newly baptized, the newly confirmed, the bride and bridegroom at a wedding, special ministers at Mass, missionaries sent on mission, those receiving *Viaticum*, the deacon at Mass, those on retreat, godparents, parents, relatives and lay catechists of newly baptized adults, relatives, friends, and special benefactors who take part in the Mass of a newly ordained priest, and members of communities at the conventual or community Mass.[7]

The next step in the development of this question came with the 1970 indult granted to the National Conference of Catholic Bishops in the United States authorizing local ordinaries to permit the distribution of Communion under both species at all Masses except Sundays and holy days.[8] The indult was eventually accompanied by an NCCB document which included a series of norms on the question under the title *This Holy and Living Sacrifice: Directory for the Celebration and Reception of Communion under Both Kinds*.

"Communion under both kinds is also permitted at parish and community Masses celebrated on Sundays and holy days of obligation in the dioceses of the United States."[9]

Seen against the backdrop of this organic evolution, paragraph 283 of the General Instruction of the third edition of the Roman Missal appears as something less than a surprise:

> 283. In addition to those cases given in the ritual books, Communion under both kinds is permitted for:
>
> a) priests who are not able to celebrate or concelebrate Mass;
>
> b) the deacon and others who perform some duty at the Mass;
>
> c) members of communities at the conventual Mass or the "community" Mass, along with seminarians, and all those engaged in a retreat or taking part in a spiritual or pastoral gathering.
>
> The diocesan Bishop may establish norms for Communion under both kinds for his own diocese, which are also to be

---

[6] *Sacrosanctum concilium* 55.

[7] Cf. *General Instruction of the Roman Missal* (1970), no. 242.

[8] Prot. N. CD 1297/78, October 13, 1984.

[9] National Conference of Catholic Bishops. *This Holy and Living Sacrifice: Directory for the Celebration and Reception of Communion under Both Kinds* (1984) no. 21.

observed in churches of religious and at celebrations with small groups. The diocesan Bishop is also given the faculty to permit Communion under both kinds whenever it may seem appropriate to the Priest to whom a community has been entrusted as its own shepherd, provided that the faithful have been well instructed and that there is no danger of profanation of the Sacrament or of the rite's becoming difficult because of the large number of participants or for some other cause.

Through experience and reflection, the Church gradually came to understand the pastoral benefit of what the council fathers first envisioned and came to apply it in new ways as the conciliar reform slowly took shape.

Organic Development in Translation Principles

A certain organic development may also be seen in regard to the translation of liturgical texts. The first postconciliar attempts at vernacularization of the Roman Liturgy were guided by the principle of dynamic equivalence, the very principle of translation that was then most popular in the secular world and in the academy. The application of this principle to the translation of Latin liturgical texts was set forth in the 1969 instruction *Comme le prevoit.* While admirable in its attempts to enthusiastically and creatively render a text in modern forms of expression, its reliance upon the subjective judgments of the translator often highlighted its defects as an adequate means of conveying liturgical texts.

As the academy and professional translators gradually moved toward an approach which would come to be known as formal equivalence, many within the Church began to reexamine the usefulness of this principle in the mid-1990s. Thus, following a period of extensive consultation, the Congregation for Divine Worship and the Discipline of the Sacraments published the fifth instruction on the implementation of *Sacrosanctum concilium* under the title *Liturgiam authenticam* on March 28, 2001.

The instruction commends "the great work of renewal of the liturgical books of the Roman Rite, a work which included their translation into vernacular languages, with the purpose of bringing about, in the most diligent way, that renewal of the sacred Liturgy which was one of the foremost intentions of the Council."[10] At the same time, it notes that "translations of liturgical texts in various localities stand in need of improvement through correction or through a new draft."11 Translations of the Roman *editiones typicae* should seek to preserve the rich patrimony of Roman liturgical texts and make clear that liturgical translation "is not so much a work of creative innovation as it is of rendering the original texts faithfully and accurately into the vernacular

---

[10] Congregation for Divine Worship and Discipline of the Sacraments, instruction *Liturgiam Authenticam* 2, March 28, 2001: *AAS* 93 (2001) 685-726.
[11] Ibid., 6.

language."12

It is, of course, the conferences of bishops which are charged by the council fathers with the approval of liturgical texts. As an act of particular law, the approval of translations requires a two-thirds vote of all *de iure* Latin rite members. For close to a decade the members of the United States Conference of Catholic Bishops have reviewed the translations of the *Missale Romanum, editio typica tertia*, first in draft form and, finally, as an amendable "Gray Book." The last vote on the last of the segments of the Roman Missal was taken by the USSB just about a year ago.

The International Commission on English in the Liturgy is a mixed commission whose role is to produce English language translations of the Latin *editiones typicae*. Each of the eleven major conferences where English is spoken holds a seat on ICEL. ICEL's chairman is Bishop Arthur Roche of Leeds and the U.S. representative is Bishop Arthur Serratelli of Paterson.

The Congregation for Divine Worship and the Discipline of the Sacraments is responsible for reviewing all liturgical translations with a view to granting the *recognitio*. Cardinal Antonio Cañizares Llovera serves as prefect to that congregation, while two native English speakers: Archbishop J. Augustine Dinoia, OP, and Reverend Anthony Ward, SM, serve as secretary and undersecretary, respectively. So important is the task of confirmation of the Roman Missal, that with the advent of the instruction *Liturgiam authenticam*, the congregation established a committee of advice on the question of the translation of English language liturgical texts. That committee is chaired by Cardinal George Pell of Sydney and is composed of senior prelates from throughout the English speaking world.

On March 25 of this year the English language edition of the Roman Missal was confirmed (Prot 269/10/LIn), an event commemorated by a luncheon with the *Vox Clara* Committee in the presence of the Holy Father.

What are some of the changes in the new translation? Many of the changes perform a function as simple as translating words which were omitted in prior renderings. Thus the triplex *mea culpa* of the *Confiteor* and several lines of the Gloria have been translated into English for the first time.

In the application of the principles of formal equivalence, however, every attempt has been made through recourse to specialists in a variety of fields (from English literature to music and from patrological latinity to systematic theology) to produce a text which is integral, proclaimable, reflective of the rhetorical form of its Latin original, and both beautiful and memorable.

It is also hoped that a more accurate translation of liturgical texts will bring many benefits to the Church, from spirituality to catechesis. A more authentic translation of liturgical texts uncovers new layers of meaning, as in the precise rendering of *meum ac vestrum sacrificium* in the *Orate Fratres*, providing a

[12] Ibid., 20.

deeper reflection on the spiritual sacrifices of the people of God. Similarly, a more precise rendering of the *Ecce Agnus Dei* highlights the contrast between the extraordinary eschatology of the invitation and the profound personalism of the response, a contrast not readily apparent in the prior rendering.

Finally, the widely known dialogue between priest and people: *Dominus vobiscum...Et cum spiritu tuo* will be more precisely translated in order to reflect the role of this important acclamation and response. From at least the early third century this dialogue has preceded every important liturgical action in both East and West and defines the roles of a priestly people in whose midst God dwells. While certain pastoral challenges in the implementation of this change are evident, its theological importance in a day and age in which priesthood is so often misunderstood, could not be more timely.

Thus, even in the translation of liturgical texts, it becomes evident that the proper renewal of the Sacred Liturgy is a matter of gradually unfolding the ways in which God's grace leads us more deeply into the celebration of the source and the summit of the Christian life. It is a process whose goal is the preservation of the Roman Rite it seeks to translate, a way of worshipping God which has evolved in dialogue with changing conditions, and which recognizes and respects the heritage it seeks to promote.

Seminar

A History of the Pastoral Provision (1980-2010)

Reverend Monsignor William H. Stetson

When I was asked a year ago to give a talk on the thirty-year history of what has come to be called the "pastoral provision," I was a bit hesitant because of my age. (In July I celebrated my seventy-ninth birthday and in the past year I have had two valves replaced in my heart and another surgery a few months later. I had reason to be hesitant.) But here I am. I hope you learn something from my presentation.

In the interest of completeness I have divided the presentation into two major sections with an introduction by way of pre-history, followed by the two sections: the first will deal with the history of the pastoral phenomena that the pastoral provision seeks to address and the process that was established to meet these new pastoral needs; and the second sets forth the juridical/canonical arrangements that were suggested to give structural stability to the provision. The second section serves as a good transition to the apostolic constitution *Anglicanorum coetibus* that extends the pastoral phenomenon to the whole church in an extraordinary way.

Introduction

My personal family situation predisposed me to have a sympathetic attitude towards the Episcopal/Anglican church. My father was a member of the local Episcopal parish, St. James, and my mother was Roman Catholic (with an Irish background). I was baptized and received the sacraments in the local Catholic Church, Holy Trinity.

During my high school years I was introduced to the writings of John Henry Newman and learned of the journey he made to the Catholic Church and the Catholic priesthood, from the Church of England, in which he had first been ordained to ministry. Also during my high school years I began the study of the organ; my teacher was the organist and choir director at my father's church, St. James Episcopal. During the summer months and at other times I substituted for him at the services. These circumstances gave me a familiarity with elements of the Anglican/Episcopal tradition, especially the music and style of worship. Anglican roots were clearly Catholic while at the same time there were definite doctrinal differences from the Catholic Church. I must add that the rector of St. James Church became a good friend and mentor to me as he was to my father.

My college years at Harvard saw a deepening of this earlier intellectual and spiritual formation. The Anglican ethos was present among faculty and students. I continued my organ studies with the organist of Trinity Episcopal Church in Boston, one of the city's more important churches; he introduced me to the rector of a small Anglo-Catholic church in the suburbs, Rev. N. Frederick Lang. I became the organist and choir director of his church, Our Savior Anglo-Catholic Church. Rev. Lang was a Harvard graduate and Air Force chaplain who was doing graduate studies at the Episcopal Divinity School in Cambridge. He would often stop by my room; and on several occasions I had dinner with him and his wife after the services at his church on Sunday.

The principal figure in my college life, however, was an upper classman whom I met at the first meeting of the Harvard Catholic Club, that as a good Catholic I dutifully attended. His name was Bernard Law. He introduced me to the chaplain, secretary to the archbishop and later auxiliary bishop of Boston. He put me to work recruiting new members of the club from the freshman class. He also presented me to one of his roommates who was Catholic and they both invited me to attend daily Mass at the parish, where the new liturgical custom of dialoguing with the celebrant was used. We became good friends. He helped me to go beyond the difficulties with the Catholic faith raised by some of the professors (gentlemen and Christians, but with the anti-Catholicism of the time).

Bernard Law and I have been friends for sixty years and have shared many interests and events during that time. Among them has been the desire to bring Anglicans and Episcopalians into the full communion of the Catholic Church, following in the footsteps of Cardinal Newman, Robert Hugh Benson, Ronald Knox, and many others.

It was in this context that in 1977, being a priest of Opus Dei in Chicago and having become friendly with a young Episcopal clergyman who wanted to come into full communion with the Catholic Church, that I introduced him to Bishop Bernard Law of Springfield, Missouri. We met in the rectory of a small Episcopal church in Park Ridge, Illinois. During that meeting the Episcopal priest spoke about a group of Episcopal priests who were seeking an appointment with the apostolic delegate with the desire of presenting a petition for being able to exercise priestly ministry in the Catholic Church after coming into full communion, with a dispensation from the norm of celibacy in the case of married men. Then and there, with characteristic forcefulness, Bernard Law contacted the apostolic delegate and arranged the meeting, which later took place at the residence of the apostolic delegate in Washington, DC.

With this I conclude my early involvement with what would become over the next few years the pastoral provision.

Section One: The Pastoral Phenomenon

Before beginning let me say that the most complete study of the pastoral provision, with documents and reports from the archives, is the doctoral dissertation of Msgr. James M. Sheehan, "A New Canonical Configuration for the Pastoral Provision for Former Episcopalians in the United States of America." In September 2005, Archbishop John Myers, the Archbishop of Newark, New Jersey, was named ecclesiastical delegate of the Congregation for the Doctrine of the Faith for the pastoral provision (succeeding Cardinal Bernard

Law). At that time the complete files of the pastoral provision, scattered in several locations, were consolidated in Newark. In 2005, Msgr. Sheehan was the secretary to the archbishop. As such he and I had frequent conversations about the work of the pastoral provision since I had been the secretary to Cardinal Law for the pastoral provision for ten years and had been asked by Archbishop Myers to continue in that capacity. After a year Archbishop Myers sent Father Sheehan (as he was then) to Rome to study for a doctorate in canon law. Father Sheehan chose a topic related to the canonical structure of the pastoral provision for his dissertation. Thus his dissertation, for which he had ready access to the archives and files in Newark, is, in my opinion, the most complete history of the pastoral provision.

Much happened in the years between 1977 and the decision of the CDF, approved by Pope John Paul II on June 20, 1980, to provide a special pastoral provision for Episcopalians seeking admission into full communion with the Catholic Church.[1]

The meeting set up by Bishop Law with the apostolic delegate took place in Washington in April 1977. "At this meeting were Rev. James Parker, the Provincial of the Society of the Holy Cross, Rev. Larry Lossing... representing southeast members of the Society, and Rev. John D. Barker of Los Angeles, California, representing the west coast members of the Society" (Rev. Barker was also an assistant to Canon Albert J. Dubois, the founder of the Diocese of the Holy Trinity that later became the Pro-diocese of St. Augustine of Canterbury).[2] The meeting was to explore what possibilities there might be for receiving Episcopal priests into the Roman Catholic Church; the stated goal was to be able to continue to function as Roman Catholic priests, even if married."[3]

As a result of this meeting and other requests of disaffected Episcopalians seeking help, addressed to the apostolic delegate and to the conference of bishops, Archbishop Joseph Bernardin, president of the NCCB, asked Bishop Law to create an *Ad hoc* committee consisting of himself and Bishop Raymond Lessard as co-chair persons.

In the course of the next three years meetings were held with various groups of disaffected Episcopalian priests, lay people, and even one bishop. Broadly speaking there were two distinct groups: priests of the Society of the Holy Cross, lead by Rev. James Parker, and groups of priests and lay faithful under the

---

[1] Much of the material for this presentation comes from the archives of the Pastoral Provision in the Archdiocese of Newark or from the personal recollections of the presenter.

[2] Canon Albert duBois was a former Episcopal priest who after the 1976 decision to ordain women as priests left the Episcopal Church with some other priests and lay people. They set about creating a new body to which he gave the name "Diocese of the Holy Trinity." He and his followers were seeking some form of "corporate re-union," hoping to retain the Anglican tradition in the Roman Catholic Church.

[3] Cf. Jack Barker, *The Pastoral Provision for the Roman Catholic Church in the USA*, 4. He is the same man mentioned above who in addition was working with Canon duBois for a form of "corporate re-union."

leadership of Canon duBois, organized in small congregations. The former sought only the possibility of exercising priestly ministry in the Catholic Church with a dispensation from the norm of celibacy; the latter were proposing some form of jurisdictional entity that would allow for the reception of congregations under its own leadership, the goal being to preserve elements of the Anglican tradition in the Catholic Church. At the request of the NCCB a canon lawyer was appointed to give his opinion on the various proposals.[4] All of this was duly reported back to the *Ad hoc* committee and to the CDF, which had been given responsibility for the question of Episcopalians in the United States seeking to enter full communion with the Catholic Church. Bishop Law, at the request of the CDF, presented to the NCCB at its May 1978 meeting in Chicago the question of allowing married men coming from the Episcopal Church to exercise priestly ministry in the Catholic Church. The vote was positive. Again, the following year the CDF asked for a repeat of the previous year's vote to allow for married priests in the Catholic Church. However, this time mention was made of some form of corporate identity. Once again the bishops voted in favor of the married priests but voted against the option for corporate identity.

This is the *status quaestionis* that led up to the decision of June 20, 1980. The decision of the CDF of June 18, 1980, approved by John Paul II was communicated to the president of the NCCB, at that time Archbishop John R. Quinn, in a letter dated June 22, 1980.

The letter, known as *Decisions* (thereafter referred to by the CDF by its Protocol Number, 66/77) became the foundational document of the pastoral provision. It contains the guiding principles for the development of the pastoral provision. *Decisions* is divided into five headings: I. General decisions; II. Elements of "common identity"; III. Steps required for admission to full communion; IV. The statute of the pastoral provision will not be definitive; V. Particulars regarding the execution of the decision.

Msgr. Sheehan aptly comments in his dissertation that the language and phraseology used in the document could have been more precise. "Statute" and "pastoral provision" are frequently used with a common meaning. The concept of "common identity" is left somewhat vague in spite of being broken down into three sub-headings: structure, liturgy, and discipline. Under the heading of "structure," mention is made of the preference of the episcopal conference for the insertion of these reconciled Episcopalians into the diocesan structures under the jurisdiction of local ordinaries. At the same time it also says, "the possibility of some other type of structure as provided for by canonical dispositions, and as suited to the needs of the group, is not excluded."

For purposes of this presentation we can conclude with Section V.2 that calls for the designation of an ecclesiastical delegate as the responsible person to oversee the practical implementation of this decision and to deal with the CDF. In January 1981 Bishop Bernard Law of Springfield-Cape Girardeau was appointed ecclesiastical delegate of the CDF for this purpose. The CDF on

[4] Henry G. Bowen, a former past-president of the CLSA.

March 31, 1981, following a meeting with Bishop Law in Rome on March 12-13, made the public announcement of the appointment. The public statement is meant to be an announcement of the decision of the Holy See to admit married Episcopal ministers to priesthood in the Catholic Church and to provide a common identity, for those who desire it, reflecting certain elements of their heritage. The latter is referred to as a "pastoral provision."

In a letter from the newly appointed ecclesiastical delegate of the CDF to the bishops of the conference of bishops, dated March 27, 1981 (immediately preceding the public announcement of the congregation), Bishop Law refers to the pastoral provision providing for the common identity as one option. He implies that priests and laity coming from Anglicanism would belong to this pastoral provision. He also presents a second option that is spelled out in greater detail to the bishops in accord with which the married priests would be incorporated into a diocesan presbyterate.

In the context of the theological preparation, called for by the *Decisions* document of those who apply, he announces that he is in consultation with Rev. Carl Peter (at that time chairman of the Department of Religious Studies at the Catholic University of America) about establishing a program for a national certification examination.

He also announces that after Easter he will have the fulltime assistance of one of the former Episcopal priests who had been responsible for presenting this request to Rome, Rev. James Parker. He also speaks of the development of the pastoral provision for the safeguarding of elements of the Anglican tradition, according to the indications of the *Decisions* document.

Following up on the structure of the possible entity for safeguarding the Anglican patrimony, Bishop Law held a meeting in St. Louis with the representatives of the Pro-Diocese of St. Augustine of Canterbury, Revs. St. John Brown and Barker. Also present was Rev. Parker and a priest of the Diocese of Springfield- Cape Girardeau, Rev. Michael Swalina. Once again Rev. Barker presented arguments similar to those that he had previously made to Cardinal Seper in Rome in 1979 and that he thought, perhaps rightly, were the basis for the reference to such a structure in the *Decisions* document of June 20, 1980.

Shortly after this meeting Bishop Law contacted me and asked me to be one of his consultants for the implementation of *Decisions* with particular reference to the question of the statute that he had been asked by the CDF to submit. He told me that he wanted me to attend a meeting of some Episcopal priests and consultants that would be held in Dallas in October.

The meeting was held at Holy Trinity Seminary at the University of Dallas. The Rector, Reverend Msgr. Michael Sheehan (later Archbishop of Santa Fe) was the host. Most of the consultants were theologians and would become the original body of examiners for the process of preparation for priestly ordination in the Catholic Church. Present also was the executive director of the NCCB

Committee on Liturgy, Rev John Gurrieri. The Episcopal or former Episcopal clergy were priests from the group of married men seeking ordination with the dispensation from celibacy and others from the so-called Pro-Diocese of St. Augustine of Canterbury, who were seeking full communion together with their congregations and hoping for a jurisdictional entity that would guarantee the preservation of elements of their Anglican tradition. Most of the discussion involved the process for ordination and the requirements. This resulted rather quickly in the list of documents for the dossier which would be presented in the CDF in Rome; and the assessment interview with theologians to be followed by a certification of *debita scientia* through an examination in two parts, written (in the sponsoring diocese) and oral. The first dossiers were subsequently quickly assembled and the assessments and certifications held.

Rev. Gurrieri gave a talk on the principles of Catholic Liturgy and its reform and how this would affect the adoption and approval of a special Anglican Liturgy in the Catholic Church.

I presented for discussion, as Bishop Law had asked me to do, a draft of the statutes for an Anglican vicariate to which the priests and their congregations could belong according to the proposed norms regarding personal jurisdictions that were presently under study in Rome. This proposal received a positive response from the men involved in the Pro-Diocese. Simply put, the vicariate notion involved giving the position of the ecclesiastical delegate a more juridically structured foundation with some form of concurrent jurisdiction over the congregations that might be established as personal parishes with the permission of the local ordinary. The primary responsibility of the ordinary/vicar would be the oversight of the special liturgy to be created. He would also oversee the process for ordination called for by *Decisions*. The priests, faithful, and parishes would be diocesan. Although the Pro-Diocese priests wanted more, I realized that Bishop Law felt that his brother bishops would not give their consent to a *uniate* style vicariate with exclusive jurisdiction, even if for the moment the vicar were to be a Catholic diocesan bishop.

In November 1981 Bishop Law presented to the CDF the statutes of the proposed vicariate. However, this was quickly withdrawn on the advice, as he wrote, of canon lawyers, theologians, and some bishops of the United States. A substitute proposal was submitted that involved the establishment of a committee of the NCCB to handle this matter, but no record exists of the reaction of the congregation. However, in the spring of 1982 a new interim statute was drawn up by Bishop Law (with my help) and quickly approved by the congregation. In September 1982 Bishop Law met with seven pastors of congregations seeking full communion and explained to them the procedures that had been approved by the CDF for the reception of their congregations and the ordination of their pastors as Catholic priests.

In fact, the norms given by the congregation, now under the leadership of Cardinal Joseph Ratzinger, were very generous. They provided for the submission of dossiers of the priests by the local ordinary sponsoring the priest and his congregation; the catechizing of the lay members of the congregations; the theological assessment and preparation of the priests; and the certification by examination of the priests. All of this was to be done while the priest continued his pastoral work under the Anglican orders he had received. After the favorable response of the congregation the priest would be received into full communion through profession of faith with the opportunity for sacramental confession. He would be confirmed, ordained deacon and priest and then receive individually the members of his congregation.

In March of 1983 the first *Rescripts* were received by the ecclesiastical delegate for the former Episcopal ministers who were requesting ordination as Catholic priests under the sponsorship of Catholic local ordinaries; among them were several who were bringing congregations with them. Before proceeding to the establishment of personal parishes using an interim liturgy, Bishop Law thought that it would be good to hold a meeting of several of the sponsoring bishops with two canon lawyers to lay out the parameters of the jurisdiction of the pastors of the parishes. This meeting was held in Reno, Nevada at the residence of the Bishop of Reno-Las Vegas, Francis McFarland, and Archbishop Patrick Flores; Bishop Anthony Bevilacqua, at the time auxiliary of Brooklyn, and myself. A set of guidelines was adopted regarding who could be members of the personal parishes and the concurrent subjection of the lay members to the jurisdictional authority of the diocesan bishop and to the pastor or the parish regarding sacramental practice. The main question was who might marry in the personal parish.

At that meeting Bishop Law mentioned that he thought it would be good for him to be represented at the Mass of priestly ordination and reception of the community. He asked me to do this and the others agreed. I attended the reception of congregations in San Antonio, Las Vegas, and Columbia, South Carolina. Parishes were also established in Houston and Austin, Texas and later in Fort Worth, Texas, without close consultation with the ecclesiastical delegate.

During the years 1983 to 1994, the work of the pastoral provision was consolidated and operated smoothly under the authority of the ecclesiastical delegate and the day-to-day supervision of Rev. James Parker. In January of 1984 a special liturgy for the "common identity" parishes was approved with the name of *The Book of Divine Worship*. A committee appointed by Bishop Law in consultation with the Congregation for Divine Worship and the Discipline of the Sacraments had worked out this liturgy. The letter of the prefect of the congregation communicating this to Bishop Law contained three documents regulating the Special Liturgy and the use of *The Book of Divine Worship* in which it is mostly expressed.

In March 1984 Bishop Bernard Law became Archbishop of Boston and the following year was named to the College of Cardinals. He continued as ecclesiastical delegate of the pastoral provision. The process of assessment and certification examination worked well, using the good offices of several Church institutions in Washington, DC and a faculty of professor-examiners, appointed by the ecclesiastical delegate, who followed the syllabus that had been adopted and the bibliography that had been suggested by the various professors. During that time I was the examiner in canon law, and occasionally in ascetical-mystical theology. In later years the facilities of Blessed John XXIII Seminary were used.

Section Two: The Canonical Itinerary

In the fall of 1993 the Episcopal Bishop of Fort Worth, Clarence Pope, a leader of the Anglo-Catholic party of the Episcopal Church in the United States, made a trip to Rome accompanied by several priests from his diocese. They had a cordial and encouraging meeting with Cardinal Ratzinger at the CDF on the possibility of coming into full communion with the Catholic Church together with several priests and congregations. They sought some form of jurisdictional entity that would assure the retention of elements of their Anglican patrimony. The result of this meeting was a 1994 letter from Cardinal Ratzinger to Cardinal Law asking that he obtain from Bishop Pope a more detailed explanation of the general outlines of the jurisdictional entity that they were seeking. At this point Cardinal Law asked me, once again, to work for him with Bishop Pope and his clerical advisors on this proposal. He also asked me to take over from Rev. Parker the work formerly handled by him in organizing the daily administration of the pastoral provision.

I made a trip to Fort Worth where I met for several days with Bishop Pope and two of his closest advisors (Rev. Jeffrey Steenson, later bishop of the Episcopal Diocese of the Rio Grand, now a Roman Catholic priest; and Rev. James Hart, now also a Catholic priest, until recently the moderator of the curia of the Diocese of Fort Worth). This meeting produced a document consisting of principles for a juridical entity modeled after the ordinariate for the military. Subsequently Cardinal Law and I realized that the only personal jurisdiction in the 1983 code is that of a personal prelature. In January 1995 Cardinal Law hand delivered to the CDF the statutes of a personal prelature for the Anglicans seeking full communion. The congregation's response came quickly and was positive. Cardinal Ratzinger asked that this be consulted with the NCCB as called for by the 1983 code (c. 294). Once again an *ad hoc* committee was established to study the proposal. After much discussion about the relationship of the prelate of the Anglican jurisdiction to the local ordinaries of the dioceses where there might be parishes and the small number of priests and parishes that were likely to come into full communion, the consensus was that it was inopportune at this time and the matter should be put off to a later date. (It should be mentioned that Bishop Pope had meanwhile entered full communion with the Catholic Church and was worshiping as a layman; however, out of discouragement at the decision, he later returned to the Episcopal Church.)

The statutes that were submitted were substantially the same as those prepared in 1981. They followed the familiar pattern of the option for a diocesan bishop to be the prelate, in which case he could request an auxiliary bishop as his vicar for the prelature. The prelature would assume the tasks, as before in the pastoral provision, of preparing former Episcopal priests for ministry in the Catholic Church at the request of a diocesan bishop wishing to sponsor and incardinate them. At the discretion of the prelate some priests could be incardinated in the prelature as needed for the congregations wishing to use *The Book of Divine Worship*. Others might be incardinated for the administrative and evangelizing work of the members of the prelature. The statutes carefully respected the authority of the diocesan bishops with regard to the establishment of parishes and worship communities. Such groups would be part of the local diocesan structure. The jurisdiction of the prelate would be concurrent with that of the diocesan bishop. The lay faithful of the Anglican prelature would be ordinary faithful of the local diocese using a special liturgy for their worship, under the jurisdiction of the prelate and the diocesan bishop. The members of the parish would be lay faithful proceeding from the Anglican communion or received into full communion through a personal parish or worship congregation. They also provided for the establishment by the prelate of a seminary or house of studies for the preparation of future priests for the Anglican use. Celibacy would be required for all future priests.

The object of this jurisdictional entity was to provide a more juridical-canonical structure for what had become the pastoral provision and to provide for its growth as requested by the Episcopal bishop of Fort Worth. It provided for the insertion of these groups into the ordinary structures of the Latin Church without creating a new species of *uniate* Anglican community with exclusive jurisdiction. This was done in a way that left room for the cultivation over time of an Anglican tradition within the English speaking Church in the United States.

There matters continued to rest until the next earthquake in the Episcopal Church in the United States, the consecration of an overtly partnered homosexual bishop. In 1995 I attended, as an observer, the convention of the Episcopal Church that took place in Indianapolis. The topic of new attitudes toward human sexuality was already being debated in the assembly. One of the Anglo-Catholic bishops said to me: "We know that we are not Catholic; but if the present direction of affairs prevails we will no longer be Christian." Thus the election of the new bishop produced a further crisis among the Episcopal Church in the United States and the worldwide Anglican communion.

This has led to a series of events and actions that are still working themselves out. The first was a convention of conservative (by Anglican standards) Episcopalians that took place in Plano, Texas in 2003. Cardinal Law, who knew one of the conservative bishops, asked me to go as his personal representative. During that assembly a letter of prayerful support from Cardinal Ratzinger was read, receiving a standing ovation. I had informal conversations with several conservative and Anglo-Catholic bishops and priests (and even women priests). Following that meeting several of the Anglo-Catholic bishops met informally with Cardinal Law and me in Washington, DC. In the fall of 2004 Cardinal Law went to Rome as the Archpriest of St. Mary Major; shortly thereafter Pope John Paul II died and Cardinal Ratzinger was elected his successor. A transition was taking place. Archbishop William Levada was appointed to succeed Cardinal Ratzinger and Archbishop John Myers was appointed to succeed Cardinal Law as ecclesiastical delegate of the pastoral provision.

Nevertheless, activity continued in the Episcopal Church in the United States and in the Anglican communion. Various suggestions were being made on re-drawing the lines of Anglicanism. Some were looking to Rome for direction. Several of the Anglo-Catholic bishops met on more than one occasion with Archbishop Myers. These meetings gave rise to a letter to the Holy Father signed by several of these bishops requesting a juridical entity for their people. A new draft of statutes was sent off to Rome in 2007. It was essentially the same as those submitted in 1995. As often happens, the reply from Rome was delayed and events in the Episcopal Church moved in another direction, leading to the creation of a schismatic (from the Episcopal Church's point of view) Anglican church in the United States. Nearly all the bishops who signed the letter to Pope Benedict XVI joined, together with their dioceses, the new Anglican Province of North America. Nevertheless, two sitting bishops resigned and became Roman Catholics and were subsequently ordained to the priesthood in the Catholic Church.

Epilogue

How does the apostolic constitution *Anglicanorum coetibus* relate to this story? My sincere answer is I do not know.

The apostolic constitution seems to be a response to petitions coming from various parts of the English-speaking world, whereas the pastoral provision is a response to individuals and groups from one country. Although England has had for several years a provision that provides for the ordination of former Church of England clergymen, married and celibate, it does not have the option of congregations with an Anglican use liturgy as was granted to the United States.

The apostolic constitution and its accompanying complementary norms go a long way in the direction of granting quasi *uniate* status, without calling it that, for those bishops, dioceses, and lay faithful, gathered in parishes, who enter full communion through a national Anglican ordinariate. Many things are granted to them, for example, election of one of their own as ordinary/bishop (if celibate); exclusive jurisdiction over their own affairs without regard to the Latin Rite diocesan bishop, and so forth. These are granted as a way of retaining and maintaining elements of their Anglican heritage. This is more than was ever considered in the context of creating the pastoral provision.

There are two crucial questions regarding the future of the national ordinariates. The first has to do with preserving unity within each ordinariate, both in a single country and worldwide, and fostering unity with the ordinary Latin Rite jurisdictions. The second is the often-faced question about the numbers of lay faithful who will follow their priests and bishops into the ordinariate. Only over time will we know the answers to these questions, and others that may occur to you.

SEMINAR

A RENAISSANCE OF CREATIVE FIDELITY IN A TIME OF RETRIEVAL AND RECONNOITERING

Sister Marlene Weisenbeck, FSPA

Introduction

This presentation proposes to look at the current apostolic visitation of U.S. Women Religious and the doctrinal assessment of the Leadership Conference of Women Religious (LCWR) through the lens of the call to creative fidelity found in *Vita consecrata* 37. Other texts about the idea of creative fidelity will also be considered. To add fascination to this exploration, the title suggests this is happening in a time of retrieval and reconnoitering. Retrieving what? And how does this relate to reconnoitering?

There is much to retrieve in a time of surprise and challenge—composure, for one thing, but more importantly a sense of spiritual, emotional and intellectual balance, and most importantly the conviction that religious life is centered in the One who calls us—the Christ, the One at the heart of our love—and the service of foot washing which is at the core of beatitude life for the sake of God's reign in our world.

Adding the word "reconnoitering" to the descriptive at this time in history provides further reflection. A number of definitions carry the day and some have meaning for us, such as: to explore, often with the goal of finding something or somebody; an exploratory survey conducted to gain or collect information. Could we admit that these inquiries have seemed like someone is scouting in territory where a sense of menace is created? Could it be that we are being observed, and that the reaction between the players in this drama is watched attentively? The derivation of the word comes from the obsolete French *reconnoître,* literally "to recognize". Webster further defines "recognize" in several ways, for example: to acknowledge formally, to admit as being of a particular status, to admit as being entitled to be heard, to acknowledge the de facto or independent existence of someone or an entity, to acknowledge or take notice of in some definite way, or finally, to perceive to be something or someone previously known.

Without question, the Vatican inquiries have given impetus for women religious in this country to identify with the aura around these words and to claim the best of their lives as consecrated women in not only the ecclesial environment but the world in general. All of us desire to be recognized for living our consecration authentically and with integrity. With this in mind, the goal of this paper is first, to provide reflection on the call to creative fidelity by specifically addressing this concept found in *Vita consecrata*, *Starting Afresh from Christ* and other related documents; and secondly to reflect on some pivotal canonical issues raised in the Vatican inquiries, why they are being raised now, and what is transpiring at the present time.

The Call to Creative Fidelity

The words "creative fidelity" are used three times in three significant Vatican documents—not a big emphasis, it could be observed or expected, in a Church that emphasizes millennial tradition. One might wonder if the writers of the documents were not much interested in imaginative, inspired, innovative or resourceful approaches to living the consecrated life in its essence or its service. Yet those words are found frequently throughout many church documents of the Second Vatican Council and the ones just cited.

The call to creative fidelity in *Vita consecrata* 37 is an invitation to respond to the ever-creating God of time and the universe. In a paragraph heading entitled "Creative Fidelity", it reads:

> Institutes of consecrated life are thus invited courageously to propose anew the enterprising initiative, creativity and holiness of their founders and foundresses in response to the signs of the times emerging in today's world. This invitation is first of all a call to perseverance on the path of holiness in the midst of the material and spiritual difficulties of daily life. But it is also a call to pursue competence in personal work and to develop a dynamic fidelity to their mission, adapting forms, if need be, to new situations and different needs, in complete openness to God's inspiration and to the Church's discernment. But all must be fully convinced that the quest for ever greater conformity to the Lord is the guarantee of any renewal which seeks to remain faithful to an institute's original inspiration.[1]

Two years later, another document, namely the instruction on Inter-Institute Collaboration for Formation issued by the Congregation for Institutes of Consecrated Life and Societies of Apostolic Life (CICLSAL) on December 8, 1998 gave a more specific definition of creative fidelity signifying a *harmoniously blending in the life and mission of the People of God, the gifts and experiences which enrich it, as well as taking care that religious not become part of the life of the Church in a vague and ambiguous way.* Emphasis is given in the text to the Holy Spirit's experience in the founders which is to be *deepened and constantly developed by them* as well as harmonized in *the Body of Christ continually in the process of growth.*

> Every institute has a primary responsibility for its own identity. In fact, "the charism of the founders, an experience of the Holy Spirit transmitted to their disciples to be lived, safeguarded, deepened and constantly developed by them, in

[1] Pope John Paul II, post-synodal apostolic exhortation *Vita consecrata* 37, March 25, 1996: *AAS* 88 (1996) 377-486.

harmony with the Body of Christ continually in the process of growth,"[2] is entrusted to each institute as its original patrimony for the benefit of the entire Church.[3] Cultivating their own identity in "creative fidelity,"[4] then, means harmoniously blending in the life and mission of the People of God, the gifts and experiences which enrich it,[5] as well as taking care that religious not "become part of the life of the Church in a vague and ambiguous way."[6]

The call to *enterprising initiative, creativity and holiness, to perseverance on the path of holiness in the midst of the material and spiritual difficulties of daily life, conformity to the Lord,* and *cultivating their own identity in "creative fidelity"* in these documents was received enthusiastically by religious institutes as clear imperatives for the renewal of religious life in the past fifty years.

In the wake of Pope John Paul II's *Novo millenio ineunte* welcoming the third millennium, a second document from CICLSAL entitled *Starting Afresh from Christ,*[7] written to religious in 2002 took its points of departure from *Vita consecrata*. The intention, the authors note, was not to produce another doctrinal document but rather to invite consecrated men and women in their particular situation and culture *to focus primarily on spirituality* (Part I), to express gratitude and wholehearted esteem *for what consecrated life is and for what it does, to look upon trials and challenges as new opportunities to rediscover more profoundly the meaning and quality of consecrated life* (Part II), to call for a renewed commitment by living the spirituality of communion in a unique way (Part III), and to accompany consecrated persons *on the streets of the world where Christ walked and today is present, where the Church proclaims him as Savior of the world, where the Trinitarian life spreads communion in a renewed mission.*

Moreover, clear emphasis was given to "constant openness" to the Spirit's action in responding to their times.

> It is fitting to remember the ability of holy foundresses and founders to respond to the challenges and difficulties of their times with a genuine charismatic creativity... to live in a constantly renewed fidelity to the call of the Spirit.[8]

---

[2] Sacred Congregation for Religious and for Secular Institutes and the Sacred Congregation for Bishops, "Directives for the Mutual Relations between Bishops and Religious," *Mutuae relationes* (May 14, 1978) 11.

[3] *Mutuae relationes*, 14b; Code of Canon Law, canon 574 §1; *Vita consecrata*, 4-5, 29, 33-34.

[4] *Vita consecrata*, 37.

[5] Cf. *Perfectae caritatis*, 1; Code of Canon Law, canon 577; *Vita consecrata*, 19, 47-48.

[6] *Mutuae relationes*, 11.

[7] CICLSAL. *Starting Afresh from Christ: A Renewed Commitment to Consecrated Life in the Third Millennium* (2002) 4.

[8] Ibid., 13, 14.

> Consecrated life itself, of its nature, calls for the constant openness of those who are called to it…open to be taught by any fragment of truth and beauty found around them... formation must be attentive to the need to plant in the hearts of young consecrated persons those human, spiritual and charismatic values necessary to make them suitable to carry out a "creative fidelity" ... an openness and docility to the Spirit's action, which is always new and creative is required.[9]

Starting Afresh from Christ echoed a pressing invitation of Pope John Paul II at the beginning of the third millennium. The document reiterated his words *Duc in altum*! "Cast out into the deep," in effect to enliven new hope and awaken a desire for a more evangelical life that would further break open the horizons for dialogue and mission. These quotes are highlighted here to set a context for the following observations about the apostolic visitation and the doctrinal assessment of LCWR.

Pivotal Canonical Issues in the Inquiries

An update on pivotal canonical issues in the Vatican inquiries is provided in as much as this is possible at this point in time and without violating the confidentiality of the processes.

"Internal Visitations" in the 1983 Code of Canon Law

Visitations are an element relating to governance in a religious institute or a diocese.[10] Canon 628 requires visitation to houses and members of an institute by an elected or appointed official. Such visitations internal to a religious institute can be traced to the twelfth and thirteenth centuries when it was considered helpful to assess and maintain discipline and to correct abuses. Canon 617 requires the superior to fulfill this duty within the norms of universal and proper law.

These personal but formal visitations have always been connected to the specific charism and form of the following of Christ. The canons do not provide areas of concern that must fall within the scope of the visitation. Potential areas of review might include the physical, psychological, and spiritual well being of the members, relational matters among the members, witness to the charism, mission and ministry, practices of the members in relation to the living of the vows, and fiscal operations. Motives for a visitation may be very serious internal divisions and insubordination, a serious abuse of authority, or of financial mismanagement, questionable practices of vocation recruitment and/or

---

[9] Ibid., 15, 20.

[10] See Sharon Holland, IHM, JCD who gives an extensive overview of this topic in "Visitation in Religious Institutes: A Service of Communion," *Proceedings of the Sixty-First Annual Convention* (Washington, DC: Canon Law Society of America, 1999) 161-178.

formation, or grave moral issues.[11]

Attention must be given to the members' right to privacy and confidentiality regarding matters of conscience and spirituality.

The nature of a visitation normally requires that the testimony gathered from individual members of the institute and from any others involved be kept confidential. Participants must have this assurance in order to respond with the truth in charity required by canon 628 §3. They would become very vulnerable if sensitive material would be revealed, and what they said was reported to anyone else. Trust and love must be the primary consideration if such a visitation is to be a graced experience (cc. 618, 619, 629 §5.)[12]

If solutions within the institute fail or are not possible, recourse to the local ordinary or the Holy See may be appropriate. The apostolic constitution *Pastor bonus* 107 and 108, in virtue of the competence given to the dicasteries of the Roman Curia, has wide authority to conduct visitations of religious institutes.[13] CICLSAL through its *congresso* may recommend a different course of action, such as an apostolic visitation. The process normally includes seeking fuller information from the general superior of the institute, possibly from the diocese, or even from the nuncio. Ultimately, recommendations are frequently made to the institute toward solutions.

"External Visitations"

Visitations conducted by anyone external to the institute would likely be concerned with similar content, but more directed with the relationship to the broader ecclesial community.

There are numerous canons pertaining to visitations by bishops, either in person or through delegates. Canon 628 §2 refers to his right and duty to visit autonomous monasteries (c. 615) and individual houses of institutes of diocesan right in his territory (cc. 579, 589, 594, 595.) The bishop must visit the entire diocese every five years (c. 396 §1, 2°). Such quinquennial visits must include

---

[11] Ibid., 172-174.

[12] Elizabeth McDonough, OP, STL, JCD, "Visitation," *Review for Religious* 58/2 (March-April 1999), 211-216.

[13] Pope John Paul II, apostolic constitution *Pastor bonus*, June 28, 1988: *AAS* 80 (1988) 841-932. English translation in *Code of Canon Law, Latin-English Edition: New English Translation* (Washington, DC: CLSA, 1998).

Art. 107: "The Congregation for its part takes care that institutes of consecrated life and societies of apostolic life grow and flourish according to the spirit of their founders and healthy traditions, faithfully follow their proper purpose and truly benefit the salvific mission of the Church."

Art. 108 §1: "It deals with everything which, in accordance with the law, belongs to the Holy See concerning the life and work of the institutes and societies, especially the approval of their constitutions, their manner of government and apostolate, the recruitment and training as well as the rights and obligations of members, dispensation from vows and the dismissal of members, and the administration of goods."

persons, all Catholic institutions, and all sacred places and things (c. 397 §1), or stated in another way, all people, apostolates, and properties within the diocese. Canon 628 §2 is a further specification of canons 396 and 397 and includes observation of religious discipline.

The diocesan bishop can also visit religious institutes of pontifical right, but only in instances expressed in law (c. 397 §2). This right is articulated in canons 683 and 806 as it pertains to schools operated by religious. More inclusively, canon 678 gives the bishop the right of visitation for churches, oratories, schools, and apostolates or ministries of charity committed to religious in his diocese. Canon 683 notes that these visitations may occur outside the ordinary pastoral visits required by canon 397 §1, that is, *in case of necessity*.

The purpose of any visitation from an external authority is intended to be an expression of concern for the whole people of God. Apostolic efficacy of the works entrusted to families of charisms are public matters in the Church as well as the communal nature of the following of Christ which relates to service to the Church and a relationship to a portion of people of God.[14]

The Apostolic Visitation

Formal canonical visitations under the auspices of the pope or a Roman dicastery are not treated in the code. They are granted competence only by the Apostolic See and thus are called "apostolic visitations". Historically, these visitations were used by the pope or a Roman dicastery as an administrative tool to gather information in order to remedy a situation that was considered problematic. There have been apostolic visitations of individual religious institutes concerning such matters as relationship with the Apostolic See, division of an institute, various aspects of community and religious life, and internal conflicts. The intention is intended to comprehensively assess and encourage the vitality of the religious institutes by focusing on specific issues such as governance, apostolate, and formation.

The most recent apostolic visitations have been directed to groups of institutes, notably the visitation of American seminaries and houses of priestly formation from 2002-2006, the visitation of apostolic institutes of women religious in the U.S. from 2008-2011, and the visitation of certain Irish dioceses, seminaries and religious congregations which will begin in autumn of this year. These visitations to groups are historically the first of their kind.

While it may be framed within the context of a pastoral motive, and thus not penal or judicial in nature, an apostolic visitation is initiated because of a perceived need for correction. Often an apostolic visitation may be initiated because a dicastery, having received complaints, desires to investigate and if necessary, resolve the situation. Because of the lack of specific norms concerning the origins for initiating an apostolic visitation, there is no way of

---

[14] Elizabeth McDonough OP, STL, JCD, "Visitation by External Authorities" *Review for Religious* 58/3 (May-June 1999) 320-324.

knowing whether or not problems existed or whether decrees proposed to remedy a perceived problem are based on information from the final report or other factors known only to the author(s). Also possible is the use of the apostolic visitation as a *pro-forma* procedure for the issuance of some decrees or exhortations already decided upon prior to its execution.[15]

Immediately after the announcement of the apostolic visitation of apostolic women religious in the U.S. on January 9, 2009, having as its purpose *to look into the quality of the life of religious women of the United States*,[16] a website was created at www.apostolicvisitation.org. According to the website, three main goals for the visitation expanded upon the purpose stated in the decree. These were articulated along with a timeline for the process of the visitation.

Goals of the Apostolic Visitation

- to look into the quality of apostolic religious life in the United States
- to learn more about the ways in which women religious contribute to the welfare of the Church and society
- to assist the Church to strengthen, enhance and support the growth of the institutes to which the women religious in the United States belong.

Timeline

- December 22, 2008: Decree initiating the apostolic visitation of apostolic women religious in the United States and naming Mother Mary Clare Millea, ASCJ, as apostolic visitator *ad inquirendum et referendum*
- January 30, 2009: News conference and press release: *"Vatican initiates study of Catholic sisters' institutes in the United States"*
- February 2, 2009: Letter from Franc Cardinal Rodé to superiors general announcing the apostolic visitation
- January 12 – July 31, 2009 - Phase I: Major superiors requested to schedule a personal visit with Mother Mary Clare or to write a letter in response to hopes and concerns for apostolic religious life
- September 18, 2009 - Phase II: *Questionnaire for Major Superiors* was made available with request to return it by November 20, 2009
- April 11 - May 30 and Sept. 12 - Dec. 12, 2010 - Phase III: Teams of visitors appointed by Mother Clare Millea to visit selected congregations

---

[15] "Apostolic Visitation," an opinion rendered by the Resource Center for Religious Institutes (2009) http://www.trcri.org/apostolicvisitation.php.

[16] Congregation for Institutes of Consecrated Life and Societies of Apostolic Life, decree Prot. 16805/2008 (Vatican City: December 22, 2008). See appendix A.

- December 2011 - Phase IV: Final reports by visitator to CICLSAL

While current technologies and professional communications strategies afforded a more public dimension for transmitting information about the apostolic visitation of women religious in the U.S., thereby implying a greater transparency in the process, it also provided an instantaneous means for a public discussion of the event. For example, it became known very early in the process that the apostolic nuncio and some members of the United States Conference of Catholic Bishops (USCCB), by their own admission, had no prior knowledge of the visitation. Although both the LCWR and the Council of Major Superiors of Women Religious (CMSWR) were informed prior to the press conference about it, they were requested to remain uninvolved and to forward any questions directly to the office of the apostolic visitation.[17]

Cardinal Franc Rodé, after hearing and reading for nine months the copious responses of the Church to this visitation, clarified further his motivation and reasons for initiating the visitation, as follows:

> For many years this Dicastery had been listening to concerns expressed by American Catholics, religious, laity, clergy and hierarchy about the welfare of religious women and consecrated life in general, and had been considering an Apostolic Visitation as a means to assess and constructively address these concerns. The multitude and complexity of these issues were made clear by speakers and participants at the Symposium on Religious Life at Stonehill College in September 2008.[18]

The same statement noted that he hoped *to encourage vocations and assure a better future for women religious*, which had not been a reason stated in the decree. Moreover, challenged with the possibility of a premeditated conclusion to the visitation, Cardinal Rodé confirmed in the same statement *that this Dicastery will formulate no conclusions or plan of action, if any, until the final report of the Visitator has been evaluated.*

As the public and internal discussions began to gain momentum about the apostolic visitation and the process outlined by the apostolic visitator began to be disseminated, women religious and canon lawyers also began their preparations to respond. Two significant things happened immediately. A spirit of solidarity among women religious like none other in church history formed among them. Additionally, they began to examine the canonical implications of how to respond appropriately within the limits of the law. While the following list of canonical issues may not be all inclusive, it represents the major canonical

---

[17] Letter from Mother Mary Clare Millea ASCJ, Apostolic Visitor, to J Lora Dambroski OSF, President of LCWR. Dated February 9, 2010.

[18] Card. Franc Rodé, C.M., Statement of the Prefect of the Congregation of Institutes of Consecrated Life and Societies of Apostolic Life, On the Apostolic Visitation of Institutes of Women Religious in the USA. November 3, 2009. See Appendix B.

questions that begged for attention by women religious.

- The canonical nature of the decree initiating the visitation *ad inquirendum et referendum* ("studied and referred")
- Obedience to the pope and bishops (cc. 576, 590, 752-754); the possibility of the removal of superior's mandate should she or the institute refuse to cooperate with the visitation
- The role of bishops; dialogue with church leaders that promotes mutual understanding and furthers unity and the mission of the church (cc. 678, 755 *Mutuae relationes*)
- The oath of fidelity and the profession of faith (c. 833 and *Ad tuendam fidem*)
- The distinctions between apostolic and monastic institutes; which ones were to be included in the visitation and which were to be excluded by the nature of the visitation and the nature of the institute (cc. 609, 613, 615, 731-734)
- The scope and limits of authority of the visitator(s);
- The obligations and rights of all the Christian Faithful and of the lay members of the Christian Faithful (cc. 208-231), with particular concern for
    - The right to canonical representation (c. 221)
    - Privacy and confidentiality; the right not to answer certain questions; the right to retain any personal notes used during the interviews (c. 630.5)[19]; the right to keep confidential personal information pertaining to members; the right to respect the personal living spaces of the members (c. 220)
    - The good name of individuals and institutes (c. 220)
    - The right to administrative recourse if corrective action is considered inconsistent with the reality of the institute's life and/or obedience to the authority of the magisterium (cc. 333 §3, 1417, 1732-1739)
- Canonical implications regarding the identity of the congregation, governance, formation, the vows and common life, mission and ministry, financial administration (cc. 573-602, 606-702 and 731-746)
- Canonical issues pertaining to the private prayer and worship by the institute; the role of proper law pertaining to the obligation of praying the Liturgy of the Hours (cc. 663-664)
- The right and obligation of participation on the part of all the superiors of an institute from general and provincial units, specifically during the interview of elected officials of the institute
- The right to see a report concerning one's institute as well as the final report
- The right of conscience (*Gaudium et spes* 16-17; apostolic letter of Pope

[19] See Daniel J. Ward, "Privacy/Confidentiality Issues in Religious Institutes" *CLSA Proceedings 61* (1999) 305-315; James H. Provost, "Rights in Canon Law: Real, Ideal, or Fluff?" *CLSA Proceedings 61* (1999) 317-342; and Rik Torfs. "Rights in Canon Law: Real, Ideal or Fluff?" *CLSA Proceedings 61* (1999) 343-384.

John Paul II *Freedom of Conscience and of Religion* [1980], c. 630 §5)

- Temporal goods of the institute (cc. 634-640; 1254-1310)
- The *Instrumentum laboris* and canonical nature of the various types of documents cited therein; the relative value of various documents issued by the Holy See or a bishops' conference. Not every pronouncement from the Vatican or a conference of bishops has juridical implications. Such documents differ in their canonical significance. For example, the most solemn form of a legal document issued by the pope in his own name is an apostolic constitution. When issued, it deals with doctrinal or disciplinary matters in relationship to very weighty questions. The Code of Canon Law was promulgated as a constitution. The Catechism of the Catholic Church and *Pastor bonus* (implications for CICLSAL) were also promulgated as constitutions. The proper law of a religious institute is in the form of a constitution. Encyclicals are next in terms of importance. They are expressions of the pope's ordinary teaching authority which shed greater light on points of doctrine. They are capable of being changed on specific points. Apostolic exhortations such as *Vita consecrata* are exhortative in nature and not considered a legislative text. Instructions are designed to clarify prescriptions of laws, elaborate on them and determine an approach to be followed in implementing them (c. 34). However, regulations found in instructions are not derogations from laws and if any of them cannot be reconciled with the prescriptions of law, they lack all force. While recognizing this, the life of religious should not be reduced to legal categories. Other dimensions need to be considered. Nonetheless, religious need to know where they stand when obligations are defined or rights are proclaimed. Frequently, the implications of these documents are not clearly understood either by the ones issuing them and/or by religious who receive them.[20]

Currently, the apostolic visitation is nearing the conclusion of Phase III. The goal is to visit approximately twenty-five percent of the apostolic institutes. Institutes are assiduously seeking the canonical assistance needed to respond faithfully to the process in solidarity with one another, with guidance from canonists, and in fidelity to calls of the Holy Spirit as discerned through fifty years of renewal and the re-imagining of religious life.

An Apostolic Visitation of the religious of a whole country, with a rather generic goal such as the current one in the U.S., if it is needed at all, should perhaps have a different name and procedure. If such visitations are to resemble accrediting processes of other institutions, as has been opined by some, then the visitators should have access to responses filed with the apostolic visitation

[20] For complete discussion on these matters see Francis G. Morrisey, O.M.I., *Papal and Curial Pronouncements: Their Canonical Significance in Light of the Code of Canon Law*, 2nd edition revised/updated by Michel Theriault (Ottawa: St. Paul University, 2001); Patrick Lagges, "The Teaching Authority of the Episcopal Conference" *CLSA Proceedings 69* (2007) 41-79 and Dr. Kurt Martens, "Nature of Authority of Roman Documents," *CLSA Proceedings 69* (2007) 131-164.

office prior to the visit. There ought to be some effort to match charisms and life forms/styles of the visitators and the institute visited. Unintended positive outcomes possibly will be related to a greater knowledge between diverse styles and forms of religious life. Women religious will have become more familiar with their rights and duties as a public actor in the ecclesial arena, and perhaps the debate about whether Vatican II resulted in continuity or rupture will have been quelled, or at least more balanced.

The Doctrinal Assessment of the Leadership Conference of Women Religious (LCWR)

Shortly after the announcement of the apostolic visitation of U.S. apostolic women religious, the LCWR was informed on February 20, 2009 of the decision of the Congregation for the Doctrine of Faith (CDF) to conduct a doctrinal assessment of the activities and initiatives of the conference. Given the requirement for confidentiality stated in most of the correspondence, it is not possible to comment specifically on the process related to the inquiries which pertain to the assessment nor to the response given at this point in time. It is possible, however, to note and reflect upon some of the canonical implications that have arisen for the LCWR.

In conversations of the LCWR presidency with Cardinal William Levada, Prefect of the Congregation for the Doctrine of the Faith, during their annual visits to the Vatican dicasteries, it was confirmed that this process would follow the nature of an assessment, but not the regulations for formal doctrinal examination.[21] However, it was noted that the process would resemble the regulations in some respects. The *verbale* of the LCWR's meeting with Cardinal Levada records:

> The "investigative" aspect is present in this assessment, but there is a way to contextualize it. When we know that our information is complete and correct, the CDF will indicate to the LCWR areas of concern. In other words, what is the status of the question now? This invites the LCWR into the CDF's role of promoting the Church's faith.[22]

Bishop Leonard Blair was appointed the delegate of CDF to initiate the process and to gather the needed information. This was done through one meeting and numerous other communications by written letter, telephone, and email. *Starting Afresh from Christ* became a context in which the presidency and executive director reflected upon the challenges of religious leadership as *a demanding and at times disputed task. It requires a constant presence which is able to animate and propose, to recall the raison d'être of consecrated life, and*

[21] Congregation for the Doctrine of the Faith, *Regulations for Doctrinal Examination*, June 29, 1997.
http://www.vatican.va/roman_curia/congregations/cfaith/documents/rc_con_cfaith_doc_19970629_ratio-agendi_en.html

[22] *Verbale* of meeting of LCWR presidency with CDF dated April 9, 2009 (Washington, D.C.: LCWR files).

to help those entrusted to them to live in a constantly renewed fidelity to the call of the Spirit.[23]

Some of the canonical issues which directed the response to CDF and which continue to be researched are:

- *The nature of a conference versus a council* (cc. 708-709)[24]: These canons are new to the 1983 code. The words "conferences or councils" appear to allow for a variety of organizations which have developed over the years to provide the wide-range of assistance that major superiors need to carry out their responsibilities. Canon 708 makes no mention of a requirement for these organizations to have the governing documents of the organization approved by the Holy See. None of these organizations such as the National Catholic Development Conference (NCDC), the National Religious Vocations Conference (NRVC), the National Conference of Vicars for Religious (NCVR), the National Religious Retirement Office (NRRO) or the Institute for Religious Life, carry the status and role of a conference of major superiors approved by the Holy See. It is only in canon 709 where the term "conference of major superiors" is used that the requirement of having "their own statutes approved by the Holy See" is stated. Thus, the wording of canons 708-709 appear to provide a distinct difference in the nature and status of a conference of major superiors from other types of conferences or councils that may be formed. Ghirlanda explains from the sources of the canons (*Ecclesiae Sanctae* II, 43 and 63 and *Perfectae caritatis* 21) that the term "council" pertains to mixed commissions made up of bishops and men and women major superiors for the purpose of dealing with questions concerning either group. As an example, he refers to the Council of 16 in Rome consisting of bishops, eight men and eight women major superiors which meets with CICLSAL periodically.[25] In the U.S. a similar "mixed commission" might be the USCCB Commission on Consecrated Life. Though it is not called a "council", it is structured like one described by Ghirlanda and is comprised of bishops and the presidents/executive directors of LCWR, CMSWR, CMSM, NRRO, NCVR and NRVC.

---

[23] CICLSAL, *Starting Afresh from Christ*, 14.

[24] Canon 708: Major superiors can be associated usefully in conferences or councils so that by common efforts they work to achieve more fully the purpose of the individual institutes, always without prejudice to their autonomy, character, and proper spirit, or to transact common affairs, or to establish appropriate coordination and cooperation with the conferences of bishops and also with individual bishops.

Canon 709: Conferences of major superiors are to have their own statutes approved by the Holy See, by which alone they can be erected even as a juridic person and under whose supreme direction they remain.

[25] Gianfranco Ghirlanda, SJ, provides a thorough explication of the history and development of canons 708 and 709 in "Nature and Institutional Ends of the Conferences of Men and Women Religious Superiors," *Consecrated Life* 19/2 (1993) 85-106 (a periodical published by CICLSAL since 1992).

- *The question of whether the approval of statutes of a conference of major superiors (c. 709) automatically confers public juridic status (cc. 113-128) by the law itself or by intentional establishment by decree:* Noted is the fact that the public juridic status and approval of statutes of LCWR and CMSWR came in two separate decrees. When public juridic status is the reality, how is this respected in the process of the doctrinal assessment?
- *Distinctions between governance structures of LCWR versus doctrinal matters:* At times questions about governance appeared to be mixed with questions about doctrine, thereby seeming to equate the relevance of distinct categories of inquiry.
- *Inferences that LCWR's assembly presenters, pastoral statements or resolutions serve as official teaching authority of the magisterium.* Doctrinal issues concern the authentic magisterium of the teaching office of the Church. According to the motu proprio *Apostulos suos*: "In order that the doctrinal declarations of the Conference of Bishops...may constitute authentic magisterium and be published in the name of the Conference itself, they must be unanimously approved by the Bishops who are members, or receive the *recognitio* of the Apostolic See if approved in plenary assembly by at least two thirds of the Bishops belonging to the Conference and having a deliberative vote."[26] Further, the same *motu proprio* states: "No body of the Episcopal Conference, outside the plenary assembly, has the power to carry out acts of authentic magisterium. The Episcopal Conference cannot grant such power to commissions or other bodies set up by it." Since these are norms governing doctrinal statements of an episcopal conference and the requirements of canon 753, it was unclear, for example, why actions of the LCWR with regard to the healthcare legislation were subject to public comment by the USCCB or included in the doctrinal assessment.
- *The tension between the prophetic role of consecrated life and adherence to and respect for the teaching office of the church* (*Vita consecrata* 84-85, *Christus Dominus* 33-35, cc. 748-755). The authors of *Starting Afresh from Christ* stated that ... they who, *in fact, are called to place their very existence at the service of the cause of the kingdom of God, leaving everything behind and closely imitating the form of life of Jesus Christ, assume a most important teaching role for the whole People of God.*[27]
- *An apparent notion that the right to engage in theological and spiritual discourse or to engage the rights of the Christian Faithful, such as hierarchical recourse (c. 221), might be considered lack of fidelity, dissent or disobedience.* The Church has a legal system that recognizes

---

[26] Pope John Paul II, motu proprio *Apostolus suos* 7, May 21, 1998: *AAS* 90 (1998) 640.

[27] CICLSAL. *Starting Afresh from Christ*, 1; quoting from JP II's Message to the Plenary Session of the CICLSAL on September 21, 2001. Quoted in *L'Osservatore Romano*, September 28, 2001.

limits to the exercise of authority and also the right of recourse.

These citations indicate the complexity of harmonizing the pastoral and legal dimensions of fidelity to church authority. Inevitably, there will be tensions between theory and practice, between the authentic promptings of the Holy Spirit and her action in the prophetic gifts of the people. Archbishop Joseph Tobin, recently stated: *If we obey, we do not go to the marginalized and excluded in order to create some sort of parallel Church. Rather, we are willing to live with an often painful, but potentially creative tension with the Pastors, who also must recognize that the consecrated life, if it is to be true to itself, will always be a little problematic for the Shepherds.*[28]

Given the response from the world over regarding these two Vatican inquiries, one is led once more to realize how the *sensus fidelium* reflects the work of the Holy Spirit and elucidates meaning. Letters of support from all over the world and media attention have created a process by which the public processing of pain and confusion is taking place. The need to "wrestle with" tradition, in both its relevance and it limits in our time witnesses the strength and commitment of many women religious who believe deeply in what God is doing right now in our midst. In her evaluation of the recent LCWR Assembly in Dallas, Texas, one member declared: *I appreciate the fact that any references to these happenings are in no way showing an angry or cowering stance, but rather a calm, deliberate, studied and prayerful spirit backed by many years of faithful service of God and the [church] by our foremothers and Sisters who have gone before us.*

Returning to the Idea of Creative Fidelity

Creative fidelity is not a concept new to Pope John Paul II in his post-synodal exhortation *Vita consecrata* of the late twentieth century. Another pope of the fourth century, Pope Athanasius of Alexandria, a Coptic Orthodox pope, in a recently discovered manuscript likewise provides us with a breath of freshness. Athanasius is a saint who told the community's most respected members that they crossed land and sea to gain one single convert only to make this convert twice as much a child of Hell as they were themselves (Matt 23:15). Athanasius was an avid fighter of the Arian heresies. He argues that creative fidelity must be centered on the faith shared by the Church from its origins. Any other argument about innovation is madness, he declares. A portion of his text reads as follows:

> What is this madness I hear about "*creative fidelity*"? For it is actually reported to me that whenever one of you talks about being faithful to tradition, his first act is to parrot mad words about how "Being Orthodox has never been a matter of mindless parrot-like repetition of the past, but always a matter

[28] Joseph Tobin CSsR, "What are we missing? What should we say?" Conference of Major Superiors of Men. Long Beach, CA: Sixth Annual Summer Conference (August 4-7, 2010) 21. Manuscript.

> of creative fidelity." *What madness is this?*
> Is creative fidelity the fundamental truth about how to be an Orthodox Christian? Then why do we only hear about this at a time when people love innovation, when the madness of too many innovators to mention poisons the air as effectively as the heretic, the Antichrist, Arius? How is it that the Fathers, who are also alleged to participate in this diabolical "creative fidelity", did not understand what they were doing, but instead insisted in one and the same faith shared by the Church since its beginning? . . .
> ... There is something the Apostle so much wants you to understand, and perhaps if you understood it better you would not go so far astray as to seek the living among the dead (Luke 24:5) in your quest for creative fidelity. How is it that you seek the living among the dead (Luke 24:5)? Christ is the head of the Church (Eph 5:23), of every man (I Cor 11:3), of every authority (Col 2:10), of all things (Eph 1:22), and God is the head of Christ (I Cor 11:3). Christ is the one head, and because of him there are many heads.
> If both incorruptible and unchangeable Heaven is the head of corruptible and changeable earth and yet earth manifests Heaven, what does this say about this strange thing you laud called "creative fidelity"? Does it not say something most disturbing? Does the one and the same faith, alive from the days of the apostles, belong to the corruptible or the incorruptible? Is it not unchangeable?
> What then of those adaptations you make—even if some are good and some are even necessary? Do they not belong to the realm of the changeable and the realm of the corruptible?
> ... Remember that you are not walking, as you say, the Orthodox System of Concepts, but the Orthodox Way. Remember that feeding the hungry (Matthew 25:35); is greater than raising the dead. Never let the lamp of your prayers go out (I Thess 5:17). Like the Father, be a father to the fatherless (Ps 68:5; Isa 1:17). All the brethren salute you (Rom 16:16; II Cor 13:13). Greet one another with a holy kiss (Rom 16:16; I Cor 16:20; II Cor 13:2; I Thess 5:26; I Pet 5:11).[29]

Philosopher Gabriel Marcel understood creative fidelity as the solution for the problem of time and change in human relationships.[30] In negotiating interpersonal relationships, he enumerates seven moral and intellectual qualities

---

[29] Athanasius, "On Creative Fidelity," trans. Christos Jonathan Seth Hayward. http://jonathanscorner.com/athanasius/printer.html

[30] Gabriel Marcel, *Creative Fidelity*, trans. Robert Rosthal (New York, NY: Noonday Press, 1964) 147 ff.

that are prerequisite for relational effectiveness: trust, respect, attentiveness, meditation on the other in silence, patience, suffering, and creative fidelity. Theologian and academician, Luke Timothy Johnson, writing of Marcel's theory, says this:

> Fidelity … is the attitude of trust [loyalty] extended through time … to be truly faithful, one must be creative. This is because the other, as free subject, always changes. Creative fidelity is the willingness to trust, be attentive to, and suffer with the other even as the other changes. It is a living process. [31]

Women religious have embraced a stewardship of the legacy of their founders and foremothers as they have reflected on their stories of faithfulness in the last fifty years. A statement released to all members and associates by the LCWR Board on February 20, 2009, urged leaders to reflect on the creative fidelity of their members at this time in history as well.

> Serious commitment to intense prayer and reflection, as well as to processes of corporate learning and analysis, have long served to make women religious keenly aware of their individual, communal and ecclesial strengths and challenges. As women religious well know, any opportunity that calls for greater reflection on our lives can be an occasion for the celebration of achievements and an examination of areas for growth... the [national] board encourage[s] continued study of the questions and challenges before U.S. religious as they seek to live religious life with depth and meaning in a pluralistic and rapidly changing culture.[32]

Creative fidelity is a commitment of the spiritual journey, the goal being to uphold our accountability in ways that really matter and in ways that honor the unpredictability of life. Marcel would emphasize that life's problems disappear once they are solved, but life's mysteries tap directly into our intuitions and linger forever. Relationships within our Church may bring forth a host of problems. They also serve as a never-ending source of mystery and spiritual awakening. The key is to keep a watchful eye on what really matters—not that which requires blind allegiances or public approvals, but the ones that flow from a wise and compassionate heart, the heart of the Christ who calls us daily into loving relationships. The LCWR National Board stated further on August 16, 2010:

> The real gift to us is around the notions of solidarity and inclusivity. We have experienced a new, deep connection with one another and a sense of real communion as we live

---

[31] Luke Timothy Johnson, *Living Jesus: Learning the Heart of the Gospel* (San Francisco, CA: 1999) 59-62.

[32] Statement by the National Board of the Leadership Conference of Women Religious on the Apostolic Visitation.
http://www.lcwr.org/lcwrpressreleases/publicstatements/Statement2-20-09.pdf

our way into new expressions of creative fidelity. We sense bonded energies and a radical openness to what is unfolding. We see ourselves as willing to wrestle with the chaos—perhaps in very public areas—cognizant of the possible cost of such discipleship.33

The Franciscan tradition offers insights for navigating creative fidelity. Helping us to understand the relationship between creativity and fidelity, John Duns Scotus appeals to justice and prudence as a way of mediating certain principles in relationships. The virtue of prudence, as moral excellence, is a type of moral artistic beauty. It functions in an artistic manner by identifying what elements ought to be present, judging actions according to a whole of beauty or completeness, and then adjusts human response in light of specific conditions present in a given reality. People learn behaviors but are invited into reflective insights; thus a correction between gut (felt) reasoning and abstract reasoning.[34] Fidelity is insufficient. It has to be coupled with creativity for the reign of God to be realized.

The notion of prudence appears four times in Clare of Assisi's writing. In her Second Letter to Agnes she speaks of travelling the path of prudent happiness,[35] inferring the necessity of learning how to compose and re-compose realities in which we are called to be faithful.

These concepts move persons to desire and to engage in dialogue. Contemplation or discernment of faithfulness to the Gospel and formation of conscience move us to options and a plan of action in responding to a situation such as Vatican inquiries. An evaluative measure of the process will surely provide evidence of how it has strengthened us in the formative elements of reverencing the other, fidelity to the gospel, and the common good.

God will not be silent as ecclesial tensions are negotiated. Rather than a static or servile obedience, creative fidelity during Vatican visitations and assessments can evidence itself by resisting caricatures and demonizing violence, by unyielding integrity and wrestling with our own transformation. Communities

---

[33] *Update*, a publication of the LCWR (Silver Spring, MD: October 2010) 6.

[34] Mary Beth Ingham, C.S.J., "The Harmony of Goodness: Mutuality as a Context for Scotus' Moral Framework," in *The Ethical Method of John Duns Scotus: A Contribution to Roman Catholic Moral Theology*, Spirit and Life 3 (1993) 60-66, 87-87, 96. Cf. Scotus, *Ordinatio* I. 17, n. 62, V, 163. 13-164.4, 9-11.

[35] Clare of Assisi, "Second Letter to Agnes of Prague," in *Clare of Assisi: Early Documents*, trans. Regis J. Armstrong, OFM Cap, 1994.

What you hold, may you always hold. What you do, may you do and never abandon.
But with swift pace, light step, unswerving feet, so that even your steps stir no dust,
go forward securely, joyfully, and swiftly, on the path of prudent happiness,
believing nothing, agreeing with nothing which would dissuade you from this resolution
or which would place a stumbling block for you on the way,
so that you may offer your vows to the Most High in the pursuit of that perfection
to which the Spirit of the Lord has called you.

of discernment and dialogue can help open us to conversion and take us beyond what is experienced as noxious authoritarianism. In this way the diversity of a religious institute's gifts to the mission will assume its proper role; it will be a public communal testimony to the responsibilities of all Christians to be the Word alive within complex social situations which cry for beatitude life of God's reign.36 Creating this beatitude life is inscribed on the heart of fidelity to be in communion with the church and to follow Christ who is always on the way with us—incarnationally—to the full creativity of Trinitarian life.

[36] Richard R. Galliardetz, *Contemporary Religious Life's Creativity to the Vision of Vatican II*, address to LCWR General Assembly (August 12, 2010) manuscript.

Appendix A

DECREE FROM THE CONGREGATION OF INSTITUTES OF CONSECRATED LIFE AND SOCIETIES OF APOSTOLIC LIFE

Prot. N. 16805/2008

DECREE

The Congregation for Institutes of Consecrated Life and Societies of Apostolic Life has the task of intervening in all that is reserved to the Holy See regarding consecrated life (cf. Pastor Bonus n. 108, §1). In order to look into the quality of the life of religious women in the United States, the Prefect of this Dicastery, with the faculties granted to him by His Holiness Pope Benedict XVI, in an audience on November 17, 2008, has decided to nominate, and with the present decree nominates,

Reverend Mother Mary Clare MILLEA
Superior General of the Apostles of the Sacred Heart of Jesus

Apostolic Visitator *ad inquirendum et referendum*

Of the General Houses, Provincial Houses and Centers of Initial Formation of the principal Religious Institutes of Women in the United States of America.

Upon completion of this Apostolic Visitation, the Apostolic Visitator will also seek information from those Diocesan Bishops in whose Dioceses the abovementioned General Houses, Provincial Houses and Centers of Initial Formation are located.

All things to the contrary notwithstanding.

Vatican City, 22 December 2008

Card. Franc Rodé, Prefect

Gianfranco A. Gardin, OFM Conv., Archbishop Secretary

Appendix B

Statement of the Prefect of the Congregation of Institutes of Consecrated Life and Societies of Apostolic Life, Card. Franc Rodé, C.M., on the Apostolic Visitation of Institutes of Women Religious in the USA

Since the Apostolic Visitation of Institutes of Women Religious was first announced in January 2009, there has been great interest in the study that the Congregation for Institutes of Consecrated Life and Societies of Apostolic Life (CICLSAL) has undertaken to look into the fundamental aspects of women religious in the United States. This Apostolic Visitation hopes to encourage vocations and assure a better future for women religious. Having read many news accounts and received various inquiries, I offer the following in response.

For many years this dicastery had been listening to concerns expressed by American Catholics, religious, laity, clergy and hierarchy about the welfare of religious women and consecrated life in general, and had been considering an Apostolic Visitation as a means to assess and constructively address these concerns. The multitude and complexity of these issues were made clear by speakers and participants at the Symposium on Religious Life at Stonehill College in September 2008. This helped me understand that such an evaluation of the challenges facing individual religious and their congregations could benefit the Church at-large as well as the sisters and institutes involved. My hope is that the Apostolic Visitation will not only provide the Holy See with a thorough analysis of the condition of religious life in the United States, but also be a realistic and graced opportunity for personal and community introspection, as major superiors and sisters cooperate with this study.

I am pleased with the voluntary response reported in Phase One of the Apostolic Visitation, during which more than three-fourths of the superiors general communicated their hopes and concerns directly to Mother Mary Clare Millea, A.S.C.J., the Apostolic Visitator. Shortly thereafter, the Instrumentum Laboris was sent to all major superiors requesting that it be given to each sister for her prayerful consideration, study and open discussion with other sisters.

Now, during Phase Two, the major superiors in the United States are responding to a questionnaire that will present a comprehensive profile of each institute's present reality and future outlook. The Center for Applied Research in the Apostolate (CARA) at Georgetown University is cooperating in the collection of information and will prepare a composite analytical report of the standard, objective data contained in Part A of the questionnaire. This report will be made public and should provide important information regarding likely future trends of religious life in the United States.

It is the practice of the Holy See that an Apostolic Visitation be conducted ad inquirendum et referendum (i.e., studied and referred). Therefore, this dicastery will formulate no conclusions or plan of action, if any, until the final report of the Visitator has been evaluated. To date, I am encouraged by the efforts to identify the signs of hope, as well as concerns, within religious congregations in the United States, which are also likely to have implications elsewhere in the world. I ask all people of good will to unite in prayer for the fruitful outcome of this effort to promote the Catholic identity and vibrancy of life of women religious.

City of Vatican, 3rd of November 2009
Original text: English

SEMINAR

INTERCHURCH MARRIAGES AND PASTORAL CARE IN SICKNESS: A CANONICAL CONSIDERATION

Doctor Myriam Wijlens

This study concerns interchurch marriages and pastoral care in sickness.[1] Two reasons prompted this topic. First, forty years ago on January 7, 1970 Pope Paul VI published the apostolic letter *Matrimonia mixta* which was to take effect on October 1, 1970.[2] The apostolic letter was the result of many new insights that Vatican II had brought to light. New insights with regard to ecclesiology, freedom of religion, ecumenism, and marriage itself asked for a rethinking of what in the world of canon law is known as "mixed marriages" and in much theological literature now as "interchurch marriages." Interchurch marriages are marriages in which both partners continue to be actively involved in their own church or ecclesial community, while at the same time participating in the faith journey of their partner.[3]

Looking back over the past fifty years, it may be noticed that within the Catholic Church the discussion topics related to mixed marriages changed as time went on: initially the focus was very much on the promises that the partners had to make with regard to the baptism and Catholic education of their children.[4]

---

[1] Originally the study was announced as mixed marriages and pastoral care in sickness and death. The term "interchurch marriage" however, reflects better the content of this study. Furthermore reflection on pastoral care in cases of death was not taken up, as this would have to be too much for one study.

[2] Pope Paul VI, apostolic letter *Matrimonia mixta*, *AAS* 62 (1970) 257-263, English translation in Austin Flannery (ed.), *Vatican Council II: the Conciliar and Post Conciliar Documents*, New Revised edition, vol. 1 (Northporth, NY: Costello, 1984) 508-514.

[3] In several countries these couples gather in associations of interchurch marriages. In particular in France and England this association has been very strong. They organize meetings to discuss and reflect about their situation and invite theologians and bishops to reflect with them. In France, for example, René Beaupère has been strongly involved with them. They publish newsletters. Pope John Paul II used the term "interchurch marriage" several times in *Familiaris Consortio* e.g. Nr. 21, 38, 48-54. For further literature see also Ecumenical Office Anglican Church of Canada, Ecumenical Commission, CCCB (eds.), *Pastoral Guidelines for Interchurch Marriages between Anglicans and Roman Catholics in Canada* (Ottawa: CCCB, 1987), George Kilcourse: *Double Belonging: Interchurch Families and Christian Unity* (Mahwah, NJ: Paulist Press, 1992) and John C. Bush, Patrick R. Cooney, *Interchurch Families: Resources for Ecumenical Hope. Catholic Reformed Dialogue in the United States* (Louisville, KY: Westminster John Knox, 2002).

[4] See for example the articles in René Beaupère e.a. (eds.), *Die Mischehe in ökumenischer Sicht: Beiträge zu einem Gespräch mit dem Weltkirchenrat* (Freiburg

Questions concerning the liturgy were discussed: What kind of liturgical celebration could be proposed for the wedding? What could be the role of the ministers of the respective church or denomination in the liturgy?[5] From a canonical perspective, the questions focused on the observance of the form: could a dispensation be requested and granted and could the celebration in the Orthodox Church also be recognized as fulfilling the form for the Catholic Church?[6] Another issue was the question of reception of the Eucharist by the baptized non-Catholic partner initially during the wedding itself and later also during the married life of the couple.[7] In these latter discussions the doctrine that a sacramental marriage could be seen as a kind of domestic church, as *Lumen gentium* 11 had said, played increasingly a role.[8] Theologians asked how the domestic church and the Eucharist, how marriage as a sign of the bond between Christ and the church on the one hand, and the Eucharist as a symbol of this unity on the other hand could be understood together and what this implied for both partners to be entitled to receive the Eucharist.[9] This was and is particularly urgent for those who live in a mixed marriage that could be qualified as a so called "interchurch marriage", because within their marriage these couples experience the communion among themselves *as well as* the brokenness of the unity of the Church of Christ simultaneously.

The suggestion in the 1993 Ecumenical Directory that bishops and episcopal

---

i.Br.: Herder, 1968).

5 The Holy See provided for celebrations in its Liturgical Books.

6 Already 1966 it was decided that the form for marriage a Catholic, whether oriental or Latins, with non-Catholic oriental faithful is only be for the liceity; for the validity the presence of a sacred minister suffices, as long as the other requirements of law are observed. Cf. Sacred Congregation for the Eastern Churches, *Crescens Matrimoniorum, AAS* 59 (1967) 165-166; English translation in Austin Flannery (ed.), *Vatican Council II: The Conciliar and Post Conciliar Documents*, vol. 1 (Northport, NY, 1984) 481-482. This was later taken up as c. 1127 §1 *CIC*; c. 835 *CCEO*.

7 During the synod on the family the then president of the Pontifical Council for Christian Unity Cardinal Johannes Willebrands emphasized that with regard to sharing the Eucharist the unity and indissolubility of a marriage might be more important than some other criteria that are mentioned for admission to the Eucharist by baptized non-Catholic. Cf. Johannes Willebrands, "Mixed Marriages and their Family Life: Cardinal Willebrands's Address to the Synod of Bishops, October 1980," *One in Christ* 23 (1987) 78-81.

8 *LG* 11 reads: "This is, as it were (veluti), the domestic church in which the parents must be for their children, by word and by example, the first preachers of the faith, encouraging each in her or his vocation and paying special attention to a sacred vocation." For an overview of the literature on the subject up till 2001 see Florence Caffrey Bourg, "Domestic Church: A Survey of the Literature," *Intams Review* 7 (2001) 182-191.

9 One of the most insightful articles is written by the German systematic theologian Peter Neuner, "Ein katholischer Vorschlag zur Eucharistiegemeinschaft," *Stimmen der Zeit* 211 (1993) 443-450 and Georg Hintzen, Peter Neuner, "Eucharistiegemeinschaft für konfessionsverschiedene Ehen?" *Stimmen der Zeit* 211 (1993) 831-840. In the spring of 2010 an international conference entitled "The Household of God and Local Households: Revisiting the Domestic Church" was held at the University of Leuven.

conferences provide particular law or guidelines for the application of sharing the sacraments[10] in combination with the increased awareness that people in interchurch marriages are asking for assistance on what to do with regard to sacramental sharing, prompted a number of episcopal conferences from around the world to address in particular the issue of sharing the Eucharist. Possibly the most impressive reaction came with the document "One Bread, One Body" issued by the three Episcopal conferences of England and Wales, Ireland and Scotland in 1998.[11]

Looking at the subjects discussed in relation to interchurch marriages one might get the impression that these couples have families with young children to look after and that there is no life beyond being a raising parent. However, forty years after the publication of *Matrimonia mixta* which implied a decrease in joining the denomination of the partner[12] and an increase in interchurch marriages, the number of couples that are now being confronted with serious sickness and death in their partnership is increasing. This then is the second reason for addressing this topic here: ministers will be confronted with this issue increasingly. The specific question of this study concerns, therefore, the topic of canonical aspects of ministry to couples (and their families) who live in an interchurch marriage and are confronted with sickness. In the reflections presented here, the focus is exclusively on the Latin rite of the Roman Catholic Church.

The urgency of the pastoral and therefore canonical aspects of this issue became clear to me when about three years ago I received a phone call from a chancery describing the following situation:

A forty-seven year old women belonging to a protestant church had died. More than twenty years earlier she had married a Catholic man and their wedding had taken place in the Catholic Church. Hence, there had not been a dispensation from the form. A minister of the protestant church had been present and had given the homily. The couple had three children who were all baptized in the Catholic Church and had made their first Communion and received confirmation. They had been attending Catholic schools. The family often went to Sunday Eucharist together. The couple lived in a rather Catholic area and thus the woman who had had cancer had been in a Catholic hospital. The hospital

[10] Pontificium Consilium ad Christianorum Unitatem Fovendam, *Directory for the Application of Principles and Norms on Ecumenism* (London: Catholic Truth Society, 1993) nr. 130.

[11] Catholic Bishops' Conferences of England and Wales, Ireland and Scotland, *One Bread, One Body: A Teaching Document on the Eucharist in the life of the Church, and the Establishment of General Norms on Sacramental Sharing* (London: Catholic Truth Society, Dublin: Veritas, 1998).

[12] Common parlance still uses the term "convert to catholicism", which is incorrect with regard to persons who are already baptized and then enter into full communion with the Catholic Church. Indeed once a person is baptized, that person is already in communion with the Catholic Church, albeit not in full communion. The Code of Canon Law rightly speaks about full communion.

chaplain, a Catholic lay minister, had accompanied her in her sickness. The woman had asked the hospital chaplain whether it would be possible that a Catholic minister would preside over her funeral. The chaplain responded in the affirmative. Upon the death of his wife, the husband called his parish priest and asked to arrange the funeral. The response of the parish priest was that this was not his "job"! She did not occur on any of his lists as a member and thus he would not do this. The husband was of course upset and mentioned the remark made by the chaplain. The priest remained with his position. The husband contacted the bishops' office which asked me for advice. I spoke with the priest who affirmed that he knew the woman and that she had regularly attended the eucharistic celebrations in his church. When I asked him how he envisioned pastoral care for the husband and children who after all "were on his list" he said that he had never given this a thought. The funeral was held in the Catholic parish with another priest.

While reflecting on this case it occurred to me that Catholic hospitals of course provide physical and yes also pastoral care to non-Catholics be they baptized or not; I thought about the seven works of mercy which includes visiting the sick and burying the dead. There is no mention that these works should be exercised vis-à-vis Catholics only. It also occurred to me that at an ecclesiastical funeral of a person who lived in an interchurch marriage, the people present would from the perspective of confessional belonging most likely display the same composition that had been present at the wedding. And finally I also asked myself the question what it means to celebrate funeral rites. Is it only for the one who died or is it also to minster to the sorrowing and console them with the comforting word of God and maybe—with the sacrament of the Eucharist? If the focus is also on the latter group how do you do that when the family members of the deceased person belong to different churches or ecclesial communities? What, so I asked myself, can the Church offer in sickness and death to people living in an interchurch marriage? What does the law say about this and above all how can the existing norms be applied with special consideration for the fact that the context is an interchurch marriage?[13]

While selecting this topic for this study I thought it would not be too difficult and expected that a focus on canon 844 which regulates the sharing of some sacraments would be the main focus of my presentation. However, as soon as the work had started it turned out to be more challenging than expected, because there are many theological and non-theological issues that changed over the years and that need to be taken into consideration. Because of the complexity of the issue I have decided to limit this study to the anointing of the sick in interchurch marriages and leave further reflections on funerals which had originally been planned as well to a future study. Furthermore, due to the complexity I have also decided to limit this presentation to listing topics that need to be taken into consideration when addressing this issue. The listing of

[13] Canonical articles often reflect about the norms only, not about the application of the norms in specific cases. The latter is a skill in itself, because it requires that the situation in which the norms are applied need to be described carefully.

different aspects is like making a list of ingredients for a dish to be cooked: there is no priority among the different ingredients because only together will they lead to a fine dish even though some might (also in a specific situation) be more important than others. This study is thus indeed a work in progress and an invitation to enter into a dialogue with each other.

The Ministry to the Sick as Such Has Changed

Over the years the ministry to the sick has tremendously changed in character. Over the past fifty years it changed from a predominantly sacramental ministry in which the focus was on the administration of sacraments—yes one could say on the *valid* administration of the sacraments—to a much more diaconal ministry. What is meant by this? Irrespective of the change from the sacrament of extreme unction to the sacrament of anointing of the sick—a topic to be addressed below—the focus in ministry to the sick was very much on administrating the sacrament not only of anointing of the sick, but also penance and Holy Communion. This focus did not only occur in hospitals it also took place in the ministry exercised in family homes. In the meantime the understanding of this ministry has received a new accent in that the focus is now predominantly on accompanying, listening and speaking to the sick person about the anxieties, fears and questions that arise. Within such a ministry there might be occasion to pray, but celebrating other rituals and in particular sacraments have diminished. The latter, so liturgists say,[14] has also to do with the fact that many sick persons are increasingly unaware of or unfamiliar with the existing rituals—in particular the sacraments—that the Church may and can offer in case of sickness and death. This implies that people simply do not ask for them.[15]

This change in the focus of the ministry implies a change in the addressees: while focusing on celebrating sacraments the ministry was primarily, yes almost exclusively geared towards Roman Catholics, but with a wider understanding of a ministry that is in particular conversational, all persons with (serious) sickness irrespective of their religious belonging come into the picture. Furthermore, this change implied that ministry to the sick was professionalized and led to courses and certificates. It also implied that lay ecclesial ministers[16] entered into this ministry which despite the change in character of the ministry

---

[14] See here the very thoughtful article by the German liturgist Stefan Böntert, "Heilssorge in Krankheit als Paradigma liturgisches Handelns: Überlegungen zur Gottesdienstkultur im Schnittfeld von Theologie, Medizin und Ritual," *Heiliger Dienst* 62 (2008) 224-244. Böntert refers to other liturgists.

[15] One may only recall that also today there is hardly any catechesis with regard to the ministry of the Church in sickness and death, something that is quite remarkable considering that each and every person will be confronted with this.

[16] The term "lay ecclesial ministers" is to be understood as in the statement by the United States Conference of Catholic Bishops, *Co-Workers in the Vineyard if the Lord: A Resource for Guiding the Development of Lay Ecclesial Ministry* (Washington; DC: USCCB, 2006). They are members of the laity who are authorized by competent authority to exercise a function or a task to serve publicly in the local church (cf. p. 5).

itself led nevertheless to questions with regard to the minister of anointing of the sick.[17] Finally, due to a different organization of the ministry in many hospitals the ministry itself has become more ecumenical.[18]

The change in accent to a more diaconal ministry does raise some questions such as a deeply theological one: what is the identity and function of liturgy in ministry to the sick if this ministry is not to end as a kind of "additional decoration" that could also be done with without. The pastoral conversation has been so much professionalized that the liturgical celebrations do not evoke as much interest. In an ecumenical context the question must be raised: if ministry not only towards Catholics but even more so towards baptized non-Catholics is limited to pastoral conversation and no liturgical celebrations are offered and celebrated, what understanding of liturgy is then displayed? If liturgy is understood as source and summit of ecclesial actions and is a presence and witness of the paschal mystery, or to say it differently as a dimension of divine salvation and consolation, then liturgy must have a place in ministry to the sick. What does that then mean for ministry to those who are baptized, but do not belong fully to the Catholic Church?

With this in mind the question about the right to receive the sacraments as expressed in canon 213 obtains an additional meaning because it relates the question concerning the right to receive the sacraments not only to the baptism of the individual, but also addresses the self understanding of the Catholic Church with regard to the liturgical celebrations in ministry to the sick.[19] The right of the baptized to receive the sacraments—a right that is of divine law and thus applies to all baptized[20]—brings with it a duty of the Church to administer the sacraments. This does not mean that the latter is unconditional, but the criteria that are set up must have a theological foundation. Of course the ecclesiological issue of belonging to the Church, the notion of *communio perfecta* and *non perfecta* and the implications for a full participation in the liturgy as celebrations of the Church are the main points here to be considered.

---

[17] This ultimately let to questions about lay ministers to be able to celebrate sacraments, a topic that was addressed at previous conventions of he Canon Law Society of America, cf. Susan K. Wood, "Anointing of the Sick: Theological Issues," *CLSA Proceedings* 63 (2001) 233-254.

[18] In many hospitals in Germany and The Netherlands the chaplain works much closer with the whole team that is responsible for all patients irrespective of their religious belonging in a specific unit. One minister is responsible for some units, the other for other ones. If a patient wishes to see a minister of his or her own denomination, this request is of course respected.

[19] Canon 213 reads: "The Christian faithful have the right to receive assistance from the sacred pastors out of the spiritual goods of the Church, especially the word of God and the sacraments."

[20] See the foundational study by Eugenio Corecco, who was on the commission that worked with Pope John Paul II on the final draft of the 1983 code, "Der Katalog der Pflichten und Rechte der Gläubigen im CIC," André Gabriels, Heinrich J.F. Reinhardt (eds.), *Ministerium iustitiae: Festschrift für Heribert Heinemann zur Vollendung des 60. Lebensjahres* (Essen: Ludgerus, 1985) 179-202, 188.

Interestingly, the connection between belonging to the Church and the Church as dispenser of grace through liturgical celebrations has always played a role in the celebration and administration of anointing of the sick even in its previous form when it was known as extreme unction. It is necessary to attend to this point because it will shed light ultimately also on the background of canon 844 which deals with sacramental sharing. Before entering the ecclesiological issue it is necessary to first understand how the sacrament used to be understood itself.

The Development of Extreme Unction

The sacrament of anointing of the sick "replaced" the sacrament of extreme unction at Vatican II. The change was not just a matter of new labeling, but of a renewed understanding of the sacrament itself. The sacrament of extreme unction has a long development. It finds its origin in the scriptural text of James 5:14-16:

> "Are anyone among you suffering? They should pray. Are they cheerful? They should sing songs of praise. Are any among you sick? They should call for the elders of the church and have them pray over them, anointing them with oil in the name of the Lord. The prayer of faith will save the sick, and the Lord will raise them up, and anyone who has committed sins will be forgiven. Therefore confess your sins to one another, and pray to one another, so that you may be healed."

Whereas early Christianity focused on the anointing with oil accompanied by a prayer and thus with a primary focus on the healing of sickness and only subsidiary—and that again in connection with sickness—on the forgiveness of sins. This changed over the centuries in particular in the Latin Church, because the phrase "and anyone who has committed sins will be forgiven" was increasingly accentuated, relating the sacrament closely to penance. Important in this development was as well the text is Mark 6:13: "They cast out many demons, and anointed with oil many who were sick and cured them." Although this text does not speak about forgiveness of sin, it associates illness and demonic possession, illness of the body and illness of the soul.

The anointing became connected to penance and Viaticum. Since doing penance was rather difficult, it was often delayed till the end of life. [21] Due to

---

[21] As of the eighth century the liturgical documents for the celebration of the anointing of the sick connect the anointing with confession by the dying person and with the related penance in case someone survives. It was not permitted for the anointed to dance for the rest of his life, eat meat, have sexual relations (for which reason in some places the spouse was asked permission for the anointing). It was indeed easier not to recover upon the anointing. High scholastics did not change this, but reflects upon it and tries to find a theological reasoning for this. For a historical overview see e.g. Theodor Schneider, *Zeichen der Nähe Gottes: Grundriss der Sakramententheologie* (Mainz: Grünewald, 1992) 220-229; see also Herbert Vorgrimmler, *Sakramententheologie* (Düsseldorf: Patmos, 1992) 252-260.

the close connection with penance anointing was thus transferred—yes one may say postponed—till the end of life as well. Furthermore, the liturgical texts for anointing with oil were put together with the ones for penance and last rites into *one* liturgical book. Moreover, there was an increased emphasis on the effect of the sacrament being the forgiveness of sins and a decreasing awareness of a bodily healing. Scholastic theology reflected on a sacrament which by the end of the twelfth century was referred to as "extreme unction" (last anointing) to be administered to dying people. The scholastic reflections implied that the anointing would wash away the final sins of the dying person and prepare this person for eternal life. At the end of the Middle Ages the sequence of "penance—anointing—Viaticum" had changed to "penance—Viaticum—anointing."[22] The Council of Trent saw anointing as "the culmination not only of penance but of the whole Christian life which itself ought to be a continual penance."[23] In the ritual anointing of the sick became part of the liturgy of the dying and was referred to as "extreme unction." As a consequence the dying became the recipients of the sacrament and the effect of the sacrament was the forgiveness of sin and the preparation for the final judgment. The idea of healing of illness lost its importance. Extreme unction and penance—or more precisely: the final forgiveness of sin—was considered to be of great importance; yes it was closely connected to what was considered to be necessary for salvation. With such an understanding it was only a matter of time, before questions would arise whether baptized non-Catholics can receive these sacraments or—and this was the question the Catholic Church struggled with—what was the obligation of the Church to administer the sacrament to the baptized if they were in danger of death even if they were not Catholic? Ultimately the issue was an ecclesiological one, as already pointed out.

Ecclesiological Aspects in the Administration of the Sacrament

Up until the eve of Vatican II Catholic doctrine taught that there is an exclusive identification of the Church of Christ with the Catholic Church: Ecclesia Christi *est* ecclesia catholica. Due to their baptism by which they were incorporated in Christ all baptized fell under the jurisdiction of the Catholic Church and had to follow all laws including the ecclesiastical ones.[24] Canon 87

---

[22] While addressing the CLSA in 2001 Susan Wood writes that "the connection between the sacrament of the sick and penance, as well as the association of the sick with a 'last anointing' of the dying was also strengthened through the practice of public penance in the patristic period. … The rigors of public penance led to the practice of postponing penance until death. Anointing was likewise postponed and was, in fact, named 'extreme unction', that is last anointing. The history of how the practice of anointing of the sick became associated with the deathbed has strong associations with this history of penance." Wood, "Anointing of the Sick," 233-234.

[23] *DS* 1694.

[24] The Council of Trent discusses the observance of the law in its seventh session, in connection with baptism. Canon 7 (=*DS* 1620): "Si quis dixerit, baptizatos per baptismum ipsum solius tantum fidei debitores fieri, non autem universae legis Christi servandae: anathema sit" and canon 8 (=*DS* 1621): "Si quis dixerit, baptizatos liberos

CIC/1917 stood in line with this as it stated that baptism would constitute a person in the Church of Christ and from this would flow the right to receive the sacraments (c. 682/*CIC* 1917). Correspondingly, the canonical norms that existed applied to all baptized unless an exception would have been made such as the one related to the observance of the form for marriage.[25] Baptized non-Catholics were considered to be heretics or schismatics who, therefore, could neither be given nor receive sacraments, as the 1917 code affirmed in canon 731 §2 when it said that it is forbidden (*vetitum est*) to administer the sacraments of the Church to heretics or schismatics, even when they err in good faith and ask for it, unless after having renouncing their errors, they have been reconciled with the Church.[26]

Yet, the *Fontes* of the 1917 code and major pre-Vatican II canonical and moral theological handbooks reveal that there were approved exceptions to the rule caused by the following problem that had been submitted to the Holy See: a heretic or a schismatic person was dying and asked a Catholic priest for the sacraments of penance and extreme unction. What could be done? The *Fontes* indicate that the Holy Office received four such replies in the nineteenth and early twentieth centuries and a reflection started: what should be done considering that these sacraments are means of salvation?[27] Would the administering of the sacrament always stipulate a renunciation of errors? The responses by the Holy Office stated that in danger of death, it would be permitted to administer these sacraments because they as well as baptism are considered to be necessary for eternal salvation. The baptized non-Catholic had to have given some sign on which the minister could base a reasonable presumption that they adhere to the Holy Catholic Church and profess the true faith. Hence, some indication of a visible unity must have been manifested. If the recipients were already unconscious the sacraments were to be administered conditionally. The minister, furthermore, had the task to see that no scandal occurred.

---

esse ab omnibus sanctae Ecclesiae praeceptis, quae vel scripta vel tradita sunt, ita ut ea observare non teneantur, nisi se sua sponte illis summittere voluerint: anathema sit" and canon 14 (=*DS* 1627): "Si quis dixerit, huiusmodi parvulos baptizatos, cum adoleverint, interrogandos esse, an ratum habere velint, quod patrini eorum nomine, dum baptizarentur, pollitici sunt, et ubi se nolle responderint, suo esse arbitrio relinquendos nec alia interim poena ad christianam vitam cogendos, nisi ut ab eucharistiae aliorumque sacramentorum perceptione arceantur, donec respiscant: anathema sit."

[25] An example of an exception were the decree from the Council of Trent *Tametsi* (*DS* 1813-1816) imposing the form for marriage on all baptized and the 1907 decree *Ne temere* modifying this requirement for marriages were one party was a Catholic.

[26] C. 731 §2 *CIC*/1917: "Vetitum est sacramenta Ecclesiae ministrare haereticis aut schismaticis, etiam bona fide errantibus eaque petentibus, nisi prius, erroribus reiectis, Ecclesiae reconciliati fuerint."

[27] For detailed report and analysis see Myriam Wijlens, *Sharing the Eucharist: A Theological Evaluation of the Post Conciliar Legislation* (Lanham, MD: University Press, 2000) 54-64.

Interesting is certainly the discussion in the literature about the kind of intention the dying person had to have. The common response was that there is no need to have an intention with regard to a particular sacrament, but the intention to be saved in general was to be considered sufficient. The theologians, furthermore, agreed that persons cannot have intentions with regard to things they do not know. Hence, it was sufficient that they intended to do what Christ would have wanted them to do had they known what God would have wanted from them. If a protestant was unconscious and he had lived a good life it could be presumed that he had such an intention.

Reading the literature of the time, one gets the feeling that the authors bend over backwards to allow for the administration of the sacraments of extreme unction and penance when heretics and schismatics were dying. The authors did so for a very good reason: they argued that if the Catholic Church believes that it has all the means of salvation—yes that it even *is* the means of salvation (*extra ecclesiam nulla salus*)[28] and that it is the only one that has this—and if these people need those means of salvation and are thus dependent on the one and true Church, how can the Church deny those means to people who through no fault of their own, do not know better? The Church could not bear the responsibility to refuse them the sacrament.

The reflections so far show the following: over the course of history the Church increasingly saw the sacrament of extreme unction in relation to penance and since penance was rather difficult, the sacrament became part of the last rites through which the final sins would be washed away and the dying person would prepare him or herself for the encounter with the Lord. The need for forgiveness was seen as necessary for all baptized. Only the Catholic Church being the true Church of Christ had been entrusted with all the means necessary for salvation, but this also implied a responsibility not to withhold them from those who needed them. Hence, when there was imminent danger of death even baptized non-Catholics could be given the sacrament provided they would be in good faith and would have wanted to do what the Lord asked from them had they known. The focus is totally on the need for salvation. The current norms on sharing the sacraments (c. 844) originate from this perspective.[29]

---

[28] At the time these discussions were held, the doctrine *extra ecclesiam nulla salus* was understood to mean that indeed outside the Catholic Church there is no salvation, but this understanding was later modified. For an excellent overview of the history of the change in doctrinal understanding see Francis A. Sullivan, *Salvation outside the Church? Tracing the History of the Catholic Response* (Mahwah: NJ: Paulist Press, 1992).

[29] The exceptions to the then existing canon 731 §2 *CIC*/1917 which determined a general prohibition of the administration of sacraments by non-Catholics, formed the basis for the text that was going to be the section on *communicatio in sacris* in the Decree on the Oriental Churches, Nn. 26-29. Remarkable about this latter text is that it did not draw extensive consequences from the new ecclesiological and ecumenical insights as expressed in the dogmatic constitution *Lumen gentium* and in the decree *Unitatis redintegratio* or from the new insights with regard to the sacrament of anointing of the sick as expressed in the constitution on the liturgy *Sacrosantum*

With Vatican II, however, a lot of the points addressed so far changed, above all the understanding of the sacrament itself and the ecclesiology.

Rediscovering the Sacrament of Anointing of the Sick

Based on research in the field of liturgy Vatican II restored the praxis on oiling. A preference for the term "anointing of the sick" was expressed and it was said it "is not a sacrament for those only who are at the point of death. If a person would begin to be in danger of death from sickness or old age, the fitting time for receiving the sacrament had certainly arrived" (*SC* 73).

It is noteworthy that the description in the Code of Canon Law about the sacrament does not even mention the forgiveness of sin when it reads: "The anointing of the sick, by which the Church commends the faithful who are dangerously ill to the suffering and glorified Lord in order that he relieve and save them, is conferred by anointing them with oil and pronouncing the words prescribed in the liturgical books" (c. 998).[30] Vatican II also returned to the original sequence of the sacrament as being penance—anointing—Viaticum. This clarified that as in the Orthodox Church anointing was not the final sacrament, but Viaticum.

Moreover, in recent times theologians have pointed out that the sacrament should not really be connected so much with penance, but with in particular with baptism and the Eucharist.[31] Both are also sacraments of reconciliation and of communion with the Church. "They are sacraments of the body, both the body of Christ and the body of the church."[32] The connection between the anointing

---

concilium. A comparison of the draft text and the final text of *OE* 26-29 reveals that the words "*fraters seiuncti*" replaces "heretics and schismatics" and "anointing of the sick" replaces "extreme unction"; there is, however, not a change of the text based on the new insights as such. The norms were governed by the need for salvation in case of danger of death. This was very clear when during the revision of the text of *OE* 26-29 the question was raised to provide for some norms with regard to *all* sacraments. This was rejected with the following argument: "De baptismo lege generali iam provisum; de matrimoniis tractat nostrum schema (n. 18); Ordo excluditur ab ipsis proponentibus; quod spectat confirmationem, non agitur de necessitate salutis." *AS* III/VIII, 604. It must be noted that the norms thus only attend to what is necessary for salvation, not to the ecumenical and ecclesiological new insights of the council. See further Myriam Wijlens, *Sharing the Eucharist*, 209-229.

[30] Of course this canon is not a definition of the sacrament, because the Code Commission did not want to provide definitions; it presents in a nutshell the theological understanding of the Legislator with regard to this sacrament. Of course theologically much more could be said. Indeed, the literary form of the canon must be respected when interpreting it.

[31] E.g. Wood, "Anointing of the Sick," 233-254.

[32] Wood, "Anointing of the Sick," 235. Wood refers in her article to other theologians who see the sacrament in light of baptism and Eucharist. See also the excellent study by Susan Wood, *One Baptism: Ecumenical Dimensions of the Doctrine of Baptism* (Grand Rapids, MI: Baker Academic, 2009) and her presentation at the 2009 CLSA Convention "Baptism: A Common Call to Service," *CLSA Proceedings* 71(2009) 1-11.

and the paschal mystery celebrated in baptism and the Eucharist, thus is more evident, because "the minister should encourage the sick person to offer his sufferings in union with Christ and to join in prayer for the Church and world."[33] If understood in this way, the anointing can give expression to a holistic view of the human person. The healing is both from physical illness and spiritual sin. "The effects of anointing touch the religious situation of the sick person: the threat to his salvation posed by religious powerlessness and weakness of soul, as well as the temptation and burden to his faith and trust. The sick person shall be 'raised up' from his weakness and saved from the threat that sickness constitutes to his salvation."[34]

Sickness not only affects the individual, but the whole ecclesial body, as scripture tells us: "If one member suffers in the Body of Christ, which is the Church, all members suffer with that member" (1 Corinthians 12:26). Indeed, all "who are united in the bond of a common baptism and a common faith are joined together in the body of Christ since what happens to one member affects all. The sacrament of anointing effectively expresses the share that each one has in the sufferings of others."[35] As the sickness affects the community, so does the celebration of the sacraments, because with Vatican II the understanding that liturgical celebrations are ecclesial celebrations was sharpened in that the whole community participates. Pope Paul VI relates this to the sacrament of anointing when he writes: "By the sacred anointing of the sick and the prayer of the presbyters, the whole church commends the sick to the suffering and glorified Lord so that he may raise them up and save them (see James 5: 14-16). The Church exhorts them, moreover, to contribute to the welfare of the whole people of God by associating themselves willingly with the passion and death of Christ (see Romans 8:17; Colossians 1:24; 2 Timothy 2: 11-12; 1 Peter 4:13)" (*LG* 15).[36]

To give expression to these insights, the 1972 Rite provides for common celebrations in parishes or in particular in homes for elderly persons. In the latter case the sacrament is celebrated as a strengthening and encouragement for elderly people. At times the sacrament is celebrated during a eucharistic celebration in a parish where the whole community is present. In such a situation the sick more easily experience the support of the whole community. A good example of such celebrations are the ones held in Lourdes.

It is here that the married couple, in particular those who live in a sacramental marriage and the immediate family come on the scene. Here the understanding of the family as being a kind of domestic church (*LG* 11) comes into play, as the sickness most deeply affects the intimate members of the family who suffer with the person and who might be longing for hope themselves. The

---

[33] The Rites of the Catholic Church, Study Edition, Pastoral Care of the Sick, 56.

[34] Charles Gusmer, "Liturgical Traditions of Christian Illness: Rites of the Sick," *Worship* 46 (1972) 531 (quoted by Wood, "Anointing of the Sick," 238).

[35] Pastoral Care of the Sick, 1998.

[36] Pope Paul VI emphasized this point in his apostolic constitution *Sacram Unctionem informorum* of November 30, 1972; English translation in *The Rites*, 603-606.

need to be raised and lifted is most acutely experienced in this small, but domestic church.

The sacrament of anointing is now to be seen in an ecumenical setting once more, but as can be imagined quite different from what it used to be.

To understand the complexity it is necessary to recall the ecclesiological understanding of the position of baptized non-Catholics as set forth in Vatican II.

The Ecclesiology of Vatican II with Regard to Belonging to the Church

Vatican II changed the doctrinal expression "Ecclesia Christi *est* ecclesia catholica" into "Ecclesia Christi *subsisti in* ecclesia catholica" to give expression to its awareness that Christians baptized outside the Catholic Church receive faith and grace in and through the community they belong to and that these communities can and must indeed be considered as churches or ecclesial communities. The terms *communio plena et non plena* or *perfecta et imperfecta, subsistit in, ecclesiae et communitates ecclesiales, fraters seiuncti* were introduced by the council and reveal ultimately their meaning only in mutual and common consideration, and while keeping in mind that they replaced words like *sectae*, heretics, schismatics, members. Indeed the council made the church aware that all the baptized first and foremost are baptized in Christ and that this brings about a *communio* among all which might lead to certain *plena cummunio*. The council also created awareness that persons belong to a community and they are not just individuals in relation to the Catholic Church. In and through their community they receive, live and nurture their faith. The Catholic Church became aware of the fact that it would be necessary not only to attend so much to the relationship of the individual to the Catholic Church, but to see the individual in relation to the ecclesial community or church he or she belongs to and subsequently focus more on the relationship between the Catholic Church and these other churches and ecclesial communities. It is because of this awareness that a different thinking about a marriage between a Catholic and a baptized non-Catholic developed. This ultimately led to the decree *Matrimonia mixta* and all the subsequent questions mentioned in the beginning.

This reasoning is also of relevance for the understanding of an interchurch marriage as a kind of domestic church: *Lumen gentium* asserts that the family that originates from a *sacramental* marriage builds the domestic church.[37] When

---

[37] *LG* 11 reads: "Finally, Christian spouses, in virtue of the sacrament of Matrimony, whereby they signify and partake of the mystery of that unity and fruitful love which exists between Christ and His Church, help each other to attain to holiness in their married life and in the rearing and education of their children. By reason of their state and rank in life they have their own special gift among the people of God. From the wedlock of Christians there comes the family, in which new citizens of human society are born, who by the grace of the Holy Spirit received in baptism are made children of God, thus perpetuating the people of God through the centuries. The family is, so to

the doctrine is accepted that every valid marriage between two baptized is by that fact a sacramental marriage, then this applies to a mixed marriage as well.[38] When over years Christians in an interchurch marriage have together been praying, reading the bible, listening to God's word, engaging in justice, peace, and the preservation of creation, carrying each other's concerns, anxieties, hopes and joy, forgiving each other for the pain caused upon the other, does this have ecclesial quality?[39] Indeed no other image renders so well the experience of the love of God for us as that of the wedding and marriage as it found expression in the doctrine of Vatican II when marriage is described with the help of terms such as "rendering mutual help and service to each other", "mutual giving and acceptance of each other", and "a partnership of the whole of life" (*GS* 48).

Considering all of this in the context of an interchurch marriage, it is possible to see that the baptized non-Catholic partner stands due to the sacramental marriage in a deep and intense relationship with the Catholic Church. It also implies that the immediate church suffering with the seriously sick person is the domestic church. Not only scripture but life itself testifies to the suffering that people experience when their most beloved one suffers. Indeed the domestic church as such suffers when one of its members suffers. Understanding this situation in the theological perspective as just described requires one to see the request for Communion and anointing of the sick by a person living in a mixed marriage from a different perspective as when this was not the case. Indeed the context must be taken into consideration. This touches on hermeneutics in the application of the law.

The Application of the Law

Canonical literature tends to focus on the interpretation of canon law unless jurisprudence itself is discussed. In the application of the law not only the law must be interpreted, but the case itself must be phrased correctly. The way a legal question is phrased will have a great impact on the answer given. On other occasions I reflected extensively on the application of the law[40] leading to the

---

speak, the domestic church. In it parents should, by their word and example, be the first preachers of the faith to their children; they should encourage them in the vocation which is proper to each of them, fostering with special care vocation to a sacred state."

[38] For a thought provoking reflection on this doctrine see the study by John Alesandro, "The Canon Law of Marriage: Ever Old, Ever New," *CLSA Proceedings* 72 (2010) 50-82.

[39] Cf. Peter Neuner, "Ein katholischer Vorschlag zur Eucharistiegemeinschaft." Professor Ratzinger wrote: "Sakrament ist nicht etwas über, neben oder an der Ehe, sondern gerade die Ehe selbst, und als solche ist sie für den, der im Glauben lebt, das Sakrament. Je mehr es ihm gelingt, die Ehe aus dem Glauben zu leben und zu gestalten, destomehr ist sie 'Sakrament'. Joseph Ratzinger, "Zur Theologie der Ehe," Gerhard Krems e.a. (ed.), *Theologie der Ehe* (Regensburg: Pustet, Göttingen: VandenHoeck & Ruprecht: 1972) 92.

[40] See for example Myriam Wijlens, "The Newness of the Council Constitutes the Newness of the Code (John Paul II): The Role of Vatican II in the Application of the Law," *Proceedings of the Canon Law Society of America* 70 (2008) 285-302.

conclusion that application of the law is not a mere technique of subsumption by which the case is—so to speak—squeezed under the law, but a more recent approach is that the case and the law stand in a hermeneutical relation: one only gets meaning in light of the other. Secondly, because of the intended close connection between Vatican II and the postconciliar legislation not only with regard to the legislation but also to the application of the law it is necessary that the situation in which the law is to be applied is described in correspondence with Vatican II. In real life this means that very often the description of the situation must be rephrased. In this study the differentiation between a mixed marriage and an interchurch marriage is of such importance.

Hence the question to be addressed here is: can a seriously ill baptized non-Catholic person who through his or her baptism stands in *communio*—albeit not in *communio plena*—with the Catholic Church and shares with his or her partner in the communion that a sacramental marriages signifies, and who by living the sacrament of marriage participating in signifying already the love of God for his people, be commended by the Church "to the suffering and glorified Lord in order that he relieve and save him or her" which is done through the sacrament of anointing of the sick (cf. c. 998)? Can this be offered to the person when indeed pastoral care should not be just diaconal in nature, but is to reveal as well that the liturgy is the source and summit of ecclesial actions and a presence and witness of the paschal mystery? Or to put it again in another way remembering the question of the time before the council: how can the Church give expression to the obligation that stems from its own ecclesiology and from its belief that liturgy is the source and summit of ecclesial actions, when a person who belongs to her trough baptism albeit not fully, who lives in a sacramental marriage which in itself constitutes the domestic church, and who is seriously sick and is thus in need to be commended to the suffering and glorified Lord in order that He relieve and save this person?

Once the question is formulated in such a way, the law can be applied.

Before doing so, it may not be forgotten that the Catholic Church owes a lot to the Orthodox and the Eastern Churches for the rediscovery of the sacrament of anointing of the sick and that this in turn inspired many churches from the Reformation to rediscover the ritual of anointing of the sick as well. Many have introduced officially rituals even though they do not refer to them as "sacraments". This awareness is important, because it also implies that asking for the sacrament might not be as foreign as it might have used to be.

Canon 844 §4

The legislator provided a new norm in the Code of Canon Law dealing with sharing the sacraments. The three sacraments concerned are penance, anointing of the sick, and Eucharist.

Unlike the norm in the 1917 code which in agreement with the ecclesiology at the time provided a norm that basically prohibited the *communication in sacris*. There were some exceptions to this, as pointed out above. The norm in the 1983 code allows for a *communicatio in sacris*, albeit under certain conditions. There is thus a change in perspective, which originates in the new ecclesiology and is also the result of the many ecumenical dialogues. It must be kept in mind, that the general perspective is that of a permission, not a prohibition!!!

The interpretation of the canon on a more general level must account for the fact that baptized non-Catholics are incorporated in the Church of Christ which *subsistit in* the Catholic Church (cf. *LG* 8, cc. 96 and 204 §2). They live their Christian existence not only in their own ecclesial communion or church but those who live in an interchurch marriage also live it in their sacramental and thus domestic church. Due to baptism each is a person in the church with duties and rights. In this regard canon 96 reads as follows: to the extent (*quatenus*) that they are in full communion with the Catholic Church (that is in faith, worship, and ecclesial life) their ontologically based belonging to the *plena communio* is activated such, that they can exercise their rights originating from baptism *subsidiary* also in the Catholic Church.[41] *Subsidiary*, writes the German canon lawyer Heinrich J. Reinhardt, in as far as they cannot exercise their right in their own church or community. If, however, other conditions are mentioned in a certain matter, these must be fulfilled.

Reinhardt points out that baptism leads to the right to receive assistance of the pastors of the Church with regard to the spiritual goods in particular the sacraments, as mentioned in canon 213 and which thus implies an obligation on the side of the Church vis-à-vis all baptized.[42] Indeed ministers may not refuse sacraments to the baptized when they seek them at appropriate times, are properly disposed, and are not prohibited by law from receiving them (c. 843 §1).[43] This is rooted in divine law, not in ecclesiastical law and thus it applies to baptized non-Catholics as well. The task to minister was entrusted to the Church and is to be executed by ordained ministers in particular. Whereas the handbooks before the council struggled with the question of what this implied for the obligation to administer sacraments, this does not seem to be the focus today. At times one might get the impression that the pendulum has moved to the other side and that there is a tendency to "make sure that all requirements on the side of the person asking for the sacrament are fulfilled." Often the requirements are of merely ecclesiastical law.

At this point it is necessary to recall that canon 844 does indeed not prohibit

---

[41] Canon 96: "By baptism one is incorporated into the Church of Christ and is constituted a person in it with the duties and rights which are proper to Christians in keeping with their condition, insofar as they are in ecclesiastical communion and unless a legitimately issued sanction stands in the way."

[42] Canon 213 reads: "The Christian faithful have the right to receive assistance from the sacred pastors out of the spiritual goods of the Church, especially the word of God and the sacraments."

[43] Canon 843 §1: "Sacred ministers cannot deny the sacraments to those who seek them at appropriate times, are properly disposed, and are not prohibited by law from receiving them."

the reception of the sacraments of penance, of anointing of the sick and of the Eucharist, but only mentions two occasions and three conditions to receive them. The occasions are danger of death and "other grave necessity". The 1993 Ecumenical Directory speaks of "grave and pressing need". The three conditions are faith in the sacrament, possessing the right disposition, and non-accessibility to one's own minister. It must be pointed out that the latter does not have the clause "for a certain time" as was in the 1967 Directory and that the requirement of accessibility to one's own minister was totally eliminated in the Catechism of the Catholic Church.[44] Cardinal Castillo Lara mentioned already during the revision of the code that such non-availability could also be due to unworthiness or another reason.

It is necessary to be aware that the conditions mentioned are of a different nature and should not be seen as all standing on an equal level. In particular the "grave and pressing need" has been a difficult subject over the past years.[45] Many episcopal conferences and diocesan bishops have indeed not been able to define what this is, simply because the "grave and pressing need" is to be seen contextually as well. Even though a mixed marriage as such cannot be seen as causing a "grave and pressing need" in itself, the interchurch marriage—and all it entails also theologically—might ask for a differentiated consideration. Actually as early as 1980 at the synod for the family Cardinal Johannes Willebrands pointed out that for mixed marriages the preservation of the unity and indissolubility of the marriage would be of a greater good than some of the requirements mentioned as a condition to receive the different sacraments and that this would need to be taken into consideration when admitting them to the sacraments.[46] Determining what "grave and pressing need" would constitute would not only take away the exercise of a discretionary power that is inherent in the application of the law, it would also imply risking that justice cannot be rendered.

Finally, there is the requirement of the shared faith. Of course it is important to recall that many ecclesial communities have rediscovered the anointing of the sick and thus those who belong to these communities might not only ask for it, the faith of their community might be such that presumptions on the faith of the individual belonging to that community might or could be made. At this point it seems good to recall the discussion in the moral and canonical handbooks at the beginning of the twentieth century: they pointed out that not more should be

---

[44] The Catechism of the Catholic Church reads in 1401: "When, in the Ordinary's judgment, a grave necessity arises, Catholic ministers may give the sacraments of Eucharist, Penance, and Anointing of the Sick to other Christians not in full communion with the Catholic Church, who ask for them of their own will, provided they give evidence of holding the Catholic faith regarding these sacraments and possess the required dispositions."

[45] Reinhardt argues that the "grave and pressing need" diminishes when there is an increasing agreement on the doctrinal level with the church or ecclesial community to which the other person belongs. The two correlate as in a scale.

[46] Willebrands, "Mixed Marriages and their Family Life," 78-81.

asked than a general belief (not knowledge) in the sacrament and an intention to do what Christ would ask them to do.

May the church refuse the sacrament to someone who asks? The response to the question will reveal how the church sees the sacrament and how it understands its own ecclesiology: Indeed, by your action you will be judged about your own faith.

An Outlook

As mentioned in the beginning the subject turned out to be more complicated than anticipated simply because so many things are to be taken into consideration. While writing this study Ravel's Boléro came to mind: many rounds had to be made, but every round implied adding new aspects to what had to be taken into consideration and thus the intensity increased as the study progressed.

The subject of this study is in many ways new: there is virtually no literature and thus this study is a work in progress that must be seen as an incentive to commence a dialogue - a dialogue in which theologians and canon lawyers not only from the Catholic Church, but also from the other ecclesial communities and churches must be involved. Anyone who had the privilege to work on ecumenical issues and who has met many couples who live in an interchurch marriage and shared their faith journey, knows that they deserve serious study of these questions leading to pastoral guidelines for ministers who then may act responsibly and with skill so that the risen Lord can lift up all who are in need.

OFFICER'S REPORT

REPORT OF THE PRESIDENT

Reverend Lawrence Jurcak

I am pleased to present the 2009-2010 annual report to the membership of the Canon Law Society of America. It is most important that this report be read in conjunction with the reports of the Executive Coordinator, the Treasurer, and the various committees for a complete understanding of the work of our Society during this past year.

CONVENTION FOLLOW-UP

Two resolutions were approved in October 2009 by the membership during the business meeting of the 71st Annual Convention of the Canon Law Society of America in Louisville, Kentucky.

The *First Resolution* concerned awarding Honorary Lifetime Membership in the CLSA to Sister Sharon Holland, I.H.M.

Be it resolved that Sister Sharon Holland, I.H.M. be honored for her lifelong service to the Church, to Canon Law and to Canon Lawyers, by giving her honorary lifetime membership in the Canon Law Society of America.

As you will recall, this resolution was unanimously approved – followed by an extended applause. After which Sister Sharon Holland, I.H.M. was presented with a memorial plaque announcing her honorary membership. Sister Sharon offered brief remarks and concluded them by challenging us to "Go forth with integrity, charity and truth." Congratulations again to Sister Sharon Holland, I.H.M. for her service and inspiration to all canonists.

The *Second Resolution* concerns a think tank to recommend changes to the Code of Canon Law.

Be it resolved that the Board of Governors organize a think tank to:

1. Gather suggestions from canonical literature, members of the Canon Law Society of America, and other sources, for changes in the *Code of Canon Law* and other legal texts.
2. Explore and evaluate the suggestions in a systematic way; and
3. Report its recommendations in a timely manner to the members of the Society and to the Pontifical Council for Legislative Texts.

The Board of Governors determined, at its January meeting to forward this resolution to the Research and Development Committee. Preliminary reactions and ideas are being generated among members of that committee.

Immediately after our last convention, in response to informal discussions in Louisville regarding Apostolic Visitation of Institutes of Women Religious in the United States, I wrote to Mother Mary Quentin, R.S.M., Chairperson of the Council of Major Superiors of Women Religious, Sister Marlene Weisenbeck, F.S.P.A., President of the Leadership Conference of Women Religious, Father Daniel Ward, O.S.B., Executive Director of the Resource Center for Religious Institutes, and Bishop Thomas J. Paprocki, Chairman of the Committee on Canonical Affairs and Church Governance of the United States Conference of Catholic Bishops. In each letter I offered the assistance of the Canon Law Society of America in the visitation process should the need arise. I am pleased to report that we were able to respond on a case by case basis from members of the Council of Major Superiors of Women Religious and the Leadership Conference of Women Religious. It appears that the offer to provide canonical assistance was greatly appreciated by both groups. Bishop Paprocki acknowledged our assistance to this important work.

In response to the letter that our Society received from Pontifical Council for Legislative Texts at our October 2008 Convention, a Board of Governors Subcommittee was charged with the task of identifying a list of experts to recommend to the Pontifical Council for the Interpretation of Legislative Texts. Following our 2009 Convention, having received the work of that Subcommittee, I contacted the canonists who were proposed see if each would be willing to allow his/her name to be forwarded to the Pontifical Council in response to the invitation the CLSA received from Archbishop Francesco Coccopalmerio. All of them were honored to be included in the list, which I sent to Archbishop Coccopalmerio in December. In my letter to Archbishop Coccopalmerio, I indicated that these individuals "were canon law experts, members of our Society, whom we recommend to the Pontifical Council for Legislative Texts as potential resource persons to assist the working groups, in Rome, that are actively exploring areas of Church law that could benefit from further specification or revisions." In a meeting with Archbishop Coccopalmerio during the biannual Rome Visit in March, he expressed gratitude for the list of canon law experts and indicated that the names would be most useful in obtaining advice on future drafts of possible changes in the law.

The resolution from our 2008 Convention calling for the establishment of a Third Instance Tribunal for the United States was given to the Committee on Church Governance. That Committee, after reviewing the report of the Officers 2010 visit to the Apostolic Signatura, believes that it would not be opportune to seek the authorization at this time (see June 2010 CLSA *Newsletter* for report on Rome visit – www.clsa.org). If a particular Diocese believes that the establishment of a Third Instance Tribunal in the United States would be appropriate in a particular case, it is free to seek authorization from the Signatura.

At the 2003 Convention in Portland, OR, a resolution was passed calling for a study of Diocesan Synods. A Task Force was appointed following the convention and made initial attempts to gather information to study the different types of synod experiences. However, for various reasons the project never moved forward. The Board of Governors discussed the project's status and, considering that it has been dormant for seven years, determined that the project should not be continued at this time. Should the topic come before the body at another time, it might be addressed in a different manner and could be referred to the Church Governance Committee for consideration at that time.

COMMITTEES

Several appointments were made to committees during the past year. These are reflected in the annual reports of the various committees. At this time all of the committees, as recommended in *Future Initiatives Project,* are now in place. The task of filling vacant positions was a challenge due primarily to the increasing responsibilities our members have in their parishes, dioceses, ministries and religious communities. On behalf of the Board, I want to express our gratitude to the many individuals who now serve on our Society's committees. Thanks also to those members of our Society who considered serving on a committee but were unable to do so at this time. I do appreciate the honesty of those who found it necessary to decline an appointment. You are always able to view a list of our committees, their mandates and membership on the CLSA website.

As you review the annual reports of the committees – I am confident that you will realize the tremendous amount of work that is being done for our Society. You will note that some of the committees have been very active this past year, some are just getting off the ground, and that the Clergy Committee has been reconstituted. I want to extend a special work of thanks to each of the Committee Chairs for the work of shepherding his/her respective committee.

While all of the committee reports are important, I take the risk of drawing your attention to two committee reports contained in this booklet. The report of Convention Planning Committee outlines what went into the planning of this year's convention, as well the work that is taking place relative to our future conventions. The report of the Publications Advisory Board clearly outlines the marvelous amount of work that is being done to address the realities associated with the ever changing world of technology and how those realities require the development of a "publication protocol" to assure that we maintain the same quality in our canonical publications that individuals have come to expect from the CLSA.

MEETINGS AND VISITS

In October I flew to Edmonton, Alberta to represent the CLSA at the annual convention of the Canadian Canon Law Society, which took place on October 19 thru October 22, 2009. I was warmly welcomed and I brought the greetings of the CLSA. It was good to see members of our Society present for this convention. From informal conversations with those who were present, as well as with the leadership of the Canadian Society, it appears that they are challenged by many of the issues that are before our Society. Namely, how to communicate with the membership given the increasing cost of mailings, mentoring new/younger members for leadership, convention costs, collaboration with Sister Societies, and responding to emerging canonical issues.

February 24 thru 26, 2010, I visited Saint Paul University in Ottawa to meet with the new Dean, Anne Asselin, JCD and the students in the faculty of Canon Law. I congratulated the new Dean in the name of our Society and assured her of our prayers and best wishes. Having graduated from Saint Paul's in 1991, I was able to renew old friendships with some members of the faculty who are still there. I am most grateful for the warm hospitality extended to me. While at Saint Paul's I delivered a lecture entitled, "The Closing and Merging of Parishes – the Cleveland Experience."

The biennial visit to Rome took place on February 27 thru March 7, 2010. Sister Sharon Euart, R.S.M., Executive Coordinator, Father Mike Joyce, C.M., Vice-President and I visited the Congregation for Divine Worship and the Discipline of the Sacraments, Congregation for Catholic Education, Congregation for Oriental Churches, Pontifical Council for Legislative Texts, Congregation for Institutes of Consecrated Life and Societies of Apostolic Life, Congregation for Clergy, Apostolic Tribunal of the Roman Rota, Supreme Tribunal of the Apostolic Signatura, and the Congregation for the Doctrine of the Faith – and were graciously received by those who met with us. The visits to the Faculties of Canon Law of the Roman Universities enabled us to touch base with the Deans of each university, update them on the work of our Society and hear their suggestions as to how our Society can address the needs of future canonists. While in Rome, we met with the English speaking students of the various Faculties of Canon Law to provide them with an overview of the CLSA. A highlight of the trip was our attendance at the Papal Audience and the opportunity to personally meet Pope Benedict and extend to him the prayers of the CLSA. Special thanks to Father Robert Geisinger, SJ, who assisted with the coordination of the Roman Visit and made himself available throughout the entire time we were in Rome. A comprehensive report on the visit to Rome was presented in the June 2010 CLSA *Newsletter*, which is available on the CLSA website.

In May I flew to Dublin, Ireland and from there embarked on a beautiful drive to Derry, Northern Ireland for the Annual Conference of the Canon Law Society of Great Britain and Ireland from May 3 thru May 7, 2010. In Derry, which is a city rich in history, I was also warmly welcomed on my first visit to the Islands and honored to be able to extend the greetings of the CLSA to another sister Society. It was good to see members of our Society present for this convention as well.

I was not personally able to meet with the Dean, faculty and students of School of Canon Law at The Catholic University of America due to scheduling difficulties. Sister Sharon Euart, R.S.M. hosted a reception at the Hecker Center for the first year canon law students, at which time she was able to brief them on our Society and what we are able to offer them as future canonists.

In April I returned to Louisville to attend the Midwest Regional Meeting. I asked the members of the Board of Governors to represent me at the other regional meetings throughout the United States. Father Manuel Viera, OFM, who is a member of the Board, represented me at the Asociación Mexicana de Canonistas in San Juan de los Lagos, Jalisco. I asked Father Thomas Anslow, C.M., who was already planning to attend the annual convention of the Canon Law Society of Australia and New Zealand, to extend to the members of that sister society our greetings at their convention. I am most grateful for their generous assistance in these visits and for the warm welcome that was extended to them.

Concluding Reflections

It has been an honor and a privilege to have served as President of the Canon Law Society of America for the past year.

I express to the Board of Governors my gratitude for their service and commitment to the work of our Society, their active participation in board meetings and their assistance as needed. I want to thank Father Daniel Smilanic, outgoing Past President of our Society. He's been a friend and generous in his counsel to me and his service to our Society. A special word of thanks to other members of the Board whose terms of service end at the close of this year's convention: Father Thomas Anslow, C.M., Father Philip Brown, S.S., and Sister Lynn McKenzie, O.S.B.

I am grateful to Father Michael Joyce, C.M. Vice President/President Elect for his work with our committees. As he anticipates serving our Society as President, I assure him of my prayers and support.

A special word of thanks to Sister Sharon Euart, R.S.M., for her work over the years for our Society and for all she does as our Executive Coordinator. With her expertise, and the ready assistance of Mrs. Katie Richards, Administrative Assistant, our Society is well served. I have relied on both of them throughout this past year – and I am grateful, not only for all that they have accomplished, but also for their patience and understanding as well. Just a look at our website is an indication of the quality of the work they are doing for our Society. I trust that any of you who have called the office in Washington have received not only a warm "hello" – but also a helpful response to your inquiry.

I thank Bishop Richard G. Lennon, Bishop of Cleveland, for giving me permission to stand for election and serve the CLSA in this manner. I also want to express deep gratitude for the cooperation of the members of the Secretariat for Clergy and Religious of the Diocese of Cleveland, with whom I have served for the last fifteen years. They understood my many absences during the past year and did a wonderful job of filling in for me each time that I was away from the office. A special work of thanks to the pastoral staff and people of Saint John Bosco Parish in Parma Heights for their understanding when I told them that I would be taking a week away from the parish just three weeks after arriving as their new pastor!

Finally, to all of you, the membership of the Canon Law Society of America – daily you have been remember as I prayed the Liturgy of the Hours and celebrated Eucharist. Each day I asked God to bless you and your ministry in the Church. Please know that you will continue to have a remembrance in my prayers in the days ahead. I ask for that same kindness from you. This year has allowed me to come to a deeper realization of your dedication to the law of the Church and your service in the various aspects of Church life and ministry. You are good people who serve the Church so very well! I am honored to stand with you. Together, may we continue the good work that God has begun in each of us.

Report of the Treasurer

Reverend Thomas C. Anslow, CM

I am pleased to present (1) the financial report for fiscal year 2009-2010 and (2) the budget for 2010-2011.

The financial report in the convention booklet consists of the end-of-year review report (not a full audit), including the auditor's statement that he is "not aware of any material modifications that should be made to the accompanying financial statements in order for them to be in conformity with accounting principles generally accepted in the United States of America." Pages 277 & 278 present the consolidated statements of our overall financial position, showing all assets and liabilities as of June 30, 2010. This "snapshot" of our financial condition presents a welcome picture. The Society not only remains financially sound for the present but managed a gain in total net assets on the order of $145,000 (see also Auditor's Report page 280). This happy circumstance is owed in part to unrealized gains on investments for both General Operations and Scholarships totaling over $85,000 (detailed on report Page 290). The remaining $60,000 is the result of Society operations during the past fiscal year.

Some noteworthy financial results are as follows:

- Publications enjoyed a net profit of some $12,000, even though gross income from sales of books was down over $24,000.
- Convention income fell nearly $6,000 over last year, but expenses declined over $12,000, resulting in a net profit for Conventions of nearly $20,000.
- General Operations contributed some $28,000 to the gain in total net assets. This reflects a small gain on membership dues ($4,000) and a greater number of reductions in expenses than increases.
- This year's net gain in assets of $145,000 compares with last year's net loss of nearly $95,000, a swing to the good of $240,000. $218,000 of this is thanks to a recovery in the value of our investment account with Christian Brothers.
- The Executive Coordinator's Office expenses increased $8,400 over last year, in keeping with expectations.
- BrightKey expenses declined some $7,300, both because of decreased inventory and the decline in sales volume.

The approved budget for next year may be found in the convention booklet behind the review report. The "budget summary" projects a modestly balanced budget. It again makes clear that the Scholarship Fund operates as a specially restricted fund.

With regard to the Society's INCOME, I would like to note the following. As happened the year before General Operations actually exceeded its budgeted income by a small amount. The new budget conservatively estimates a small decline, relying on a fairly stable number of members who in turn are faithful in paying their dues. Publications income fell notably short of expectation this year. The new budget anticipates a return to better times, and so may be overly optimistic. Conventions income fell short last year once again owing to the fewer number of attendees. The new budget actually projects greater attendance in view of both location and meeting simultaneously with the Canadian Society. On the Scholarship front, the new budget again anticipates slightly reduced income compared to last year's experience. Given the tightness of financial circumstances all around, this year's income was really pretty good.

As of the time of writing this report, the investment markets having been treading water on average (with some real bobbing up and under), and the economic recovery continues at a very weak and precarious pace. I expect the market value of the Society's investment portfolio to remain volatile without much change in the income it generates. The improvement or deterioration of the Society's financial health will depend to a large extent then on dues collected, convention and workshop fees and publications sales.

In regard to EXPENSES it is again easiest to work backwards through the budget, starting with the Scholarship Fund. The budget projects an average of three recipients being funded each year, so that for the time being expenses will exceed anticipated income. The Scholarship endowment (restricted) funds are healthy enough to sustain a little bleeding for two or three years of reduced investment income without impairing its future growth.

Conventions expenses are expected to be somewhat higher than last year but still below anticipated income. Our experience with Nix & Associates has been beneficial in getting good value for the hotel and service fees.

With regard to Publications, expenses are projected to be higher this year to the tune of $15,000 in view of new book production costs. The auditor's review report (see Note 10) shows from an accounting standpoint that the cumulative available profit as of last June 30 increased some $12,000 from last year to $48,086.

Under General Operations, the most significant budgetary change is the anticipated savings of roughly $5,000 in the cost of operating the CLSA website, since the setup fees were a one-time expense. Other savings should be realized in areas such as printing and mailing costs, to be offset by modest increases in other items such as salary and benefits. Overall, expenses are projected to total about $8,000 less than last year but still in excess of projected income by about $12,000.

At the risk of instilling inertia I again repeat the summation I have written the last two years: The usual tug of war between income and expenses continues to challenge the Society's creativity as it plans its future. We are in good shape financially, but with little margin for inattention or indecisiveness.

As my term of office draws to its end, I take this opportunity to thank the membership for the opportunity to serve as the Society's treasurer. It has been an honor to be trusted with such a responsibility, and both an education and a pleasure to work with the members of the Board of Governors and the Executive Coordinator's Office these three years.

I am also happy to repeat my concluding words of recognition: The reports which you have received are the culmination of the work of many people. I especially wish to recognize Mr. Joseph Godbout, CPA, for his professional assistance in preparing them; Mrs. Katie Richards, our Administrative Assistant, for her enthusiasm, hard work and creativity in finding better ways to do things and in learning the ropes of bookkeeping; and Sr. Sharon Euart, RSM, for her insightful management and keen eye for the bottom line. I am also grateful to the Board of Governors for their prudence, insights and support, and to the Resource and Asset Management Committee for their wisdom and invaluable assistance. The generous collaboration I have experienced with all these people provides clear evidence of their commitment to the mission of the Canon Law Society.

May God continue to bless the Society in its mission to the People of God.

INDEPENDENT AUDITOR REPORT

Joseph E. Godbout, CPA

To the Board of Governors
and Executive Coordinator
Canon Law Society of America
Washington, D.C.

I have reviewed the accompanying statements of financial position of Canon Law Society of America (a District of Columbia not-for-profit professional corporation) as of June 30, 2010 and June 30, 2009, and the related statements of activities and changes in net assets and cash flows for the year then ended in accordance with Statements on Standards for Accounting and Review Services issued by the American Institute of Certified Public Accountants. All information included in these financial statements is the representation of the management of Canon Law Society of America.

A review consists principally of inquiries of company personnel and analytical procedures applied to financial data. It is substantially less in scope than an audit in accordance with generally accepted auditing standards, the objective of which is the expression of an opinion regarding the financial statements taken as a whole. Accordingly, I do not express such an opinion.

Based on my reviews, I am not aware of any material modifications that should be made to the accompanying financial statements in order for them to be in conformity with accounting principles generally accepted in the United States of America.

My review was made for the purpose of expressing limited assurance that there are no material modifications that should be made to the financial statements in order for them to be in conformity with generally accepted accounting principles. The information included in the accompanying schedules is presented for supplementary analysis purposes. Such information has been subjected to the same inquiry and analytical procedures applied in the review of the basic financial statements, and I am not aware of any material modifications that should be made to these schedules.

Joseph E. Godbout
Certified Public Accountant

Silver Spring, Maryland
August 26, 2010

Statements of Financial Position
as of June 30, 2010
with comparative figures as of June 30, 2009

ASSETS

	June 30, 2010	June 30, 2009
Current Assets:		
Cash and cash equivalents	$ 170,567	$ 87,905
Royalties receivable	2,400	600
Accounts receivable-books	-0-	569
Accounts receivable-dues	200	200
Current inventory of books and publications, at cost (Note 3)	15,068	17,282
Prepaid postage	3,399	3,520
Prepaid insurance	1,070	1,191
Prepaid expenses, other	11,292	12,189
Total Current Assets	203,996	123,456
Non-current Assets:		
Furniture, phone equipment, computers, and leasehold improvements, at cost, less accumulated depreciation of $6,216 ($5,362 at June 30, 2009)	7,751	9,232
Long-term inventory of books and publications, at cost (Note 3)	84,710	98,831
Investments, cost $471,630 ($463,647 at 6/30/09), at market value (Note 4)	426,382	370,094
Investments, cost $403,810 ($402,401 at 6/30/09), at market value, temporarily restricted in Scholarship Fund (Note 5)	353,951	316,816
Total Non-current Assets	872,794	794,973
Total Assets	$1,076,790	$918,429

See Accountant's Review Report.

LIABILITIES AND NET ASSETS

		June 30, 2010	June 30, 2009
Current Liabilities:			
Accounts payable	$	-0-	$ 100
Royalties payable		158	188
Deferred revenue – convention		19,625	4,325
Deferred revenue - membership dues		1,200	3,400
Total Current Liabilities		20,983	8,013
Net Assets: (Statement-page 282)			
Unrestricted			
Board designated restricted reserve fund (Note 9)		55,412	55,412
Board designated for special projects/ publications (Note 10)		48,086	36,063
Other unrestricted		598,358	502,125
Total unrestricted		701,856	593,600
Temporarily restricted-scholarship fund		353,951	316,816
Permanently restricted		NONE	NONE
Total Net Assets (Statement-page 280)		1,055,807	910,416
Total Liabilities and Net Assets		$1,076,790	$918,429

See Accountant's Review Report.
The accompanying notes are an integral part of these financial statements.

Statements of Activities and Changes in Net Assets
for the year ended June 30, 2010
with comparative figures for the year ended June 30, 2009

	June 30, 2010	June 30, 2009
Changes in unrestricted net assets:		
Revenues and Gains:		
Membership dues	$252,500	$248,650
Investment income (Note 16)	8,007	13,264
Sales of publications and books	77,995	102,108
Royalties	9,782	6,479
Convention and pre-convention workshops fees	112,929	118,791
Reprint permissions	700	100
Unrealized gains on investments (Note 16)	48,305	-0-
Total unrestricted revenues and gains	510,218	489,392
Net assets released from restrictions:		
Scholarship fund expenses	14,752	19,134
Total unrestricted revenues, gains, and other support	524,970	508,526
Expenses:		
Program services (Schedules-pages 280 &281)	220,265	271,808
Supporting services (Schedules-page 282)	196,449	192,684
Net unrealized losses on investments (Note 16)	-0-	75,531
Total expenses and losses	416,714	540,023
Increase/(decrease) in unrestricted net assets	108,256	(31,497)
Changes in temporarily restricted net assets:		
Contributions to the scholarship fund	$ 9,815	$ 9,744
Income on long-term investments (Note 16)	6,347	9,672
Net realized gains/(losses) on sale of investments (Note 16)	-0-	(4,954)
Net unrealized gains/(losses) on appreciation of investments (Note 16)	35,725	(58,701)
Net assets released from restriction (Page 282)		
Scholarship fund expenses	(14,752)	(19,134)
Increase/(decrease) in temporarily rest. net assets	37,135	(63,373)

	June 30, 2010	June 30, 2009
Changes in permanently restricted net assets:	NONE	NONE
INCREASE/(DECREASE) IN NET ASSETS	145,391	(94,870)
Net Assets at Beginning of Year	910,416	1,005,286
Net Assets at End of Year	$1,055,807	$ 910,416

See Accountant's Review Report.

Schedules of Program Services

	June 30, 2010	June 30, 2009
Publications		
Cost of publications sold	$ 22,741	$ 26,270
Executive Coordinator Office	9,844	13,230
Royalty expense	1,927	2,401
Advertising	13	1,227
Loss on inventory reduction	-0-	16,612
BrightKey	41,929	49,233
Total Publication Expenses	76,454	108,973
Convention and Pre-convention Workshop		
Coordination (Note 14)	67,763	69,028
Pre convention expenses	3,614	4,696
Food service	1,859	1,451
Honoraria	4,700	3,965
Speakers' travel	1,041	1,658
Printing	4,140	8,924
Freight	203	491
Other	816	35
Postage	2,021	3,594
Convention Chair	1,649	2,149
Liturgy	950	2,447
Supplies	2,198	5,852
Convention planning	1,443	1,685
Convention company	145	600
Liturgy Chair	537	939
Adjustment to 2008	-0-	(1,685)
Total Convention and Pre-convention	93,079	105,829

	June 30, 2010	June 30, 2009
Projects		
Total Projects Expenses	-0-	-0-
Membership services		
Postage	4,574	6,024
Printing	3,963	8,769
Newsletter	11,110	13,217
Total Membership Services	19,647	28,010
Committees		
Church Governance	2,965	-0-
Resource & Asset Management	1,620	526
Publications Task Force	1,088	68
Nominations	1,071	1,705
Laity	739	-0-
Other	281	-0-
Regional Workshops for Advocates	250	1,861
Sacramental Law	31	-0-
Marriage Research	-0-	128
Future Initiatives	-0-	137
Clergy procedure handbook	-0-	3
Budget	-0-	958
Professional responsibilities	-0-	1,330
Total Committees	8,045	6,716
Visit to Holy See and Australia trip	8,288	3,146
Scholarship Fund		
Scholarships paid	14,000	18,000
Scholarship expenses	752	1,134
Total Scholarship Fund	14,752	19,134
Total Program Services	$220,265	$271,808

See Accountant's Review Report.
The accompanying notes are an integral part of these financial statements.

Schedules of Supporting Services

	June 30, 2010	June 30, 2009
Board of Governors		
Rental housing	$ 9,412	$ 9,761
Travel	6,206	7,643
Food service	3,410	5,235
Other expenses	568	535
President	5,862	6,528
Vice President	568	661
Treasurer	242	409
Executive Coordinator Office	149,151	140,714
Depreciation expense	2,262	2,430
Rent expense (Note 12)	18,768	18,768
Total Supporting Services	$196,449	$192,684

Statement of Changes in Net Assets by Fund
for the year ended June 30, 2010

	Special Projects Fund	Restricted Reserve Fund	Scholarship Fund	Other Unrestricted	Total
Balance, July 1, 2009	$36,063	$55,412	$316,816	$502,125	$ 910,416
Add: Increases					
Membership dues				252,500	252,500
Investment income			6,347	8,007	14,354
Sales of publications	77,995				77,995
Royalties	9,782				9,782
Convention, workshops				112,929	112,929
Reprint permissions	700				700
Contributions			9,815		9,815
Gains on investments			35,725	48,305	84,030
	88,477	-0-	51,887	421,741	562,105
Less: Decreases					
Publication expenses	(76,454)				(76,454)
Convention, workshops				(93,079)	(93,079)
Projects expenses	-0-				-0-
Membership services, committees and other			(14,752)	(35,980)	(50,732)
Supporting services				(196,449)	(196,449)
	(76,454)	-0-	(14,752)	(325,508)	(416,714)
Balance, June 30, 2010	$ 48,086	$55,412	$353,95	$598,358	$1,055,807

	June 30, 2010	June 30, 2009
Cash Flows From Operating Activities:		
Membership dues	$250,300	$249,750
Publications and book sales	78,564	101,539
Convention and workshops	128,229	79,711
Royalties	7,982	9,379
Investment income	24	2,210
Reprint permissions	700	100
	465,799	442,689
Less: Cash paid to suppliers and employees	382,356	(439,440)
Net Cash From Operations	83,443	3,249
Cash Flows From Investing Activities:		
Purchase of furniture, equip. & leasehold imprvmnts	(781)	(2,538)
Purchase of investments	-0-	(219,449)
Net Cash (Used In) Investing Activities	(781)	(221,987)
Cash Flows From Financing Activities:	NONE	NONE
Increase/(Decrease) In Cash During Year	82,662	(218,738)
Cash and Cash Equivalents at Beginning of Year	87,905	306,643
Cash and Cash Equivalents at End of Year	$170,567	$ 87,905

Reconciliation of Increase/(Decrease) in Net Assets to Net Cash Provided By Operating Activities:

Increase/(Decrease) in Net Assets (Statement-pg. 279)	$145,391	$(94,870)
Adjustments to Reconcile:		
Depreciation	2,262	2,430
Gains/losses on long-term investments	(84,030)	139,186
Contributions to the scholarship fund	(9,815)	(9,744)
Investment income - scholarship fund	(79)	(197)
Dividend income reinvested-CUIT	(14,251)	(20,529)
Loss on inventory reduction	-0-	16,612
(Increase)/decrease in accounts receivable - book sales	569	(569)
(Increase)/decrease in royalties receivable	(1,800)	2,900
(Increase)/decrease in accounts receivable - dues	-0-	(200)
(Increase)/decrease in inventory of books	16,335	(16,513)
(Increase)/decrease in prepaid postage	121	364
(Increase)/decrease in prepaid insurance	121	(136)
(Increase)/decrease in prepaid expenses, other	897	3,179
Increase/(decrease) in accounts payable	(100)	100
Increase/(decrease) in royalties payable	(30)	(118)
Increase/(decrease) in deferred revenue – conv.	15,300	(39,080)

Adjustments to Reconcile (continued):		
Increase/(decrease) in deferred revenue - dues	(2,200)	1,300
Expenses paid from scholarship fund	14,752	19,134
Net Cash From Operations	$ 83,443	$ 3,249

Supplemental Disclosures
Schedule of Non-Cash Investing and Financing Transactions

Dividends reinvested-CUIT Balanced Fund	$14,251	$20,52

See Accountant's Review Report.
The accompanying notes are an integral part of these financial statements.

NOTES TO FINANCIAL STATEMENTS

JUNE 30, 2010
AND
JUNE 30, 2009

Note 1. Summary of Significant Accounting Policies

This summary of significant accounting policies of Canon Law Society of America (CLSA), a District of Columbia not-for-profit professional corporation, is presented to assist in understanding the financial statements. The financial statements and notes are representations of the organization's management, who is responsible for their integrity and objectivity. These accounting policies conform to accounting principles generally accepted in the United States of America and have been consistently applied in the preparation of the financial statements.

Accounting Basis

CLSA prepares its financial statements on the accrual basis of accounting; that is, income is recognized when earned and expenses are recognized when the obligation is incurred.

Accounts Receivable - Books and Publications

Books and publication receivables are considered uncollectible if not collected within 90 days after sale.

Accounts Receivable - Dues

Dues are billed to members at the beginning of each fiscal year (July 1). CLSA records dues income on the basis of dues actually collected. Dues not collected by the issue date of the annual report are considered uncollectible and are written off.

Deferred Revenue

Membership dues, book sales, workshop and convention registrations, collected in advance have been included in deferred revenue in the accompanying balance sheets under current liabilities. This deferred revenue is all recognizable within one year.

Inventory of Books and Publications

The inventory of books and publications is valued at cost, on the first-in, first-out method. CLSA carries a 5 year supply of some books and publications. Because of this long-term supply, there is the possibility that part of the inventory will become obsolete and never be sold. The inventory has been separated on the balance sheet between the estimated current portion which management believes will be sold in the next twelve months and the estimated long-term portion which management expects will be sold in the remaining four years as detailed in Note 3.

The write off for obsolete inventory for the fiscal year ended June 30, 2009 was $16,612. There was no write off for obsolete inventory for the fiscal year ended June 30, 2010.

Capitalization and Depreciation Policy

Expenditures for fixed assets of $300 or more per item are capitalized and depreciated using the straight-line method over the estimated useful lives of the assets which is five years for the furniture, phone equipment and computers and ten years for the leasehold improvements. Depreciation is computed for six months on asset additions during the year. Fully depreciated assets and their related reserves are removed from the accounts. Repairs are expensed as incurred.

Fixed assets additions during 2009-2010 were:

	2009-2010		2008-2009
Letter Folder	$781	Computer	$1,891
		Desk	328
		Conference call center	319
			$2,538

Depreciation expense for the years ended June 30, 2010 and June 30, 2009, was $2,262 and $2,430, respectively.

Investments

Investments are carried at their fair market value on the balance sheet date. Gain or loss on investments during the year is measured by the difference between the sales price or the fair market value at the end of the year and their cost if acquired during the year or their fair market value at the end of the preceding year.

Restricted Funds

Restricted funds are recorded as either temporarily or permanently restricted in the net assets. Temporarily restricted gifts are reclassified to unrestricted net assets and reported in the statement of activities as net assets released from restrictions when the stipulated restriction is accomplished.

Board Designated Net Assets

The Board has designated that part of the unrestricted net assets be set aside for special purposes as described in Notes 8 & 9 below.

Expenses for Convention and Workshops

Expenses for the convention and workshops have been charged with direct costs only, and do not include overhead costs which may be associated with these functions.

Income Taxes

CLSA is a nonprofit organization exempt from federal income taxes under Section 501 (c) (3) of the Internal Revenue Code, and contributions to it are deductible by donors for income tax purposes. The organization is also exempt from state income taxes.

Cash Equivalents

For purposes of the statement of cash flows, CLSA considers only highly liquid investments with an original maturity of three months or less at the time of purchase to be cash equivalents.

Current Assets and Current Liabilities

Current assets and current liabilities are those items expected to be or which may be realized or liquidated during the next twelve-month period.

Fund Accounting

CLSA uses fund accounting because this method allows the organization to readily keep track of the various monies under its control and the purposes of those funds.

Use of Estimates

The preparation of financial statements in conformity with generally accepted accounting principles requires the use of management estimates and assumptions. Accordingly, actual results may differ from those estimates.

Note 2. Organization

Canon Law Society of America (CLSA) is a national, not-for-profit corporation, established in November, 1939 in Washington, DC to promote canonical and pastoral approaches to significant issues within the Roman Catholic Church. In addition to a publication service, CLSA convenes an annual convention and other symposia to promote a better understanding of church law and its pastoral applications. Major sources of gross income are from membership dues (56%), sales of publications and books (19%) and annual convention (25%).

Note 3. Inventory

Total inventory at June 30, 2010, at cost, was $99,778 ($116,113 at June 30, 2009) of which $15,068 ($17,282 at June 30, 2009) is reported on the statement of financial position under current assets as the estimated portion of the inventory which management believes will be sold in the coming fiscal year. The balance of the inventory of $84,710 ($98,831 at June 30, 2009) is reported under non-current assets. Thirteen recent publications make up 82% of this long-term portion.

Note 4. Investments-Canon Law Society

These investments are subject to market risks, and their values fluctuate daily. At June 30, 2010 and June 30, 2009, the investments consist of an individually managed portfolio with Religious Communities Trust in the CUIT Balanced Fund.

	2010		2009	
	Cost	Value	Cost	Value
CUIT Balanced Fund	$471,630	$426,382	$463,647	$370,094

Note 5. Scholarship Fund

At June 30, 2010 and June 30, 2009, the Scholarship Fund consisted of cash in Wachovia Bank, N.A. and an individually managed portfolio with Religious Communities Trust in the CUIT Balanced Fund. These investments are subject to market risks, and their values fluctuate daily.

	2010		2009	
	Cost	Value	Cost	Value
Cash	$ 25,647	$ 25,647	$ 24,505	$ 24,505
CUIT Balanced Fund	384,193	334,334	377,927	292,341
Less: Accounts Payable	(6,000)	(6,000)	-0-	-0-
Less: Deferred – Schaaf	(30)	(30)	(30)	(30)
	$403,810	$353,951	$402,402	$316,816

Note 6. Significant Concentrations of Credit Risk

The organization maintains deposits at two banks that occasionally exceed the amount that would be covered by federal insurance.

Note 7. Operating Lease Payable-Toshiba

The organization leased a new Toshiba copier with a four-year lease beginning on August 21, 2008. The lease is $230.00 per month and includes supplies and maintenance up to 25,000 copies per month.

Because this lease includes supplies and maintenance as a major part of the monthly payments, it is considered an operating lease, even though there is an option to purchase the copier at the end of the lease.

Estimated minimum future lease payments at June 30, 2010 are as follows:

June 30, 2011	$2,760
June 30, 2012	2,760
June 30, 2013 – 2 months	460
	$5,980

Note 8. Operating Lease Payable

The organization leased a new postage machine with a fifty-four month lease payable to Pitney-Bowes beginning May 1, 2006 to November 1, 2010. The lease is for $127 per quarter.

Minimum future lease payments under this lease are as follows:

June 30, 2011 – 4 months	$169

Note 9. Restricted Reserve Account

The Board has designated $55,412 as a Restricted Reserve Account to be set aside for future purposes. The income of this Restricted Reserve Account, formerly the Quasi-Endowment Fund, is to be used for operations.

Note 10. Publications Sales

The Board of Governors has also voted to use the net income from sales of publications and books to fund Special Projects.

The changes in Board Designated For Special Projects are as follows:

	6/30/10	6/30/09
Balance, beginning of year	$ 36,063	$ 36,349
Add: Publication income	77,995	102,108
Royalty income	9,782	6,479
Reprint permissions	700	100
Less: Publication expenses (Schedule-page 16)	(76,454)	(108,973)
Balance, end of year	$ 48,086	$ 36,063

Note 11. Annual Meeting Site Reservation Agreements

The organization has reserved hotel space for future annual meetings. The terms of these reservation agreements provide that a fee will be assessed to CLSA if the reservation is canceled due to a site change, within a specified period prior to the meeting dates.

Note 12. Office Rental Commitments

The corporation has leased office space in Washington, DC under the terms of a lease dated January 2, 2007, for the 10-year period January 2, 2007 through December 31, 2016. Annual rent payments for the first through the fifth year are $18,766. Annual rental payments for the sixth through the tenth year will be increased by the CPI each July 1.

Estimated minimum future payments as of June 30, 2010 are as follows:

June 30, 2011	$18,766
June 30, 2012	18,766
June 30, 2013	18,766 (Subject to CPI increase)
June 30, 2014	18,766 (Subject to CPI increase)
June 30, 2015	18,766 (Subject to CPI increase)
Thereafter – 1½ years	28,149 (Subject to CPI increase)
	$121,979

Note 13. Reclassification

The allocation of the respective balances in the CUIT between General Operations and the Scholarship Fund were changed from those reported on the June 30, 2009 financial statements.

Note 14. Convention Coordination Company

Beginning in October of 2001, CLSA hired an outside company to coordinate its annual convention.

Note 15. Executive Coordinator's Contract

The organization has contracted with Sisters of Mercy of the Americas South Central Community and Sister Sharon Euart, R.S.M. for Sr. Euart to serve as the Executive Coordinator of the Canon Law Society of America beginning August 1, 2008 until July 31, 2011. This Agreement shall remain in force, even beyond its original foreseen term, until its termination is effected in writing.

This Agreement may be terminated by either the Sisters of Mercy or Sr. Euart upon 60 days written notice to the Canon Law Society.

Note 16. Investment Income

The elements of investment income are as follows:

	6/30/10	6/30/09
Interest and dividend income		
Interest Capital One F.S.B. money markets	$ -0-	$ 1,413
Interest-RCT Flex Cash account	24	797
Dividends-CUIT Balanced Fund	7,983	11,054
	$ 8,007	$ 13,264
Net unrealized gains/(losses) on investments		
Unrealized gains/(losses)-CUIT Balanced Fund	$48,305	$(75,531)
Dividends and gains/(losses) on long-term investment- Temporarily Restricted Scholarship Fund		
Interest and dividend income		
Interest on Wachovia checking	$ 79	$ 197
Dividends-CUIT Balanced Fund	6,268	9,475
	$ 6,347	$ 9,672
Net realized gains/(losses) on investments		
Realized gains/(losses) CUIT	$ -0-	$(4,954)
Net unrealized gains/(losses) on investments		
Unrealized gains/(losses)-CUIT Balanced Fund	$35,725	$(58,701)

Letter of Comments on the 2009-2010 Review Audit

August 31, 2010

Sr. Sharon Euart, RSM
Executive Coordinator
Canon Law Society of America
The Hecker Center
3025-4th Street, NE, Suite 111
Washington, DC 20017-1102

Dear Sr. Sharon:

Here are my comments about the corporation's fiscal year ended June 30, 2010:

1. The financial statements show an increase in net assets on page 280 of $145,391. This is the same as a net profit. $37,135 of this belongs to the Scholarship Fund, $48,305 is the result of unrealized appreciation in the CUIT, and the rest, $59,951 is a result of the operations of the corporation during the year.

2. Publications had gross income of $88,477 on page 279 and costs and expenses of $76,454 on page 180, for a net profit of 12,023.

3. Conventions had gross income on page 279 of $112,929 and costs and expenses on page 280 of $93,079, for a net profit of $19,850.

4. The rest of the profit of $28,078 belongs to General Operations. This is gross income from dues on page 279 of $252,500, plus dividend income from the CUIT of $8,007, minus various expenses on page 17 of $35,980 and the supporting services expenses on page 281 of $196,449.

5. This net profit of $145,391 compares to a net loss from last year of $94,870, a swing to the good of $240,000. $218,000 of this is from the CUIT going up this year as opposed to down last year.

6. The dues income of $252,500 on page 279 is an increase of about $4,000 over last year $248,650 due to an increase in new members.

7. Publication gross income from sales of books is way down, $77,995 this year as compared to $102,108 last year. But costs on page 280 are also down, $76,454 this year as compared to $108,973 last year. Bright Key costs were down $7,304 this year. Last year you also had a write off of obsolete inventory of $16,612, as you cleaned up Bright Key's inventory. Bright Key's costs were 54% of publication sales this year, close to the percentage of previous years, 48% in last year, and 57% the year before.

8. On page 281, the Member Services expenses were down $8,363 this year, mostly due to a reduction in the cost of printing of $4,806. The cost of Proceedings was that much less this year. The newsletter looks like it cost

$2,000 less this year.

9. The long-term portion of book inventory on page 277 has decreased from $98,831 to $84,710, a reduction of $14,121. This is you cleaning up the inventory, I suppose.

10. The CUIT on page 277 of $426,382 has climbed back to within $50,000 of the original monies that you put into it plus reinvested dividends of $471,630.

11. The same with the Scholarship CUIT. See the details in Note 5 on page 287, $334,334 vs. $384,193.

12. Your cash in the bank on page 277 has increased from $87,905 last year to $170,567 this year, an increase of $82,662. This is mostly from the net profit in item #1 above of $59,951, plus the convention prepays on page 278 of $19,625.

13. I noticed that you are being charged insurance of $32.48 each month on the lease of the copier. It seems to me that, since you carry your own property protection insurance, the $32.48 is for double coverage. Could someone please check with the leasing company to see if you can provide them with proof of your coverage. Then maybe they can cancel this $32.48 each month and refund to you what you have paid up until now.

14. The Internal Revenue Service has once again lowered the mileage rate that can be paid to employees and Board members for 2010 to 50 cents per mile.

15. Once again this year, there were no special projects to be charged against the Projects Fund.

16. One last item. I found that I had made an error last year in the allocation of the CUIT monies between General Operations and Scholarship. I corrected this allocation on these statements. See note on page 289. You do not need to do anything about this, as the transfer we made in September of this year was correct and Katie has the correct balances for each entity on her books.

Very truly yours,

Joseph E. Godbout
Certified Public Accountant

BUDGET SUMMARY

Fiscal Year July 1, 2010 – June 30, 2011

GENERAL OPERATIONS		
Income	$	246,050
Expenses	$	258,248
Excess/(Deficit)	$	(12,198)
PUBLICATIONS		
Income	$	115,400
Expenses	$	102,909
Excess/(Deficit)	$	12,491
CONVENTIONS		
Income	$	124,225
Expenses	$	119,500
Excess/(Deficit)	$	4,725
Subtotal Gen. Ops., Pub. & Conv. *	$	5,018
SCHOLARSHIP FUND		
Income	$	14,650
Expenses	$	22,300
Excess/(Deficit)	$	(7,650)
Grand Total *	$	(2,632)

* Note: Since Scholarship income by definition belongs to the Scholarship Fund, it can not be used to balance the overall budget. Hence, the first three CLSA "companies" as a whole need to achieve a balance independently, and the number labeled as "Grand Total" is not a simple "operational" profit. An "Excess" in the Scholarship Fund represents an increase in the fund, which is needed for the fund to grow.

General Operations

	Budget FY 08-09	Actual FY 08-09	Budget FY 09-10	Actual FY 09-10	Budget FY 10-11
INCOME					
Investment Income/CBIS	$15,000	$11,461	$6,000	$7,986	$6,000
Interest Income/RCT	$5,000	$797	$3,000	$24	$50
Dues Income (Note 1)	$240,000	$248,650	$246,000	$252,500	$240,000
TOTAL INCOME	**$260,000**	**$260,908**	**$255,000**	**$260,510**	**$246,050**
EXPENSES					
Staff Expenses (Note 2)	$111,980	$100,184	$115,680	$114,023	$117,430
Service Charges					
Bank Service Charges				$1	$50
Flex Fund Service Charges				$38	$100
Credit Card Fees	$6,029	$4,345	$7,500	$2,983	$6,500
Sub-total	$6,029	$4,345	$7,500	$3,021	$6,650
OEC Expenses					
Books and Periodicals	$740	$756	$500	$273	$400
Copier Lease & Maintenance	$5,500	$3,286	$3,750	$3,577	$3,700
Furniture & Equipment	$2,000	$931	$1,200	$1,006	$1,000
Hospitality	$750	$575	$500	$359	$500
Insurance & Workers Comp.	$3,000	$2,206	$2,000	$2,103	$2,500
Office Supplies	$3,000	$2,329	$3,500	$2,956	$2,800
Postage Meter	$700	$594	$900	$568	$900
Postage/UPS/FedEx	$1,000	$908	$750	$713	$1,000
Collaboration w/ Nt'l Orgs.				$1,278	$500
Rent	$18,768	$18,768	$18,768	$18,768	$18,768
Taxes	$100	$45	$200	$135	$100
Telephone/ISP/DSL	$2,700	$3,035	$3,800	$2,778	$3,500
Travel	$4,000	$1,002	$3,000	$1,554	$3,000
Sub-total	$43,258	$34,635	$39,868	$36,267	$39,668
Professional Services					
Accountant/Auditor (Note 3)	$7,875	$7,875	$6,000	$6,000	$6,000
Web Design & Maintenance	$8,300	$12,893	$11,300	$8,925	$6,500
Legal Services	$2,000	$-	$1,000	$-	$500
Sub-total	$18,175	$20,768	$18,300	$14,925	$13,000
Member Services					
General Printing	$500	$219	$100	$-	$100
General Postage	$2,000	$1,556	$1,800	$350	$1,500
Newsletter Printing (Note 4)	$8,000	$8,982	$8,000	$6,778	$5,500
Newsletter Postage (Note 4)	$8,000	$4,235	$3,000	$4,332	$4,000
Proceedings Printing	$8,600	$8,550	$8,500	$3,963	$6,500
Proceedings Postage	$6,500	$4,468	$4,500	$4,225	$5,500
Sub-total	$33,600	$28,010	$25,900	$19,647	$23,100

General Operations continued

	Budget FY 08-09	Actual FY 08-09	Budget FY 09-10	Actual FY 09-10	Budget FY 10-11
Board of Governors, Mtgs					
Food	$3,500	$5,234	$5,600	$3,410	$5,500
Lodging	$6,000	$9,761	$9,000	$9,412	$11,000
Meeting Space	$500	$500	$500	$500	$500
Postage/UPS	$500	$-	$250	$38	$100
Supplies	$350	$35	$100	$30	$100
Telephone	$400	$-			
Travel	$11,000	$7,643	$9,000	$6,206	$8,500
Rome or Australia Trip	$10,000	$3,146	$10,000	$8,288	$10,000
Sub-total	$32,250	$26,319	$34,450	$27,884	$35,700
Board of Governors, Officers					
President	$8,000	$6,528	$7,000	$5,862	$7,000
Vice President/Past President	$500	$661	$1,500	$568	$1,000
Treasurer	$500	$409	$600	$242	$600
Secretary	$200	$-	$100	$-	$100
Sub-total	$9,200	$7,598	$9,200	$6,672	$8,700
Committees					
Constitutional Committees					
Nominations	$3,000	$1,705	$3,000	$1,071	$1,500
Resolutions	$100	$-	$100	$-	$100
Resource & Asset Mngmt	$2,000	$958	$2,000	$1,620	$1,500
Professional Responsibility	$100	$-	$100	$-	$200
Standing Committees					
Church Governance				$2,965	$2,000
Clergy		$4	$200	$-	$500
Institutes of Cons. Life.	$400	$-	$100	$-	$400
Laity				$739	$2,500
Publications Adv. Board	$2,000	$68	$2,500	$1,088	$2,400
Advisory Opinions	$100	$-	$100	$-	$100
Canon Law Digest	$2,000	$-	$2,000	$-	$1,000
Roman Replies	$100	$-	$100	$-	$-
Research & Development			$750	$-	$100
Sacramental Law	$1,200	$128	$1,200	$31	$1,200
Apprvd Cmte Contingency.	$1,000	$-	$1,000	$281	$1,000
Sub-total	$12,000	$2,863	$13,150	$7,795	$14,500
Miscellaneous					
General Operations Contingencies	$1,000	$-	$1,000		$500
Sub-total	$1,000	$-	$1,000	$-	$500

General Operations continued

	Budget FY 08-09	Actual FY 08-09	Budget FY 09-10	Actual FY 09-10	Budget FY 10-11
Additional Transactions - Previous FY					
Advisor Fees - CBIS	$1,000	$-			
Contribution to Conventions		$24,950			
Former Committees					
Advocacy Procedures	$200	$-			
Can. Asp. of Sex. Abuse	$225	$-			
Civil and Canon Law	$500	$-			
Diocesan Synods	$500	$-	$100	$-	
Eastern Canon Law	$100	$-			
Future Initiatives		$137			
Professional Resp. Rev.	$2,300	$1,330	$2,100	$-	
Workshps for Advocates	$2,400	$1,861	$100	$250	
Grant Request Writing	$3,000	$-			
Sub-total	$10,225	$28,278	$2,300	$250	$-
TOTAL EXPENSES	**$276,717**	**$252,800**	**$266,348**	**$230,286**	**$258,248**
EXCESS/DEFICIT	**$(16,717)**	**$8,108**	**$(11,348)**	**$30,224**	**$(12,198)**

Note 1: This line includes all income from dues (past dues, current dues and new member dues).

Note 2: This line item includes the Executive Coordinator & Administrative Assistant Salaries, all EC & AA benefits, payroll taxes and a minimal cost for outsourcing the payroll for one employee.

Note 3: This item is apportioned between General Ops and Publications, at a distribution rate of 75% and 25% respectively.

Note 4: These line items are based on two printed Newsletters mailed and two Newsletters distributed electronically.

Publications

	Budget FY 08-09	Actual FY 08-09	Budget FY 09-10	Actual FY 09-10	Budget FY 10-11
INCOME					
Publication Sales	$80,000	$84,713	$65,000	$62,915	$90,000
Reprint Permissions	$300	$100	$300	$700	$400
Royalty Income	$9,000	$6,479	$9,000	$9,782	$5,000
Shipping/Restocking - BrightKey	$20,000	$17,395	$20,000	$15,080	$20,000
TOTAL INCOME	**$109,300**	**$108,687**	**$94,300**	**$88,477**	**$115,400**
EXPENSES					
Staff & Professional Services					
Staff Salary (Note 1)	$5,720	$5,720	$3,342	$3,342	$3,509
Accountant/Auditor	$2,625	$2,625	$2,000	$2,000	$2,000
Sub-total	$8,345	$8,345	$5,342	$5,342	$5,509
Royalties Paid					
Royalties/CCEO	$600	$355	$450	$192	$400
Royalties/CIC	$1,000	$1,071	$1,400	$1,229	$1,200
Royalties/Dignitas Connubii	$1,000	$675	$600	$339	$500
Royalties/Selected Issues	$200	$222	$200	$119	$100
Royalties/Recp. & Communion	$100	$78	$50	$48	$100
Sub-total	$2,900	$2,401	$2,700	$1,927	$2,300
Publication Expenses					
Advertising - Printing	$1,200	$1,210	$1,000	$13	$1,500
Advertising – Electr. (Note 2)			$1,000	$-	$500
Book Production	$30,000	$41,264	$25,000	$1,005	$40,000
Copyright Applications	$210	$105	$150	$175	$150
Outsourcing - BrightKey	$45,000	$49,233	$47,000	$41,929	$47,000
OEC Expenses					
Storage of Negatives	$100	$48	$100	$78	$100
Postage	$400	$33	$400	$104	$200
Supplies	$100	$-		$39	$100
Service Charges					
Bank Service Charges	$50	$17	$50	$-	$50
Credit Card Fees	$4,500	$4,681	$4,500	$3,101	$5,000
Publications Contingencies	$500	$-	$500	$-	$500
Sub-total	$82,060	$96,592	$79,700	$46,444	$95,100
Additional Transactions - Previous FY					
Advertising - Postage	$1,000	$17			
Sub-total	$1,000	$17	$-	$-	$-
TOTAL EXPENSES	**$94,305**	**$107,355**	**$87,742**	**$53,713**	**$102,909**
EXCESS/DEFICIT	**$14,995**	**$1,332**	**$6,558**	**$34,765**	**$12,491**

Note 1: Publications is responsible for 10% of the Executive Assistant salary.

Convention

	Budget FY 08-09	Actual FY 08-09	Budget FY 09-10	Actual FY 09-10	Budget FY 10-11
INCOME					
Convention Fees (Note 1)	$114,000	$98,921	$99,125	$94,300	$105,625
Pre-Convention Fees (Note	$22,500	$15,750	$18,750	$15,875	$15,000
Exhibitors' Fees	$3,400	$3,940	$4,500	$2,700	$3,600
Additional Banquet Fees		$180		$54	$-
Sponsors' Donations			$1,000	$-	$-
Gen Ops contribution		$24,950			$-
TOTAL INCOME	**$139,900**	**$143,741**	**$123,375**	**$112,929**	**$124,225**
EXPENSES					
Professional Services					
General Convention Chair	$1,800	$2,149	$1,800	$1,649	$1,800
Convention Liturgy Chair	$200	$939	$500	$537	$600
Convention Planning Cmte	$4,000	$1,685	$2,000	$1,443	$2,000
Convention Company	$500	$600	$700	$145	$700
Sub-total	$6,500	$5,373	$5,000	$3,773	$5,100
Pre-Convention					
Honoraria	$3,000	$3,000	$3,000	$3,000	$3,000
Liturgy	$1,000	$-	$400	$400	$400
Postage	$100	$2			$50
Printing	$3,000	$742	$1,000	$45	$500
Shipping	$500	$10	$100	$27	$50
Speaker's Travel	$900	$943			$300
Supplies	$500	$-		$142	$200
Sub-total	$9,000	$4,697	$4,500	$3,614	$4,500
Convention					
Convention Company	$89,821	$69,028	$80,000	$67,763	$76,000
Food		$1,452	$1,500	$1,859	$1,200
Honoraria	$5,400	$3,965	$4,800	$4,700	$3,900
Liturgy	$2,800	$2,447	$2,500	$950	$1,500
Postage	$3,000	$3,594	$1,500	$2,022	$2,200
Printing	$8,000	$8,925	$9,000	$4,140	$6,000
Shipping	$1,000	$491	$600	$203	$500
Speaker's Travel	$700	$1,658	$2,000	$1,041	$2,500
Supplies	$6,700	$5,852	$5,500	$2,198	$4,000
Telephone/Internet				$60	$150
Translation Services					$10,400
Sub-total	$117,421	$97,412	$107,400	$84,935	$108,350
Service Charges					
Bank Service Charges	$50	$35	$50	$35	$50
Credit Card Fees				$642	$1,000

Convention continued

	Budget FY 08-09	Actual FY 08-09	Budget FY 09-10	Actual FY 09-10	Budget FY 10-11
Miscellaneous					
Conventions	$500				$500
OEC Office Supplies					$80
Sub-total	$550	$35	$50	$677	$1,630
Additional Transactions - Previous FY					
Audio Visuals	$2,000	$-			
Exhibitors' Expenses	$800				
Sub-total	**$2,800**	**$-**	**$-**	**$-**	**$-**
TOTAL EXPENSES	**$136,271**	**$107,517**	**$116,950**	**$92,999**	**$119,580**
EXCESS/DEFICIT	**$3,629**	**$36,225**	**$6,425**	**$19,930**	**$4,645**

Note 1: Assume 325 attendees @ $325 each

Note 2: Assume 60 attendees @ $250 each

Note 3: This contribution from General Operations was made to cover the hotel bill; therefore the actual excess for FY 08-09 is $11,275.

Scholarship Fund

	Budget FY 08-09	Actual FY 08-09	Budget FY 09-10	Actual FY 09-10	Budget FY 10-11
INCOME					
Investment Income					
Investment Income/CBIS	$30,000	$10,481	$8,250	$6,268	$6,000
Interest Income/Wachovia	$600	$197	$300	$79	$150
Sub-Total	$30,600	$10,678	$8,550	$6,347	$6,150
Scholarship Donations (Note 1)					
Donations from Dues		$1,425	$-	$2,085	$1,500
Donations from Appeal	$16,000	$8,319	$7,000	$7,330	$6,000
Donations from Convention				$400	$-
Donations from Regionals					$1,000
Sub-Total	$16,000	$9,744	$7,000	$9,815	$8,500
TOTAL INCOME	**$46,600**	**$20,422**	**$15,550**	**$16,162**	**$14,650**
EXPENSES					
Service Charges					
Money Market Fees	$50	$38	$50	$-	$50
Postage					
General Postage	$100	$15	$150	$2	$50
Appeal Postage	$1,000	$674	$700	$641	$800
Printing					
General Printing	$200	$-	$600	$-	$200
Appeal Printing	$800	$408	$50	$108	$200
Domestic Awards (Note 2)	$18,000	$12,000	$14,000	$14,000	$21,000
Additional Transactions - Previous FY					
Advisor Fees (Note 3)	$1,500	$-			
Scholarship Committee	$100	$-			
International Awards	$6,000	$25,000			
TOTAL EXPENSES	**$27,750**	**$38,135**	**$15,550**	**$14,751**	**$22,300**
EXCESS/DEFICIT	**$18,850**	**$(17,713)**	**$-**	**$1,411**	**$(7,650)**

Note 1: At the April 2009 BOG Meeting it was decided to donate the entire International Scholarship Fund to the Antonium in Rome for international scholarships. Therefore, for this year's budgeting purposes I have divided the income from FY 08-09 by the same categories as we are budgeting for FY 10-11. Total domestic donations collected in FY 08-09: $7,842; total international donations collected in FY 08-09: $1,902

Note 2: Assumes 3 awards at $7,000 each

Note 3: There are no advisor fees with CBIS

REPORT OF THE EXECUTIVE COORDINATOR

Sister Sharon A. Euart, RSM

During the past year the Office of the Executive Coordinator has continued to address challenges, initiate changes, and facilitate communication among our members and with other important publics. I am most grateful to the Board of Governors and CLSA members for your ongoing support and assistance in addressing the needs of the Society. We have learned much from the experience of the past two years and it is my hope that we have served you well.

Again this year I will comment on some of the challenges, changes and initiatives that have occurred in the four areas of service: general operations, conventions, publications and scholarship. I will also offer observations on progress in accomplishing the goals outlined in our 2009 report.

GENERAL OPERATIONS

OEC Staffing

Kathleen Richards continues to serve the Society as the Administrative Assistant in the Office of the Executive Coordinator. Many of you have come to know Katie, her gracious manner, and her competence in responding to questions, requests for assistance and resources. Over the two years during which she has worked with us, her responsibilities have increased enormously to include administration of the website, design and formatting of publications, updating of office procedures, and monitoring our financial transactions. Our student intern, Susan Mulheron, will be with for another year as she completes the JCL program next summer. We are most fortunate to have both women on staff and grateful for their service to the Society and its members.

Website Development, Management and Membership

A year ago July the new CLSA website went "live." Since that time we have made numerous improvements in the site including the addition of resources available to both members and non-members. With Katie's knowledge of websites as well as Susan's experience we have been able to generate a significant amount of "traffic" throughout the site. The members' services on the website are numerous and we continue to look for new ways to encourage members and groups such as committees to utilize its features.

As you are aware one issue of the 2009-2010 *CLSA Newsletter* was published in electronic form only. Though this did result in a cost savings, it also enabled us to publish a larger issue, with increased content, sharper photos and an enhanced appearance. The feedback we received was quite favorable.

We anticipate publishing two electronic issues in the coming year. The design and formatting for the Newsletter are done in-house by staff giving us greater flexibility in style and appearance.

With the introduction of the new website in July 2009, we have experienced a tremendous growth in the number of members utilizing the website for convention and workshop registration and for dues payments. We expect this trend to continue as more members become accustomed to accessing the website on a regular basis.

Based on the experience of the past year and half, I believe the increased awareness of the CLSA website has several implications for the Society and its mission in the future. Let me mention three implications.

First, the increase in the number of new members of the Society this past year far exceeded our projection. Ninety-four (94) new members joined during the past fiscal year and, as of this writing (September 9) an additional 25 have joined since July 1, 2010, more than one quarter of whom come from countries other than the United States. This international diversity among the membership is a positive development which enables the Society to reach out to canonists throughout the world. Most of these new members found out about the Society from the website and the vast majority applied through the website. Additionally, the increasing number of new student memberships (36%) bodes well for the future of the Society. These student members are generally electronically astute and quite familiar with navigating the website and utilizing many of its features.

Second, as we heard from the both the faculty and students we met with in Rome during our March visits to the canon law faculties, the availability of English-language canon law resources is a critical need. The accessibility of CLSA publications electronically on the website is a major attraction for new members, especially those from countries other than the United States. The more electronic resources the CLSA can provide the greater the awareness of the Society and the greater our service to the broader canonical community. See the section below on CLSA publications for more information on publications and the website.

A third implication of the increased awareness of the CLSA website is the need for the Society to remain in the forefront of electronic technology in order to provide the necessary upgrades to maintain a high quality of service. This necessarily requires staff skilled in the use and administration of website technology, familiar with new advances and able to respond to members' questions and requests for information. This competence will become increasingly important in the years ahead.

The chart below shows the overall number of unique visitors to the website on a daily basis from October 1, 2009 until June 30, 2010 (the end of the past fiscal year). The peak date with 306 different visitors was June 9, 2010, the day the first e-newsletter was mailed to members.

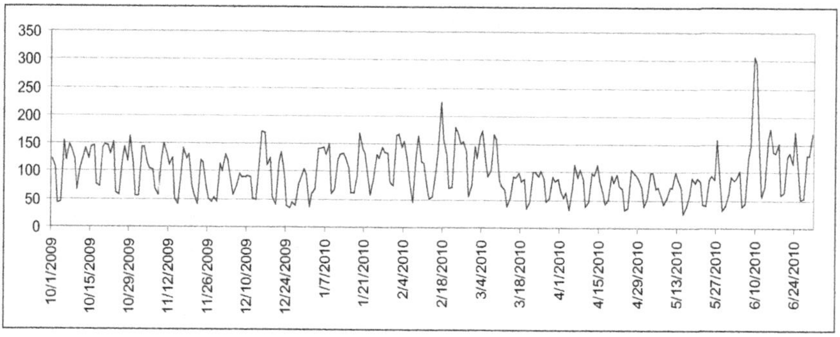

The chart below reflects the website's international visitors; displaying visitors from the top ten international countries.

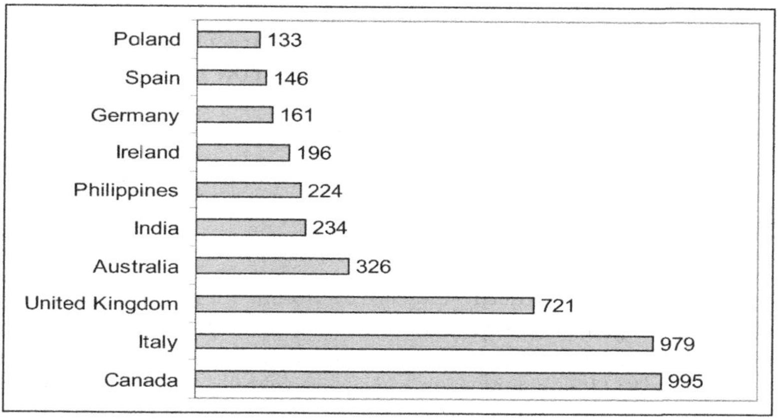

Efforts to Reduce Operational Costs

Again this year we have sought ways to reduce expenses that are both effective and efficient. The areas in which this was effective included, for example, introducing new procedures for printing and mailing for the CLSA *Newsletter*, convention brochure, and *Proceedings*; obtaining additional printing and formatting alternatives for publications; utilizing lower cost options for Board of Governors meeting arrangements; scheduling conference calls rather than in-person meetings when possible; and limiting travel. We were able to reduce costs significantly over the past year, which is reflected in the end of the year financial statements.

Collaboration with other groups

Over the course of the year we have initiated communication and increased our collaboration efforts with the USCCB with assistance in internet technology, human resources, publications, making available bishops' documents to our membership, and especially the 2010 Canon Law Seminar for Media held in May. We participated in a Staff Day Retreat for staff of the many national Catholic organizations located in the Washington, DC area. In addition the Society participated in the planning meeting for the 2011 Symposium on Lay Ecclesial Ministry to be held at St. John's University in Collegeville.

During the March 2010 visits to the dicasteries in Rome, we established contacts that have facilitated our follow up on various projects and enabled us to communicate more quickly and effectively with the various offices of the Holy See. This has proven to be a most valuable outcome of the 2010 Rome visit.

Tribunal Review Procedure

In the past, the CLSA worked closely with the USCCB Committee on Canonical Affairs and Church Governance on the Tribunal Review and Evaluation Process. As a result of the recent conference restructuring process the USCCB is no longer able to provide assistance in the Tribunal review process. Reviews continue to take place and are now organized through the Executive Coordinator's Office. If your bishop wishes to have a review of the Tribunal, he should contact the Executive Coordinator to initiate the process. The procedure for review will follow the same steps as previously outlined by the USCCB and the CLSA.

Annual Tribunal Statistical Reports

For many years the Office of Executive Coordinator has been compiling an annual report of statistics concerning activity in U.S. tribunals. Over time the form has been modified for clarity and precision. Nonetheless, for various reasons, the instrument continues to cause some confusion on the part of those completing the forms. Following discussion with the Board of Governors in April 2010, and in an effort to improve the quality and accuracy of the reports, we will ask those completing the 2010 reports to submit copies pages 5 and 6 from the (arch)diocesan report submitted annually to the Apostolic Signatura, a practice utilized by the Canon Law Society of Great Britain & Ireland. Since the forms from the Apostolic Signatura do not request financial information, we will include a separate form with the letter requesting the statistical information. It is anticipated that collecting the same data that is submitted to the Holy See will eliminate potential discrepancies between the CLSA summary report and the report sent by the (arch)diocese to the Apostolic Signatura.

Requests for Canonical Assistance

We continue to receive requests for canonical assistance from individuals and/or groups. Increasingly the requests come from the website from individuals who may have been told to obtain the services of a canonist without knowing very much about canon law. Often diocesan officials, parish staff and canonists recommend that individuals contact the CLSA for canonical service. I am most grateful to those who have offered to be available to respond to such requests and welcome others who may be willing to speak to someone seeking canonical advice. We currently have a limited number of canonists whose names we are authorized to make available to those requesting assistance.

Hecker Center

During the past year the Office of the Executive Coordinator hosted several CLSA meetings. The Board of Governors met at the Center in January and April, Convention Planning Committee in January, Resource & Asset Management Committee in February, the Church Governance Committee in April, and the Presidential Transition Meeting in September. Several individuals visited the Office while in the Washington, DC area as well as new students at the beginning of the school year. We welcome members and committees to the OEC and to the Hecker Center. Accommodations are available and the Center is only a short walk to the DC Metro.

We are interested in expanding our capability for alternatives to face-to-face meetings not only in an effort to reduce costs but also to enable committees, work groups, etc. to meet more frequently for shorter periods of time in order to work more effectively. We are looking into the possibility of utilizing webinars and video conferencing and providing the technical assistance needed to make these formats available to our membership.

CONVENTIONS

We continue to work closely with the Convention Planning Committee and with the Convention Chairperson for the 2010 convention in Buffalo. Our new procedures for contacts with presenters that provide necessary information and outline expectations and responsibilities on the part of the CLSA and the presenter have proven most beneficial. The 2010 convention planning has been unique and required more staff time due to the joint nature of the convention. Our office prepares in advance the materials for distribution at registration and throughout the meeting. By doing this in-house, we have reduced convention printing costs significantly. We will be working on a Convention Manual that will outline the key roles and responsibilities in the planning and execution of CLSA conventions. It is likely that attendance at annual conventions will continue to decrease, due primarily to the economic situation in our dioceses. Planning for future conventions as well as for regional conferences will need to take this into consideration.

PUBLICATIONS

A full report of the activity around CLSA publications can be found in the report of the Publications Advisory Board. The PAB continues to offer valuable assistance to the OEC. Working with the PAB has facilitated both the preparation of publications and their timely distribution. The Board's recommendations regarding reprinting publications, formatting options, printing costs, and new initiatives for printing have proven most helpful. The PAB developed a protocol for committees on how to proceed when initiating a publication including a clarification on the responsibilities of the committee, the PAB, and the OEC. The efforts of the PAB to coordinate the publication function of the CLSA have and will continue to enable the Society to move forward in an organized and effective manner.

This year we were able to make several CLSA publications available on the website. Issues of *Proceedings* from 1983-2000 can now be downloaded from the website at no cost for members and at a minimal cost for non-members. Similarly, issues of *Roman Replies and CLSA Advisory Opinions* from 1983-2000 will be shortly available on the website. Out of print publications will also be made available for downloading from the website. In addition, several CLSA publications are available on Amazon.com. We generated over $1000 from Amazon sales since October 2009.

We continue to work with BrightKey as our book distributor. With the concurrence of PAB new shipping rates have been put in place that will reduce costs for members ordering directly from BrightKey.

SCHOLARSHIPS

As we reported in the recent CLSA *Newsletter* we are pleased to have offered one scholarship this year to a student beginning studies in canon law at St. Paul's in Ottawa. The appeal was held this year during Lent of 2010. We received several contributions made in memory of members who have served the Society and are now deceased. We want to acknowledge these memorials in a meaningful way on the website, in the CLSA *Newsletter*, and in our annual report.

Scholarship contributions were made in memory of the following:

Rev. Dennis Burns
Rev. Richard Cunningham
Rev. Bertram F. Griffin
Rev. Ellsworth Kneal
Msgr. Frederick McManus
Rev. James Provost
Msgr. Charles Schettler
Msgr. William Varvaro

May they rest in peace

Goals for the Office of the Executive Coordinator

As I begin the third year of my term, I continue to focus my efforts on making the Office of the Executive Coordinator a locus of service to the membership and those seeking our assistance. To this end we have introduced new procedures, updated services and enhanced communication with committees and other groups.

In 2008, I identified the following goals for 2008-2011 Goals:

1. To hire the staff necessary to carry out administrative and financial responsibilities, including, but not limited to, computer proficiency, data entry/management, means of communication such as website and newsletter development, and bookkeeping procedures;
2. To initiate contact with Catholic organizations and groups whose mission and agendas include canonical matters or issues having canonical implications;
3. To seek opportunities to collaborate and cooperate with other groups whose educational goals might benefit from the CLSA's canonical input and expertise;
4. To be present to groups and/or activities with and in which the CLSA might have an interest and through which the Society's service to the broader Church might be enhanced;
5. To assist in implementation of the recommendations of the *Futures Initiative Project* as approved by the Board of Governors.

For the most part, I continue to see these goals as viable directions for the coming year with an emphasis on increasing the availability of canonical resources in conjunction with CLSA committees and/the Public Advisory Board. With your assistance we have accomplished much in two years; there remains much to do. I look forward to serving to the Society in the coming year. I am grateful for your support and welcome your suggestions or comments on how the Office of the Executive Coordinator might better serve you and the canonical needs of our Church.

Constitutional Committees

Committee:	Nominations
Constituted:	Constitution, Article X
Charge:	The mandate of the Committee is: *1. To submit to the active members, at least one month prior to the date of election, the names of nominees as provided for in Article IX of the Constitution; (and)* *2. To formulate and recommend to the Board of Governors plans for maintaining and increasing the membership of the Society.*
Members:	Sr. Maureen A. McPartland, OP, *Chair* Rev. Msgr. Ricardo E. Bass Dr. Diane Barr Rev. Daniel A. Smilanic, *ex officio*

Annual Report

The Nominations Committee met in Chicago on February 23-25. All members of the committee were present for the meeting.

During the afternoon and evening of February 23rd, lists of possible candidates for various offices were compiled from recommendations to the committee from the membership at large, those identified by members of the committee and those suggested by the Board of Governors. Attention was paid to selecting candidates who would offer sound leadership to the committee while representing diverse constituencies and regions.

The following day committee members contacted prospective candidates. By the evening of the 24th the slate of nominees was complete.

On February 25th the following slate of candidates was forwarded to the Board of Governors for presentation to the members gathered at the 2010 convention in Buffalo, New York:

Vice President/President Elect:
Rita Ferko Joyce
Rev. Msgr. Mark Plewka

Treasurer:
Rev. Gregory Bittner
Rev. Kelly Vandehey

Consultor:
Rev. Thomas Cronkleton
Rev. Thomas Fransiscus. C.SS.R.
Rev. Joseph Matt
Margaret Poll Chalmers

The Nominees' *Curricula Vitae* and Photographs were complied by the Executive Coordinator's office. That office published the booklet regarding the 72nd Annual Convention and included the information pertaining to the candidates.

During the February meeting, the committee members also discussed maintaining and increasing the membership of the Society. While no new strategies were formulated, two points were highlighted: first, the importance of networking with other organizations of church professionals; second, the need to strengthen personal relationships among the members. These insights were forwarded to the BOG for their April meeting.

The Committee wishes to thank those who have been willing to consider serving the Society as an elected officer.

Maureen McPartland, OP

* * * * * * * * *

Committee:	Resolutions
Constituted:	Constitution, Article X
Charge:	The mandate of the Committee is: *1. To solicit, develop and draft proposed resolutions which will express the concerns of the Canon Law Society of America;* *2. To consult with the membership at large and, in particular with the Board of Governors, the standing and ad hoc committees of the Society, and the organizers of the convention;* *3. To formulate resolutions on given points in response to requests of the members of the Society;* *4. To compose differences in the formulation of similar proposals and to revise all proposals so that the meaning of each is clear; (and)* *5. To encourage resolutions which authentically express in a positive way the activities and concerns of the Society.*
Members:	Br. Patrick T. Shea, OFM, *Chair* Ms. Rita Joyce Rev. Gregory T. Luyet

Annual Report

The bulk of the Committee's work occurs immediately prior to and during the annual convention. At the last convention, the committee assisted in the formulation of two resolutions both of which were subsequently adopted

Members of the committee have been in occasional e-mail contact and a meeting by means of conference call is planned on August 17, 2010 at which time a determination can be made as to which role each committee member plays.

Brother Patrick T. Shea, O.F.M.

* * * * * * * * * *

Committee:	Resource and Asset Management
Constituted:	Constitution, Article X, as last amended in 2008
Charge:	The mandate of the Committee is: *1. To develop a comprehensive budget for all the activities of the Society and report on the funding available for projects;* *2. To submit the proposed budget for the coming fiscal year to the Board of Governors for approval at its spring meeting;* *3. To conserve, invest and disburse the monies of the Scholarship Fund in accord with the criteria established by the Society;* *4. To select recipients for the CLSA scholarships based on criteria approved by the Board of Governors; (and)* *5. To advise the Treasurer on all matters pertaining to the Society's investments.*
Members:	Rev. Thomas C. Anslow, CM, *Chair* Rev. Phillip J. Brown, SS Rev. Michael Joyce, CM, *ex officio*

Annual Report

The committee members met with Sr. Sharon Euart, Executive Coordinator, and Ms. Katie Richards at the CLSA offices on 17 February 2010 to draft the proposed budget for the CLSA for the fiscal year 2010-2011. The committee succeeded in arriving at a balanced budget to present to the full BOG for its consideration at its April meeting.

The BOG accepted and approved the proposed budget at its April meeting.

During the April BOG meeting, an ad hoc subcommittee consisting of Sr. Lynn McKenzie, OSB, and Fr. Michael Padazinski reviewed the two applications submitted for scholarship awards commencing in the fall of 2010. In approving the budget the BOG decided to award a single scholarship this year. Accepting the recommendation of the ad hoc subcommittee, the BOG voted to award the scholarship to the nominated applicant.

The tenuous economic recovery both at home and abroad and corresponding tenuous financial markets this past year have rewarded a conservative wait-and-see stance regarding the Society's investments, especially since the bulk of the Society's funds were in as safe and prudent hands (Christian Brothers Investment Services) as one could reasonably expect to find.

Once again I take the opportunity to commend both Sister Sharon and Katie for their excellent work in managing our administrative expenses frugally while improving the efficiency of our operations. This good stewardship allowed the committee to arrive at a balanced budget at a time of financial stress and uncertainty. Their efforts in this regard will continue to play a crucial role in the challenging fiscal year to come.

Rev. Thomas C. Anslow, CM

* * * * * * * * * *

Committee: Professional Responsibility

Constituted: Constitution, Article X, as last amended in 1995, and the Code of Professional Responsibilities, canon 9c(1), d(1)

Charge: The mandate of the Committee is:

1. Regarding complaints:

a) To receive complaints of any party aggrieved with respect to provisions of the Code of Professional Responsibility originally adopted by the CLSA in October 1983, and its can. 9d(1)

b) To make an initial finding that the complaint is not frivolous but is serious in character; (and)

c) By majority vote to refer the matter to the hearing officers.

2. To issue advisory opinions and decisions on the application of the Code of Professional Responsibility; (and)

3. To advise on all other questions concerning the professional responsibility of canonists.

Members: Rev. Phillip Brown, SS, *chair*
Very Rev. C. Michael Padazinski, *ex officio*
Rev. Michael Joyce, CM, *ex officio*

Hearing Officers:

Very Rev. William J. King
Rev. Msgr. Frederick C. Easton
Rev. Msgr. Michael A. Souckar

Annual Report

1. There were no reports of professional misconduct or referrals to the Committee during the past year.

2. The Professional Responsibility Committee has been reviewing the existing Code of Professional Responsibility and Statement of Professional Courtesies and the Report of Task Force for the Revision of the Code of Professional Responsibility submitted by its Chair, Melanie De Pietro, S.C., on October 7, 2009 along with a proposed revision of the Code. The Committee continues to work toward developing a recommendation regarding the Report and proposed revisions. The Committee hopes to complete its work in the near future.

Rev. Phillip J. Brown, S.S.

* * * * * * * * * *

COMMITTEE REPORTS

ON-GOING COMMITTEES

Committee: Church Governance
Constituted: 2009
Charge: The mandate of the Committee is:

1. To initiate as needed any projects pertinent to the study of canon law pertaining to Church structures and governance or the implementation thereof, including but not limited to the following:

a) diocesan and parish temporalities;
b) consultative bodies;
c) diocesan and parish structures;
d) power of governance;
e) comparative law issues;
f) inter-ritual matters;
g) Eastern canon law and institutions

2. To oversee projects referred to the committee by the BOG
3. To oversee its subcommittees working on projects concerning Church governance; (and)
4. To collaborate with national organizations and other groups dealing with issues of Church governance.

Members: Rev. Msgr. Daniel F. Hoye, *Chair*
Sr. Ann F. Rehrauer, OSF
Rev. Msgr. Steven J. Raica
Dr. Patricia M. Dugan
Chorbishop John D. Faris

Annual Report

The Committee met at The Hecker Center on April 28-29, 2010. Among the items we wish to report to the membership are the following:

- We recommended that the Committee's mandate be amended slightly so that the wording of section 1.g read "Eastern canon law". We noted that "traditions" are not a component of Eastern canon law.
- At a recent meeting between the CLSA officers and the Congregation for Oriental Churches it was suggested that the Society translate into English the book "Latin Pastor and Oriental Faithful" by Lorenzo Lorusso, OP. A member of the committee, Chorbishop John Faris, was familiar with the book and thought this would be a worthwhile project. He offered to do the translation himself. We have sent our recommendation to the Publication Advisory Board. Included in our recommendation was the thought that poor countries like India be given permission to publish the book but with a restriction on selling it outside their own country.

- We received a proposal from Research and Development suggested by an individual member of the Society to the effect that a pastor of a merging or closing parish be obliged to seek hierarchical recourse. We are recommending that the issue of hierarchical recourse be contained in a publication on the closing and merging of parishes (see below). Moreover, we suggested to the Board of Governors that consideration be given to offering a seminar at the 2011 convention on hierarchical recourse. At the same time, our Committee does not favor making it obligatory for a pastor to appeal a closing or merging of a parish. We noted that oftentimes the pastor is part of the process that results in a closing or merger and while he retains the right to appeal, it may not be something he would want to do in conscience.
- At a recent meeting between the CLSA officers and certain officials of the Apostolic Signatura, the topic of the closing and merging of parishes was discussed. One official suggested that it would be useful to have a modest publication that would summarize the canonical aspects of mergers and closures.
- The committee favors this project in principle and will consult with the Publications Advisory Board when it is more developed.
- The Committee received from the President a resolution from the 2008 Convention that called for the establishment of a third instance tribunal in the United States. The officers talked about this possibility at the Signatura. They were told that while individual requests for a third instance tribunal would be considered, it was not envisioned that an ordinary third instance tribunal be established in the United States. Moreover, our Committee was informally told that the Canonical Affairs and Church Governance Committee of the USCCB had recently considered a request to seek the necessary authorization from the Holy See to establish a third instance tribunal and did not deem it opportune to pursue this at this time.
- Our Committee is also considering the possibility of preparing a publication on consultative bodies.
- On an agenda for a future meeting will be the issue of what can be done by an administrator during a vacancy in a diocese.
- We may also consider research into the role of the Promoter of Justice.

The Committee will meet again during the Convention in Buffalo.

Msgr. Daniel F. Hoye

* * * * * * * * * *

Committee: Clergy
Constituted: 2008
Charge: The mandate of the Committee is:

1. To initiate as needed any projects pertinent to the study of canon law pertaining to the life and ministry of bishops, priests and deacons or the implementation thereof, including, but not limited to, the following:

a) canonical issues related to the sexual abuse of minors

b) clergy personnel issues and resources

c) advocacy for clergy in penal cases

2. To oversee projects referred to the committee by the BOG;

3. To oversee its subcommittees working on projects concerning clergy; (and)

4. To collaborate with national organizations and other groups dealing with clergy issues.

Members: Msgr. Ricardo E. Bass, *Chair*
Rev. Gregory T. Bittner
Rev. Gary D. Yanus
Rev. Daniel J. Ward, OSB
Rev. James I. Donlon

Annual Report

The membership of the Committee was re-constituted in July 2010.

The members will have two conference calls previous to the October Convention and will meet during the time of the Convention. The first order of business will be to share ideas and establish a procedure for the revision of the Clergy Procedural Handbook in coordination with the Publications Advisory Board.

Other items for the committee include: Special Faculties (2009), Revised *Normae de gravioribus delictis* (2010), the practice of appointing priests as administrators of parishes instead of appointing them as pastors, rights and responsibilities of senior (retired) priests.

The Committee for the *Regional Workshops for Advocates in Penal Cases* has completed its work.

Msgr. Ricardo E. Bass

* * * * * * * * * *

Committee:	Convention Planning
Constituted:	2008
Charge:	The mandate of the Committee is: *1. To receive from the Board of Governors the approved general theme of the next convention as well as any suggestions from the Committee on Research & Discussion for the development of the theme;* *2. To recommend to the BOG, in accord with the general theme, topics for major addresses, seminars or other presentations at a future convention, as well as a list of potential speakers and the honoraria for such speakers;* *3. Following BOG approval, to arrange for the speakers, addresses and seminars for the annual convention;* *4. To plan all convention liturgies and prayer services; (and)* *5. To review the evaluations of the most recent Convention and assist the Convention Chairperson in planning future arrangements, as needed.*
Members:	Rev. Patrick J. Cogan, SJ, *Chair* Very Rev. Anthony E. Bawyn Very Rev. Paul J. Hachey, SM Sr. Sharon A. Euart, RSM, *ex officio* Rev. Daniel A. Smilanić, *ex officio* Rev. Michael A. Boccaccio, *General Convention Chairperson* Ms. Barbara Bettwy, *Convention Liturgies Co-chair* Rev. Msgr. Peter Polando, *Convention Liturgies Co-chair*

Annual Report

The committee met at the CLSA office on January 5, 2010. The agenda was focused on three conventions:

1. 2009 – A brief review of the 2009 presentations and speakers.

2. 2010 - A review of the speakers and topics. Some updates were provided. Msgr. James Moroney, who had to withdraw from the 2009 program has been confirmed for the 2010 program with his presentation on the translation of the new sacramentary. With the notice that Archbishop Coccopalmerio from the Pontifical Council for Legislative Texts could not be present for the convention, Bishop Juan Ignacio Arrieta, Secretary of the same pontifical council will deliver the opening address. The appearance of the motu proprio *Anglicanorum coetibus* in October 2009 will likely impact on the seminar on the Pastoral Provision to be presented by Msgr. William Stetson. Since the 2010 convention is a simultaneous convention with the Canadian Canon Law Society, the chair of the Convention Planning Committee will attend the planning session for the Canadian program.

3. 2011 - This principal task of this meeting was to identify speakers and

topics for the previously selected theme "Safeguarding the Rights of the Christian Faithful."

Rev. Patrick Cogan, SA

General Convention Chairperson Report

The Present

Welcome to our 72nd convention, here in Buffalo, NY. This will be a special experience for us, since we and the Canadian Canon Law Society are simultaneously gathering. The interchange, professionally and socially, will be of benefit to all, I am sure.

I wish to thank the volunteers from the local Tribunal and Chancery offices for their valuable help and care. I single out Msgr. David G. LiPuma, Secretary to the Bishop/Vice-Chancellor, Rev. Salvatore Manganello, Judicial Vicar and his Administrative Assistant, Nicole Ball. I also want to thank Julie Chartrand who serves as CCLS Secretary/Treasurer for her assistance to both Katie Richards and me in planning this special convening.

As ever, I am eager to do what I can to facilitate a smooth running of this 2010 convention. May your participation in this convention and your delighting in this unique and attractive corner of the USA that so closely borders Canada be quite rewarding. Make every effort, if possible, to allow yourself extra time beyond/before the convention to get to Niagara Falls ... absolutely spectacular!

FYI: [1] While CLSA has gathered in NY, NY for 10 conventions ['40 - '47, '50 & '63], this is our first convention elsewhere in the state. [2] As a result of our having booked this and the next two Hyatts, CLSA's master bill will be reduced by 5%; our use of hotel points will further a discount. Together, this can mean a minimum savings of $5000.

Upcoming: 2011

2011: As printed in last year's Report Book [pp. 38-39], CLSA will gather in Jacksonville, FL, [Pre] Convention October [9] 10 - 13. This is our first gathering in J'ville; but our 5th in Florida: Miami, '06, Orlando, '80 & '98; & Tampa, '05. We will be at the Hyatt Regency Jacksonville Riverfront, www.jacksonsville.hyatt.com. The hotel, build in 2001, houses 966 rooms within its 19 floors. Room rates are $149 for single, double, triple, quadruple – yes all the same rates! Waterfront view costs more, of course. Within a mere 3 minute waterside walk is Jacksonville Landing with eateries, shops, entertainment venue, etc. [www.jacksonvillelanding.com]. The waterside walk is well lit at night and provides for a lovely stroll. A first for me is an "Ambassador" team, recognizable in their orange T-shirts and straw 'jungle' hats, who go out of their way to assist anyone, especially visitors, with any questions http://downtownjacksonville.org/downtown-vision/ambassadors. A water taxi service, just outside the hotel, is handy and pleasant. Some major upscale restaurants are just across the waterway, e.g., Ruth's Steak House!

Plans were noticeably underway, during my November 2008 visit, to have a walkway connecting J'ville Landing to two other 'center/malls,' i.e., Laura St. StreetScape www.metrojacksonville.com and Hemming Plaza http://downtownjacksonville.org/directory/detail/1594. These other two 'centers' are rather attractive both providing outdoor spaciousness and tempting eateries. The restored Library, now a mini mall, is rather unique.

Immaculate Conception Church [www.immaculateconceptionjax.org] is about a 7 minute walk. It is wheelchair accessible and even has a bookstore. FL is very tax-exempt friendly. If any payment is received via a Diocesan/Institution check or credit card, the tax-exempt policy would be applied, be it for one person or a group.

In time, CLSA will approach the J'ville Tourism Development Council for a grant up to $2000; the Council wants to encourage visitors! Then there's the Hyatt points and 5% rebate, too, all of which will be used to keep costs to a minimum. So, start saving time and money to enjoy this beach side, marvelous and welcoming cities, which by the way, boasts "*At 840 square miles, J'ville is the largest city in the continental USA*."

The Future- 2012 & 2013

2012: Our 74th [pre] convention, October [7] 8 - 11 is at the 'Chicago's' Rosemont Hyatt, which indeed has a 'big city' feel about it, www.rosemontsomethin.com/org! With 1100 rooms and 2 different designs of 10 floors each, there is a 'metropolitan' ambiance, along with a typical Hyatt open air atrium. Across the street is an Expoteria Cafeteria [& that is what it is]. Within a mile radius are the following: two strip malls; entrance to "L" [Chicago's 'subway' - a 35 minute to downtown center]; Stephens' waterfall park leading into a large forest preserve; a feast of fast to fine eateries [e.g., pizza slices, gourmet crab burgers, tossed salads]; etc. Also, in this 1 mile compound one will find a post office, Kinko's/Fed-Ed [one in hotel too], '7/11' convenience, liquor & bakery stores. An eighteen screen 'Muvico' with its 'Bogart' restaurant and a legit Rosemont Theatre are directly across the street.

A trend developing in the area is free van rides to/from local restaurants. Beyond the mile are drug, gift, book, grocery & department stores [read: taxi or hotel van]. Best 'future' projection for the immediate RH area is a Fashion Outlet Mall, 2012 is earliest opening. Convention attendees would be able to locate it from hotel windows. More info: www.rosemont.com. A casino is expected to be opened in the neighboring Des Plaines about 1.5 miles away. Finally, there are pre-Chicago stops on the "L" where one will find more eateries, malls, entertainment, etc.

The local [and only] Church is 1.5 miles away, Our Lady of Hope – hence transportation is necessitated, if convention Mass is celebrated there. It is a unique and lovely modern designed 'Romanesque' building, www.ourladyofhopechurch.com.

Room rate is $158 for single, double, triple, quadruple. Pricey? Yes, but this is a BIG city; also, review some concessions: [1] 10% discount for hotel restaurants, not in-room service; [2] tax exempt policy applicable to payment made by a Diocese/Institution; [3] O'Hare, perhaps USA's busiest airport, means inexpensive and frequent flights; [4] free to/from airport shuttle service – hardly a 10 minute ride; [5] free shuttle van service to/from any mall within 1 mile; [6] Visitors' Convention Bureau is arranging for a discount voucher program. Considering, then, being in the outer circle of a major city, we have a bargain! FYI: We have held conventions in Chicago itself: '51, '65 & '81. Rosemont is our 4th visit to IL.

2013: CLSA holds its 75th convention in Sacramento, CA; [Pre] Convention is October [12] 13 - 16. Once more we shall be at a Hyatt Regency www.sacramento.hyatt.com. A little background: During its October 15, 2009 Louisville meeting, BOG assigned me to "Go West" for 2013. There was a total of 15 proposals received from CA, NV, UT and AZ; the 15 became 6, because of price, distance from airport, isolation, travel accessibility, not tax-exempt friendly, calendar, etc. For the same reasons the 6 became 4, then 2, i.e., a Hilton and a Hyatt in Sacramento.

Part of my June 7, 2010 report to Past/Present/Future Presidents and to Executive Coordinator reads: "*The Hilton is located in the middle of an industrial park. The nearest eateries, shops, etc. are in Arden Fair Mall, a 20 minute walk, under the freeway; nearest church is about 2 miles. The Hyatt, recently renovated, is located directly across the street from the State Capital, which has a very picturesque park. Blessed Sacrament Cathedral is a 3-5 minute diagonal walk from the hotel www.cathedralsacramento.org – a fine building. Within a 2-block walk are many eateries. "K" street, adjacent to the hotel, is now a pedestrian mall going East to West. It travels through a Westfield Shopping Mall www.westfield.com/downtownplaza and directly into Old Sacramento – a tourist's 'must,' www.oldsacramento.com. Paralleling Old S'mento and going beyond – endlessly it seemed – is a promenade walkway along the river. I have never been to S'mento before; I was pleasantly surprised; it is an appealing, clean place.*"

In other words, it was a 'no-brainer'! But more than that, it is a financial investment, since Hyatt now sees us as a 'regular' customer. Among the benefits: [1] 20% – not 10% – discount for in house [not in room] meals; [2] $5/rebate to master account on ALL paid room nights, which alone could approach $6000; [3] Double points to use toward billing; etc. A further factor in choosing the Hyatt over the Hilton – round trip airport shuttle to Hilton is $32; to Hyatt, $24, since it is 3 miles closer! Room rate: $149/night single or double; $174, triple; $194 quadruple ... and as always, taxes.

The hotel, built in 1988, has 15 floors and 503 rooms, so CLSA could be the major occupant, please God! This will be our 7th visit to California [Los Angeles '59, San Francisco '64 & '83, San Diego '75, La Jolla '97 and Orange County '07]. To return to my comments about Sacramento: it is a lovely city in its own right, with so much within a 5 minute walk. On the west of the hotel is Old

Sacramento ... again, 'a MUST'; there may not be enough time to walk it, visit its museums, different shops, eateries, etc. The very clean Capital park, across the street, provides very attractive and restful settings and sittings! I believe our convention attendees will enjoy this city.

Conclusion

CLSA's next 3 convention sites provide very exciting and different environments. Ranging from the Atlantic Ocean shore of Florida to the banks of the California's Sacramento River, stopping along the way in 'the windy city, Chicago', variety and vibrancy await us. As ever, please know how eagerly I welcome your input and involvement; let alone being able to assist and serve you as General Convention Chair.

Rev. Michael Boccaccio

Convention Liturgies

The Co-Chairs of the committee attended the June 22 Convention Planning Meeting at the Hyatt Regency Buffalo, site of the 2010 convention. The following issues were decided at this meeting:

1. The opening prayer service on Monday and the cathedral liturgy on Wednesday afternoon will be jointly celebrated by both the CLSA and the CCLS. The two celebrations will incorporate French as well as English. Specifically, the cathedral liturgy will include a reading in French, the intercessions in French and English, and part of the Eucharistic Prayer in French. The homily will be in French and English.

2. The CLSA will have liturgies in English at a designated area of the hotel on Sunday, Monday, Tuesday and Thursday. The CCLS will have liturgies in French in another designated area of the hotel on Tuesday and Thursday. The English and French liturgies will be celebrated simultaneously at 7:30 AM on Tuesday and Thursday. The CLSA liturgy committee will provide the items needed for the celebration of the liturgies except for the French Sacramentary, Lectionary, and hymnals that will be provided by the CCLS.

3. The officers of both societies will be installed after the homily at the cathedral liturgy on Wednesday afternoon. The CLSA liturgy committee will work out the details.

4. The larger liturgical space in the hotel will be configured as last year with a "sacristy" and chairs arranged to encourage good community celebration.

5. Specific needs were addressed with the personnel from Diocese of Buffalo regarding music ministers and the liturgy at the Cathedral.

Monsignors David LiPuma and Sal Manganello have been more than generous in offering their resources and assistance for all the liturgical details.

The Co-Chairs are in regular communication as the final preparations for the convention liturgies are being worked out. The committee is especially interested in incorporating some of the local culture, specifically from the Iroquois Confederacy, in the gathering prayer.

Ms. Barbara Bettwy

* * * * * * * * * *

Committee:	Institutes of Consecrated and Apostolic Life
Constituted:	2009
Charge:	The mandate of the Committee is: *1. To initiate as needed any projects pertinent to the study of canon law pertaining to the life and ministry of Institutes of Consecrated and Apostolic Life of the implementation thereof, including, but not limited to, the following:* *a. sponsorship;* *b. mergers and restructuring of institutes;* *c. governance;* *d. membership;* *e. new forms of consecrated life.* *2. To oversee projects referred to the committee by the BOG;* *3. To oversee its subcommittees working on projects concerning Consecrated and Apostolic Life; (and)* *4. To collaborate with national organizations and other groups dealing with issues of Consecrated and Apostolic Life.*
Members:	Sr. Mary Catherine Wenstrup, OSB, *Chair* Sr. Dominica Brennan, OP Sr. Sharon L. Holland, IHM Rev. Kevin W. Niehoff, OP Br. Patrick T. Shea, OFM

Annual Report

The committee was formed this past summer. Currently we are in the process of sending a survey to members of CLSA regarding ways the committee can be of service to the members. The results will assist the committee in fulfilling its mandate.

Sr. Mary Catherine Wenstrup, OSB

* * * * * * * * * *

Committee: Laity
Constituted: 2009
Charge: The mandate of the committee is:

1. To initiate as needed any projects pertinent to the study of canon law pertaining to the life and ministry of lay persons of the implementation thereof, including, but not limited to, the following:

a. lay ecclesial ministry;
b. collaboration with clergy;
c. rights of the lay faithful

2. To oversee projects referred to the committee by the BOG;
3. To oversee its subcommittees working on projects concerning the laity;
4. To collaborate with national organizations and other groups dealing with the role of the laity in the Church.

Members: Ms. Zabrina R. Decker, *Chair*
Mrs. Mary C. Edlund
Rev. Msgr. James M. Sheehan
Mr. Jay M. Conzemius
Mr. Mark L. Raper

Annual Report

The committee met in June in Milwaukee. Two project ideas surfaced from this meeting.

We are exploring ways to support and mentor lay canonists graduating from the various schools of canon law, especially those who are not sponsored by an archdiocese/diocese. This could take many forms but one discussed was a summer internship. In this way, the student would receive practical experience in the workings of a diocese so that they would have greater level of success once hired.

The second project surrounds a certification program for secretaries in parishes and others who are responsible for sacramental record keeping (i.e. archivists). It would be a very practical explanation of how and why we retain what we retain and how and why we annotate…etc. The committee would work with the Publications Advisory Board to determine the best publishing format.

Thank you for your support.

Zabrina Decker

* * * * * * * * * *

Committee: Publications Advisory Board
Constituted: Board of Governors, 2007; revised in 2008, assumes the responsibilities of the following committees: Canon Law

	Digest, Roman Replies, Advisory Opinions, Electronic Media
Charge:	The mandate of the committee is: *1. To advise the BOG about all aspects of current, periodic and proposed CLSA publication projects, including financial, literary, educational and marketing issues;* *2. To monitor the progress of all CLSA publication projects;* *3. To implement the procedures for peer review of CLSA publications;* *4. To review the coordination and management of the CLSA's publications activity on the part of the Office of the Executive Coordinator; (and)* *5. To provide a written report to the CLSA membership at the annual convention.*
Members:	Rev. Msgr. John A. Alesandro, *Chair* Very Rev. Lawrence DiNardo Very Rev. Paul B. R. Hartmann Rev. Msgr. Kevin E. McKenna Dr. Barbara Anne Cusack, *ex officio* Rev. Patrick Cogan, *Canon Law Digest Chair* Rev. Msgr. Frederick Easton, *Canon Law Digest* Mr. William Daniel, *Canon Law Digest*

Annual Report

During the past year, the members met in person and by conference call at the Convention in Louisville, Kentucky, and carried on discussion throughout the year by e-mail and conference call. A 24-hour meeting scheduled for July 2010 at the CLSA office in Washington was cancelled because of unavoidable schedule conflicts. In lieu of the summer meeting, the members agreed to meet in the morning and afternoon of October 11, 2010, prior to the start of the Convention in Buffalo. The chair also attended the BOG meetings in January and April, 2010, to offer progress reports on publications.

CLSA Budget

PAB's participation in drafting the FY 2011 budget (7/1/2010-6/30/11) followed the previous year's process and seemed to go well again. PAB's assumptions were presented to the CLSA Finance Committee in February and to the BOG in April.

1. The current year saw little in the way of new publications. Most of the revenue came from existing publications. During the next fiscal year, however, it is anticipated that *Rotal Jurisprudence* and *Canon Law Digest 14* will become available for sale, leading PAB to recommend an increase in the book sales and book production estimates.

2. In April PAB recommended to the Executive Coordinator to use

the following assumptions for the Publications Portion of the FY2011 budget:

	2010 budget	6-mo. actuals	2011 budget
INCOME			
Book Sales:	$65,000	$46,000	$90,000
Additional Income:	$29,000	$14,000	$25,400
Total Income:	$94,000	$60,000	$115,400
EXPENSES			
Book Production:	$25,000	$5,250	$40,000
BrightKey/Office:	$62,700	$29,300	$62,900
Total Expenses:	$87,700	$34,550	$102,900

3. Timetable for the budget process: The finance committee meets in Washington in February. Prior to that, after the first six months of experience, PAB examines the following to develop a projection for the next fiscal year:
   - the six-month report of sales and inventory
   - a discussion with the Executive Coordinator about the status of all pending publications
   - information from the BOG meeting and the chair of R&D (an ex officio member of PAB) about the activity of the committees and what publications we can anticipate from them for the next fiscal year.

Inventory

Consolidation of Inventory

PAB continues to monitor and manage the inventory, reducing it where there is little likelihood of additional sales of any significance, in order to consolidate the volumes into fewer pallets and thereby reducing the monthly storage expenses. In August and September the chair met with the executive coordinator and the auditor to review such decisions.

Individual Texts in Inventory

- Translation of the Latin Code
  - This is a major item of discussion for PAB. Inventory analysis shows that the volumes will be depleted in two years.
  - In preparation for a decision about reprinting, the following information and items are being addressed:
    - Ongoing review of sales and current stock
    - Abrogations and other changes made in the Latin Code since promulgation
    - Corrections needed in translation
    - Anticipated changes in the near future.

        - Content of appendices.
        - The size of the reprinting: how many volumes and whether hardback or soft cover or both.
        - Timetable of steps to be taken to accomplish this project.
    - Suggestions from the CLSA members will be gratefully received regarding the above points.
- *Eastern Code*: Efforts continue to be made to reduce this inventory, which currently stands at around 2,300 volumes.
- *Advisory Opinions Collections*: Volume 2 is depleted. The next volume will cover *Advisory Opinions* from 2006 to 2010. These collections have sold well, but a decision must be made about this series before the next volume is due (2011). Right now the second volume of the three is out of print and unavailable. One possibility: put the volumes on a CD as was done with *American Jurisprudence.*
- *RR&AO & Proceedings*: PAB recommended that *Roman Replies & Advisory Opinions* should appear on the CLSA website, including volumes up to the year 2000. The same strategy should be applied to the annual *Proceedings.* As of March 2010, volumes *1983-2000* of out-of-print *Proceedings* have been put on the website. The next stage is to do the same with volumes of *RR&AO* up to year 1996.
- *Canonical Standards for Parish*. This publication, which is now out-of-print, is still in demand. As of March 2010 it has been placed on the website and has already generated revenue in that format.
- *Clergy Handbook*: This work is out-of-print, but there is a regular demand for it. This situation is currently under consideration by the Clergy Committee in consultation with PAB and the Executive Coordinator.
- *American Jurisprudence*: This work, which offers decisions from American tribunals, is now out-of-print. It will be placed on a CD and sold in that format by the CLSA office.

Shipping and Handling

New rates for S&H have been put into effect this past year and will be reviewed by PAB at its next meeting. PAB has also worked with the CLSA office to set up a limited use of an *Amazon* account as a pilot project to see whether some sales can be handled directly out of the office. At the moment, this has been limited to five or six selected titles. After review, this experiment may be expanded in the future to assist in marketing CLSA publications worldwide.

Roman Replies & Advisory Opinions

The Executive Coordinator's office worked with PAB this year to solicit and coordinate the publication of replies and other relevant documents issued by the Apostolic See as well as a series of interesting opinions from members of the

Society on specific canonical questions.

Canon Law Digest

CLD 14 is progressing nicely under the editorship of Pat Cogan. He has noted the improvement in obtaining texts thanks to the availability of many of the documents on-line. The CD put together by Bill Woestman of volumes 1-12 has been selling well.

Rotal Jurisprudence

The project to translate sixteen Rotal decisions has been continuing. It is anticipated that the book will be completed within the current fiscal year. Further details on the project can be found in the separate report by the editor of this work.

Pastoral Resources

PAB has been discussing the idea of the CLSA's publication of a series of "pastoral resources" that would bring canonical expertise into the wider audience of the Church: particularly, parish priests, lay ecclesial ministers, pastoral staffs, and parish volunteers. There is a real need for concise summations of the law with good interpretations that apply the norms to everyday life in the church. This is a concrete goal that various committees of the CLSA are pursuing. PAB is hoping to list topics that might be addressed from a canonical perspective (e.g., parish pastoral councils; parish finance councils; role of the parochial vicar; duties of the vicar forane; the vacant see – to name a few). The idea is to develop brief publications, perhaps fifty pages or so in length, that could be printed in paperback and could be widely marketed, to CLSA members and many others.

Publication Protocol

At the Buffalo Convention PAB will be reviewing a recommended protocol for all CLSA publications that includes the following.

1. PAB will review all proposed publications at an early stage to make a recommendation to the BOG about the proposed concept. The main purpose of such a review is to determine that the concept of the proposed work is appropriate for the CLSA to publish.

2. Once the proposal is approved in principle, the author/editor must submit the manuscript to the EC and PAB in *Word for Windows* (a format that will permit the EC to build up an electronic database of all publications).

3. PAB will arrange for peer review of the manuscript during its development or, at the latest, at the point of receiving the entire manuscript. (Sometimes, peer review will be done piecemeal, especially when the book consists of various articles or discrete

chapters.)

4. PAB will interact with the EC and make recommendations to the EC about the usual elements of publication such as formatting, size of the book, design of the cover. All such technical decisions will be made by the EC in consultation with PAB.

Future Meetings

PAB has been accomplishing its mandate with a minimum of expenditures. It is monitoring all publications, working closely with the CLSA office on all aspects of publication, making recommendations, when needed, to the Executive Coordinator and the BOG and interacting with the R&D committee about activities that may result in publications. PAB's schedule during the current year will be as follows

5. Meeting of PAB with Executive Coordinator on Monday, October 11, 2010, 9:00 a.m. to 3:00 p.m. All members will participate.
6. Chair's Report at the BOG meetings in January and April.
7. Conference Call in February to discuss budget assumptions for the next fiscal year.
8. Summer meeting to review all activities: date and place to be determined

If members of the CLSA have comments or suggestions about the Society's publication activity, please feel free to communicate with any of the members of PAB, all of whose contact information can be found on the CLSA website.

Msgr. John Alesandro

Canon Law Digest Report

The preparation of Canon Law Digest 14 (1996-2000) is now in the final stages. All entries have been collected and entered into the computer. Presently the entries are being proof-read and the bibliographical citations are being verified. This is a very detailed process, but moves forward steadily. Once these editorial tasks are finalized, the index will be prepared by a professional indexer. Once the index has been completed, then the project can be sent for printing. It is anticipated that the text will be ready for printing and distribution by December 2010. Once again, appreciation is extended to Saint Paul University, Ottawa for its generous grant for the preparation of this volume.

With the increasing availability of documentation on the internet, their retrieval and downloading are greatly facilitated. The Committee continues to have need of at least one more member. Efforts to recruit a new member have not been successful thus far. The members assist in the identification of entries and to review their editorial preparation.

Rev. Patrick J. Cogan, SA

* * * * * * * * * *

Committee:	Research and Development
Constituted:	2008
Charge:	The mandate of this Committee is as follows: *1. To initiate or cooperate in all CLSA research projects such as seminars, symposia and special studies;* *2. To design and implement Think Tanks that will allow for diverse views on issues of ecclesial life having canonical implications;* *3. To develop and recommend themes for the annual Conventions for submission to the Board of Governors for approval and subsequent referral to the Convention Planning Committee for implementation;* *4. To maintain close communication with all the committees of the Society in order to facilitate needed research and discussion; (and)* *5. To interact with the Publications Advisory Board in order to assess the current and contemplated publications of the CLSA and offer suggestions and guidance for publication planning.*
Members:	Dr. Barbara Anne Cusack, *Chair* Very Rev. Patrick R. Lagges Rev. Robert W. Oliver Rev. John P. Beal Rev. Michael P. Joyce, CM, *ex officio*

Annual Report

The R&D Committee referred the following projects to other CLSA Committees in October 2009:

- The *Bonum Coniugum* Project: The Marriage Research Committee originally proposed this project for a publication, listing articles that would illustrate various aspects of the use of *bonum coniugum* as a ground of nullity. This project was referred to the chair of the Sacramental Law Committee.
- *Clergy Procedural Handbook*: This publication has been useful to members but is currently out of date and does not include important developments of the last ten years. The updating of this handbook was referred to the chair of the Committee on Clergy.

A research proposal was forwarded to the R&D Committee concerning the right to, and obligation of, hierarchical recourse by a pastor for his parish when the parish is proposed for suppression or merger. In searching for the ecclesiological basis for the relationship between a priest and his bishop, some Ordinaries have suggested that if a pastor were to lodge such recourse, it would constitute the delict of non-cooperation with the ministry of the Ordinary. Other opinions hold that, as administrator of a juridic person presumed to be perpetual, a pastor would have a responsibility to seek recourse against any such decree. It was decided by the R&D Committee that this topic should be expanded to include research into the whole concept of hierarchical recourse. It was further recommended that the research proposal be submitted to an existing committee for research consideration. In January 2010, it was sent to the Chair of the Church Governance Committee.

The R&D Committee had been asked by the PAB to conduct a survey of teachers of canon law to ascertain what published materials would be of benefit to them. The survey was prepared and posted on the CLSA website with the expert assistance of Katie Richards. Thirty respondents completed the survey. The R&D chair has organized the data received and sent it to the committee members and the PAB chair. Further analysis will need to be completed prior to a referral report to PAB for their October meeting.

The BOG referred a resolution from the 2009 Convention to the R&D Committee. The resolution calls for the organization of a Think Tank to recommend changes to the Code of Canon Law. This resolution and the supporting discussion report from the 2009 *CLSA Proceedings* have been distributed to the R&D committee members. Preliminary reactions and ideas are being generated by e-mail among the members.

Barbara Ann Cusack

* * * * * * * * *

Committee:	Sacramental Law
Constituted:	2008
Charge:	The mandate of this Committee is as follows: *1. To initiate as needed any projects pertinent to the study of canon law pertaining to the sacramental life of the Church or the implementation thereof;* *2. To oversee projects referred to the committee by the BOG;* *3. To oversee its subcommittees working on projects concerning the sacramental life of the Church;* *4. To offer suggestions to the BOG for marriage topics for pre-convention workshops; (and)* *5. To collaborate with national organizations and other groups dealing with the sacramental life of the Church.*
Members:	Sr. Victoria Vondenberger, RSM, *Chair* Rev. John J.M. Foster Ms. M. Margaret Gillett Rev. Bruce Miller Rev. Mark A. Plewka Rev. Michael A. Vigil

Annual Report

Regarding # 1 of the mandate, the SLC continues the project initiated by the Marriage Research Committee to publish English translations of rotal sentences. The chair of the committee is serving as editor working with three rotal auditors and fifteen translators. In May 2010, the BOG urged that priority be given to the publication of the English translation of Rotal Sentences. As of this August 2010 report,

- All 16 sentences/decrees have been translated. Each one was reviewed by a second translator who made suggestions about possible improvement.
- All 16 have been sanitized to remove identifying names and places. All sixteen have been edited for compliance with the CLSA style sheet.
- 3 are waiting to be put into book format for another review by the editor.
- 1 is ready but has not yet been sent to be formatted until the others are finished.
- 1 with translator for review before going to the rotal auditor. [A second sentence was at this stage however, I went ahead and sent the translation to the rotal auditor before the August break in Rome although I did not yet have corrections from the translator.]
- 6 are with rotal auditors for review and any changes.
- 2 await incorporation of the changes sent by rotal auditors.
- 3 are ready for publication.

Results of a previous suggestion: the SLC report in the 2009 convention booklet indicated that the committee suggested to the BOG that the Code might be divided among the various committees of CLSA with the SLC responsible for canons 840-1165 or the whole of book IV to gather specific suggestions from members of CLSA for revision of the Code as requested by the Pontifical Council For Legislative Texts, paying particular attention to the PCLT's request to fill *lacunae*. In a letter dated 3 Feb. 2010 the committee was pleased to be commended by the BOG for being so active. The same letter informed the committee that the BOG created a committee from its own membership to determine how to proceed with the request from PCLT. The SLC was told not to act on this matter until directed otherwise by the BOG. No such BOG direction about this was received by the SLC.

Regarding # 1 of the mandate, SLC members considered issues for research and possible publication.

We think that some of these ideas may evolve into smaller publications such as booklets rather than full books. It would be good to have publications include academic research and practical experience so we may want to find two authors for each issue or topic. Some of the academics who need to "publish or perish" may not be working in tribunals or parishes and some of those in the vineyard may not have easy access to libraries.

1. How to write a good sentence

This could be related to issues about publication particularly if a copy of the Sentence is given to the parties. Some tribunals have the published Sentence and then a much longer judicial memo sent with it to second instance which argues the case in much more detail. Does that violate procedural law? *Studia canonica* 2008-2 had an article by Bill Daniel about publication of the Sentence.

Discuss moral certitude, what is needed, how to achieve it, and the Allocution to the Rota in 1942 by Pius XII.

Discuss publication of the acts especially regarding expert opinions and related issues. If civil law prevents sharing these reports with the parties, can they be used in the Sentence published to the parties? If the tribunal has the acts of a case evaluated by an expert, do not the parties have a right to review that evaluation?

2. RCIA issues

Advice is sometimes requested by those who accept candidates to the RCIA program about how to find out about previous marriages which may prevent a person now in an irregular marriage situation from becoming Catholic. Should a person be admitted to RCIA if there is no hope of regularizing a current civil union?

Do those who are to be baptized make an auricular confession of their sins before baptism (see 1988 document # 461; 1974 # 342 and 1988 # 303) without receiving absolution since baptism entails the forgiveness of actual sins? Canon 11 says ecclesiastical law applies only to the baptized but catechumens and the elect are governed by Church law. Do the three scrutinies replace confession of sins? If so, what about dispensations from scrutinies (1974 - # 66 and 1988 #

34.3 not included in later documents)? What is the canonical and/or liturgical basis for any response? Is there enough experience since 1977 that a thorough canonical review now would be appropriate? Consider canon 865 §1, Navarre commentary and 1890 response of the Holy Office, the 1974 (# 25) general instruction and the 1988 (#141) RCIA document. Is our committee the right one in CLSA to do/oversee this research and publication?

Would it be useful to have an actual survey of US dioceses about current RCIA practices related to marriage situations? Informally, some folks report people being baptized or received into the Church with no remedy for irregular marriage situations.

3. New bishops

What appointments need to be made by a new diocesan bishop? Include a check list. A source is in the back of the Directory for the Pastoral Ministry of Bishops, *Apostelorum Successores.* Several questions about this came to the SLC Chair but would this research and publication be for our committee or another? (The list requested by the committee from the BOG – see the end of # 3 below – about which canons are covered by which committees would have been helpful here!)

4. Sacramental record keeping:

Discuss problems and solutions. Include evaluations of storing such information in computers.

5. How to begin a marriage case

Present ideas about providing assistance to help people write formal petitions; describe information about various tools used to gather information (perhaps including Bruce Miller's use of a marriage assessment tool to determine grounds for nullity).

Advocacy: information about field advocates, procurator/advocates, people in parishes who help people present cases and how to train them, how to use them, etc.

6. Right of defense

Focus this on marriage cases especially for non-cooperating respondents and include information about the absent respondent, needed reasons for declaring absence, (Is hostility a solid reason?) grounds focused on an absent respondent, etc. [Perhaps combine this with the previous topic regarding initial assistance for petitioners determining what kind of case is needed and appropriate grounds for nullity.]

7. Baptism

May those who are not validly married in the Church be godparents? It is very important for Hispanics who is named godparent since the civil courts look to that person for custody if the parents are killed. There is difficulty in regularizing marriages in some states because many local jurisdictions require a valid form of ID and many states will not issue drivers licenses to undocumented immigrants so they cannot obtain civil marriage licenses. Clerics are very cautious about witnessing marriages without civil licenses keeping in mind Canon 22 and deferring to civil law. Related issues?

8. Appeal concerns

Explain issues around appeal to second instance and third instance by the defender or a party, challenge of sentence, plaints of nullity...what can be appealed, who may appeal, time limits for appeal, differences if appealed by a party or the defender of the bond.

Vetita and *monita*: the need for confirmation of these since *Dignitas Connubii,* procedures for imposing these cautions or restrictions and proceeding after they are placed.

9. Appeals to the Rota

This should include what to do about a respondent who just wants to hinder the petitioner moving on in life. Include how to file, how to communicate with Rome noting CLSA newsletter (Sept. 2008, Pat Lagges) item saying that a party must ask that the case be moved forward unlike appeals according to law to ordinary second instance, etc. Who may appeal and what may be appealed?

10. Eastern law

Include defects of form for the Orthodox, Eastern marriage law and its interaction with the Latin Church

11. Impotence

Research this impediment especially in light of recently developed medications: viagra, cialis, etc. Is it still an impediment if the condition can be remedied by medication or surgery or implants? What if penetration is possible but conception is impossible? [One of the rotal Sentences soon to be published in English translation is related to this issue.]

12. Condition

Good information about this ground for nullity may increase use of it in marriage cases. Include practical checklists indicating what to look for in a case.

13. Long marriages

Discuss handling cases for long marriages. Some tribunals question whether they can accept cases when the married life was say 30 or 45 years; some even informally tell priests not to submit those cases for long marriages.

After receiving this list of items the committee thought would be worthy of research and publication, the BOG responded in May 2010 that as the committee considers various topics to research, it should submit them as they are developed to the BOG. If the Board decides that the topic and its development can be possibly published, it will refer the matter to the Publications Advisory Board. The PAB will then determine how to proceed in consultation with the Office of the Executive Coordinator and the BOG.

Regarding # 2 of the mandate, no projects were referred to the SLC by the BOG since the 2009 convention. In May 2010 the BOG mentioned a *Bonum Coniugum* Project that had been referred to the Committee by the Research and Development Committee. No such referral was received by this committee. Current committee members know that before several of us were involved as members of the previous Marriage Research Committee, there was some discussion of possible research about the *bonum coniugum* as a ground for nullity. Since that time there have been several presentations at regional conventions and at the national convention which offered research on that topic.

Regarding # 3 of the mandate, there has been confusion for the committee. Before the January 2010 BOG meeting the SLC asked whether the committee mandate covers everything in Book IV of the Code which would include parts II and III beyond sacraments *per se.* A response in February from the BOG said that we are not to consider matters that involve liturgical law. If such issues arise, the BOG said it will determine the committee best suited to work on the matter. Since several sacraments necessarily involve liturgical law, the committee faces some confusion. There has been some informal contact with members of the BOG but no official response about that concern.

Regarding # 3 of the mandate, the SLC asked the BOG in April 2010 to consider dividing the canons of the Code among the existing committees so that CLSA members will know to whom to address suggestions for research or concerns as ideas arise. Such division of the canons could also alert the BOG if there are areas of law not being addressed in our structure since FIP went into place. In a response in May 2010, the committee learned that the BOG decided not to accept the suggestion. The board concluded that such an action would not allow the flexibility that currently exists for the BOG and the committees of CLSA to respond to various situations.

Regarding # 4 of the mandate, the committee offered detailed suggestions for a pre-convention workshop. Specific content for six sessions was suggested along with possible presenters. The SLC suggested that the presenters, prior to the workshop, question working canonists from a variety of tribunals (large urban as well as small rural in different parts of the country) to gather varied suggestions for fulfilling procedural requirements.

Due to the wonderful offer of Msgr. Punderson to present a workshop about defending the bond, the suggestion presented below was not considered for 2010. If there is interest, the proposed format could be considered for 2011. Here is a draft of a possible publicity blurb:

Sticky Issues in Tribunal Practice *...and some suggested solutions*

The workshop will address recurring issues related to the processing of marriage nullity cases. The presentations will focus on developments in procedural law especially after the promulgation of *Dignitas Connubii*. The presenters will suggest solutions, based on careful study coupled with creativity and practical experience, to some of the issues that arise as cases are processed. Opportunities will be given to those attending also to propose issues and offer solutions. Networking often is the most valuable part of these pre-convention workshops especially when the format raises key issues and begins the process of finding possible solutions

The SLC asks that members of CLSA let the committee chair know if they would be interested in such a workshop and also if they have other suggestions for a pre-convention workshop related to sacraments or tribunal ministry. Please send your responses to victoriav@catholiccincinnati.org. Please also feel free to indicate your interest in being a possible presenter for such workshops.

Regarding # 5 of the committee mandate, the SLC identified the following organizations for collaboration: Federation of Diocesan Liturgical Commissions, National Association of Pastoral Musicians, North American Forum on the Catechumenate, National Catholic Cemetery Conference, Association for Consultants of Liturgical Space, Form/Reform, and the USCCB Committee on Divine Worship We were advised by the BOG that the committee may make informal contact in our own name but any formal collaboration must be approved by the BOG. If members of CLSA have additional suggestions of groups with whom this committee of CLSA could network regarding sacramental life/law, please tell a member of the committee or e-mail ideas to the Chair of the committee victoriav@catholiccincinnati.org.

Sr. Victoria Vondenberger, RSM, JCL

TRIBUNAL STATISTICS 2009

Since 1975, the CLSA has published Tribunal Statistics annually in *Proceedings*. These statistics are provided voluntarily by participating tribunal offices in the United States. Beginning next year, the CLSA will be requesting tribunals to submit copies of the annual report each tribunal submits to the Apostolic Signatura, rather than using custom statistics forms. This change is being made to help establish greater consistency between yearly reports and to make it easier for tribunals to provide this information.

For 2009, 88% of tribunals contacted provided statistical information. The tribunals of Albany, Atlanta, Baltimore, Boston, Denver, Fort Wayne-South Bend, Las Vegas, Lubbock, Miami, New Orleans, the eparchy of Newton, Philadelphia, Phoenix, San Francisco, Santa Fe, the eparchy of St. Maron of Brooklyn, Tucson, Tulsa, the eparchy of Van Nuys, Washington DC, Wichita, and Winona did not participate.

In first instance, an analysis of totals for each category since 2006 shows a gradual decline in the number of cases being presented and decisions being made. Conversely, the total expenses reported indicates a gradual increase while the amount of fees received is a slight decline.

Second instance statistics are also provided for 2009. Some discrepancies are apparent due to variations in appellate court structure and reporting practices.

2006-2009 First Instance Data

The chart below reflects total data reported for the last four years.

Year	Documentary Cases	Formal Cases (Previous Yr)	Formal Cases (This Year)	Cases Abated	Formal Decisions	Fees Received	Diocesan Subsidy	Total Expenses	Percent of tribunals reporting
2009	12239	17457	19039	1846	17106	$4,980,461	$26,104,591	$31,123,946	88.11%
2008	14089	18704	19805	2002	18503	$5,551,648	$26,434,692	$32,465,062	88.11%
2007	12593	19168	19864	2451	18644	$5,411,389	$25,444,135	$30,950,916	86.49%
2006	14246	20466	21850	2603	20117	$6,109,704	$22,381,454	$27,936,716	86.49%

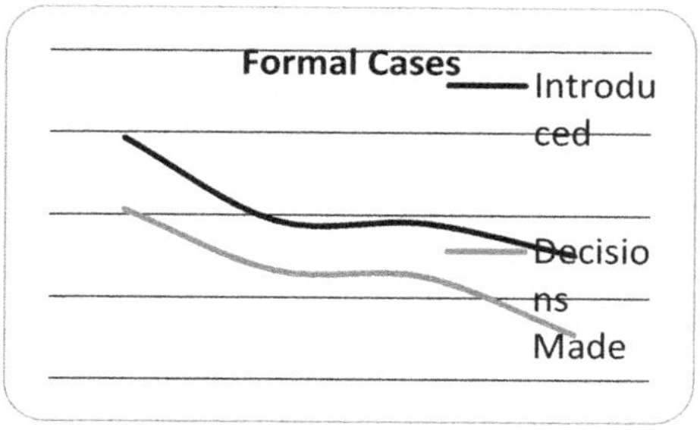

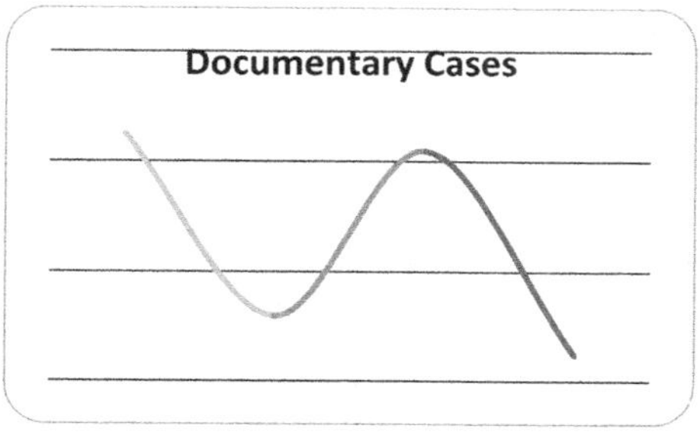

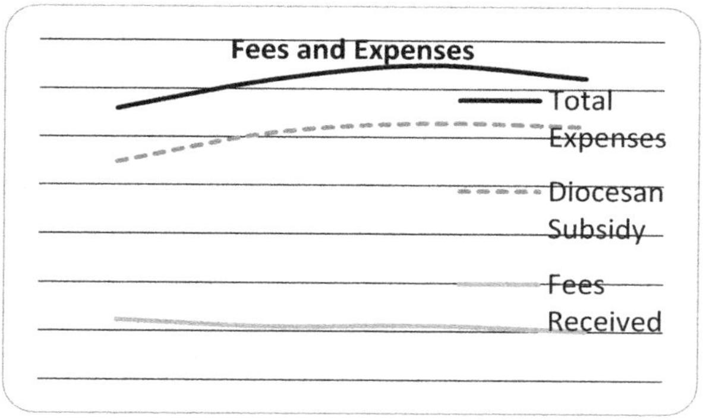

****

Tribunal Statistics 2009: First Instance Tribunals by (Arch)Diocese

Arch/Diocese	Documentary Cases	Formal Cases (Previous Yr.)	Formal Cases (This Year)	Cases Abated	Formal Decisions	Fees Received	Diocesan Subsidy	Total Expenses
Alexandria	0	81	55	1	42	$8,947	$155,638	$164,585
Allentown	99	241	168	27	141	$61,945	$325,793	$387,738
Altoona-Johnstown	6	60	71	10	101	$1,200	$65,475	$60,000
Amarillo	36	3	41	0	45	$9,200	$26,500	$35,750
Anchorage	31	38	39	0	33	$12,775	$60,211	$72,986
Arlington	267	246	227	3	219	$78,023	$351,022	$429,993
Austin	194	130	210	15	185	$48,321	$264,136	$314,252
Baker	8	112	48	48	37	$8,920	$95,777	$104,697
Baton Rouge	11	128	134	10	117	$46,825	$250,448	$297,273
Beaumont	71	114	72	10	71	$25,660	$156,121	$181,781

Arch/Diocese	Documentary Cases	Formal Cases (Previous Yr.)	Formal Cases (This Year)	Cases Abated	Formal Decisions	Fees Received	Diocesan Subsidy	Total Expenses
Belleville	42	87	62	7	60	$19,105	$92,295	$111,400
Biloxi	66	99	62	11	23	$3,645	$125,604	$123,806
Birmingham, Alabama	50	59	68	7	54	$18,630	$135,970	$149,247
Bismarck	35	47	37	4	47	$12,072	$192,104	$204,176
Boise	114	85	129		96	$28,395	$142,706	$171,101
Bridgeport	1	38	64	3	71	$25,886	$428,183	$424,164
Brooklyn	268	200	77	81	116	$127,600	$230,000	$350,000
Brownsville	180	91	85	22	76			
Buffalo	86	38	129	0	128	$62,357	$203,632	$265,990
Burlington	0	69	52	3	47			
Camden	0	97	62	8	42			
Charleston	89	66	82	6	110	$62,391	$300,148	$362,539
Charlotte	221	147	142	5	159	$78,308	$364,709	$443,017
Cheyenne	7	50	61	8	59	$36,000	$116,000	$152,000
Chicago	29	390	427	19	452			
Cincinnati	234	203	291	17	222	$75,365	$417,008	$514,012
Cleveland	251	240	517	25	366	$167,133	$442,096	$630,983
Colorado Springs	58	80	56	17	51	$15,685	$241,367	$257,052
Columbus	20	156	195	8	164	$0	$337,837	$431,608
Corpus Christi	167	199	187	2	76	$35,955	$92,679	$128,634
Covington	5	37	39	2	44	$1,950		
Crookston	16	55	56	2	47	$0	$139,602	$139,602
Dallas	25	204	315	84	200	$0	$362,885	$362,885
Davenport	67	87	84	12	63	$32,700	$103,695	$136,395
Des Moines	46	40	99	1	78	$39,050	$95,717	$134,767
Detroit	324	49	509	44	494	$11,625		
Dodge City	36	19	48	6	37	$3,045	$66,365	$69,410
Dubuque	94	104	157	8	155	$59,424	$176,118	$235,542
Duluth	24	69	27	8	33	$5,490		$59,642

Arch/Diocese	Documentary Cases	Formal Cases (Previous Yr.)	Formal Cases (This Year)	Cases Abated	Formal Decisions	Fees Received	Diocesan Subsidy	Total Expenses
El Paso	0	115	87	4	74			
Erie	6	68	152	3	131	$39,858	$304,755	$344,613
Evansville	50	4	73	5	64	$17,148	$209,926	$227,074
Fairbanks	1	6	9	0	9			
Fall River	59	14	65	4	54			
Fargo	51	39	59	0	44	$9,830	$165,956	$175,786
Fort Worth	211	507	222	17	63			
Fresno	237	90	198	21	160			
Gallup	28	28	20	7	20	$28,697		$1,575
Galveston-Houston	279	390	328	27	292	$155,000	$312,276	$467,276
Gary	0	36	35	12	93	$30,603	$180,582	$214,370
Gaylord	8	48	56	2	33		$95,584	
Grand Island	33	62	44	4	49	$4,294	$182,616	$186,910
Grand Rapids	83	100	152	3	147	$10,325	$277,273	$287,598
Great-Falls Billings	37	20	22	5	15	$3,775	$107,055	$110,830
Green Bay	94	42	98		98	$35,480	$76,557	$172,491
Greensburg	53	26	84	1	83			
Harrisburg	138	240	211	25	149	$110,000	$425,481	$535,481
Hartford	139	131	93	16	93			
Helena	30	116	54	25	61	$900	$100,000	$100,900
Honolulu	2	37	53	5	59	$23,000	$121,000	$144,000
Houma-Thibodaux	55	30	42	3	41	$15,570	$91,950	$91,736
Indianapolis	12	169	95	21	113	$61,075	$308,337	$369,412
Jackson	54	11	62	13	51	$0	$139,000	$139,000
Jefferson City	70	161	110	10	114	$0	$149,558	$142,307
Joliet in Illinois	22	286	189	23	94	$27,500	$501,000	$570,000
Juneau	0	3	1	1	2	$600	$25,000	$30,000
Kalamazoo	3	76	63	4	73	$14,600	$42,555	$57,155
Kansas City - St. Joseph	127	134	112	6	106			

Arch/Diocese	Documentary Cases	Formal Cases (Previous Yr.)	Formal Cases (This Year)	Cases Abated	Formal Decisions	Fees Received	Diocesan Subsidy	Total Expenses
Kansas City in Kansas	135	251	265	20	265	$72,807	$115,197	$188,004
La Crosse	81	70	193	21	163	$57,990	$101,186	$195,874
Lafayette, Indiana	61	70	111	22	79	$0		
Lafayette, Louisiana	6	299	174	2	182	$44,670	$159,280	$225,366
Lake Charles	66	107	56	5	67	$23,960	$156,938	$180,898
Lansing	115	113	178	21	123	$40,150	$407,029	$447,179
Laredo	39	38	19	0	30	$9,808	$73,582	$83,390
Las Cruces	1	104	65	7	51	$27,905	$76,771	$104,676
Lexington	28	101	59	9	55	$0	$240,378	$240,378
Lincoln	0	61	44	26	22			
Little Rock	35	85	261	12	235	$40,716	$167,898	$208,614
Los Angeles	25	477	407	22	399			
Los Angeles, Our Lady of Lebanon Eparchy	14	22	34	0	36	$17,850	$0	$21,800
Louisville	10	12	115	2	117	$26,865	$219,929	$246,794
Madison	48	49	83	4	73	$33,000	$94,200	$127,200
Manchester	2	309	98	12	95			
Marquette	30	36	36	0	29			
Memphis, Tennessee	59	87	83	4	86	$600	$168,519	$172,519
Metuchen	1	69	111	4	69	$52,780	$260,756	$128,903
Military Services, Archdiocese of the	144	193	149	22	117	$49,025	$111,464	$160,855
Milwaukee	2	199	261	14	172	$100,291	$462,611	$364,182
Mobile	5	62	75	12	37			
Monterey, California	56	43	40	7	19	$16,135	$91,569	$107,703
Nashville	33	186	121	2	124	$0	$371,934	$371,934
New Ulm	14	37	32	3	27	$5,100	$165,292	$170,392
New York	328	105	133	3	117	$174,424	$1,230,423	$1,404,847
Newark	3	208	167	36	130	$89,045	$382,798	$471,843

Arch/Diocese	Documentary Cases	Formal Cases (Previous Yr.)	Formal Cases (This Year)	Cases Abated	Formal Decisions	Fees Received	Diocesan Subsidy	Total Expenses
Norwich	37	41	48		45	$18,000		$265,000
Oakland	196	190	126	11	95	$77,210	$405,003	$482,213
Ogdensburg	33	97	53	7	53	$16,070	$101,772	$117,842
Oklahoma City	101	270	216	2	188	$0	$213,690	$213,690
Omaha	108	139	155	5	169	$46,109	$189,021	$235,130
Orange	11	130	189	61	161			
Orlando	321	69	325	15	315	$157,434	$265,098	$389,536
Owensboro	23	58	69	2	54	$10,510	$236,057	$246,567
Palm Beach	153	70	124	1	123			
Parma, Byzantine Eparchy	0	6	11	0	1			
Passaic, Byzantine-Ruthenian	0	15	0	0	6	$2,800	$14,000	$16,800
Paterson	105	121	77	17	73	$37,425	$239,885	$277,310
Pensacola-Tallahassee	91	31	62	4	71	$7,500	$65,495	$72,995
Peoria	94	100	151	6	120	$73,596	$326,710	$289,114
Philadelphia, Ukrainian Archeparchy	8	0	8	3	5			
Pittsburgh, Archeparchy	2	4	16	0	4	$1,750	$500	
Pittsburgh	6	117	318	15	283	$162,000	$557,000	$719,000
Portland, Maine	82	121	136	22	159	$31,785	$323,211	$354,996
Portland, Oregon	99	401	171	6	123	$23,349	$155,049	$178,397
Providence	90	97	108	4	130	$39,021	$277,017	$347,833
Pueblo	60	46	33	6	36	$6,244	$118,438	$124,682
Raleigh	165	107	115	15	93	$33,115	$174,148	$206,834
Rapid City	26	60	27	3	42	$6,980	$53,471	$60,456
Reno	57	65	44	3	48	$51,922	$112,653	$164,575
Richmond	229	102	192	11	211	$0	$476,108	$476,108
Rochester	66	52	67	6	83	$48,988	$225,292	$274,280
Rockford	141	59	209	7	203	$66,458	$279,849	$376,360

Arch/Diocese	Documentary Cases	Formal Cases (Previous Yr.)	Formal Cases (This Year)	Cases Abated	Formal Decisions	Fees Received	Diocesan Subsidy	Total Expenses
Rockville Centre	111	289	256	68	216			
Sacramento	183	277	156	31	126			
Saginaw	5	40	71	5	80	$0	$104,780	$108,781
Saint Paul and Minneapolis	159	264	283	81	211	$86,350	$502,290	$588,640
Salina	41	72	79	16	40	$14,394	$44,302	$58,696
Salt Lake City	133	22	80	3	55	$20,000	$80,035	$100,035
San Angelo	0	41	63	4	41	$14,235	$237,219	$251,454
San Antonio	18	135	287	2	298	$100,598	$186,468	$291,565
San Bernardino	244	152	125	15	134			
San Diego	363	187	196	11	213	$66,000	$271,000	$337,000
San Jose	150	126	102	2	76	$48,344	$416,898	$465,242
Santa Rosa	64	25	31	1	33	$17,875	$122,251	$140,126
Savannah	96	10	104	7	79	$24,800	$212,385	$176,947
Scranton	77	107	154	11	136	$69,204	$214,110	$283,314
Seattle	36	398	161	33	304	$80,153	$405,153	$535,957
Shreveport	50	34	33	3	26	$11,350	$167,457	$178,807
Sioux City	44	76	67	2	81	$24,029	$88,798	$112,827
Sioux Falls	61	51	82	4	88	$26,345	$114,185	$140,530
Spokane	88	25	59	0	60	$8,595	$29,740	$38,335
Springfield, Illinois	112	143	146	3	115	$78,666	$232,826	$311,492
Springfield, Cape Girardeau	56	195	113	61	105	$19,946	$164,454	$184,400
Springfield, Massachusetts	74	107	87	10	87	$29,155	$197,347	$226,502
St. Augustine	140	167	134	19	114			
St. Cloud	54	77	87	5	95	$17,655	$107,260	$124,987
St. Louis	193	301	261	34	232	$155,246	$271,386	$426,632
St. Petersburg	245	19	240	3	210			
Stamford, Ukrainian Eparchy	2					$50		$300
Steubenville	10	41	36	8	42	$6,900	$32,346	$39,246

Arch/Diocese	Documentary Cases	Formal Cases (Previous Yr.)	Formal Cases (This Year)	Cases Abated	Formal Decisions	Fees Received	Diocesan Subsidy	Total Expenses
Stockton	118	86	77	5	89	$20,458	$51,199	$71,656
Superior	34	20	50	2	39	$4,200	$113,034	$117,234
Syracuse	0	34	133	4	149	$72,800	$32,484	$105,284
Toledo	132	103	154	5	169	$42,842	$186,843	$229,685
Trenton	6	150	144	0	98	$75,150	$233,100	$308,474
Tyler	36	40	57	7	40	$12,802	$59,775	$72,577
Venice	101	34	147	22	77	$50,663	$232,853	$283,515
Victoria, Texas	0	12	82	0	66	$19,000	$49,590	$67,590
Wheeling-Charleston	73	141	72	6	50	$42,913	$0	$146,237
Wilmington	9	120	79	4	92	$53,400	$272,752	$327,392
Worcester	42	2	47	1	87	$44,078	$123,795	$167,872
Yakima	9	55	31	10	32	$25,000	$125,000	$150,000
Youngstown	65	71	80	3	62	$19,996	$295,953	$318,005

****

Tribunal Statistics 2009: Second Instance Tribunals by (Arch)Diocese

Appeal Court	Cases Remaining from	New Cases Appealed	Ratified by Decree	Cases Admitted to 2nd Instance Trial	Cases Decided by Formal Decisions	Decisions Affirming	Decisions Reversing	Fees Received	Diocesan Subsidy	Total Expenses
Boise	0	184	182	2	2	2				
Bridgeport	20	53	52	53	9	6	3			
Camden	10	54	54	7	7	0	7			
Cincinnati	11	97	91							
Cleveland	1	309	295	3	3	1	2			
Columbus	36	72	86	4	7	6	1			
Covington	0	74	53	0	0	0	0			

Appeal Court	Cases Remaining from Prev. Year	New Cases Appealed	Ratified by Decree	Cases Admitted to 2nd Instance Trial	Cases Decided by Formal Decisions	Decisions Affirming	Decisions Reversing	Fees Received	Diocesan Subsidy	Total Expenses
Davenport	1	56	55	0	1	1	0			
Des Moines	0	55	55	0	55	55	0	$39,050	$95,717	$134,767
Detroit	42		473	2	2	1	1	$11,900		
Dubuque	19	219	214	6	6	2	4			
Evansville	0	89	86	3	2	2	0			
Fargo	0	50	40	1	41	41	0	$1,000	$174,786	$175,786
Fresno	4	0	89	97	89	88	1			
Gary	2	0	60	2	0	0	0	$1,800	$180,582	$214,370
Grand Rapids	1	369	369	0	0	368	0	$10,325	$0	$3,075
Green Bay			192							
Hartford	10	120	120	7	7	5	2	$0		
Indianapolis	33	45	25	15	17	9	8			
Kansas City in Kansas	4	224	223	1	1	1	0	$5,575	$1,985	$7,560
Lafayette in Indiana	18	2	110	2	1	1	0	$0		
Lafayette in Louisiana	21	26	38	0	0	0				
Lexington	6	42	47	0	0	0	0	$0	$240,378	$240,378
Los Angeles	45	194	213	3	3	3	0			
Louisville	13	111	107	0	0	0	0			
Memphis in Tennessee	4	110	108	2	2	1	1	$0		
Milwaukee	10	374	388	3	1	1	0	$8,950	$3,875	$5,075
Missouri	89	706	702	702	18	10	0	$109,175	$0	$127,951
Mobile	18	119	108	4	4	0	4			
Nashville	4	2	1	0	2	0	2			
Newark	0	0	151	151	151	151	0			
Norwich	0	56	50	6	6	6	0		$265,000	
Oakland	5	0	127	12	12	12	0	$3,550		
Omaha	0	65	61	0	0	61	0			

Appeal Court	Cases Remaining from Prev. Year	New Cases Appealed	Ratified by Decree	Cases Admitted to 2nd Instance Trial	Cases Decided by Formal Decisions	Decisions Affirming	Decisions Reversing	Fees Received	Diocesan Subsidy	Total Expenses
Orange	73	398	460	1	1	459	1			
Owensboro	8	46	39			39				
Paterson	2	42	38	1	1	1	0			
Philadelphia, Ukranian Archeparchy	0	0	4	4	4	4	0	$1,200		
Pittsburgh	47	225	327	0	2	2	0			
Portland in Maine	26	139	149	2	2	2	0			
Portland in Oregon	124	300	295	1	1	0	0			
Providence	7	84	73	13	12	12	0			
Saginaw	0	107	106	1	1	1	0	$2,675		
San Bernardino	0	1	116	0	134	116	0			
San Diego	57	280	330	2	332	0	0			
San Jose	2	140	130	8	5	5	1	$3,625	$461,617	$465,242
Seattle	21	2	265	3	1	0	0	$5,840		
Sioux City	2	47	46	0	0	46	0			
Sioux Falls	0	66	57	4	4	2	2	$1,200	$1,500	
Springfield, Massachusetts	27	281	271	271	6	6	0			
St. Cloud	6	49	46	9	9	7	2	$2,000		
St. Paul and Minneapolis	241	447	506	28	28	12	16	$18,925	$107,180	$126,105
Steubenville	2	61	59	0	2	1	1			
Stockton	10	0	0	187	177			$2,025		
Texas	386	1601	1578	5	3	2	0	$160,000		$151,007
Toledo	21	279	272							
Trenton	1	55	53	1	1	1	0			
Youngstown	8	118	114	1	0	0	0			

CANON LAW SOCIETY OF AMERICA SEVENTY-SECOND ANNUAL BUSINESS MEETING

Buffalo, New York
October 13, 2010

MINUTES

CALL TO ORDER AND OPENING PRAYER

Reverend Lawrence Jurcak, President, called to order the Seventy-Second Annual Business Meeting of the Canon Law Society of America (CLSA), on October 13, 2010 at 11:00 a.m., at the Hyatt Regency Hotel in Buffalo, New York. He presided over the meeting as Chair.

The Chair then invited Reverend Michael P. Joyce, C.M., CLSA Vice-President/President-Elect, to lead the assembly in an opening prayer.

Following the opening prayer, it was announced that Reverend Phillip J. Brown, S.S. would serve as Parliamentarian for the Business Meeting, and that *Robert's Rules of Order* would resolve matters not provided for in the CLSA's *Constitution* or *Bylaws*.

The Chair then gave instructions on the voting procedures to be observed for the election of Officers and Consultors during the Business Meeting. The procedures were adopted as described by the Chair.

The Chair then reviewed the procedures for addressing the assembly, and the CLSA's practices for presenting resolutions. The procedures and practices were adopted, as presented by the Chair.

The Chair then entertained a motion that Associate Members present at the meeting have the opportunity to address the assembly, as called for in Article 5.3 of the CLSA's *Constitution*. The motion was seconded and approved unanimously by the assembly.

The Chair then called upon the Secretary, Ms. Siobhan M. Verbeek, to read the Minutes of the Seventy-First Business Meeting of the CLSA, unless there was a proposal to accept the Minutes as published in the 2009 CLSA *Proceedings*. A motion to accept the Minutes was presented and seconded. The motion was accepted, with one objection.

Election of Officers and Consultors

The Chair next called upon Sister Maureen A. McPartland, O.P., Chair of the Nominations Committee, to present the slate of Officers and Consultors. Sister McPartland announced the candidates for Officers and Consultors. No additional nominations were added to the slate, as is provided for in the CLSA's *Constitution*.

Reverend Jurcak then read the provisions of the CLSA's *Bylaws* regarding elections. The active members of the CLSA were instructed to cast their votes. The tellers collected the ballots and retired to a separate room to count them. Later in the meeting Sister McPartland returned to the Business Meeting and informed the Chair of the election results. The Chair then announced that:

For the Office of Vice-President/President-Elect:

208 valid ballots were cast, with 105 votes needed for election. There were 0 abstentions and 0 invalid votes. The votes cast were:

Mrs. Rita F. Joyce: 152

Rev. Msgr. Mark A. Plewka: 56

The Chair declared an election with Mrs. Rita F. Joyce selected as Vice-President/President-Elect. The election was received with applause.

For the Office of Treasurer:

207 valid ballots were cast, with 105 votes needed for election. There was 1 abstention and 0 invalid votes. The votes cast were:

Rev. Gregory T. Bittner: 145

Rev. Kelly Vandehey: 62

The Chair declared an election with Reverend Gregory T. Bittner selected as Treasurer. The election was received with applause.

For the Office of Consultor:

207 valid ballots were cast, with 105 votes needed for election. There was 1 abstention and 1 invalid vote. The votes cast were:

Reverend Thomas E. Cronkleton, Jr.: 110

Reverend Thomas J. Franciscus, C.SS.R.: 72

Reverend Bruce Miller: 97

Dr. Margaret Poll Chalmers: 120

The Chair declared an election with Reverend Thomas E. Cronkleton, Jr. and Dr. Margaret Poll Chalmers selected as Consultors. The election was received with applause.

President's Report

Reverend Lawrence Jurcak informed the assembly that a written copy of the President's Report could be found on pages 1-5 of the *2010 Annual Reports Booklet* that was distributed with the registration materials for the convention. He then proceeded to highlight several items contained in the President's Report. In particular, he noted that the resolution approved by the CLSA at the 2009 convention, for the development of a think tank to recommend changes to the *Code of Canon Law*, had been referred to the Research and Development Committee. The Committee was in the process of finalizing its response for submission to the Board of Governors at its January 2011 meeting. He then added that, following the CLSA's 2008 convention, he forwarded to the Pontifical Council for Legislative Texts a list of experts who had been recommended by a working group of the Board of Governors to serve as potential resource persons to the Pontifical Council for the various working groups that had been assigned to explore areas of the Code that could benefit from further specification or revision. He reported that during the 2010 visits to the Roman dicasteries, Archbishop Francesco Coccopalmerio had expressed gratitude for the list of experts that had been provided by the CLSA. Reverend Jurcak concluded his Report by noting that all of the Committees that had been recommended by the Future Initiatives Project were now in place. He expressed gratitude to the CLSA members who had agreed to serve on committees, and then called for questions or observations on the President's Report.

Reverend James A. Coriden, of The Washington Theological Union, referred to the description on page 2 of the Report of the resolution passed at the CLSA's 2003 convention, calling for a study of diocesan synods. He noted that the study appeared to have been lost, and he asked what it would take to find it again. Reverend Jurcak responded that another resolution would be required in 2011 to move the item forward.

Reverend Patrick J. Cogan, S.A., of Saint Paul University in Ottawa, Canada, referred to the CLSA's custom of visiting the Roman dicasteries every two years. He asked the President to comment on whether this was a good idea, and whether it was worth the time and the expense. Reverend Jurcak responded that the interactions with Vatican representatives was indeed helpful, not only in terms of the information that was received from them, but as an opportunity to provide insights into the work of the CLSA and possible areas where research provided by the CLSA could benefit the work of the Holy See. He added that the Board of Governors would revisit the question of the advisability of continuing to schedule the visits every two years, or to consider a longer duration between scheduled visits.

Reverend Jacques M. Roland, O.M.I., of Saint Paul University in Ottawa, Canada, observed that members of the Canadian Canon Law Society (CCLS) who had registered for the 2010 simultaneous CCLS-CLSA convention did not receive all of the information that had been included in the registration packets for CLSA members, even though they were members of both Societies. Reverend Jurcak responded that, following the Business Meeting, the CLSA's Executive Coordinator's Office would make available the information to any CLSA member who did not receive it. He then thanked Reverend Roland for the observation.

Executive Coordinator's Report

Reverend Jurcak next invited Sister Sharon Euart, R.S.M. to present the Executive Coordinator's Report. Sister Euart informed the assembly that a written copy of the Executive Coordinator's Report could be found on pages 33-38 of the *2010 Annual Reports Booklet*. With respect to the Executive Coordinator's Office's commitment to website development and management, she observed that one of the immediate results of the expanded website had been a growth in the membership's usage of the website for convention registration, dues payment, and access to documents online. In light of the experience over the past year, she then offered three implications for the CLSA in the future: (1) The substantial increase in the CLSA's membership as a result of the website was a positive development, enabling the CLSA to reach out to canonists throughout the world; (2) CLSA members were continuing to look for more English-language resources in canon law on-line; (3) The increased reliance on its website will require the CLSA to remain at the forefront of technological advances. This direction, moreover, will require the Executive Coordinator's Office to have competent staff who possess the necessary skills to administer, design, and use the website, and to answer technological questions from the membership.

Sister Euart next recalled that for several years the CLSA had worked with the United States Conference of Catholic Bishops (USCCB) to implement a Tribunal Review and Evaluation Process. She reported that under the recent reorganization of the USCCB, the USCCB was no longer able to provide this service. However, the CLSA will continue to provide it in accord with the approved procedure. She encouraged dioceses to contact the Executive Coordinator's Office directly if they are interested in arranging a Tribunal Review and Evaluation.

Sister Euart concluded her Report by noting that several CLSA members had made contributions over the past year to the CLSA's Scholarship Fund in memory of past CLSA members. She proceeded to read the names of the past CLSA Members in whose names such contributions had been given: Reverend Dennis Burns, Reverend Richard Cunningham, Reverend Bertram Griffin, Reverend Ellsworth Kneal, Reverend Monsignor Frederick McManus, Reverend James Provost, Reverend Monsignor Charles Schettler, and Reverend Mosignor William Vavaro. She then invited questions or observations on the Executive Coordinator's Report.

Reverend James A. Coriden, of The Washington Theological Union, asked for an update on the CLSA's study of marriage and undocumented immigrants. He recalled that at the 2009 CLSA convention it was reported that the publication of this study was imminent. Sister Euart responded that the project had not been, and will not be, completed. Of the chapters that were completed, efforts were being made to obtain the permissions from the authors to post their essays on the CLSA's website.

Treasurer's Report

Reverend Jurcak next invited Reverend Thomas C. Anslow, C.M. to present the Treasurer's Report. Reverend Anslow reported that, in the area of General Operations, the CLSA took in more money than it had spent. In addition, a profit had been made on the 2009 convention, which was a positive development in light of the increased costs associated with the 2010 simultaneous convention with the Canadian Canon Law Society. He likewise noted that CLSA committees had not spent all of the funds that had been allotted to them. In some cases this was because the committee's members were newly appointed in 2010; in other cases, committees had been savvy in utilizing cost-saving measures, such as the use of modern technologies for conducting regular meetings. He concurred with the Executive Coordinator's observation that the CLSA's continued use of technology, and the need for competent staff to oversee the new direction, will also require a sustained financial commitment into the future.

In the area of investments, Reverend Anslow reported that the CLSA had recovered what had been lost in previous years due to fluctuations in the stock market nationally. He predicted that the return on investments would likely continue to be a roller coaster over the coming few years. He then invited questions or observations on the Treasurer's Report.

There being no questions or observations, Reverend Anslow then thanked the assembly for the opportunity and the privilege to have served as Treasurer. He commended the staff of the Executive Coordinator's Office for the many ways that they had exercised sound stewardship and fiscal responsibility. On behalf of the entire CLSA, Reverend Jurcak thanked Reverend Anslow for his service as Treasurer, which was met with applause.

Committee Reports

The Chair then invited questions or comments on the Committee Reports that were contained in the *2010 Annual Reports Booklet*. Brother Patrick T. Shea, O.F.M., of the Diocese of Cleveland, and a member of the Committee on Institutes of Consecrated and Apostolic Life, reported that a survey had been sent to members of the CLSA regarding ways that the Committee on Institutes of Consecrated and Apostolic Life could be of service to the membership. He expressed gratitude to those who had already responded to the survey, and then gave instructions on how to complete the survey online, via the CLSA's website, for those who still wished to do so.

Reverend Martins C. Emeh, of the Diocese of Rockford, asked to speak to the liturgies at the 2010 convention. He expressed gratitude for the preparation that had gone into the planning for the convention, but indicated that he had been deeply offended by the Opening Prayer Service to Earth Mother, river, corn, sister beings, etc. Having been raised in a family where pagan worship was common, he expected that in a gathering of priests and bishops of the Catholic Church the Prayer Service would reflect Christian prayer, and not the prayer of the Iroquois Native Americans. Reverend Jurcak responded that the point had been well taken, and that it would be shared with the Convention Liturgies Committee following the convention.

Most Reverend R. Daniel Conlon, of the Diocese of Steubenville, asked if the Chair would entertain a request for the Clergy Committee. Reverend Jurcak responded in the affirmative. Most Reverend Conlon then stated that, in light of the penal trials for priests and deacons who have been accused of sexual abuse of minors, it would be helpful to know how many trials there have been, while still respecting the pontifical secret. In addition, he encouraged the CLSA to develop a list of experts who were willing to serve as promoters of justice and judges in such cases, as was being done by the CLSA for those willing to serve as advocates.

Resolutions

Reverend Jurcak then read the applicable CLSA *Bylaws* that governed the proposing of resolutions from the floor and asked if there were any such resolutions to be presented. There being none, he called upon Brother Patrick T. Shea, O.F.M., Chair of the Resolutions Committee, and Reverend Gregory T. Luyet, Time-keeper, to approach the podium and to present the resolutions previously submitted to the Resolutions Committee. Ms. Katie Richards of the CLSA Executive Coordinator's Office, served as secretary for the redaction of the proposed resolutions.

The full texts of the previously submitted resolutions were projected onto screens in the hall. In addition, printed copies of the resolutions were distributed to those in attendance.

Brother Shea thanked the presenters for submitting their resolutions well in advance of the convention, and the members of the Committee on Resolutions for their service to the CLSA.

Resolution I: Provide the Canon Law Digest On-Line

Proposed by: Reverend James A. Coriden.

Be it resolved that the Board of Governors direct the Publications Advisory Board to expedite its investigation of providing the *Canon Law Digest* on-line, and, if the project seems feasible and affordable, proceed with all deliberate speed to set in motion the process of on-line conversion, indexing documents by canons, chronology, source, and subject matter, maintaining permanent access, constant updating, and easy down loadability. The Publications Advisory Board shall report its finds to the Board of Governors and membership within a year.

Implementation by means of intensified consultation and study by the Publications Advisory Board.

Anticipated Cost: $5,000.00. Cost supplied by the CLSA from unrestricted, general operations funds.

Discussion: The Resolutions Committee moved the resolution. Reverend James A. Coriden, of The Washington Theological Union, was called forward to present the rationale. Reverend Coriden referred to page 55 of the *2010 Annual Reports Booklet*, wherein it was stated that the next volume of *Canon Law Digest*, volume 14 was in the final stages of development, but covered the years 1996-2000. The publication cycle resulted in a ten year delay in the publication of the material; yet, the information to be included in *Canon Law Digest* is already readily accessible. His proposed resolution was an attempt to fill the lacuna regarding the instantaneous availability of the information.

Reverend Phillip J. Brown, S.S. spoke on behalf of the Board of Governors in support of the resolution. He recognized its inherent value and indicated its congruity with the direction of the Board of Governors for the past several years. He also noted that it was probable that some hard copies of the publication would still be maintained, if only for archival purposes.

The question was then called from the floor. The Chair called for a voice vote. The resolution was approved unanimously.

Resolution II: Canonical Assistance for the Creation and Organization of the Anglican Ordinariate in the United States

Proposed by: Dr. Margaret Poll Chalmers, Reverend Monsignor James Sheehan, and Reverend Monsignor William Stetson.

Be it resolved that the CLSA offers its assistance to the delegate from the Congregation for the Doctrine of the Faith to the United States and the Anglican Ordinariate after its creation, in assisting in the creation and initial formation of the Anglican Ordinariate and the juridic persons associated with it, until such time as the Ordinariate is able adequately to supply its own canonists.

Be it further resolved that the CLSA compile and maintain a list of canonists willing to assist the delegate from the Congregation for the Doctrine of the Faith to the United States, the Ordinary, and the Ordinariate and individual Ordinariate parishes, clergy, and other juridic persons to help them with their creation and their ongoing canonical needs.

Implementation by means of the Board of Governors.

Anticipated Cost: $0.00.

Discussion: The Resolutions Committee moved the resolution. Dr. Margaret

Poll Chalmers, of the Diocese of Charleston, was called forward to present the rationale. Dr. Chalmers noted that many questions had been raised about the Anglican Ordinariate. It was not known how it will work or what it will look like, but the CLSA should be a part of the process from the very beginning. The resolution was asking that names be provided to assist, as is needed, in the process. She concluded her observations by stating that she was aware that Most Reverend Donald W. Wuerl, the Congregation for the Doctrine of the Faith's delegate to the United States, supported the resolution.

Very Reverend Paul D. Counce, of the Diocese of Baton Rouge, expressed support for the resolution in principle, but asked that the final phrase of the first *Be it resolved* clause be deleted ("until such time as the Ordinariate is able to adequately supply its own canonists."). The question was called from the floor, and the emendation to the resolution was approved unanimously.

Mrs. Meg Romano-Hogan, of the Diocese of Fort Worth, commended the timeliness of the resolution. She stated that local churches were experiencing a great number of Anglican clergy and laity who desired to come into full communion with the Catholic Church. She cited St. Thomas Aquinas' maxim that "A small error at the beginning becomes a huge error in the end." The ability to be a part of the processes from the very beginning will enable the CLSA to have a great impact on the development and maintenance of the Ordinariate.

The question was then called from the floor. The Chair called for a voice vote. The resolution was approved unanimously.

New Business

The Chair opened the floor to any New Business of interest to the assembly. There was none.

Varia

Greetings by Officials of Canon Law Societies and Distinguished Guests

Reverend Jurcak then invited the visiting officials of Canon Law Societies and other distinguished guests to come to the podium to address the assembly.

Monsignor David Hogan, President of the Canon Law Society of Great Britain and Ireland (CLSGB&I), expressed sincere gladness at the opportunity to be with the CLSA. He extended the good wishes of the CLSGB&I. In a particular way, he expressed gratitude for the generosity and hospitality of Reverend Lawrence Jurcak. He reported that the 2011 convention of the CLSGB&I would be held in Harrogate, North Yorkshire, England, and that all were welcome. He concluded his remarks by asking God's blessings on the CLSA, and on the great nation of the United States of America.

Very Reverend Anthony Kerin, President of the Canon Law Society of Australia and New Zealand (CLSA&NZ), extended greetings from the canonists of Australia and New Zealand. He observed that attendance at the CLSA's convention provided an irreplaceable link between the two professional societies, and was an opportunity to share common experiences. He stated that the warm welcome that he had received was a sign of the CLSA's respect for the CLSA&NZ. He reported that the CLSA&NZ had re-launched its Newsletter as a peer review journal entitled *The Canonist*. In addition, the CLSA&NZ and Catholic Religion Australia had recently conducted a Canon Law for Leadership course for those who had been elected to leadership in religious institutes. Sister Sharon L. Holland, I.H.M. was a presenter during the course. He concluded his remarks by reporting that the CLSA&NZ convention in 2011 would be held in Melbourne, Australia, and its 2012 convention would be held in Christ Church, New Zealand. Further details about the conventions could be found on the Society's website at clsanz.catholic.org.au.

Reverend Rogelio Ayala Partida noted that it was a special privilege to attend the convention on behalf of the Asociación Mexicana de Canonistas. He extended the greetings of the association, and expressed gratitude for the hospitality extended to him by the CLSA. He noted the common interest between the two professional Societies because of the large Mexican population within the United States. He reported that the association's convention would take place from July 11-15, 2011 and he encouraged those who were proficient in Spanish to attend.

Reverend Lawrence Jurcak then reported that, due to the simultaneous Business Meeting of the Canadian Canon Law Society (CCLS), Reverend Alain Guevremont was unable to attend the CLSA's Business Meeting, but had asked that the greetings of the CCLS be brought to the convention.

Adjournment

There being no further business, Reverend Jurcak entertained a motion to adjourn the meeting, which was seconded. The motion passed unanimously.

At 11:50 a.m., Reverend Jurcak then formally closed the Seventy-Second Business Meeting of the Canon Law Society of America.

Respectfully Submitted,
Ms. Siobhan M. Verbeek
Secretary

Convention Mass Homily

Reverend Alain Guevremont

One Sunday morning, on her way back from church, little Suzy asked her mother, "Mom, what was Father Greg talking about this morning? He mentioned that God was big, so big he could hold me in his hand? Yes, her mother replied, that is true. Well, he also said that God lives in every one of us. Yes her mother said, what don't you understand? Well, how can he be big, hold us in his hand but also be in everyone of us? Wouldn't we be big and fat if that was true? Wouldn't Jesus show through everything?

Wouldn't Jesus show through everything? Good question. And that is exactly what the Gospel tells us today. That is exactly what Jesus is teaching his followers through his Sermon on the Mount. And that is what God has been teaching his people since the beginning of time "*Let me shine through you... let me show through your actions and words*." Do you remember the little book called "Imitation of Christ", well I'll venture out and say, that God does not expect us to imitate him but to be him. The Beatitudes are a self-portrait of Jesus, of God and they are our marching orders.

I do not believe that the Beatitudes are a standard by which we must live by. That would be too easy... trying to reach for the "stars", trying to imitate what a Christian should be. NO. The Beatitudes are a way of life, it's what we must be, it's the way we must live. It is not trying to be poor in spirit or be meek but we must be poor in spirit and we must be meek. In an excerpt I read that the Beatitudes are "not to be produced by the Christian, but in the Christian". It is basically surrounding to the Lord, being the Lord for our sisters and brothers of the world.

In the time of Jesus, such teachings were foreign to the ears of his countrymen. Everything was very clear in society; everyone had their place and knew their place. So you can be absolutely sure that when Jesus started to talk and used such words as "blessed", people listened. People listened because it was the first time they were told to be happy, told that they were somebody. For ages, they had only heard the Scribes and Pharisees tell them they were nobodies, worth nothing. The word "happiness" was only used to refer to the wealthy because money seemed to put them above all problems. Happiness was linked to the three "P"s : popularity, prosperity and power. And still is today.

But here we have this Jesus telling them quite the opposite.

So, why should we listen to this teachings by Jesus, why should we care?

Because of the first word in every phrase: "Blessed." We want to be blessed. God wants us to be blessed. It's a promised of happiness from God. And who doesn't want to be happy?

Wanting to be happy is a common desire and a normal feeling. Unfortunately, because of this, the world takes advantage of our vulnerability and defines for us what happiness truly is. For example, the next time you are standing at the super market waiting for your turn at the cash, just look at all the magazines that talk about the life of the rich and famous... how they lost wait, what trip they took, their new look. Wow, they must be happy with all this attention and all the money they have. That is what the world tells us that happiness is. But is that truly being happy? The world through publicity tells me that if I buy a certain aftershave, I will have all the women going crazy for me. I don't think my Bishop would appreciate this. If I buy a certain underwear, I'll have the body of the Renaldo's and Beckam's of this world. But is that true happiness? Is God showing through me when I follow that philosophy? There is no doubt that such teachings pushes people to associate happiness with the wrong things and to look in the wrong places.

That is why we should listen to the teachings of Jesus. The beatitudes do not represent individual qualities, but a complete picture of the person mastered by God. It's just a complete package of qualities needed to be a true Christian. And so, we must not imitate Christ but be Christ for our sisters and brothers.

Here is a challenge: how would your life be different if Jesus was to walk in your shoes? If he was to take your job or be the parent to your children? Thinking like this makes us wonder, doesn't? Is God showing through me? Can anyone se Him?

When you go back to your room tonight, take a good look in the mirror. Do you see God showing through? Are the Beatitudes shinning through? You know what it should look like because the Beatitudes are a self-portrait of Christ.

Let us finish with a prayer from St. Theresa of Avila:

Christ has no body now, but yours.
No hands, no feet on earth, but yours.
Yours are the eyes
through which Christ looks compassion into the world.
Yours are the feet
with which Christ walks to do good.
Yours are the hands
with which Christ blesses the world.

Amen.

VARIA

Role of Law Citation

Reverend Lawrence Jurcak

Each year the Canon Law Society of America presents its distinguished Role of Law Award to an individual considered to be outstanding in the field of canonical science. The By-Laws of the Society directs the Board of Governors to select a person who demonstrates in his or her life and legal practice the following characteristics:

> Embodiment of pastoral attitude, commitment to research and study, participation in the development of law, response to needs or practical assistance, facilitation of dialogue and the interchange of ideas within the Society and with other groups.

These qualifications are merely a concise re-statement of the constitutionally-expressed purposes of the Society.

The person to whom this award is given is viewed by us as one who embodies all that we, as members of the Society hold dear, as one to whom we can look for guidance and inspiration. Such an official statement alone is, perhaps the greatest honor that can be bestowed on anyone – to be selected by one's friends and peers as outstanding among them.

The 2010 honoree is a priest who was born in Detroit, Michigan in 1947. He was educated in the public school system of Detroit, and having completed his years of priestly formation, was ordained a priest of the Archdiocese of Detroit in 1974. Active in his archdiocese, he has served many capacities: as associate pastor and pastor in various parishes in the archdiocese. He has taught in local colleges and seminaries, held various offices in the archdiocesan tribunal, and assisted as called upon be it for the cause of the canonization of Father Solanus Casey, OFM, Cap., moderator for various archdiocesan organizations and causes, including dealing with cases of clergy sexual misconduct.

In addition to involvement with his archdiocese, this year's recipient of the Role of Law Award has been an active member and representative of our Society for almost thirty years. He served as a member of the Task Force on Due Process in 1985, Consultor in 1988-1990, Vice-President in 1992-1993., and President in 1993-1994. He has been a presenter at conventions and contributed generously to the ongoing formation of canonist in various aspects of the law – most recently as Chair of our Regional Workshops in Penal Cases. Accessible is a word used by many canonists to describe this year recipient – a shepherd and a mentor for younger canonists.

This year's recipient of the Role of Law Award is well know to all as a committed churchman who serves his parish community with the heart of a shepherd, a dedicated teacher, and a person convinced of the pastoral nature of the Church's law as it is grounded in service to the people of God. Yet he knows how to take care of himself – as his parish secretary indicated when I called to inform him of our desire to award him this honor. "If you knew our pastor, you would know that when he's on vacation, not much interrupts his time away – so understand that he won't be calling you until he gets back." Yet another lesson some of need to learn, the importance of maintaining a healthy balance in life!

Tonight we honor a friend, a colleague, an educator, a pastor, and a fellow canonist. It my privilege to present the 2010 Role of Law Award, on behalf of the Canon Law Society of America and the Board of Governors, to Reverend Monsignor Ricardo E. Bass.

ROLE OF LAW AWARD RESPONSE

Reverend Monsignor Ricardo E. Bass

As you can well imagine, I am deeply honored to have my name joined to the 37 previous recipients of this Role of Law Award which was first presented in 1973. I am particularly honored at this Convention which is meeting simultaneously with the Convention for the Canadian Canon Law Society. My thanks to the Board of Governors, to our President, Rev. Lawrence Jurcak, for his gracious and generous remarks, and to you in whose name they acted.

When Rev. Robert T. Kennedy was named as the fifth recipient of this Award 33 years ago, in 1977, he began with a brief story which I would like to repeat this evening. I repeat it because after 33 years I am hoping that most of you either never heard it or, if you did, that you have forgotten it. I am also repeating it because it is far more fitting for me than it ever was for Fr. Kennedy.

There was a little donkey who was entered in the Kentucky Derby. As the horses paraded onto the track, and the band played the beautiful strains of "My Old Kentucky Home", the little donkey was chugging along trying as best he could to keep up with the thoroughbreds. As they neared the starting gate, one of the thoroughbreds looked down at the donkey and asked, "What are you doing in here?" The little donkey replied, "I entered not because I expected to win anything, but only because I thought the association would do me good."

My association with the Canon Law Society has, indeed, "done me good" over the years. Because of this association during the past quarter of a century, I have ministered with and learned from the real canonical thoroughbreds – I have made lifetime friendships with a number of member of this Society – and I have come to value deeply the ministry in which we all share.

The Most Reverend Timothy Dolan, Archbishop of New York, at this year's annual Los Angeles Catholic Prayer Breakfast which was held on September 2nd, quoted the great British historian, Lord Macauley: "After considerable study and with some admitted regret as a Protestant, I must confess that I consider the Roman Catholic Church to be of divine origin because no mere human institution run with such knavish imbecility could have survived two weeks." The context of this remark was Archbishop Dolan speaking about the need for our Church, which we all love and for whom we all minister, to admit of its own sinfulness – the Church we love which, Dolan said, can be "…imperfect, sloppy, awkward and corrupt." His was a clarion call for the Church we all love to admit not only its own sinfulness – but also its own woundedness. He referred to Chapter 20 of John's Gospel – when Christ first appears to the disciples in the Upper Room, and after greeting them he then "…showed them his hands and his side..." – the wounds of his crucifixion. These were the wounds – the stripes - by which we were healed. These wounds which today are still shared by His

Church and by each of us who are the ministers of that Church.

Henri Nouwen in his classic work, *The Wounded Healer* writes: "For the minister is called to recognize the sufferings of his time in his own heart and make that recognition the starting point of his service."[1] In recent years we most clearly see the "sufferings of our time" - our own wounds and the wounds of our beloved Church - in the sexual misconduct scandals which have plagued our Church and continue to plague Her. These scandals which have caused ceaseless numbers of Catholics to flee from the Church. These scandals which have clearly shown the woundedness of our entire Church: our hierarchy, our clergy, countless numbers of those who have been victimized and even ourselves.

Those of us who have chosen to minister as advocates for the accused and those of us who have been appointed to minister as delegates for our dioceses or religious congregations and those of us who, like myself, have chosen or been appointed to do both – are painfully aware of these wounds and the need for healing. But the path to such healing has proven to be long and complicated and frustrating. Yet in spite of some members of the hierarchy – in spite of norms which often raise more questions than they do provide answers – and in spite of processes which can drag on for years - healing has begun to take place – but the wounds are still ugly and gaping and there is much healing left to do.

The wounds are ugly and gaping for those who are accused and have not had their rights adequately protected – for those who have not had recourse to trained advocates – for those who have had their rights denied by overzealous bishops or untrained Episcopal delegates. As Sr. Rose McDermott so rightly pointed out in her acceptance of the 30th Role of Law Award in 2002:

If we, trained in the law, stand in silence while: allegations are treated as crimes, reputations are irretrievably lost before a formal trial, grave complaints are reviewed by unskilled persons, the rights of the accused to advocacy, defense, and recourse are denied; therapeutic evaluations are ordered prior to a penal process, statutes of limitation and the non-retroactivity of the law are forgotten, and the mitigating circumstances lessening imputability and tempering penalties are neglected, we have failed in our ministerial vocation.

These words ring as true today as they did when she first spoke them eight years ago.

As Episcopal Delegate in the Archdiocese of Detroit for over five years first for Adam Cardinal Maida and then for Archbishop Allen Vigneron for cases involving the sexual misconduct of the clergy, I had the opportunity of sitting with 22 different individuals who were proven to have been victims of such heinous acts. Most of those 22 had tried unsuccessfully for years to tell their story to someone in authority in the Church who would listen, but no one would – to speak with someone in authority in the Church who would believe them, but they could find no one – to approach some figure of authority in the church

[1] Nouwen, Henri. *The Wounded Healer*. Image Books: 1972.

who would share in their woundedness but no one was willing to do so.

During those same years, I had the opportunity of also being an advocate for eight priests who had been accused of sexual misconduct with minors in dioceses outside my own. Through being their advocate, I saw the other side of the coin and experienced how a diocese can pass judgment on one of its own before any process has taken place – how a bishop can completely cut himself off and make himself unavailable for a priest who has been accused – and how files and important information can be withheld by a diocese in any number of ways.

By having a foot on each side of the fence and being both an Episcopal delegate and an advocate, I learned that as a Church we have not always done enough for many of those who were truly victims and we have not always done enough for many who have been accused but who have, in some cases, been denied protection of their rights and access to adequate canonical representation. We can and we must do better as a society of professional canonists and as a Church. The way is neither easy nor clear – but that should not – indeed must not – prevent us from entering into the woundedness of so many: both the accusers and the accused. We must become the wounded healers if we are to be true to our canonical tradition and to our vocation in the Church. We do this not for ourselves but for these our sisters and brothers in Christ and for our Church.

In the words of the great 20th century spiritual master, Carlos Carretto:

> How baffling you are, oh Church,
> And yet how I love you!
> How you have made me suffer,
> And yet how much I owe you!
> I should like to see you destroyed, and yet I need your presence.
> You have given me so much scandal
> And yet you have made me understand sanctity.
> I have seen nothing in the world more
> Devoted to obscurity, more compromised,
> More false, and I have touched nothing more pure,
> More generous, more beautiful.
> How often I have wanted to shut the doors of my soul in your face,
> and how often I have prayed to die in the safety of your arms.
> No, I cannot free myself from you, because
> I am you, although not completely.
> And where should I go?[2]

Thank you and God bless you.

[2] Carretto, Carlos. *The God Who Cares.* Orbis Books: 1974.

Contributors

Reverend Monsignor John A. Alesandro, JCD, JD, Vicar General, Diocese of Rockville Centre, New York

Reverend Thomas C. Anslow, CM, JCL, Vicar for Canonical Services, Archdiocese of Los Angeles, California, Treasurer of the Canon Law Society of America

Most Reverend Juan Arrieta Ochoa de Chinchetru, JCD, Secretary of the Pontifical Council for Legislative Texts, Vatican City State

Reverend Monsignor Ricardo E. Bass, JCL, Pastor, Prince of Peace Parish, West Bloomfield, Michigan, 2010 recipient of the Role of Law Award

Reverend Phillip J. Brown, SS, JD, JCD, Économe Générale, Society of St. Sulpice, Baltimore, Maryland

Reverend Paul D. Counce, JCL, MCL, Judicial Vicar, Diocese of Baton Rouge, Louisiana

Mister William L. Daniel, JCL, Judge and Vice-Chancellor, Diocese of Winona, Minnesota

Doctor Patricia M. Dugan, JCL, JD, MA maintains civil and canon law practices from her law offices in Philadelphia, Pennsylvania, and President of Canon Law Books, Inc.

Reverend Monsignor Frederick C. Easton, JCD, Judicial Vicar, Archdiocese of Indianapolis, Indiana

Sister Sharon A. Euart, RSM, JCD, Executive Coordinator, Canon Law Society of America, Washington, District of Columbia

Most Reverend Joseph A. Galante, DD, JCD, MA, Bishop of the Diocese of Camden, New Jersey

Reverend Alain Guevremont, JCD, Lieutenant-Colonel Commandant, Canadian Forces Chaplain School and Centre, Ontario, Canada, President of the Canadian Canon Law Society

Reverend Lawrence A. Jurcak, JCL, Pastor, St. John Bosco Parish, Parma Heights, Ohio, President of the Canon Law Society of America

Reverend Monsignor James P. Moroney, STB, STL, Rector, Cathedral of St. Paul, Worcester, Massachusetts and Faculty Member, St. John's Seminary, Brighton, Massachusetts

Reverend Monsignor William H. Stetson, LLB, JCD, Secretary of the Pastoral Provision, Houston, Texas

MOST REVEREND V. JAMES WEISGERBER, PHL, STL, DD, immediate Past President of the Canadian Conference of Catholic Bishops and Archbishop of the Archdiocese of Winnipeg, Manitoba, Canada

SISTER MARLENE WEISENBECK, FSPA, PHD, JCL, MM, immediate Past President of the Franciscan Sisters of Perpetual Adoration, La Crosse, Wisconsin

DOCTOR MYRIAM WIJLENS, JCD, PHD, HABIL., professor of canon law and Vice-President, University of Erfurt, Germany

PARTICIPANTS

Joseph Abraham
Reno, NV
Jane Adolphe
Naples, FL
Robert Ahlin
Pittsburgh, PA
John Alesandro
Rockville Centre, NY
Oliver Angel
Laredo, TX
Steve Angi
Cincinnati, Ohio
Thomas Anslow
Los Angeles, CA
Charles Antonicelli
Washington, DC
Gary Applegate
Kansas City, KS
Christopher Armstrong
Cincinnati, OH
Juan Ignacio Arrieta
Pontifical Council for Legislative Texts
James Auth
Toledo, OH
Alberto Avella
Grants, NM
Rogelio Ayala Partida
Asociacion Mexicana de Canonistas
Renata Babicz-Baratto
Lexington, KY
Diane Barr
Baltimore, MD
Mark Bartchak
Erie, PA
Mary Ann Bartolac
Kansas City, KS

Virginia Bartolac
Kansas City, KS
Carlotta Bartone
Bryn Mawr, PA
Ronald Barusefski
Minersville, PA
Ricardo Bass
Detroit, MI
Anthony Bawyn
Seattle, WA
John Beal
Erie, PA
John Bell
Allen/Plano, TX
Charles Benoit
St. Benedict, LA
Barbara Bettwy
Erie, PA
Gregory Bittner
Birmingham, AL
Mary Gen Blittschau
Evansville, IN
Michael Boccaccio
Bridgeport, CT
James Bonke
Indianapolis, IN
John Boyle
Southwark, England
Michael Bradley
Chicago, IL
Sean Bransfield
Philadelphia, PA
Patrick Brennan
Portland, OR
R. Richard Brickler
Rochester, NY
Phillip Brown
Baltimore, MD
Steven Brown
Cincinnati, OH

Thomas Brundage
Anchorage, AK
Anne Bryant
Houston, TX
Michael Burchfield
Fresno, CA
Thomas Burke
Odessa, TX
Marianne Burkhard
Peoria, IL
Jesus Cabrera
Milwaukee, WI
Michael Cariglio
Youngstown, OH
Michael Carter
Camden, NJ
Timothy Cavanaugh
Washington, DC
Anthony Celino
El Paso, TX
Deborah Cerullo
Providence, RI
Charles Chaffman
Los Angeles, CA
Margaret Chalmers
Greenville, SC
Cherry Clark
Shenandoah, VA
Paul Clark
Harrisburg, PA
John Cody
Columbus, OH
Patrick Cogan
Ottawa, ON
Rick Conason
Biloxi, MS
Daniel Condon
Rochester, NY
R. Daniel Conlon
Steubenville, OH
Jay Conzemius
Pittsburgh, PA

Patrick Cooney
Saint Meinrad, IN
Joe Corbett
Atlanta, GA
James Coriden
Washington, DC
Luis Corneli
Baltimore, MD
Paul Counce
Baton Rouge, LA
John Crerand
Columbus, OH
Thomas Cronkleton
Cheyenne, WY
Barbara Anne Cusack
Milwaukee, WI
Catherine Darcy
Camden, NJ
Jamin David
Baton Rouge, LA
Zabrina Decker
Milwaukee, WI
Robert DeLand
Saginaw, MI
Louis DeNinno
Pittsburgh, PA
John Dermond
Trenton, NJ
Lawrence DiNardo
Pittsburgh, PA
James Donlon
Glenmont, NY
Patricia Dugan
Philadelphia, PA
Frederick Easton
Indianapolis, IN
Mary Edlund
Dallas, TX
Peter Eke
Gaylord, MI
William Elder
New York, NY
Martins Emeh
Rockford, IL
Jace Eskind
Lake Charles, LA
Sharon Euart
Office of the
Executive
Coordinator
John Faris
Utica, NY
Thomas Feeney
Corpus Christi, TX
David Fellhauer
Victoria, TX
Timothy Ferguson
Detroit, MI
Christopher Ferrer
Austin, TX
William Finnegan
Anchorage, AK &
Phoenix, AZ
Brian V Finnigan
Brisbane,
Queensland,
Australia
Daniel Firmin
Savannah, GA
Kenneth Fortener
New Hope, KY
John J. Foster
Washington, DC
Thomas Fransiscus
Reno. Nevada
Matthew Frisoni
Albany, NY
Canuto Emeritus
Fuentebella
Aruba
Leonardo Gajardo
Gary, IN
Joseph Galante
Camden, NJ
Engelberto Gammad
San Jose, CA
Ricardo Garcia
Brownsville, TX
M. Margaret Gillett
Dallas, Texas
Catherine Gilligan
Little Rock, AR
Garry Giroux
Brasher Falls, NY
Raymond Goehring
Lansing, MI
Paul Golden
Denver, CO
Mary Ellen Goverts
Rochester, NY
William Graham
Baltimore, MD
Thomas Green
Washingto, DC
Janice Grochowsky
Dodge City, KS
Ralph Gross
Milwaukee, WI
Paul Hachey
Atlanta, GA
Michael Hack
Chicago, IL
Edward Hankiewicz
Grand Rapids, MI
Mary Hauck
Indianapolis, IN
Leo Hausmann
Wall, SD
Robert Hayes
San Jose, CA
R. Paul Heiting
Winona, MN
Amy Hereford
Saint Louis, MO
Marie Hilliard
Philadelphia, PA
Viet Peter Ho
Orange, CA
Thuan Hoang
San Francisco, CA
Michael Hoeppner
Crookston, MN
Thomas Hofmann
Charleston, SC
David Hogan
Canon Law
Society of Great
Britian & Ireland

Daniel Hoye
Fall River, MA
Eduardo Huerta
Tucson, AZ
Andrea Imburgia
Rochester, NY
James Innocenzi
Trenton, NJ
Jolene Jasinski
Beaver Falls, PA
William Jerse
Cleveland, OH
Anila John
Bronx, NY
Bernard Johnson
Vina, CA
Gerald Jorgensen
Dubuque, IA
Rita Joyce
Pittsburgh, PA
Michael Joyce
Memphis, TN
Jerome Jung
Berkeley, CA
Lawrence Jurcak
Cleveland, OH
Thomas Kadera
Cheyenne, WY
Robert Kaslyn
Catholic University of America
Connie Kassahn
Cheyenne, WY
James Kee
Mobile, AL
Anthony Kerin
Canon Law Society of Australia & New Zealand
Elaine Kerscher
Joliet, IL
Rita Killackey
Kansas City, MO
Adela Maria Kim
Peoria, IL

Robert Kincl
Austin TX
David Klein
Camden, NJ
Joseph Klos
Buffalo, NY
Jose Kochuparambil
Lubbock, TX
K.S. Kopacz
Fargo, ND
Richard Kosisko
Greensburg, PA
Joseph Koury
Portland, ME
Heidi Krupp
Saginaw, MI
Kate Kuenstler
Pawtucket, RI
Rose Mary Kuklok
Santa Rosa, CA
Patrick Lagges
Chicago, IL
Bonnie Landry
Lake Charles, LA
Jennie Latta
Memphis, TN
Daniel Laurita
Athens, AL
Richard Lelonis
Pittsburgh, PA
Herman Leong
Oakland, CA
Andres Ligot
San Jose, CA
Judene Lillie
New Orleans, LA
Timothy Lindenfelser
Jacksonville, FL
Paul Litwin
Buffalo, NY
Douglas Loecke
Dubuque, IA
Eugene Lozinski
Sleepy Eye, MN
William Lum
Rochester, NY

Gregory Luyet
Fort Smith, AR
John Lynch
Rochester, NY
Richard Lyons
Metuchen, NJ
Elyn Macek
Atlanta, GA
Sandra Makowski
Charleston, SC
Edward Malesic
Harrisburg, PA
Michele Mangan
San Jose, CA
Salvatore Manganello
Buffalo, NY
Wojciech Marat
Chicago, IL
Tomas Marin
Miami, FL
Ricardo MartÃ-n
Alexandria, VA
Kurt Martens
Washington, DC
Peggy Martin
Denver, CO
Michael Martine
Staten Island, NY
Jose Martinez
Las Cruces, NM
Reb Materi
Saskatoon, SK
Joseph Matt
Kansas City, MO
Valerie Maxineau
Grand Rapids, MI
John McAllister
Little Rock, AR
Jeremiah McCarthy
Savannah, GA
Robert McClory
Detroit, MI
Rose McDermott
Washington, DC
Kevin McKenna
Rochester, NY

Mary McKenzie
Charleston, SC
Lynn McKenzie
Birmingham, AL
Maureen McPartland
Dubuque, IA
Brian McWeeney
Pleasant Valley, NY
Mark Mealey
Arlington, VA
Gerard Mesure
Philadelphia, PA
George Michalek
Lansing, MI
Bruce Miller
Alexandria, LA
Christopher Moore
Baltimore, MD
Robert Nalley
Gaylord, MI
Luis Navarro
Pontifical University of the Holy Cross
Marilyn Newman
Oklahoma City, OK
Steve Nguyen
Honolulu, HI
Thu Nguyen
Houston, TX
Kevin Niehoff, O.P.
Albuquerque, NM
Mark O'Connell
Boston, MA
Thomas O'Donnell
Pittsburgh, PA
Kelly O'Donnell
San Diego, CA
Lawrence O'Keefe
Gallup, NM
James Oliver
Philadelphia, PA
Robert Oliver
Boston, MA
Thomas Olson
St. Cloud, MN
Thomas Olszyk
Washington, DC
George Oonnoonny
New York, NY
Agustin Opalalic
Vista, CA
Henry Orszulak
Buffalo, NY
Sinclair Oubre
Port Arthur, TX
Evelyn Ovalles
Crown Point, IN
C. Michael Padazinski
San Francisco, CA
William Palladino
Boston, MA
Carl Pallasch
Chicago, IL
Duaine Pamment
Laingsburg, MI
Stanislaus Pang Nghee Seng
Singapore
Peggy Paoli
Orange, CA
Thomas Paprocki
Springfield, IL
F. Stephen Pedone
Worcester, MA
Phu Phan
Amarillo, TX
Anthony Pileggi
Kansas City, MO
Mark Plewka
Pueblo, CO
Peter Polando
Youngtown, OH
John Porter
Grand Rapids, MI
Joseph Punderson
Rome, Italy
John Putnam
Charlotte, NC
Kevin Quirk
Wheeling, WV
Steven Raica
Lansing, MI
Margaret Ramsden
Orange, CA
William Rathgeb
Greensburg, PA
Santiago Raudes
Sacramento, CA
Ann Rehrauer
Green Bay, WI
Richard Reidy
Worcester, MA
Charles Renati
San Francisco, CA
Mark Richards
Sacramento, CA
Thomas Richstatter
Saint Meinrad, IN
George Rigazzi
Oklahoma City, OK
Michael Riley
Des Moines, IA
Kenneth Riley
Kansas City, MO
J. Michael Ritty
Feura Bush, NY
Christine Rody
Cleveland, OH
Marie Roldan
San Jose, CA
Meg Romano-Hogan
Fort Worth, TX
Wilmer Rosario
Manila, Philippines
Eloise Rosenblatt
San Jose, CA
Patricia Ruiz
Fresno, CA
Marvin Samiano
Honolulu, HI
Mary Santi
Seattle, WA
John Santone
Simsbury, CT

Maria Amparo Santos
Pangasinan, Philippines
Eugene Sawicki
New York, NY
Edward Schaefer
St. Rose, IL
Joseph Scheib
Pittsburgh PA
Jerry Scherkenbach
St. Paul, MN
J. Gerard Schreck
Savannah, GA
John Schuster
Calgary
David Schuyler
Cupertino, CA
Gilbert Seitz
Baltimore, MD
John Sekellick
Jessup, PA
John Shamleffer
Saint Louis, MO
Donetta Shaw
Kansas City, MO
Patrick Shea
Cleveland, OH
James Sheehan
Newark, NJ
Sean Sheridan
Washington DC
Langes Silva
Salt Lake City, UT
Christopher Singer
Erie, PA
Louis Sirianni
Rochester, NY
Harmon Skillin
Stockton, CA
Kevin Slattery
Jackson, MS
H. Roberta Small
Camden, NJ
Daniel Smilanic
Chicago, IL
Rosemary Smith
Convent Station, NJ
Patricia Smith
Aston, PA
Harry Snow
Ogdensburg, NY
James Socias
Woodridge, IL
Richard Stansberry
Oklahoma City, OK
James Steiger
Hilton, NY
William Stetson
Houston, TX
Charles Strebler
Cleveland, OH
Therese Sullivan
Cleveland, OH
W. Jerome Sullivan
Buffalo, NY
Margaret Sullivan
Boston, MA
David Szatkowski
Hales Corners, WI
Amy Tadlock
Washington, DC
Allison Townley
Kansas City, MO
Gregory Trawick
Cloverport, KY
Francis Tse
Hong Kong, China
Ann Tully
Indianapolis, IN
Benedetto Vaghetto
Pittsburgh, PA
Arquimedes Vallejo
Rockford, IL
Irene Valles
Las Cruces, NM
Kelly Vandehey
Portland, OR
Marilyn Vassallo
Shreveport, LA
Desmond Vella
New York, NY
Siobhan Verbeek
Washington, DC
Manuel Viera
Cincinnati, OH
Victoria Vondenberger
Cincinnati, OH
Richard Wahl
Houston, TX
Aidan Walsh
Boston, MA
John Ward
Baltimore, MD
Rosanne Warner
Rochester, NY
Ian Waters
Victoria, Australia
Marlene Weisenbeck
La Crosse, WI
James Weisgerber
Winnipeg, MB
Lynn Marie Welbig
Sioux Falls, SD
Brian Welding
Pittsburgh, PA
Rick Wells
St. Petersburg, FL
Emmett Wells
Rochester, NY
Daniel Welter
Chicago, IL
Robert Wendelken
Cleveland, OH
Mary Catherine Wenstrup
Covington, KY
Ralph Wiatrowski
Cleveland, OH
Myriam Wijlens
Erfurt, Germany
Thomas Wisniewski
Darby, PA
Nicholas Wolfla
Atlanta, GA
Gary Yanus
Cleveland, OH